SOUL EATER NOT!

ATSUSHI OHKUBO

1

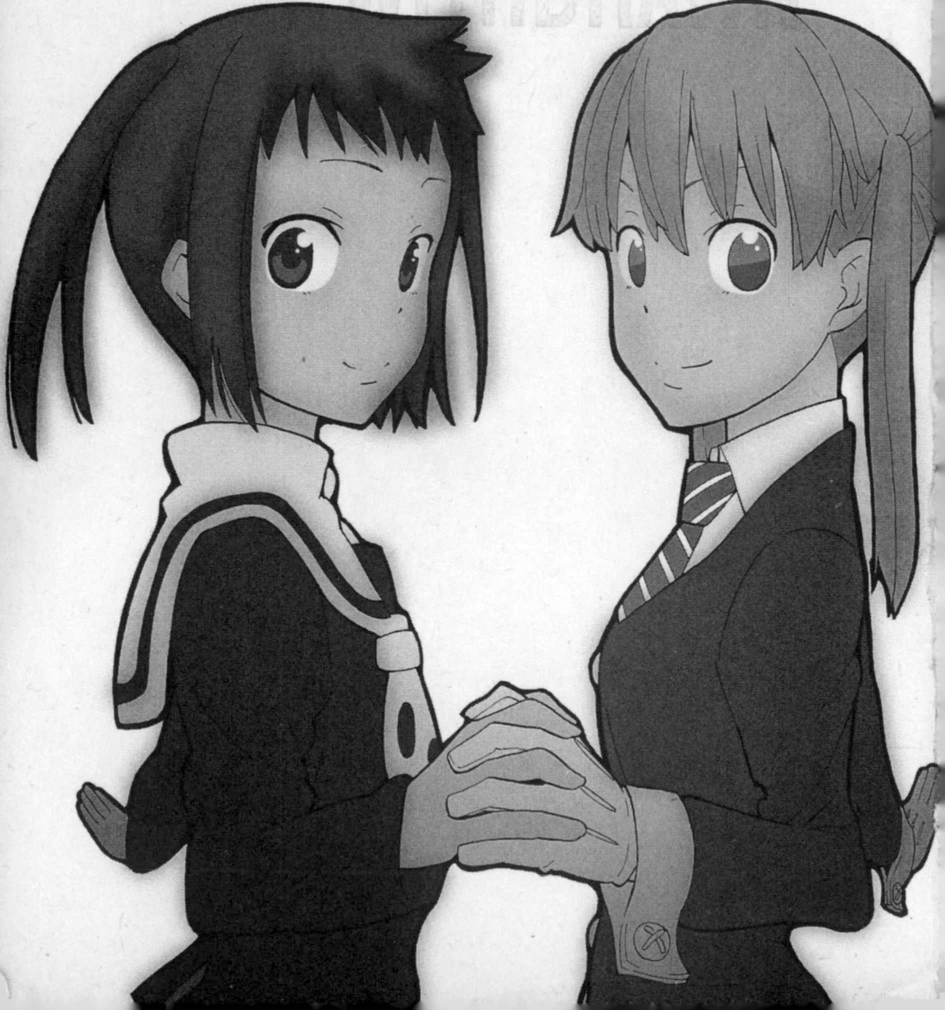

EATER

ATSUSHI
OHKUBO

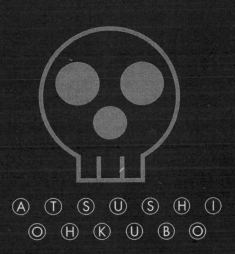

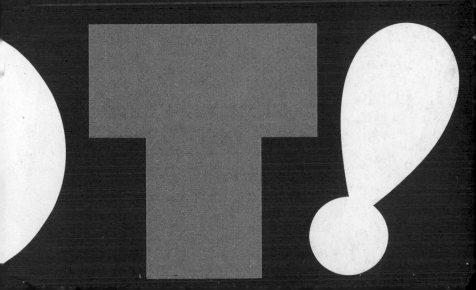

SOUL

01

NO

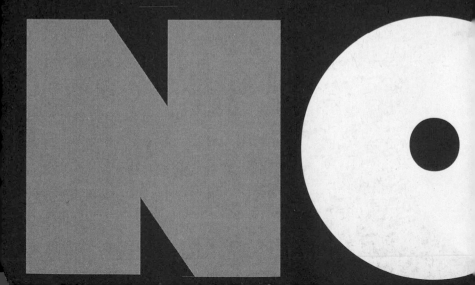

NOT!

SOUL EATER NOT!

01

CONTENTS

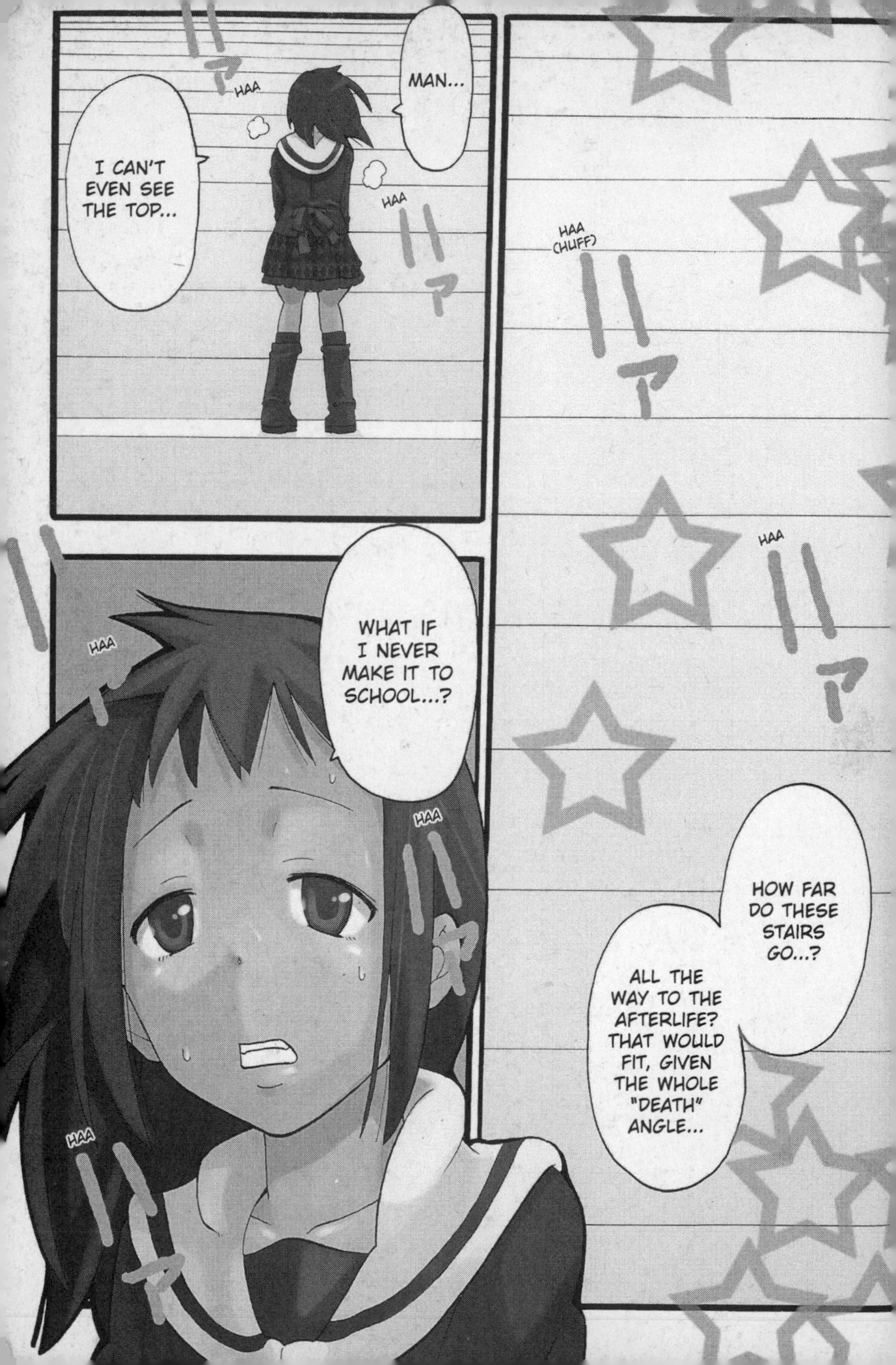
HAA (HUFF)
HAA
HOW FAR DO THESE STAIRS GO...?
ALL THE WAY TO THE AFTERLIFE? THAT WOULD FIT, GIVEN THE WHOLE "DEATH" ANGLE...
MAN...
HAA
I CAN'T EVEN SEE THE TOP...
HAA
WHAT IF I NEVER MAKE IT TO SCHOOL...?
HAA
HAA
HAA

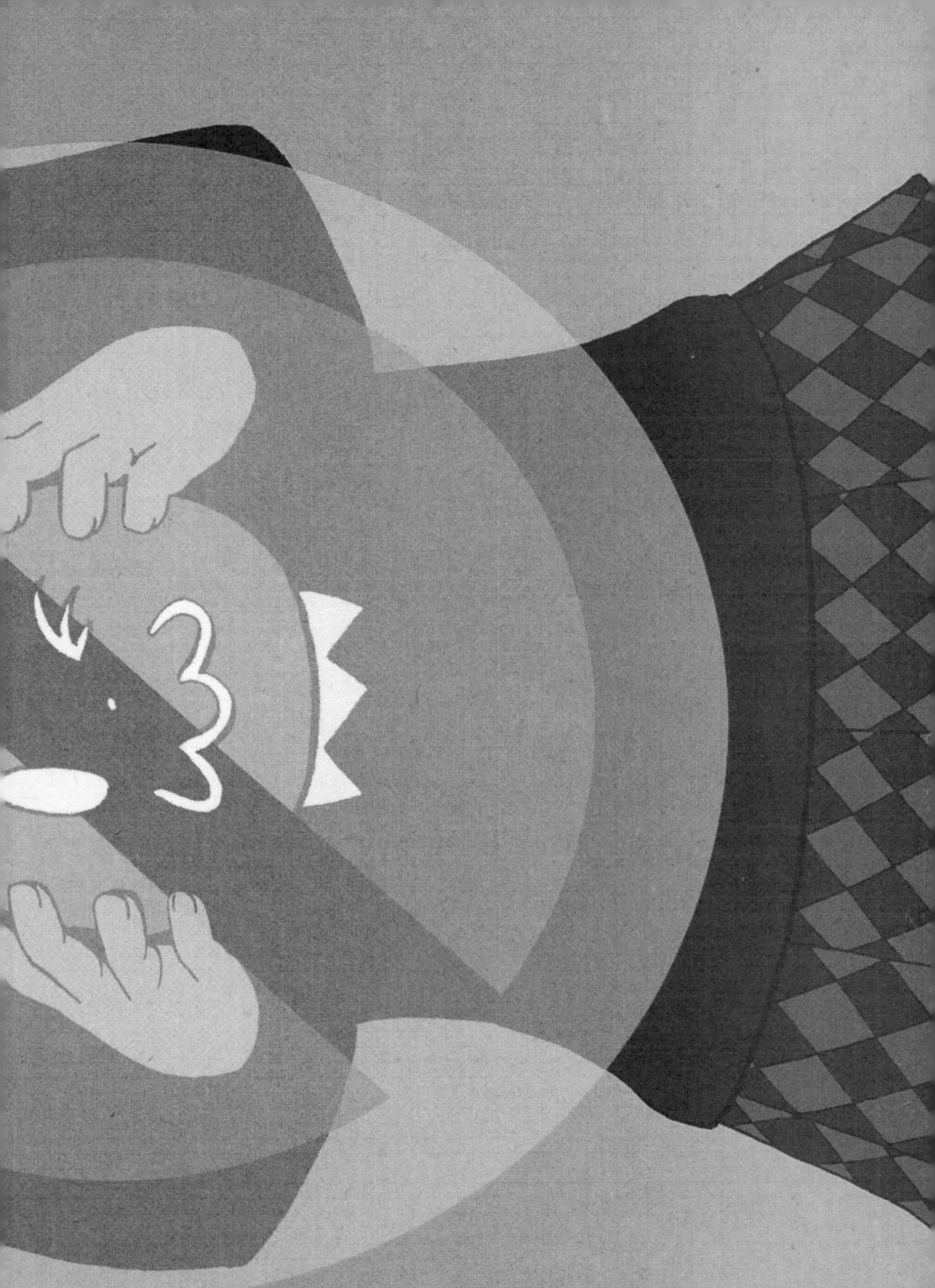

CHAPTER 1: STARTING SCHOOL!

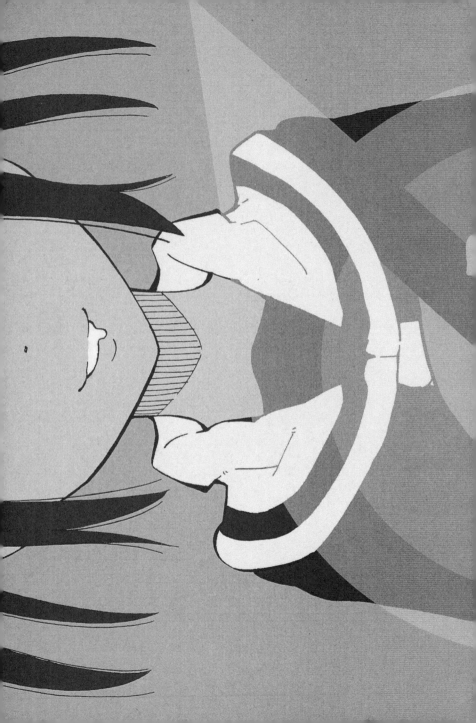

SOUL EATER NOT!

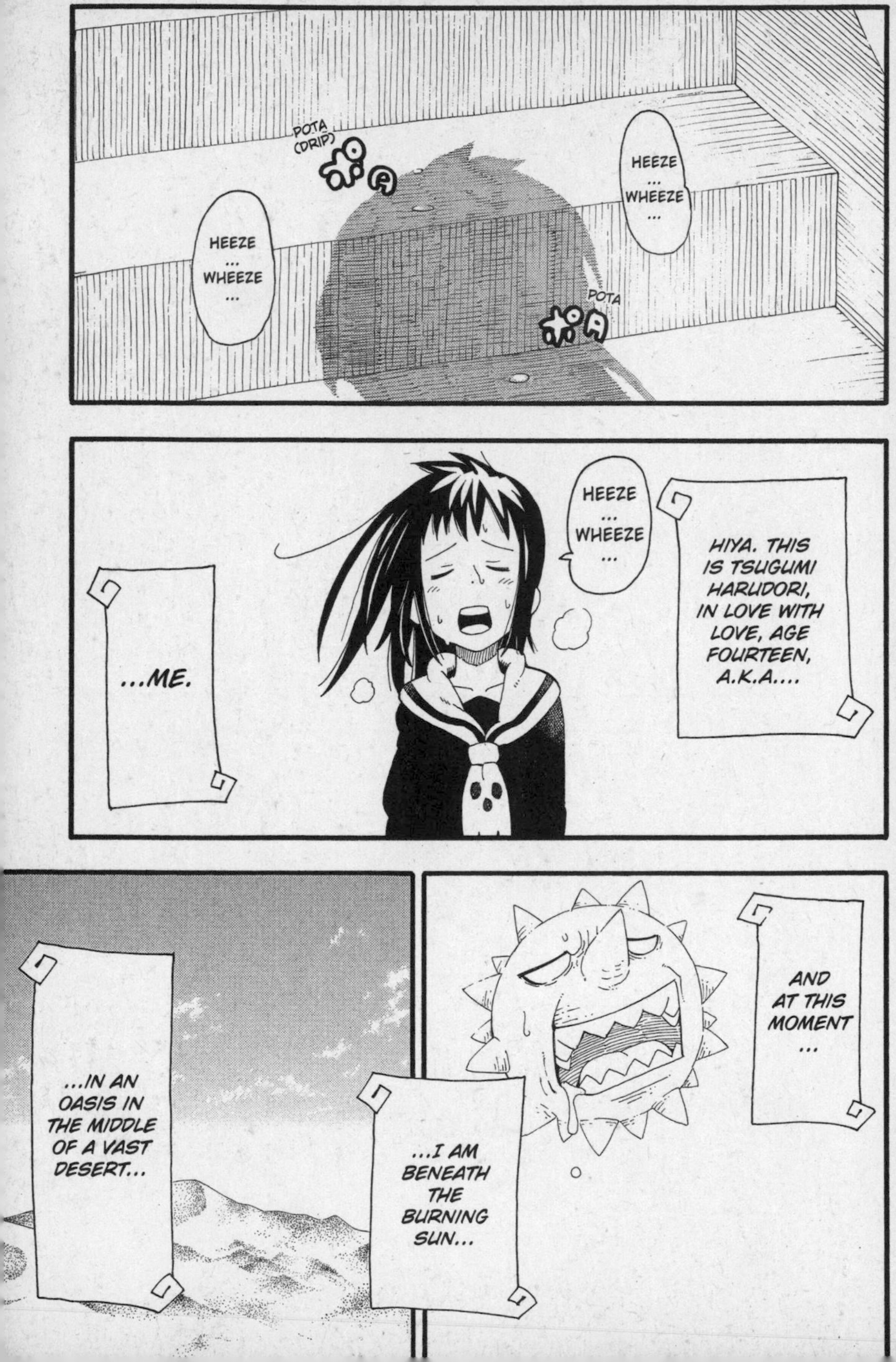
HEEZE ... WHEEZE ...
POTA (DRIP)
HEEZE ... WHEEZE ...
POTA
HIYA. THIS IS TSUGUMI HARUDORI, IN LOVE WITH LOVE, AGE FOURTEEN, A.K.A....
HEEZE ... WHEEZE ...
...ME.
AND AT THIS MOMENT ...
...I AM BENEATH THE BURNING SUN...
...IN AN OASIS IN THE MIDDLE OF A VAST DESERT...

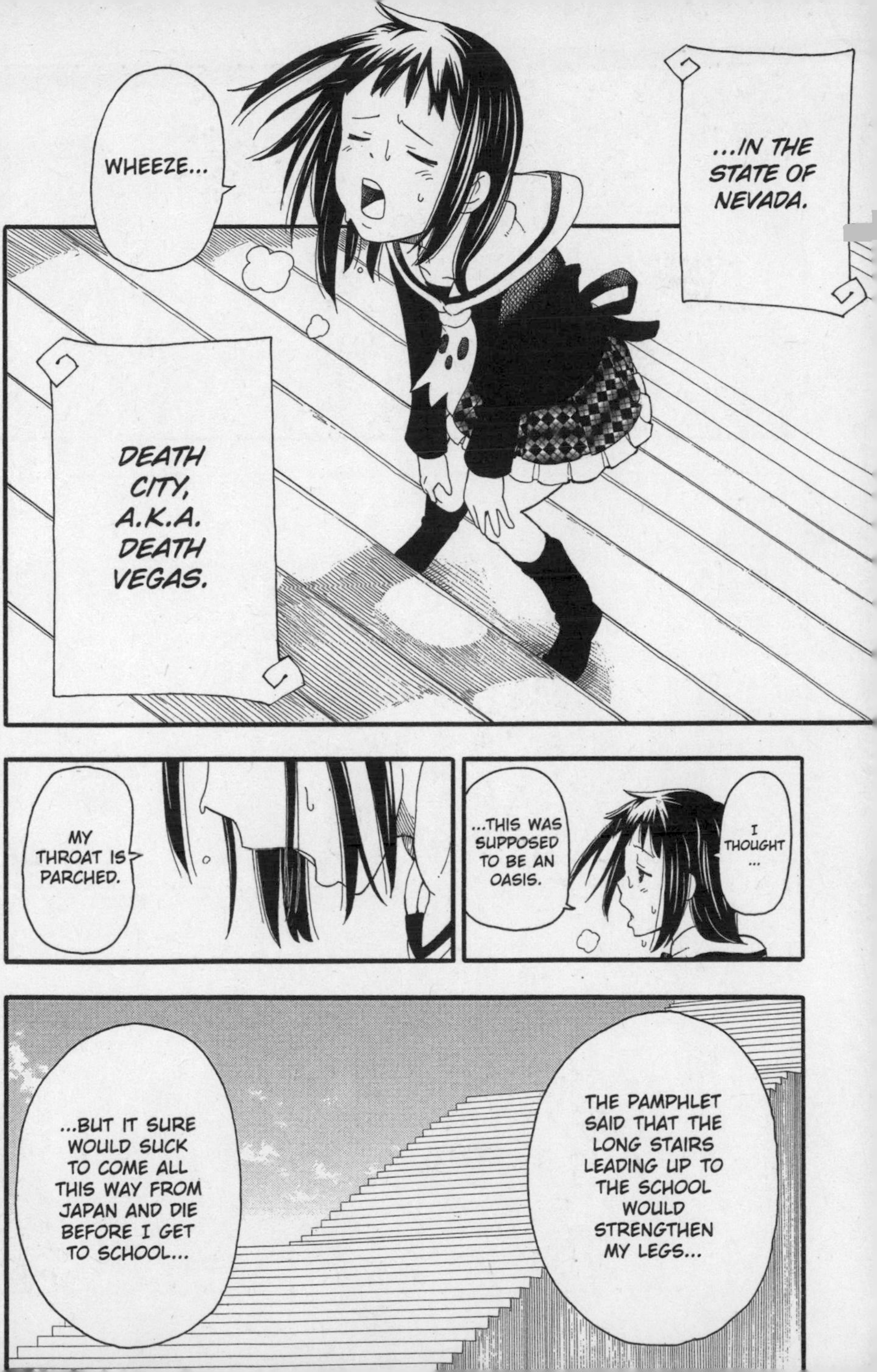
...IN THE STATE OF NEVADA.
WHEEZE...
DEATH CITY, A.K.A. DEATH VEGAS.
I THOUGHT...
...THIS WAS SUPPOSED TO BE AN OASIS.
MY THROAT IS PARCHED.
THE PAMPHLET SAID THAT THE LONG STAIRS LEADING UP TO THE SCHOOL WOULD STRENGTHEN MY LEGS...
...BUT IT SURE WOULD SUCK TO COME ALL THIS WAY FROM JAPAN AND DIE BEFORE I GET TO SCHOOL...

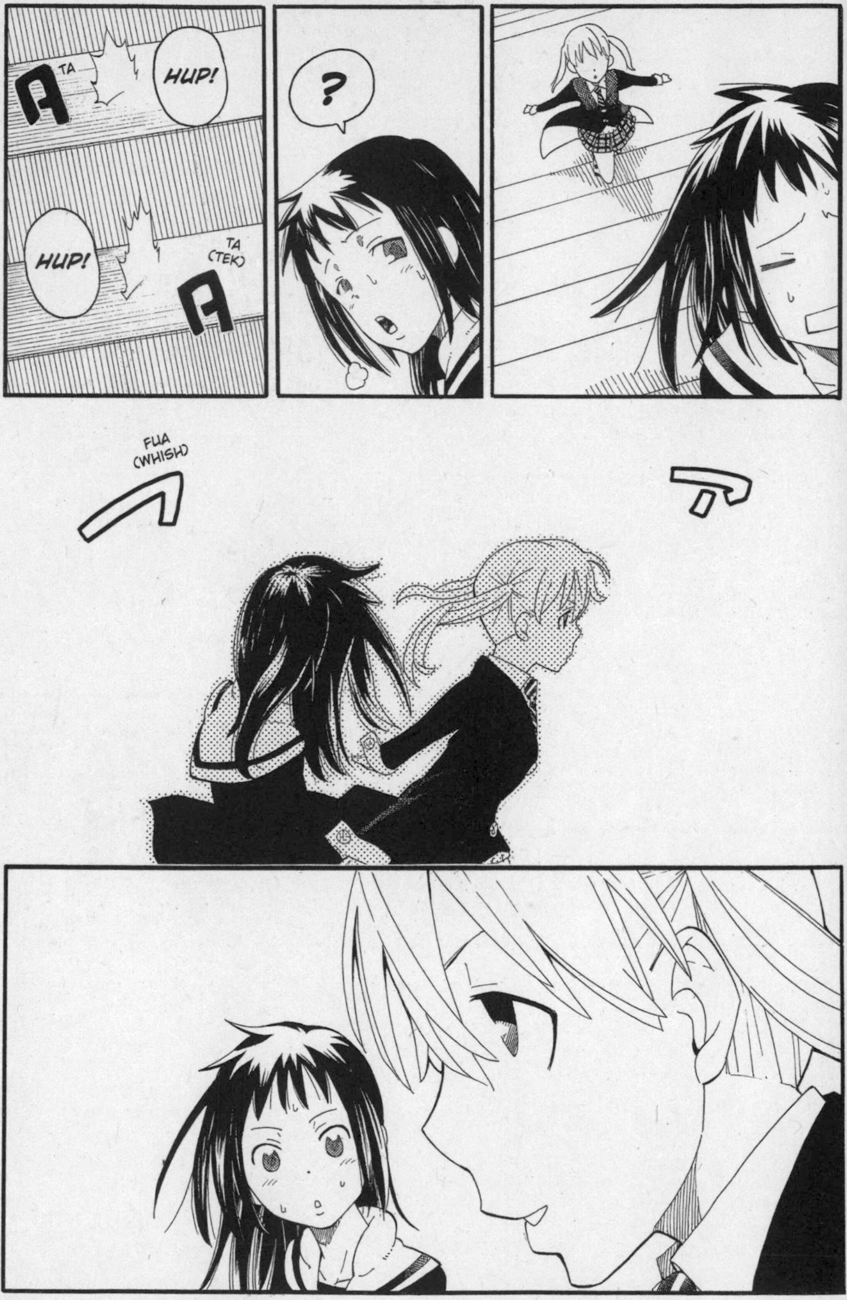
?
HUP!
TA
TA (TEK)
HUP!
FUA (WHISH)

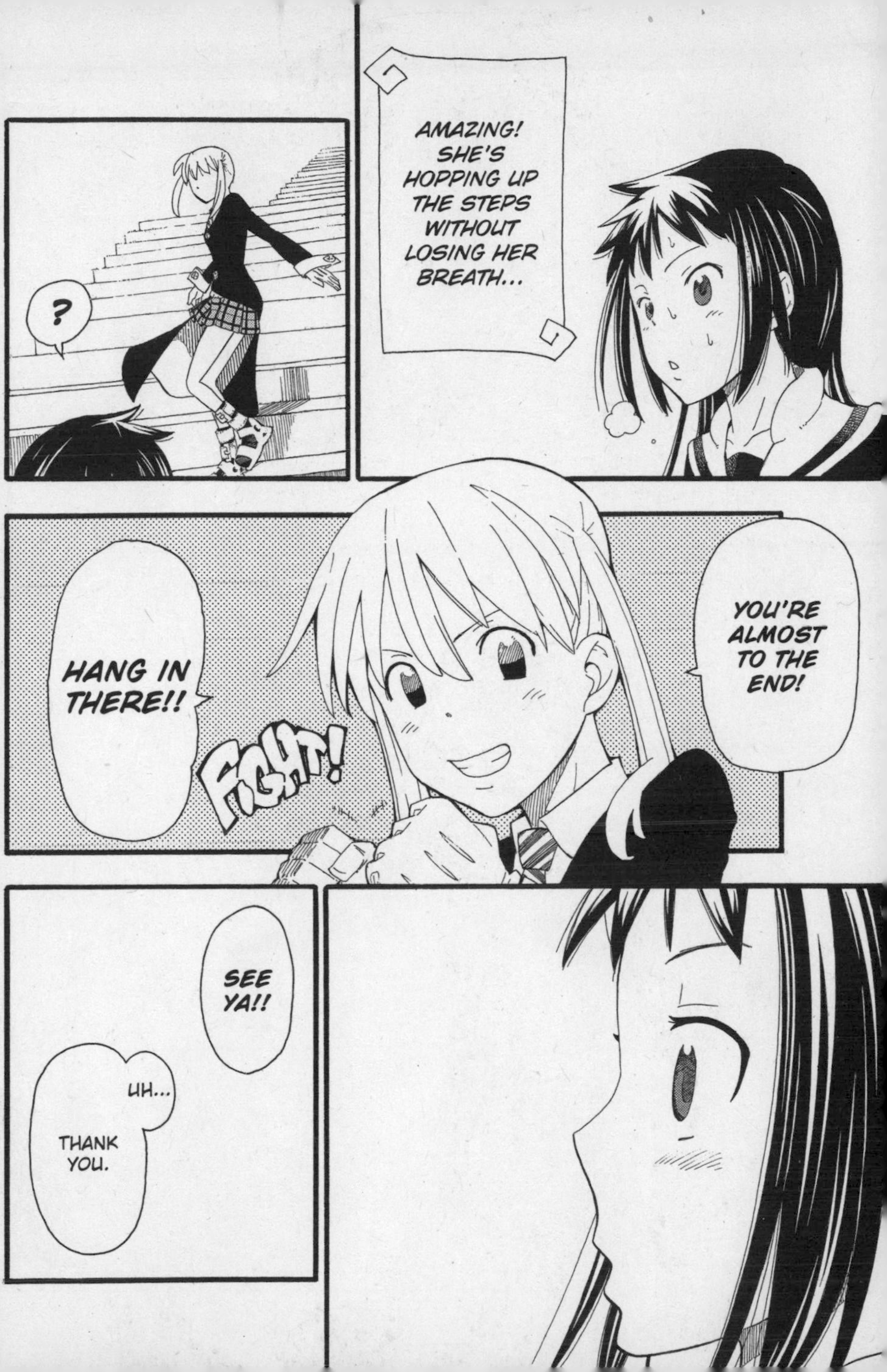
AMAZING! SHE'S HOPPING UP THE STEPS WITHOUT LOSING HER BREATH...
?
YOU'RE ALMOST TO THE END!
HANG IN THERE!!
FIGHT!
SEE YA!!
UH... THANK YOU.

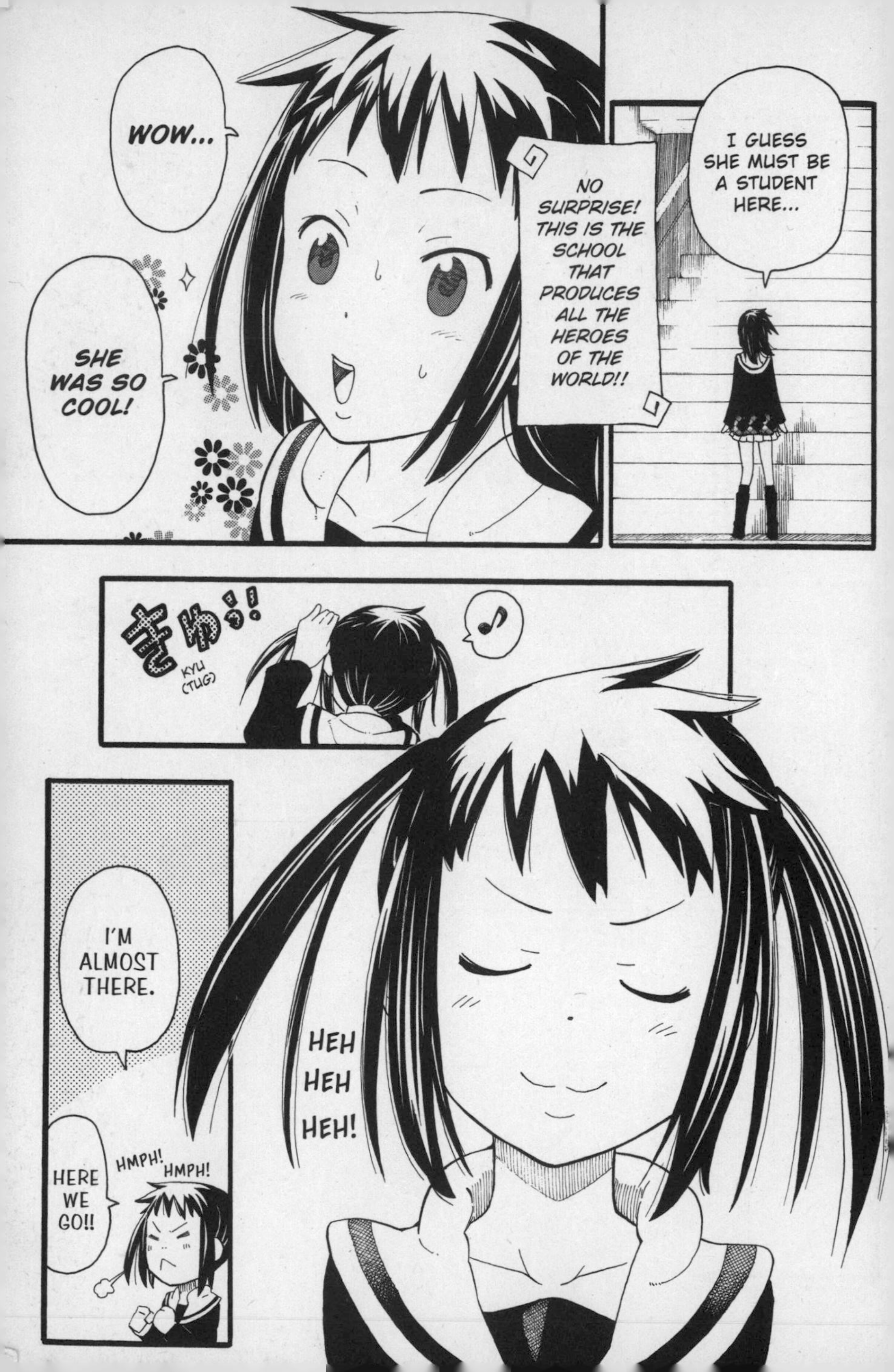
I GUESS SHE MUST BE A STUDENT HERE...
NO SURPRISE! THIS IS THE SCHOOL THAT PRODUCES ALL THE HEROES OF THE WORLD!!
WOW...
SHE WAS SO COOL!
きゅっ!!
KYU (TUG)
♪
HEH HEH HEH!
I'M ALMOST THERE.
HMPH! HMPH!
HERE WE GO!!

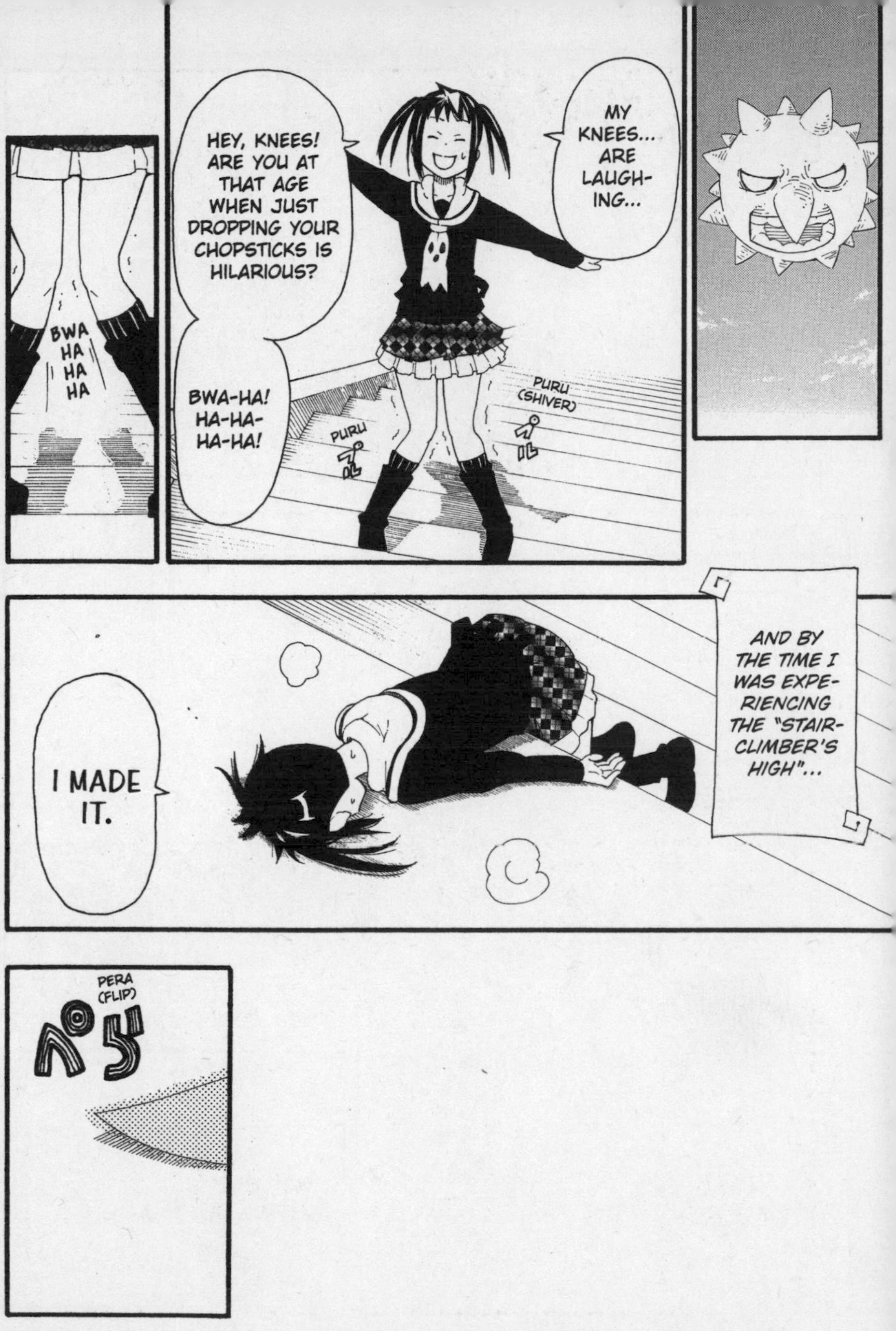
MY KNEES... ARE LAUGHING...
HEY, KNEES! ARE YOU AT THAT AGE WHEN JUST DROPPING YOUR CHOPSTICKS IS HILARIOUS?
BWA-HA! HA-HA-HA-HA!
PURU (SHIVER)
PURU
BWA HA HA HA
AND BY THE TIME I WAS EXPERIENCING THE "STAIR-CLIMBER'S HIGH"...
I MADE IT.
PERA (FLIP)
ぺら

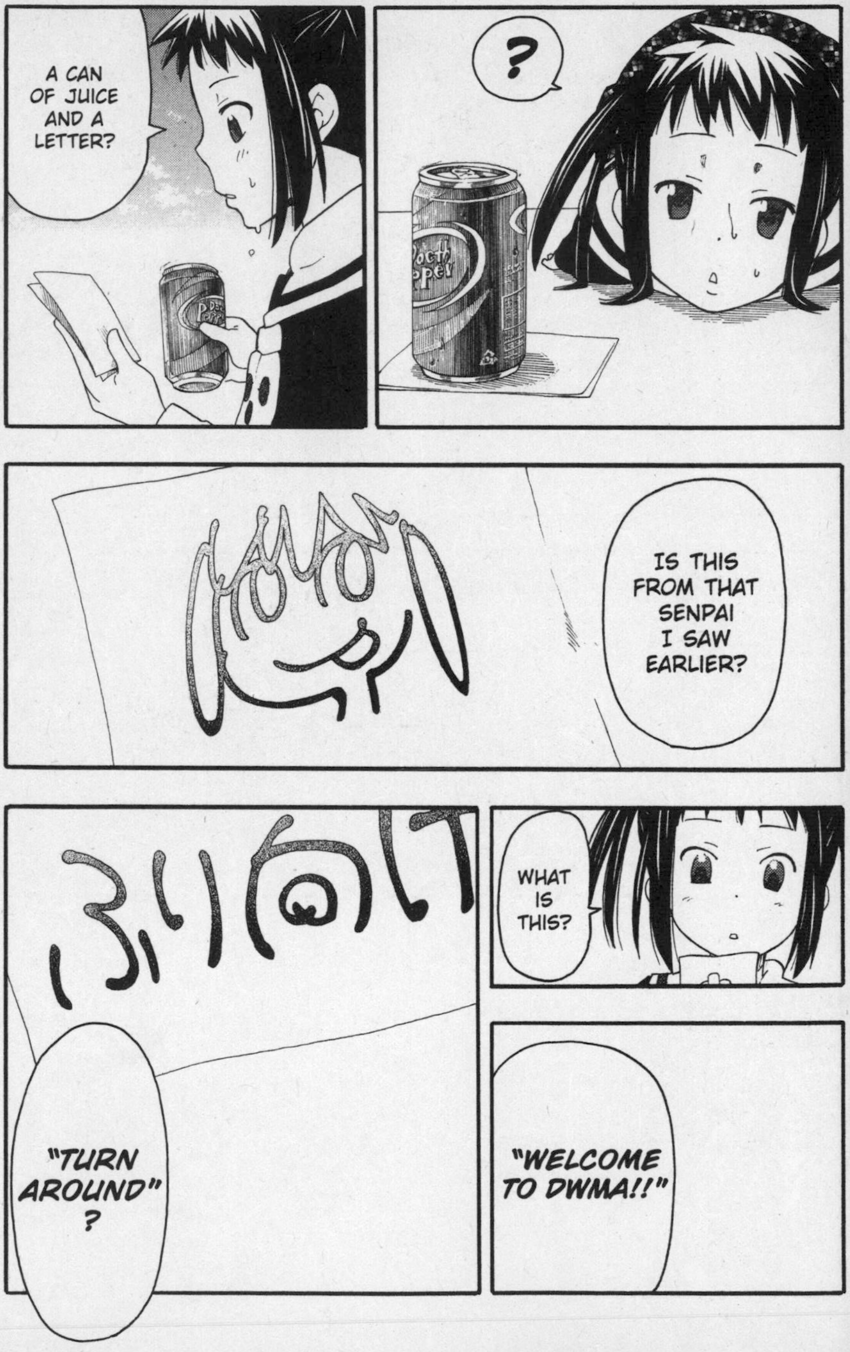
?
A CAN OF JUICE AND A LETTER?
IS THIS FROM THAT SENPAI I SAW EARLIER?
WHAT IS THIS?
"WELCOME TO DWMA!!"
ふり向いて
"TURN AROUND"?

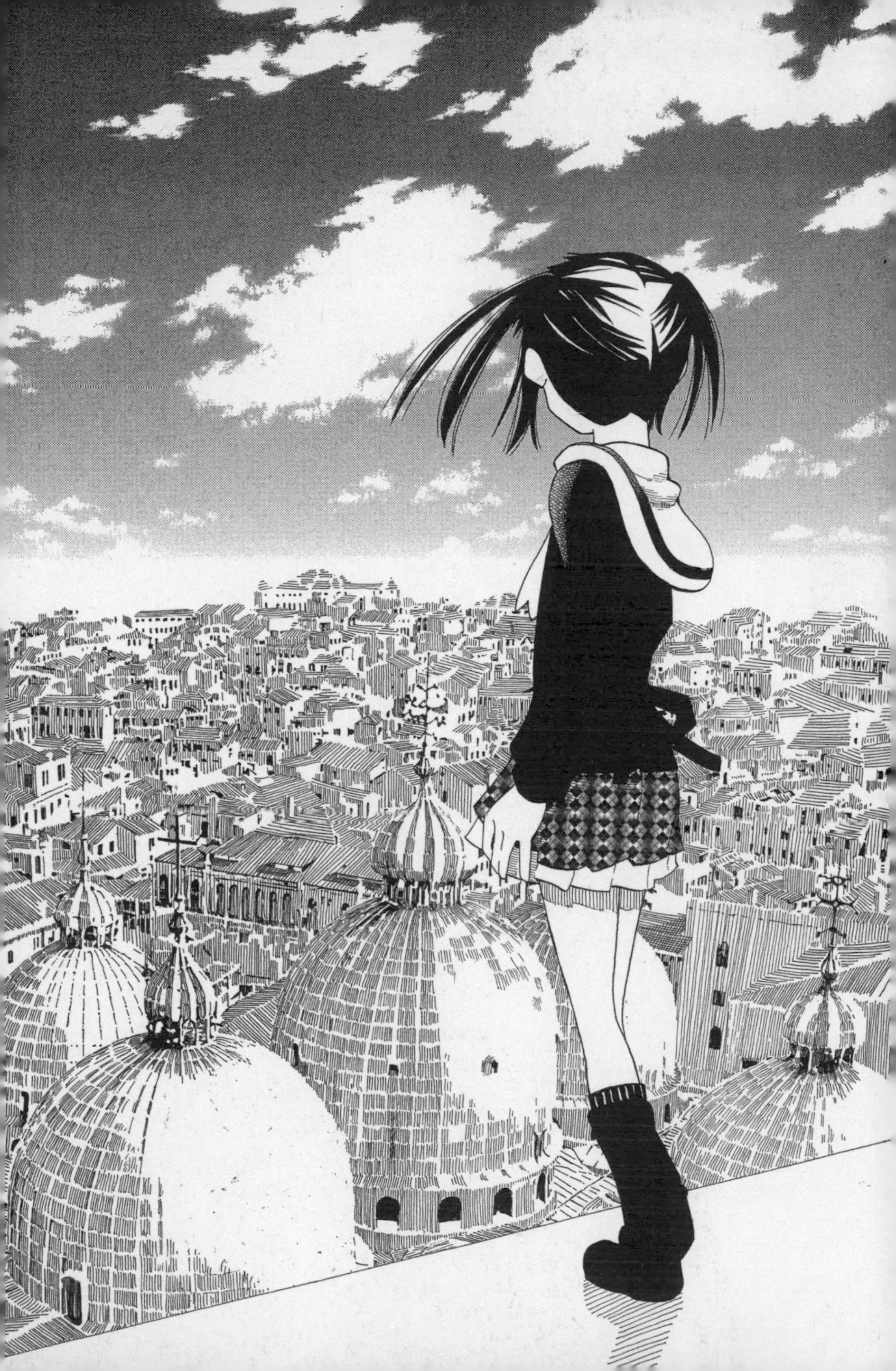

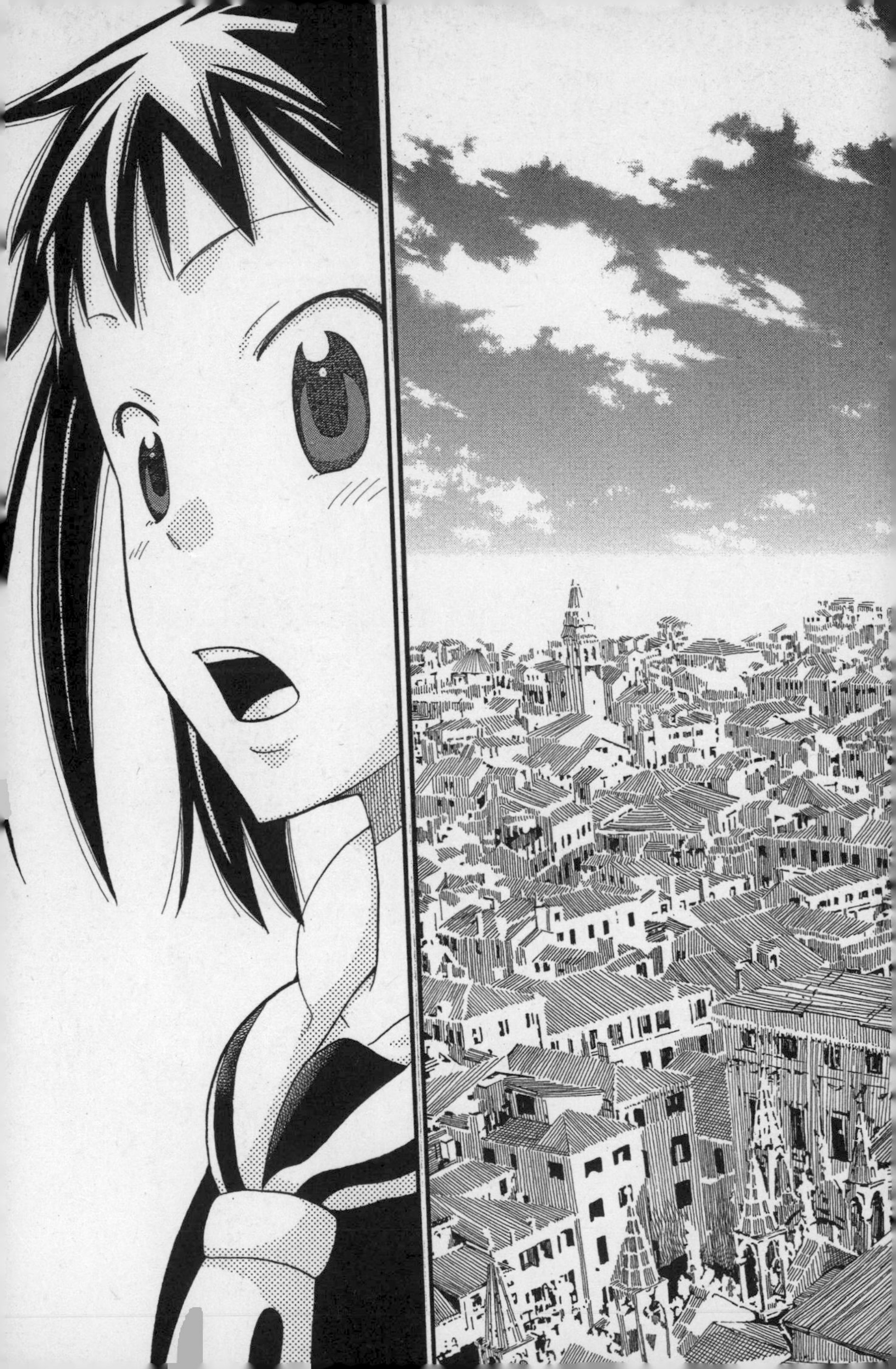

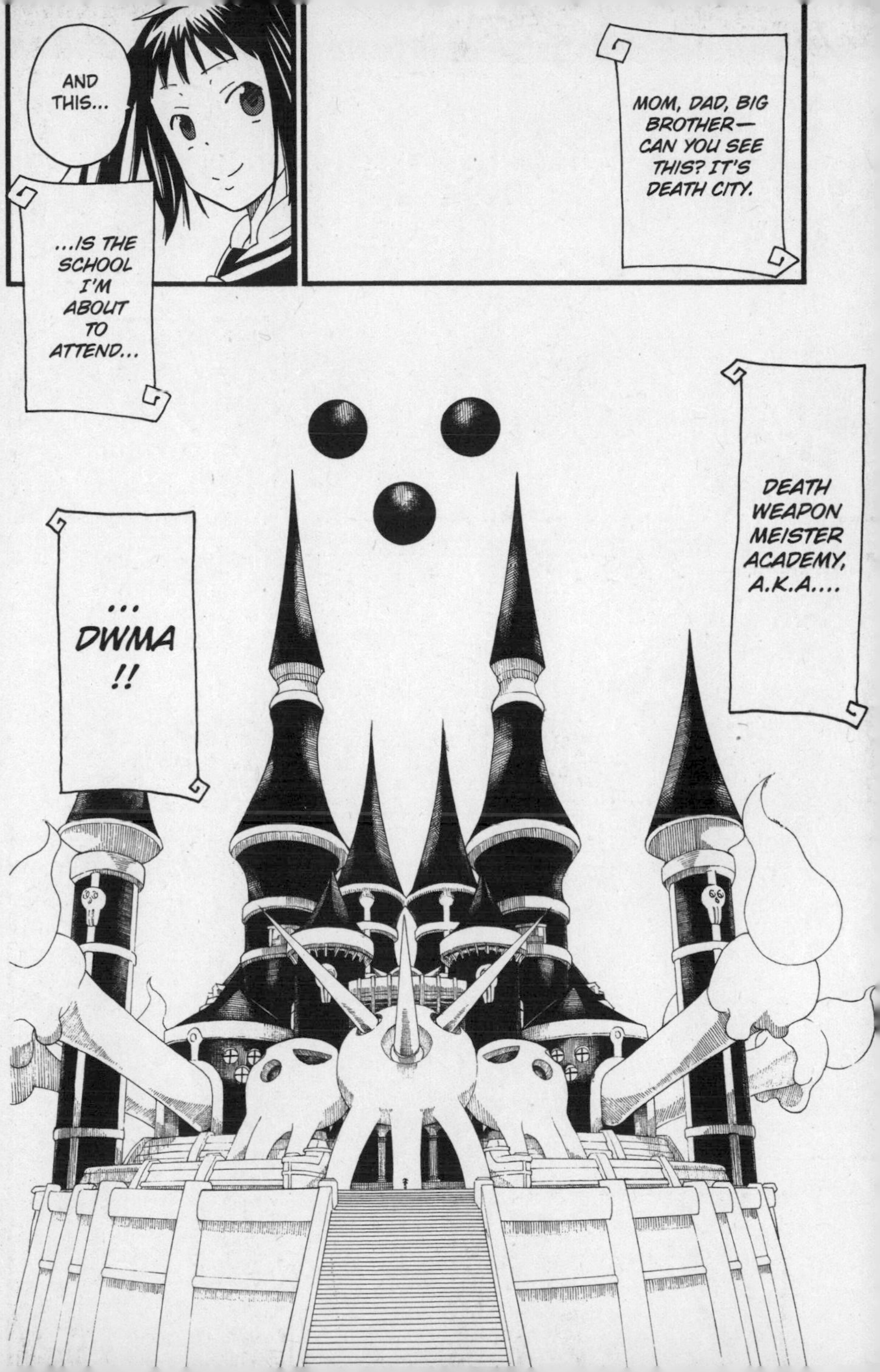
MOM, DAD, BIG BROTHER—CAN YOU SEE THIS? IT'S DEATH CITY.
AND THIS...
...IS THE SCHOOL I'M ABOUT TO ATTEND...
DEATH WEAPON MEISTER ACADEMY, A.K.A....
...DWMA!!

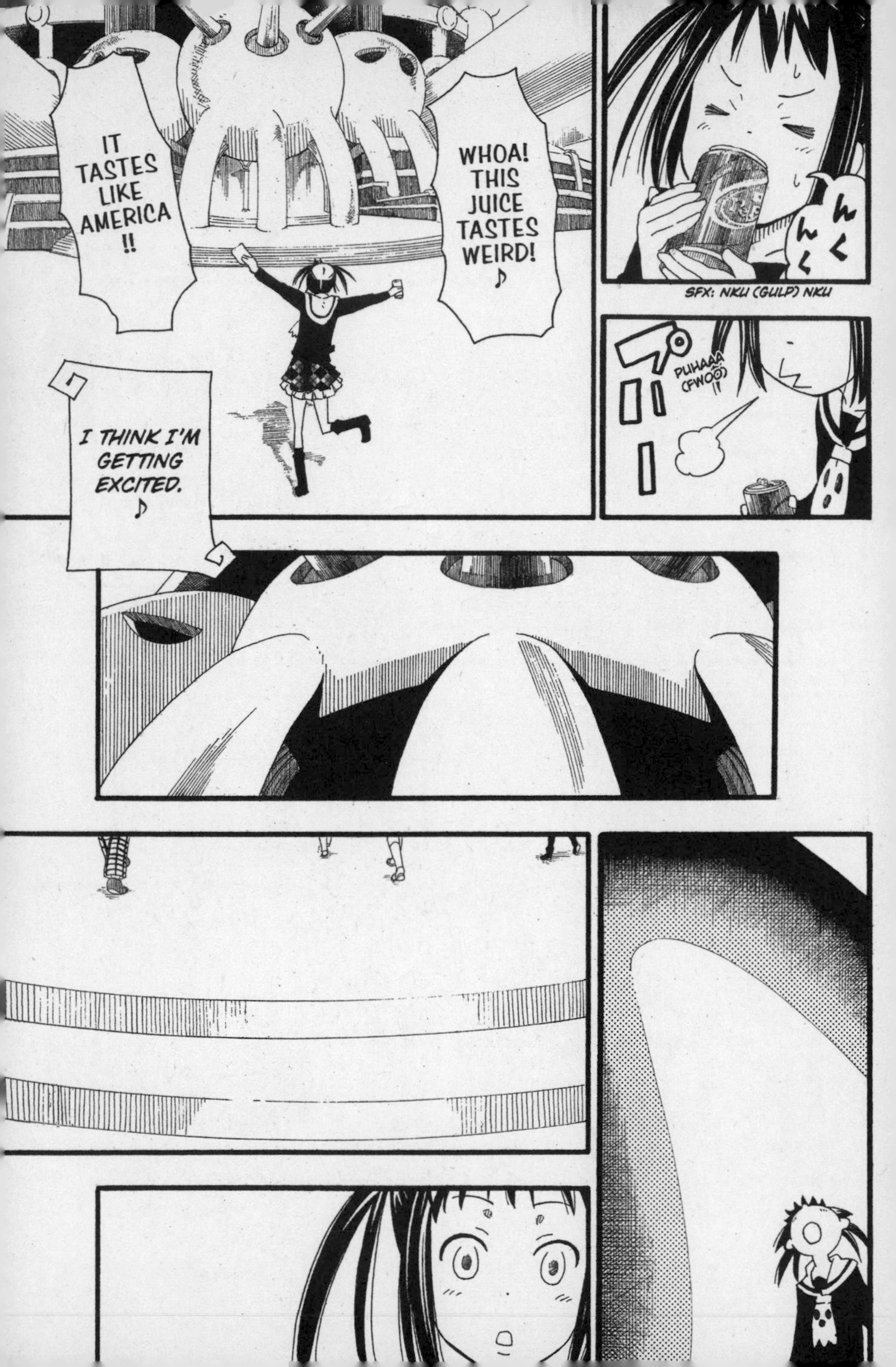
SFX: NKU (GULP) NKU
PUHAAA (FWOO)
WHOA! THIS JUICE TASTES WEIRD! ♪
IT TASTES LIKE AMERICA !!
I THINK I'M GETTING EXCITED. ♪

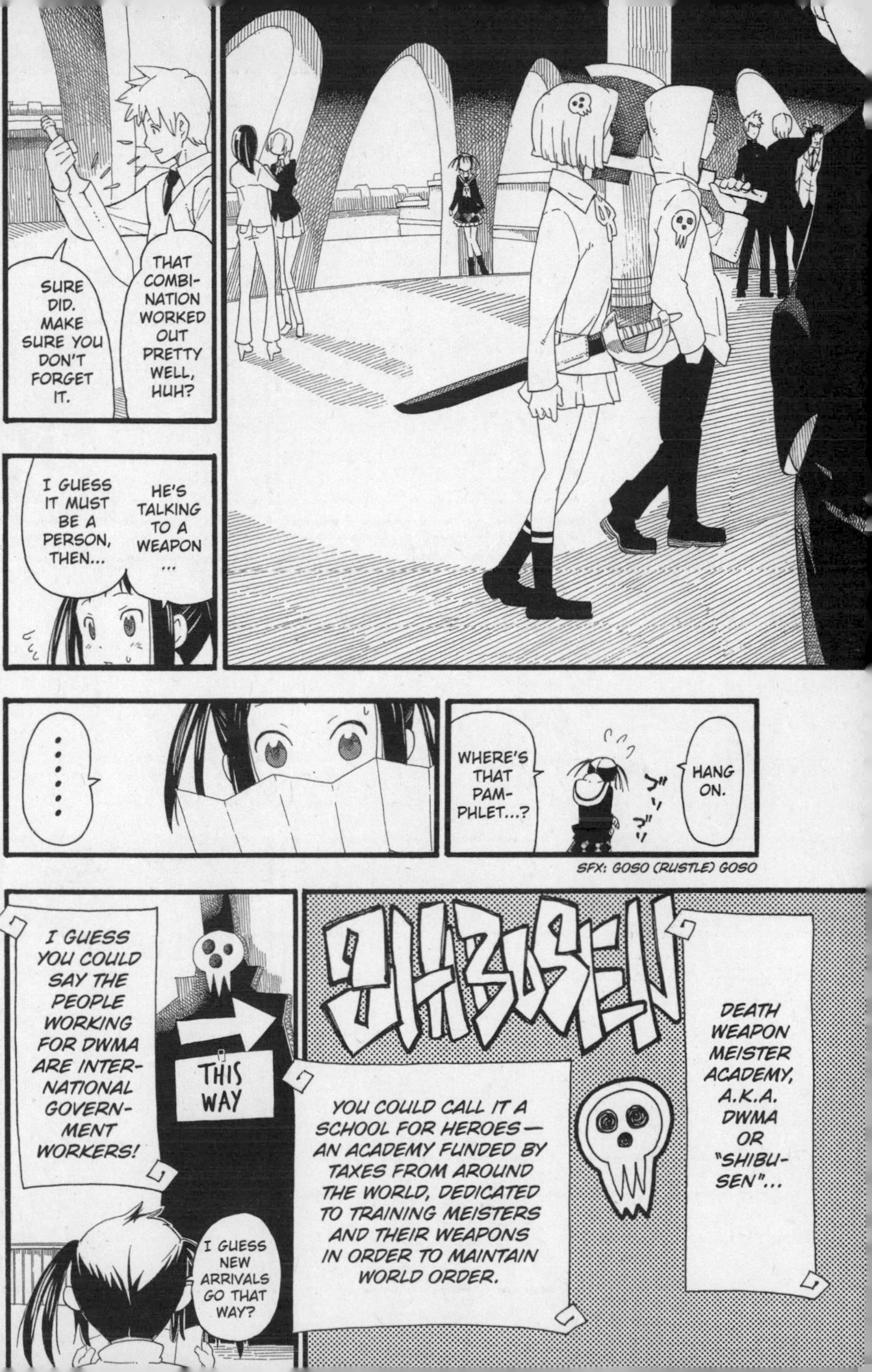
THAT COMBINATION WORKED OUT PRETTY WELL, HUH?
SURE DID. MAKE SURE YOU DON'T FORGET IT.
HE'S TALKING TO A WEAPON...
I GUESS IT MUST BE A PERSON, THEN...
HANG ON.
WHERE'S THAT PAMPHLET...?
SFX: GOSO (RUSTLE) GOSO
......
DEATH WEAPON MEISTER ACADEMY, A.K.A. DWMA OR "SHIBUSEN"...
SHIBUSEN
YOU COULD CALL IT A SCHOOL FOR HEROES—AN ACADEMY FUNDED BY TAXES FROM AROUND THE WORLD, DEDICATED TO TRAINING MEISTERS AND THEIR WEAPONS IN ORDER TO MAINTAIN WORLD ORDER.
I GUESS YOU COULD SAY THE PEOPLE WORKING FOR DWMA ARE INTERNATIONAL GOVERNMENT WORKERS!
THIS WAY
I GUESS NEW ARRIVALS GO THAT WAY?

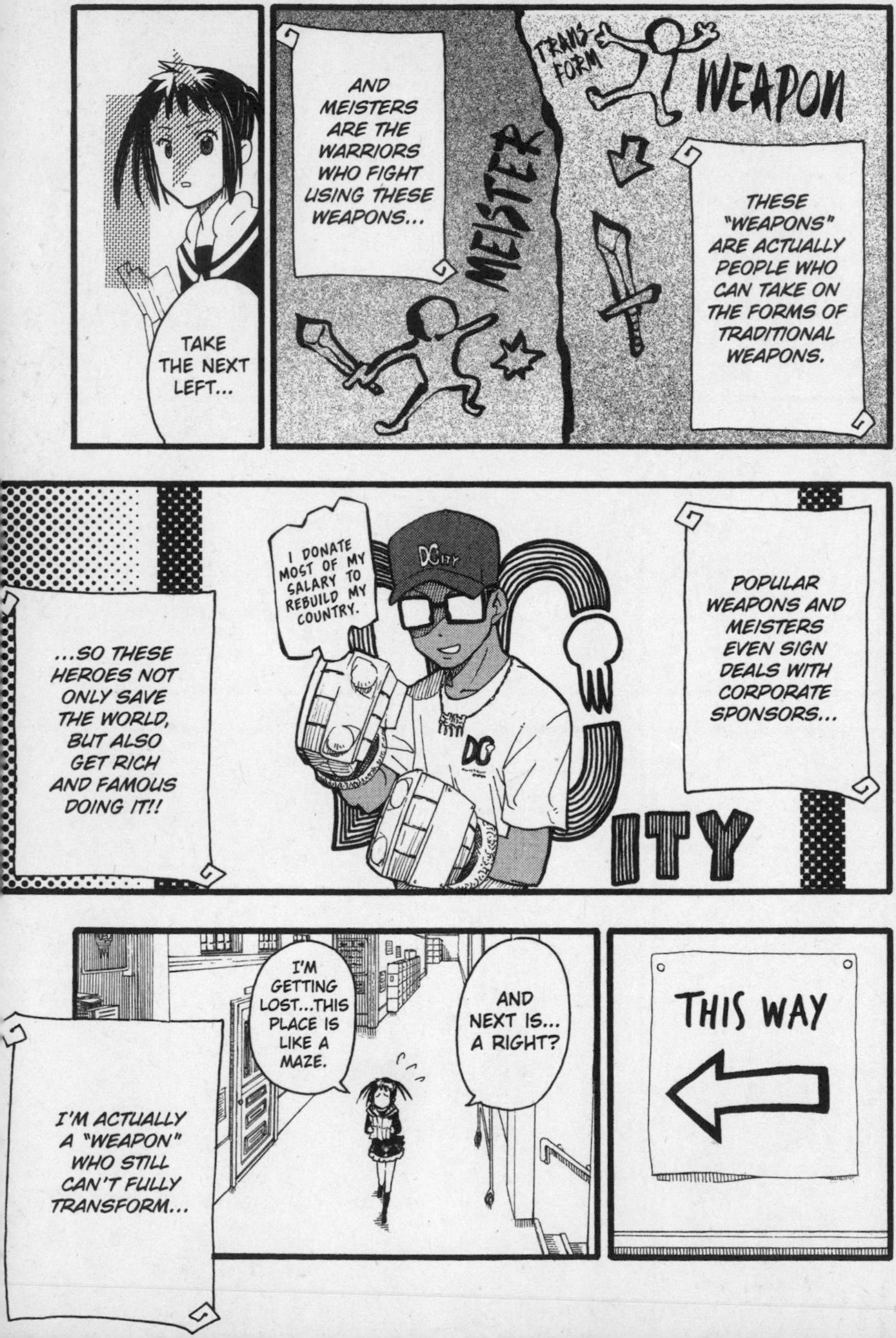
TRANS-FORM
WEAPON
THESE "WEAPONS" ARE ACTUALLY PEOPLE WHO CAN TAKE ON THE FORMS OF TRADITIONAL WEAPONS.
AND MEISTERS ARE THE WARRIORS WHO FIGHT USING THESE WEAPONS...
MEISTER
TAKE THE NEXT LEFT...
POPULAR WEAPONS AND MEISTERS EVEN SIGN DEALS WITH CORPORATE SPONSORS...
I DONATE MOST OF MY SALARY TO REBUILD MY COUNTRY.
...SO THESE HEROES NOT ONLY SAVE THE WORLD, BUT ALSO GET RICH AND FAMOUS DOING IT!!
ITY
THIS WAY
AND NEXT IS... A RIGHT?
I'M GETTING LOST...THIS PLACE IS LIKE A MAZE.
I'M ACTUALLY A "WEAPON" WHO STILL CAN'T FULLY TRANSFORM...

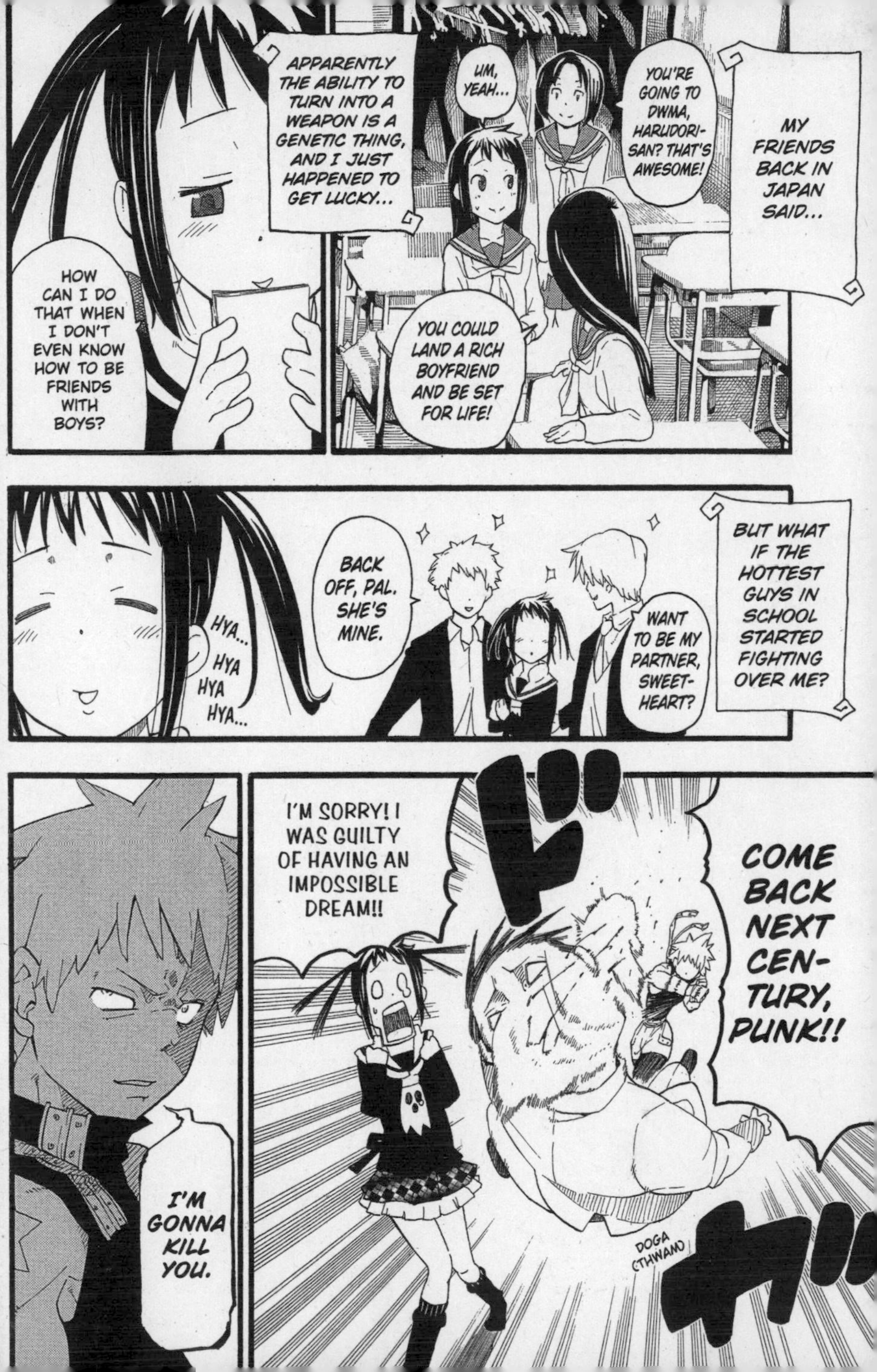

MY FRIENDS BACK IN JAPAN SAID...
YOU'RE GOING TO DWMA, HARUDORI-SAN? THAT'S AWESOME!
UM, YEAH...
APPARENTLY THE ABILITY TO TURN INTO A WEAPON IS A GENETIC THING, AND I JUST HAPPENED TO GET LUCKY...
YOU COULD LAND A RICH BOYFRIEND AND BE SET FOR LIFE!
HOW CAN I DO THAT WHEN I DON'T EVEN KNOW HOW TO BE FRIENDS WITH BOYS?
BUT WHAT IF THE HOTTEST GUYS IN SCHOOL STARTED FIGHTING OVER ME?
WANT TO BE MY PARTNER, SWEET-HEART?
BACK OFF, PAL. SHE'S MINE.
HYA... HYA HYA HYA...
COME BACK NEXT CEN-TURY, PUNK!!
I'M SORRY!! I WAS GUILTY OF HAVING AN IMPOSSIBLE DREAM!!
DOGA (THWAM)
I'M GONNA KILL YOU.

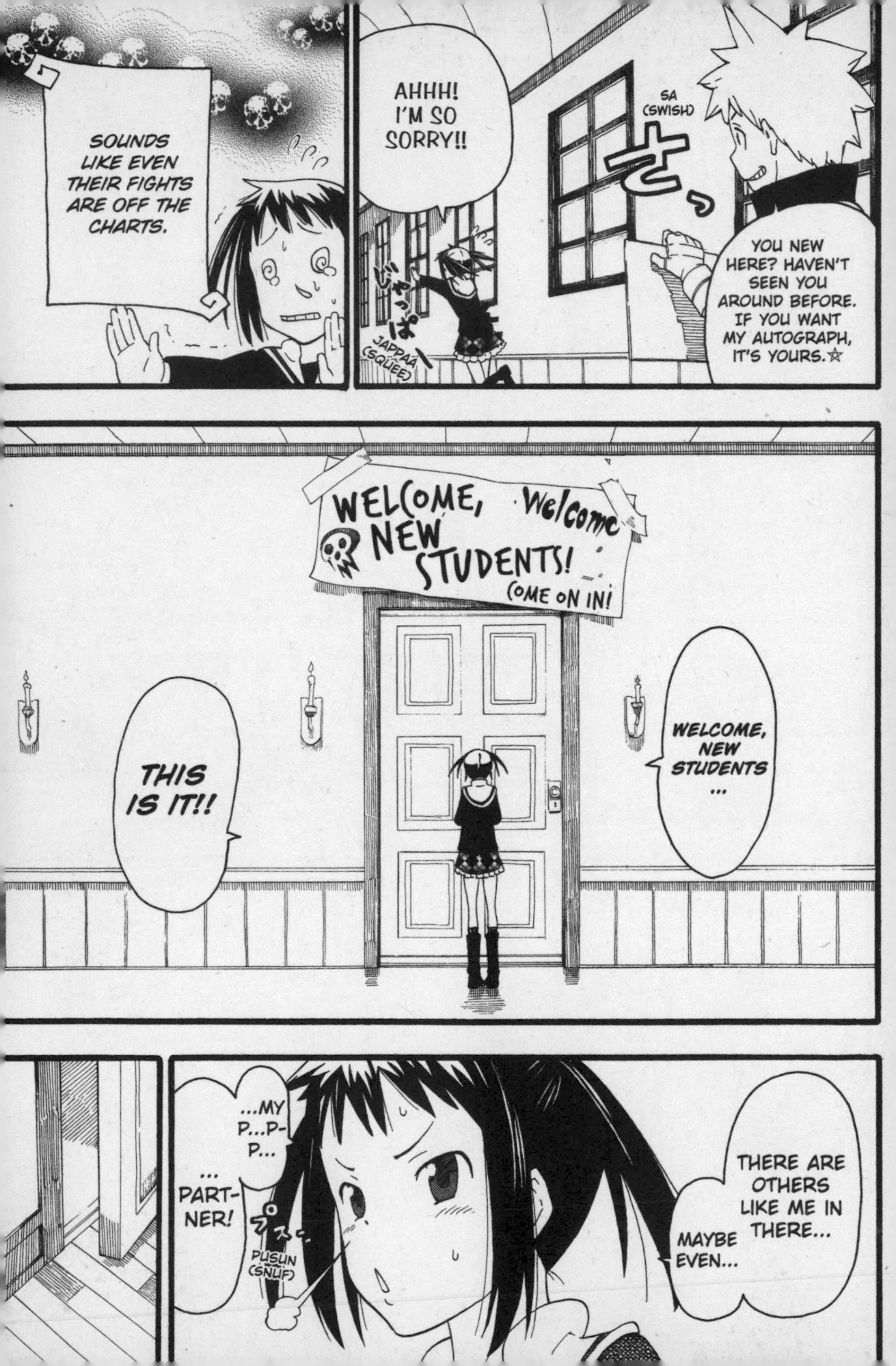
SA (SWISH)
YOU NEW HERE? HAVEN'T SEEN YOU AROUND BEFORE. IF YOU WANT MY AUTOGRAPH, IT'S YOURS.☆
AHHH! I'M SO SORRY!!
JAPPAA (SQUEE)
SOUNDS LIKE EVEN THEIR FIGHTS ARE OFF THE CHARTS.
WELCOME, Welcome NEW STUDENTS! COME ON IN!
WELCOME, NEW STUDENTS ...
THIS IS IT!!
THERE ARE OTHERS LIKE ME IN THERE...
MAYBE EVEN...
...MY P...P-P... ...PART-NER!
PUSUN (SNUF)

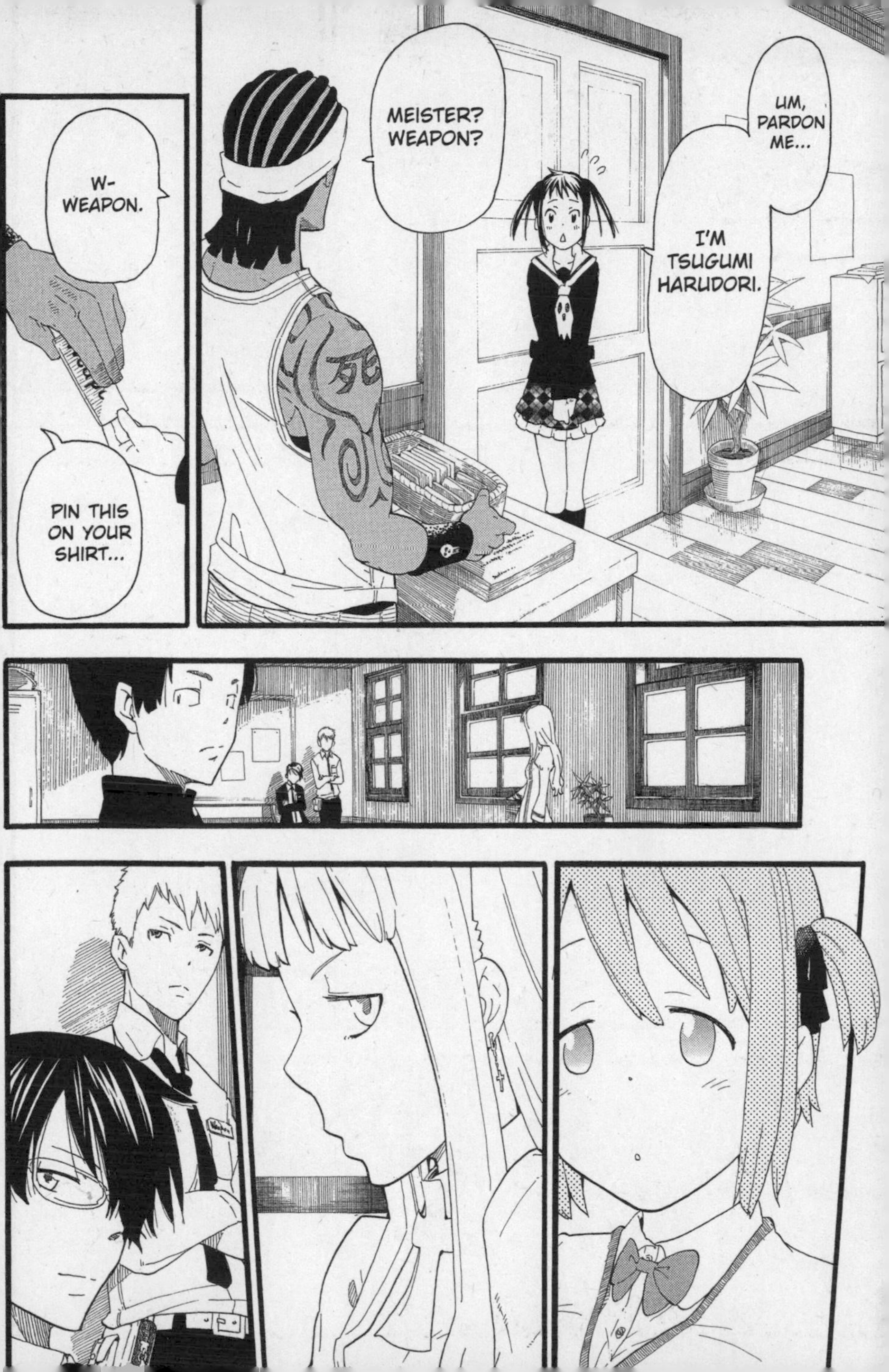
UM, PARDON ME...
I'M TSUGUMI HARUDORI.
MEISTER? WEAPON?
W- WEAPON.
PIN THIS ON YOUR SHIRT...

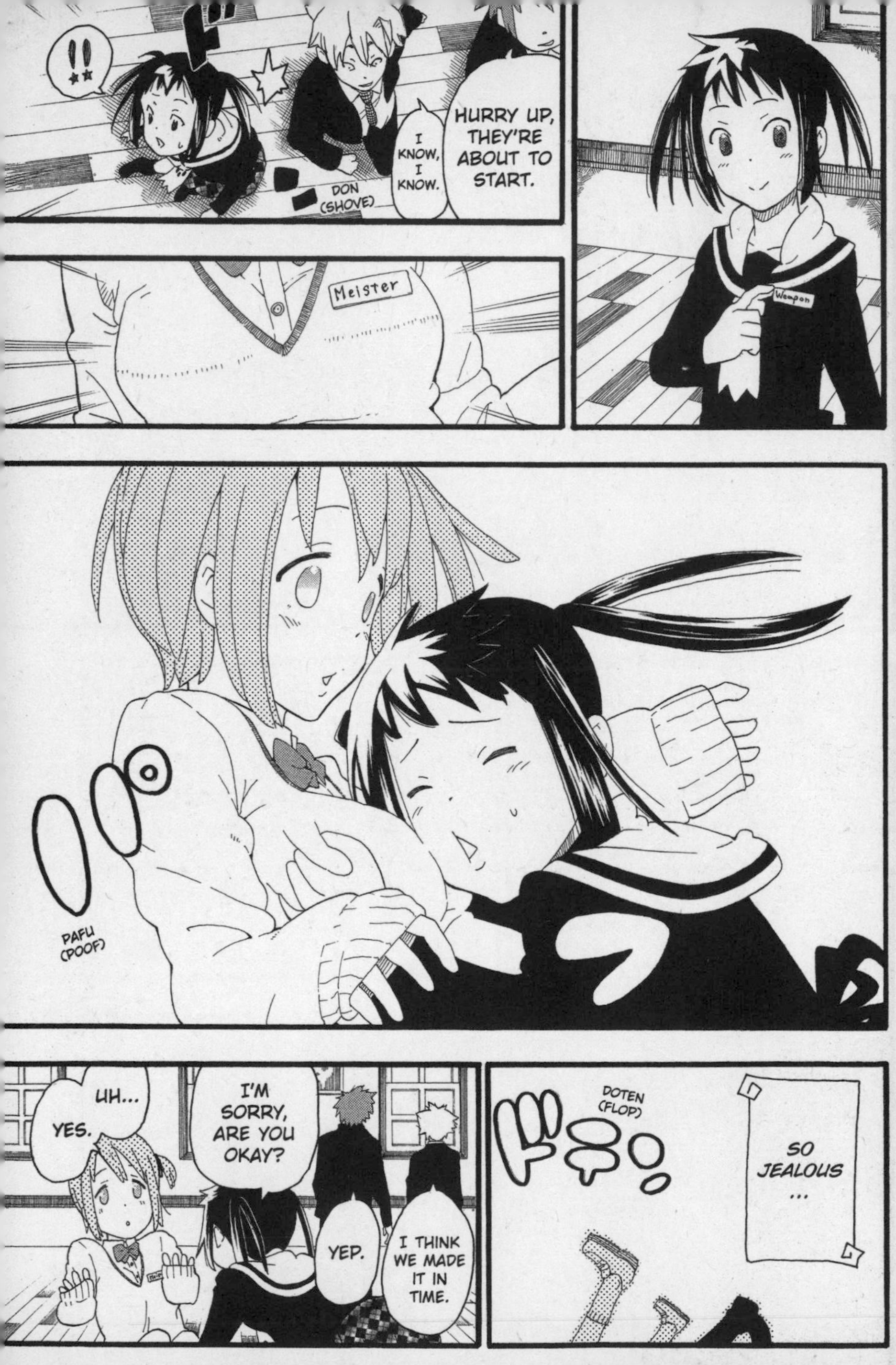

Weapon
HURRY UP, THEY'RE ABOUT TO START.
I KNOW, I KNOW.
DON (SHOVE)
!!
Meister
PAFU (POOF)
DOTEN (FLOP)
SO JEALOUS ...
I'M SORRY, ARE YOU OKAY?
UH... YES.
I THINK WE MADE IT IN TIME.
YEP.

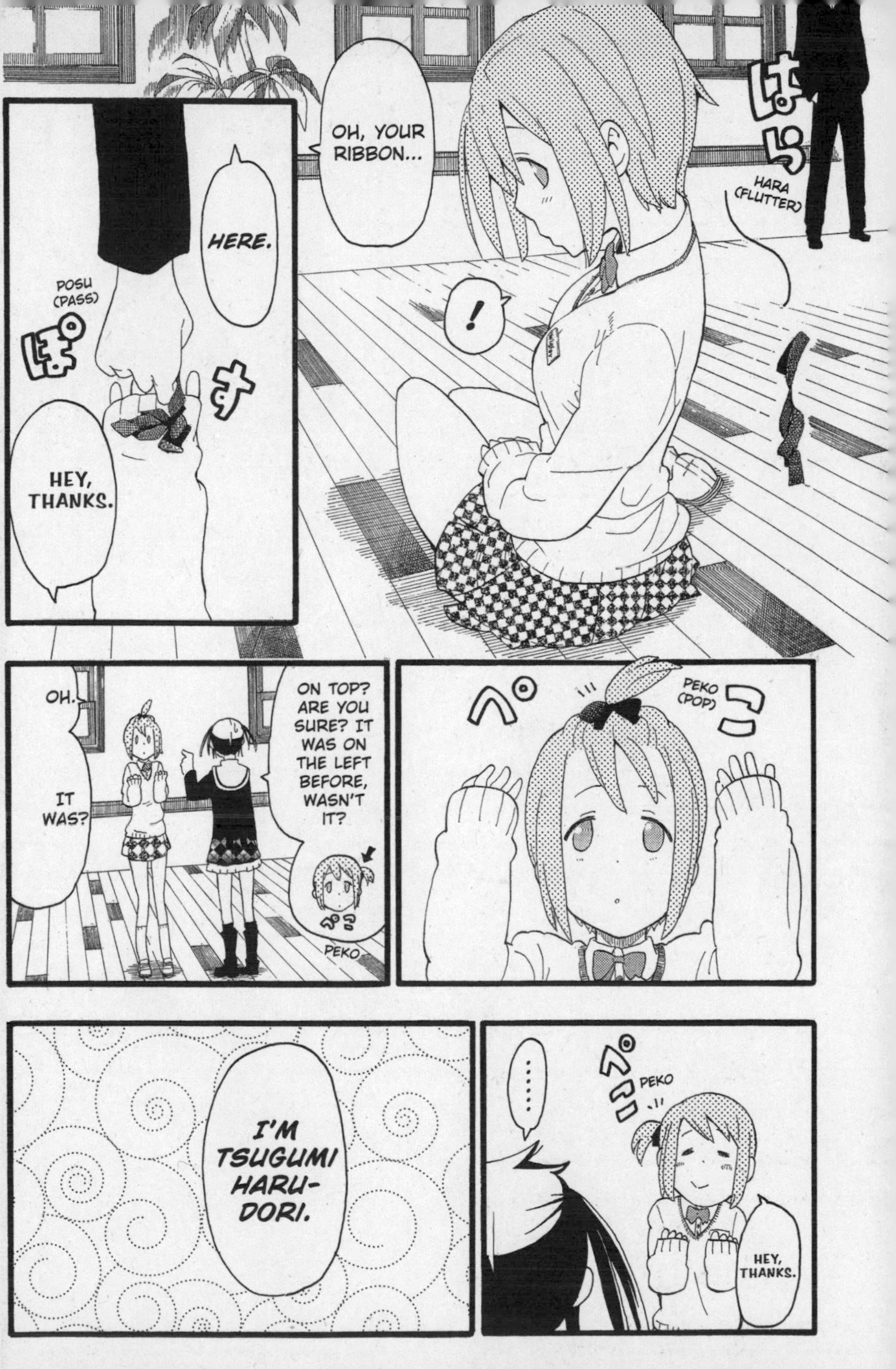
ぱら
HARA (FLUTTER)
OH, YOUR RIBBON...
!
HERE.
ぽす
POSU (PASS)
HEY, THANKS.
ぺこ
PEKO (POP)
ON TOP? ARE YOU SURE? IT WAS ON THE LEFT BEFORE, WASN'T IT?
ぺこ
PEKO
OH.
IT WAS?
ぺこ
PEKO
......
HEY, THANKS.
I'M TSUGUMI HARU-DORI.

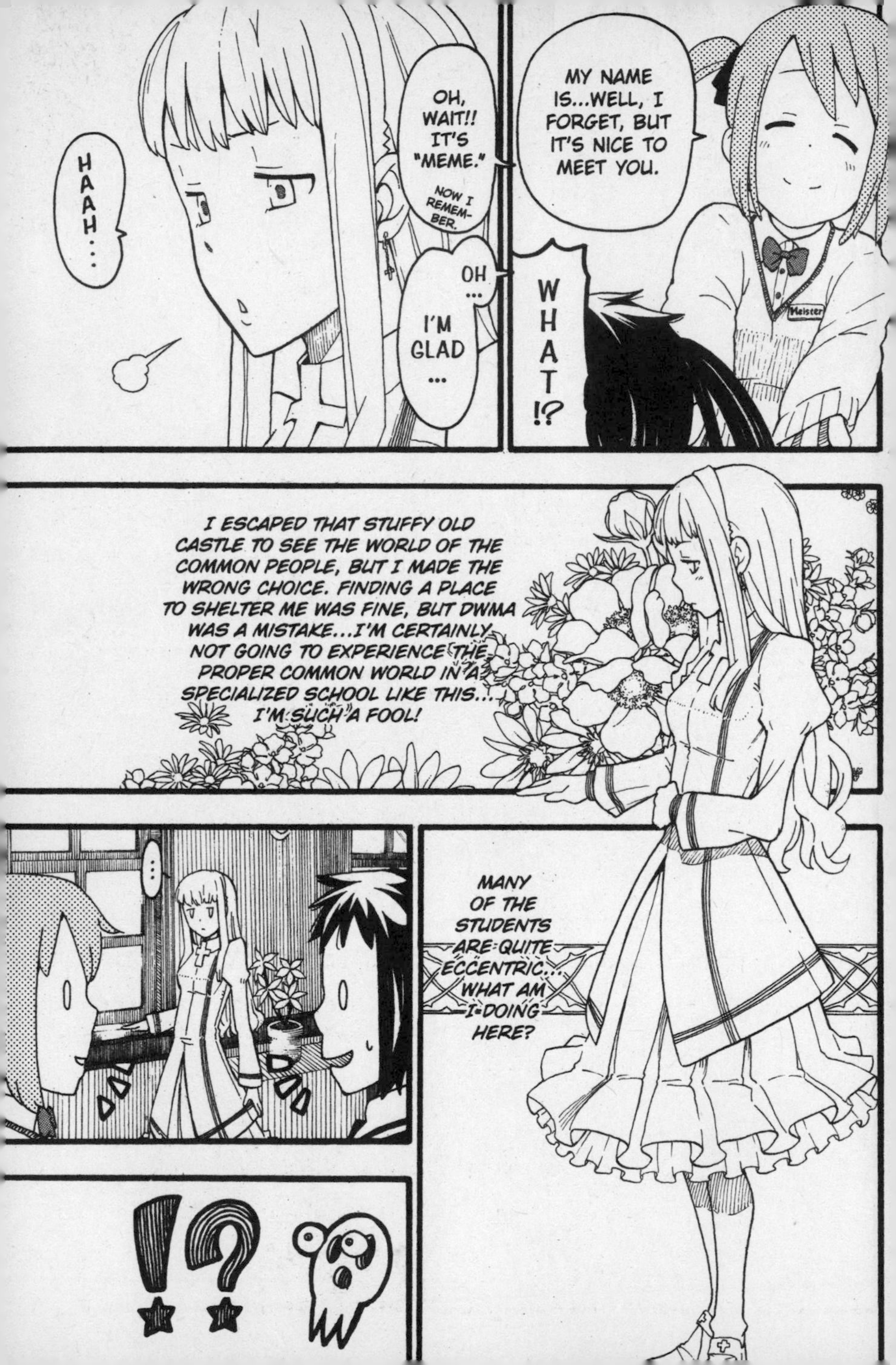
MY NAME IS...WELL, I FORGET, BUT IT'S NICE TO MEET YOU.
WHAT!?
OH, WAIT!! IT'S "MEME."
NOW I REMEMBER.
OH...
I'M GLAD...
HAAH...
I ESCAPED THAT STUFFY OLD CASTLE TO SEE THE WORLD OF THE COMMON PEOPLE, BUT I MADE THE WRONG CHOICE. FINDING A PLACE TO SHELTER ME WAS FINE, BUT DWMA WAS A MISTAKE...I'M CERTAINLY NOT GOING TO EXPERIENCE THE PROPER COMMON WORLD IN A SPECIALIZED SCHOOL LIKE THIS... I'M SUCH A FOOL!
MANY OF THE STUDENTS ARE QUITE ECCENTRIC... WHAT AM I DOING HERE?
...
Meister

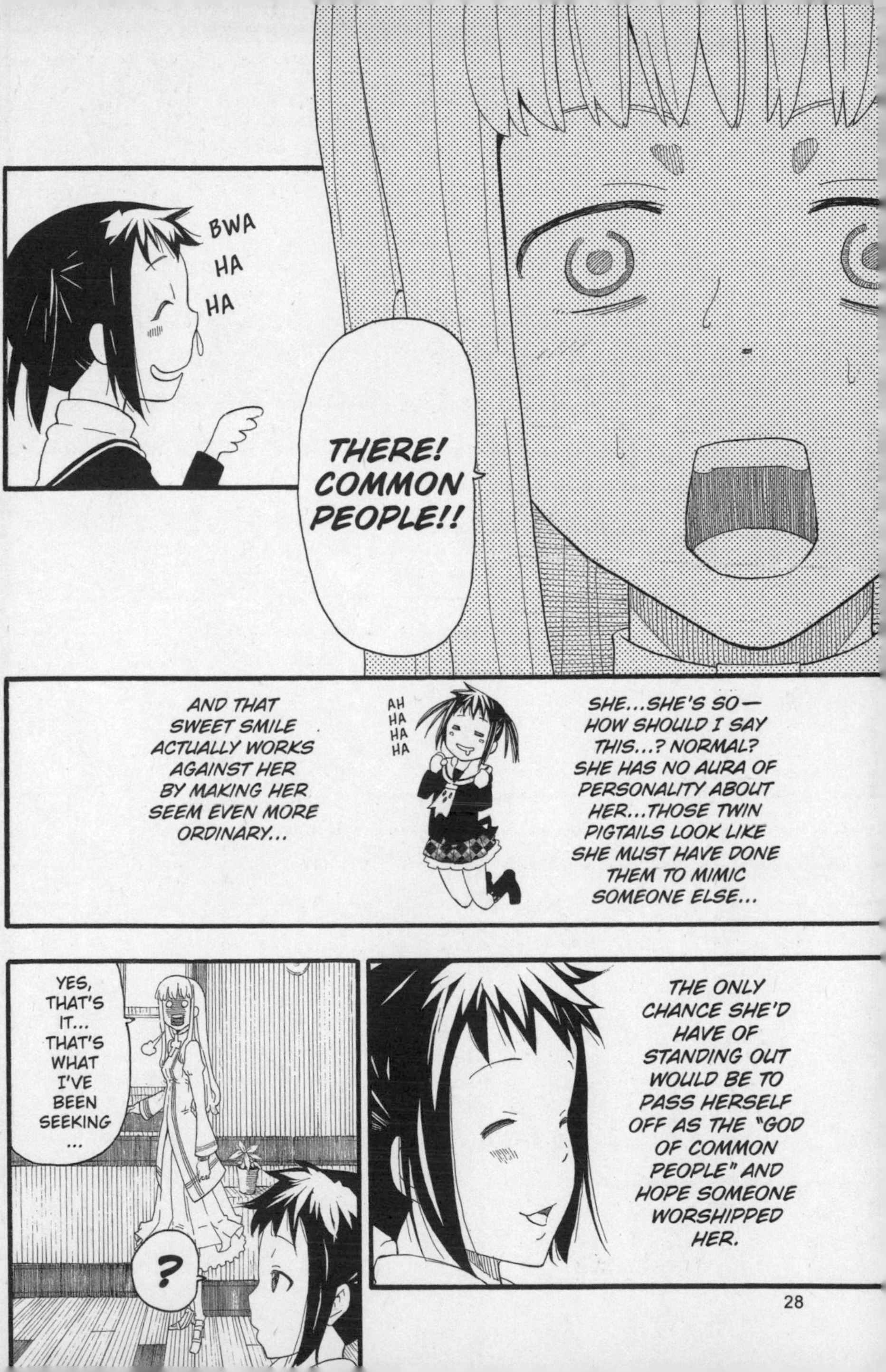
THERE! COMMON PEOPLE!!
BWA HA HA
SHE...SHE'S SO—HOW SHOULD I SAY THIS...? NORMAL? SHE HAS NO AURA OF PERSONALITY ABOUT HER...THOSE TWIN PIGTAILS LOOK LIKE SHE MUST HAVE DONE THEM TO MIMIC SOMEONE ELSE...
AH HA HA HA
AND THAT SWEET SMILE ACTUALLY WORKS AGAINST HER BY MAKING HER SEEM EVEN MORE ORDINARY...
THE ONLY CHANCE SHE'D HAVE OF STANDING OUT WOULD BE TO PASS HERSELF OFF AS THE "GOD OF COMMON PEOPLE" AND HOPE SOMEONE WORSHIPPED HER.
YES, THAT'S IT... THAT'S WHAT I'VE BEEN SEEKING...
?

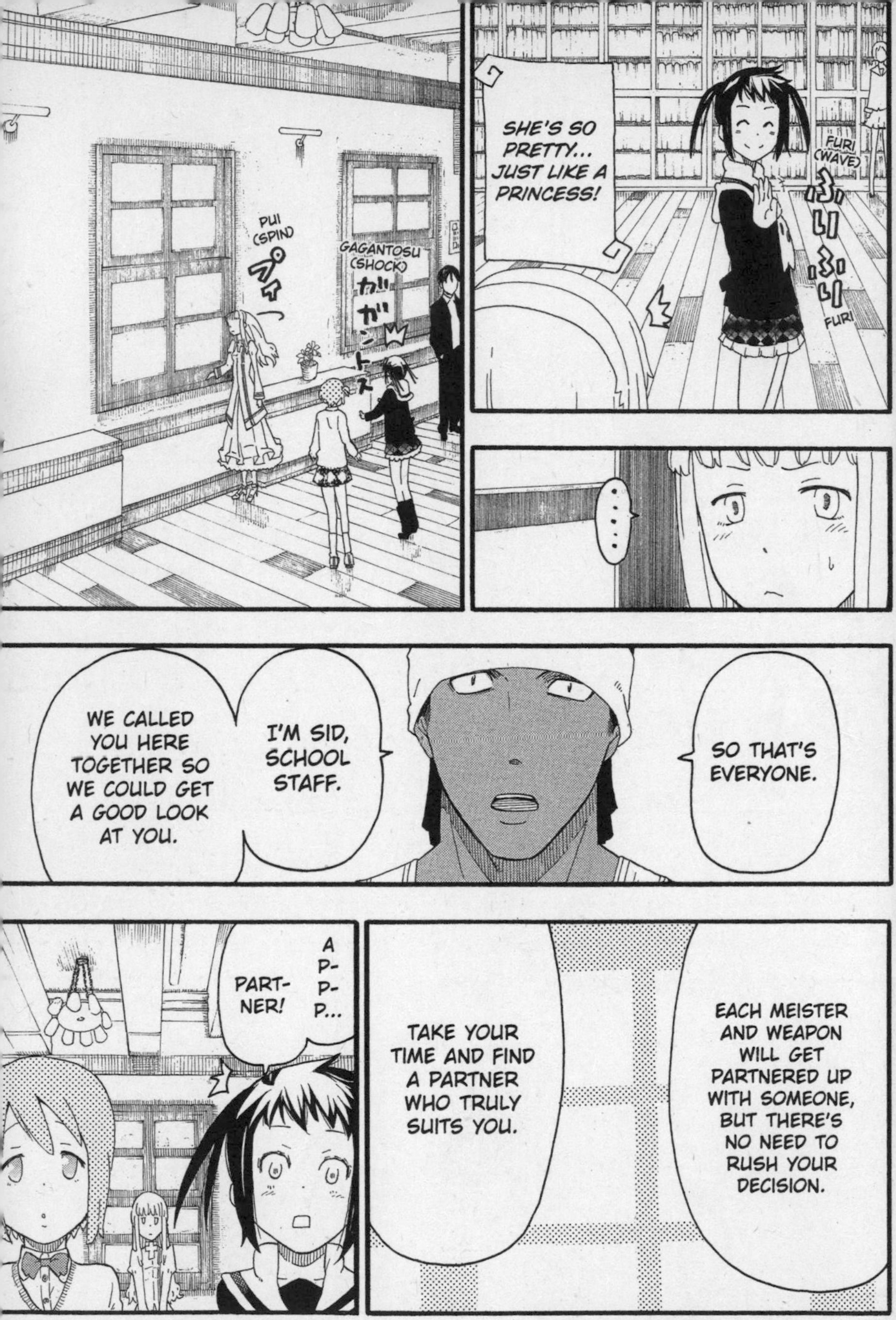
SHE'S SO PRETTY... JUST LIKE A PRINCESS!
FURI (WAVE)
FURI
...
GAGANTOSU (SHOCK)
PUI (SPIND
SO THAT'S EVERYONE.
I'M SID, SCHOOL STAFF.
WE CALLED YOU HERE TOGETHER SO WE COULD GET A GOOD LOOK AT YOU.
EACH MEISTER AND WEAPON WILL GET PARTNERED UP WITH SOMEONE, BUT THERE'S NO NEED TO RUSH YOUR DECISION.
TAKE YOUR TIME AND FIND A PARTNER WHO TRULY SUITS YOU.
A P- P- P...
PART- NER!

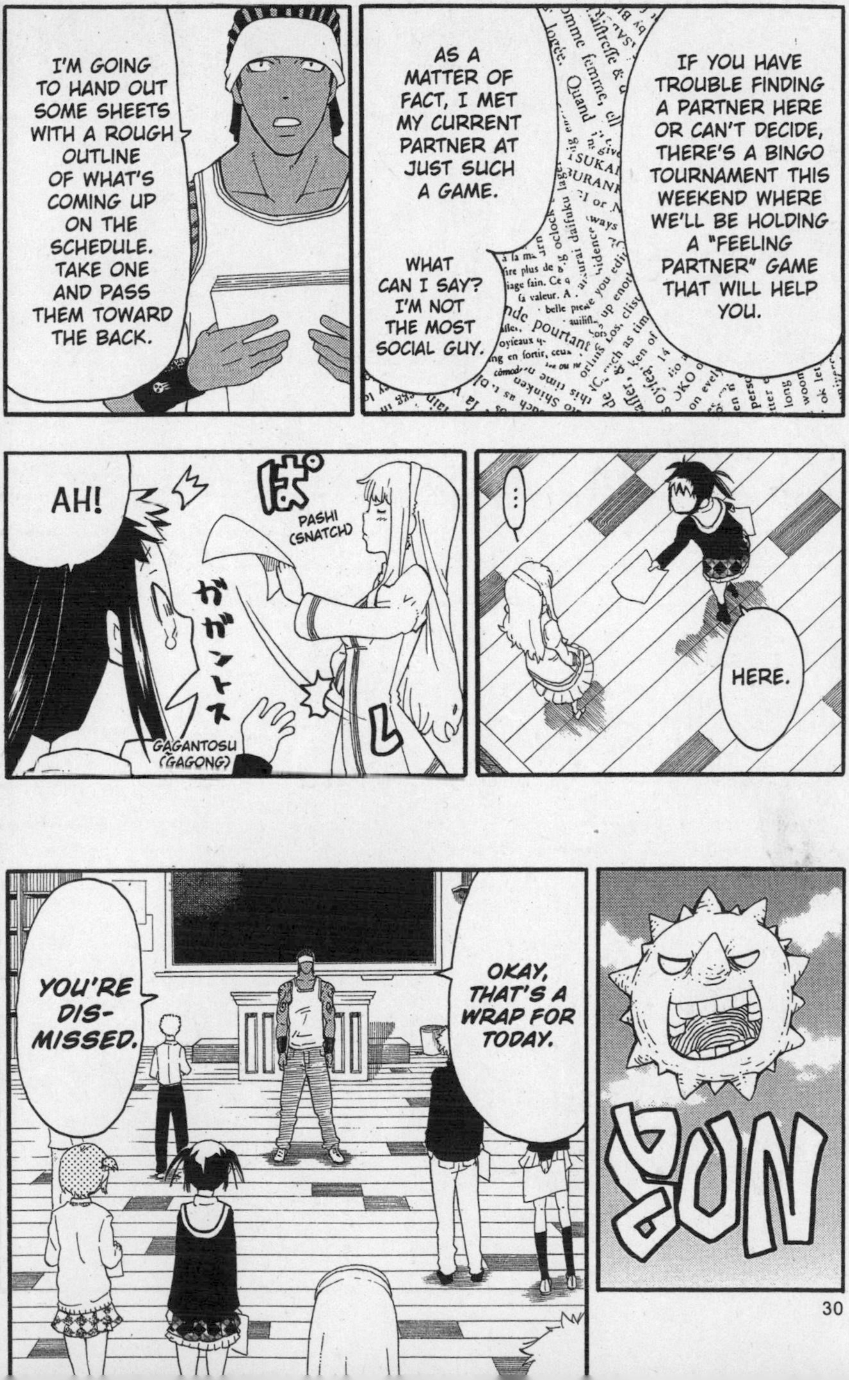

IF YOU HAVE TROUBLE FINDING A PARTNER HERE OR CAN'T DECIDE, THERE'S A BINGO TOURNAMENT THIS WEEKEND WHERE WE'LL BE HOLDING A "FEELING PARTNER" GAME THAT WILL HELP YOU.
AS A MATTER OF FACT, I MET MY CURRENT PARTNER AT JUST SUCH A GAME.
WHAT CAN I SAY? I'M NOT THE MOST SOCIAL GUY.
I'M GOING TO HAND OUT SOME SHEETS WITH A ROUGH OUTLINE OF WHAT'S COMING UP ON THE SCHEDULE. TAKE ONE AND PASS THEM TOWARD THE BACK.
...
HERE.
ぱ
PASHI (SNATCH)
AH!
ガガントス
GAGANTOSU (GAGONG)
SUN
OKAY, THAT'S A WRAP FOR TODAY.
YOU'RE DIS-MISSED.

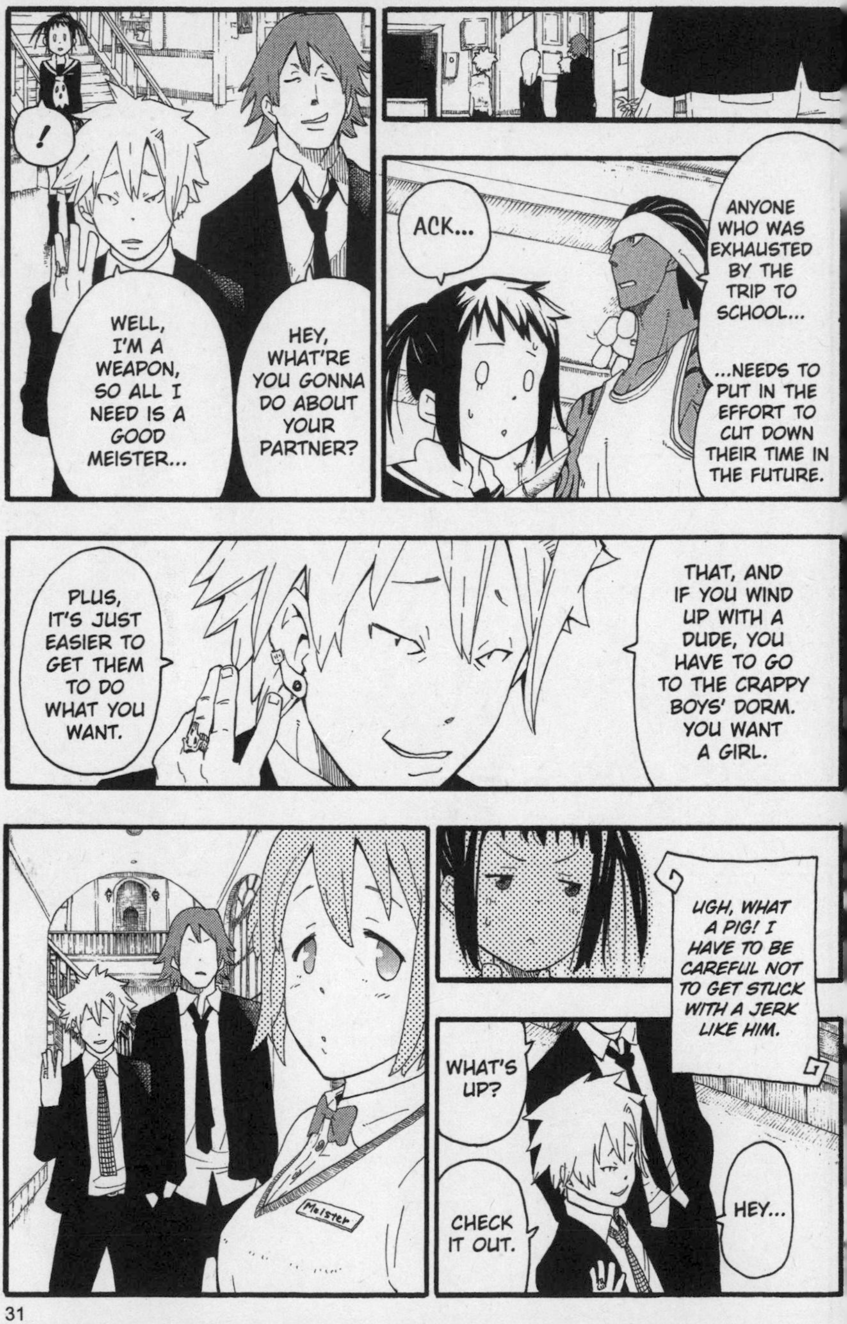
ANYONE WHO WAS EXHAUSTED BY THE TRIP TO SCHOOL...
...NEEDS TO PUT IN THE EFFORT TO CUT DOWN THEIR TIME IN THE FUTURE.
ACK...
!
HEY, WHAT'RE YOU GONNA DO ABOUT YOUR PARTNER?
WELL, I'M A WEAPON, SO ALL I NEED IS A GOOD MEISTER...
THAT, AND IF YOU WIND UP WITH A DUDE, YOU HAVE TO GO TO THE CRAPPY BOYS' DORM. YOU WANT A GIRL.
PLUS, IT'S JUST EASIER TO GET THEM TO DO WHAT YOU WANT.
UGH, WHAT A PIG! I HAVE TO BE CAREFUL NOT TO GET STUCK WITH A JERK LIKE HIM.
HEY...
WHAT'S UP?
CHECK IT OUT.
Meister

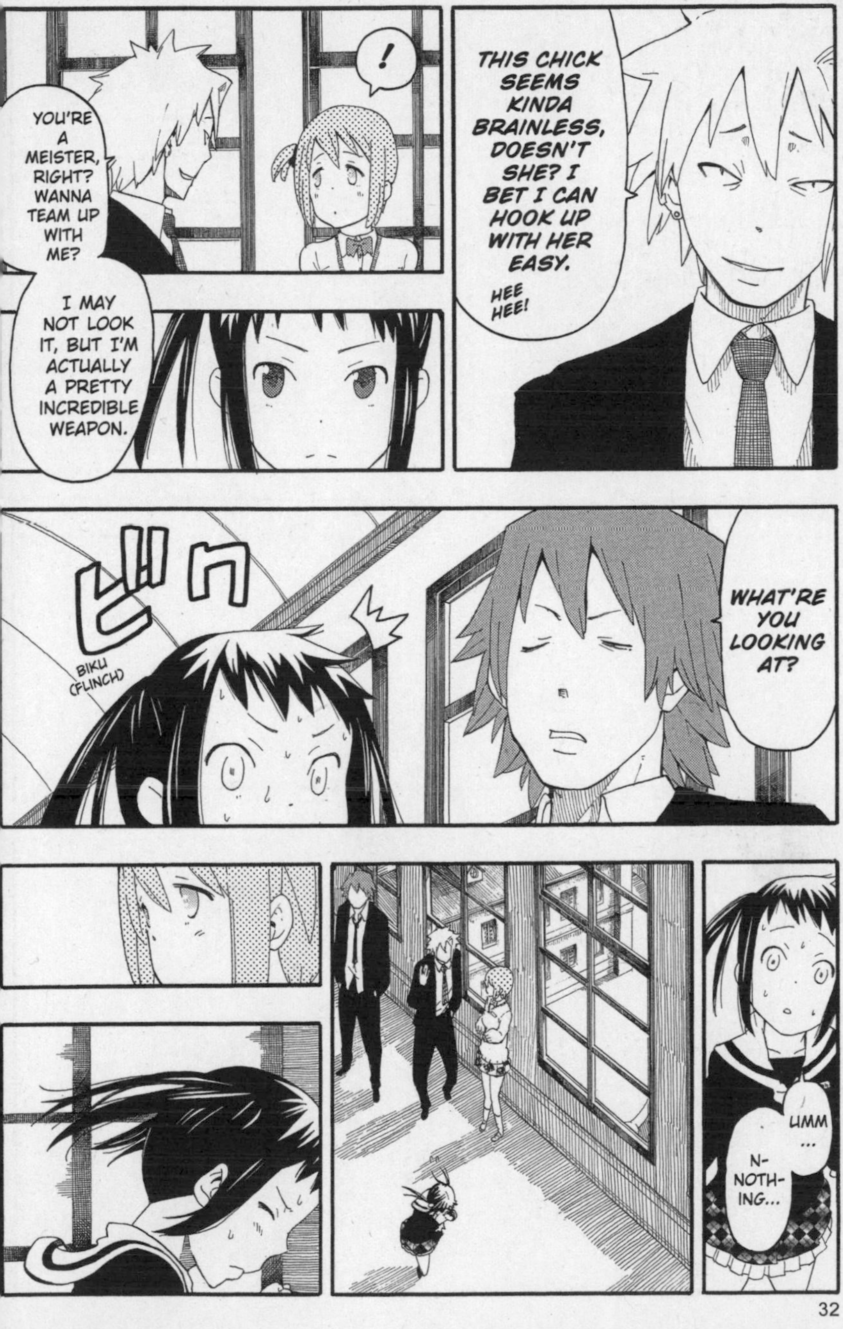

THIS CHICK SEEMS KINDA BRAINLESS, DOESN'T SHE? I BET I CAN HOOK UP WITH HER EASY.
HEE HEE!
!
YOU'RE A MEISTER, RIGHT? WANNA TEAM UP WITH ME?
I MAY NOT LOOK IT, BUT I'M ACTUALLY A PRETTY INCREDIBLE WEAPON.
WHAT'RE YOU LOOKING AT?
BIKU (FLINCH)
UMM...
N-NOTHING...

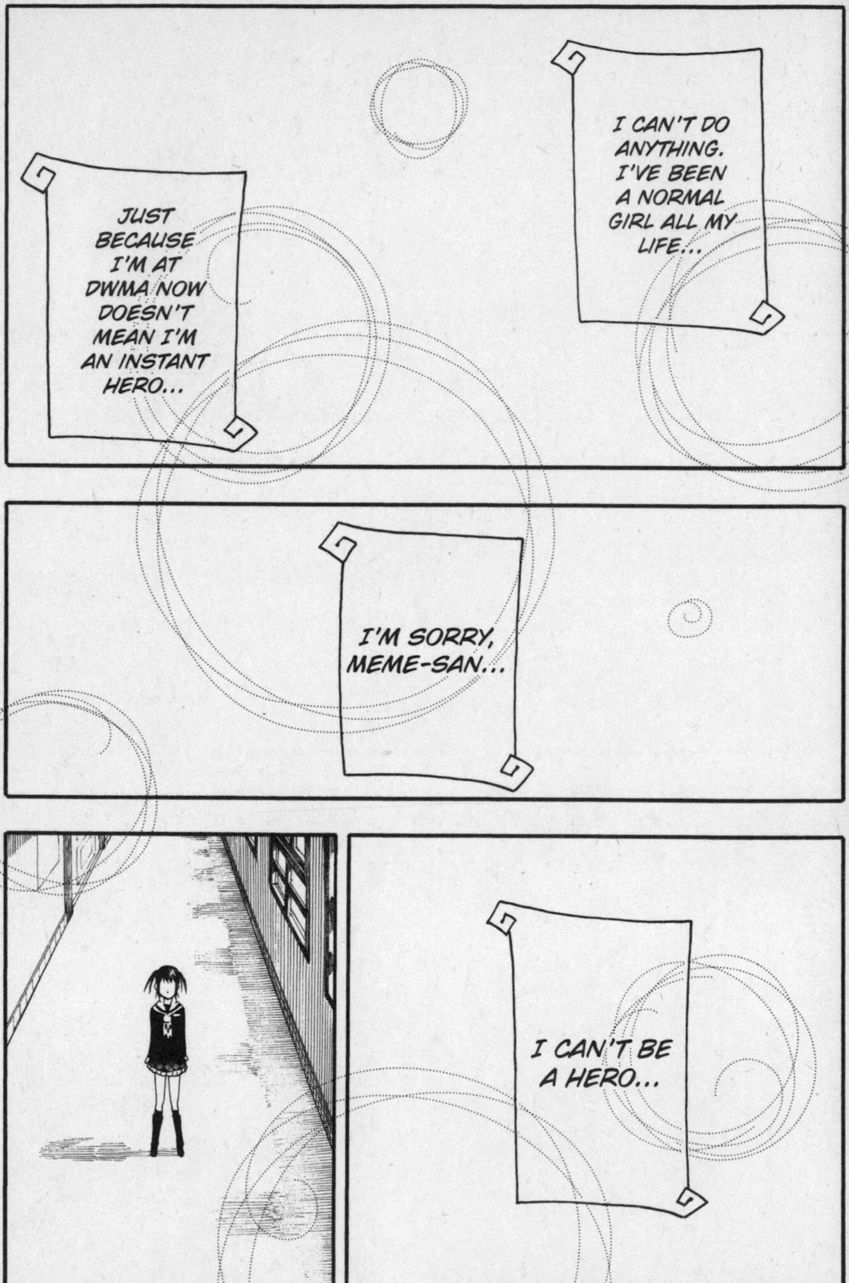
I CAN'T DO ANYTHING. I'VE BEEN A NORMAL GIRL ALL MY LIFE...
JUST BECAUSE I'M AT DWMA NOW DOESN'T MEAN I'M AN INSTANT HERO...
I'M SORRY, MEME-SAN...
I CAN'T BE A HERO...

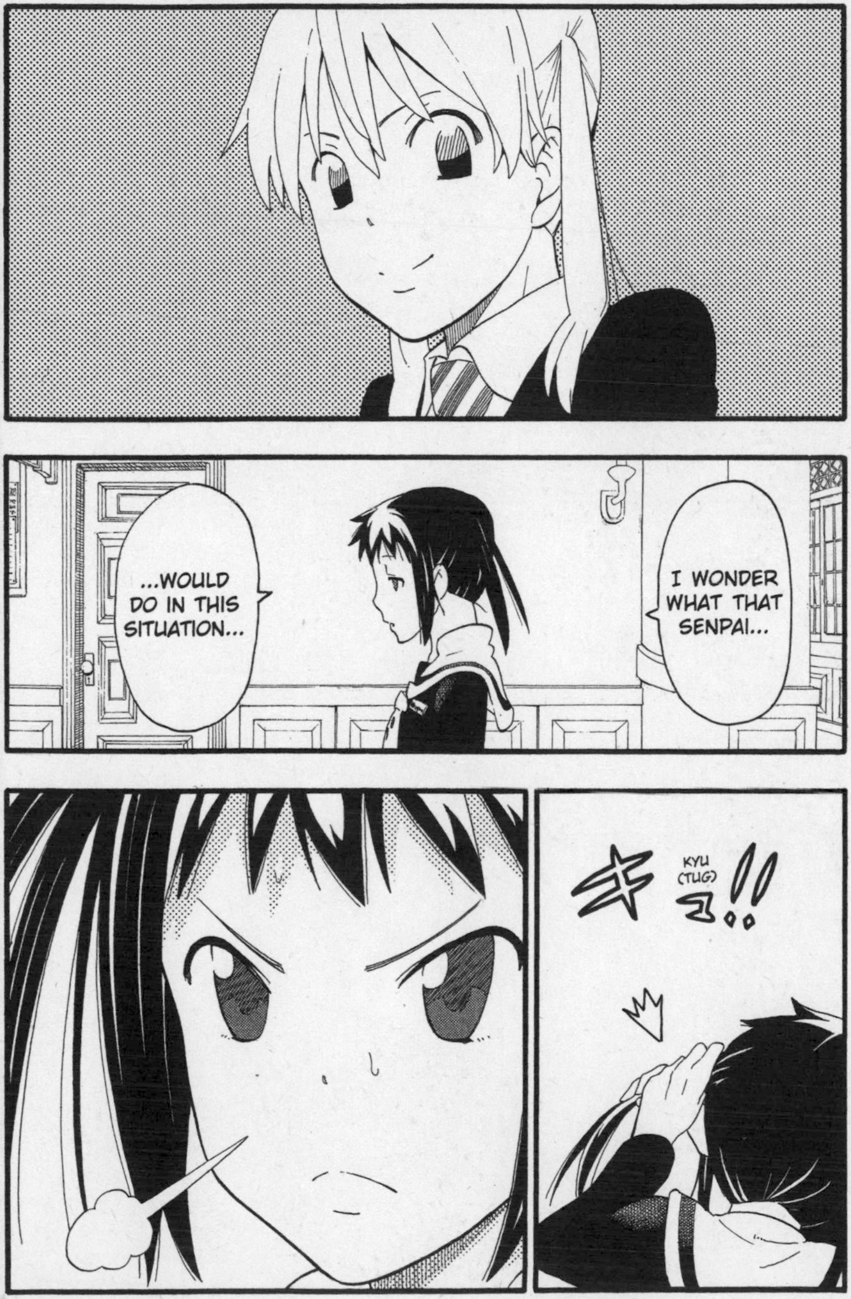
I WONDER WHAT THAT SENPAI...
...WOULD DO IN THIS SITUATION...
KYU (TUG)

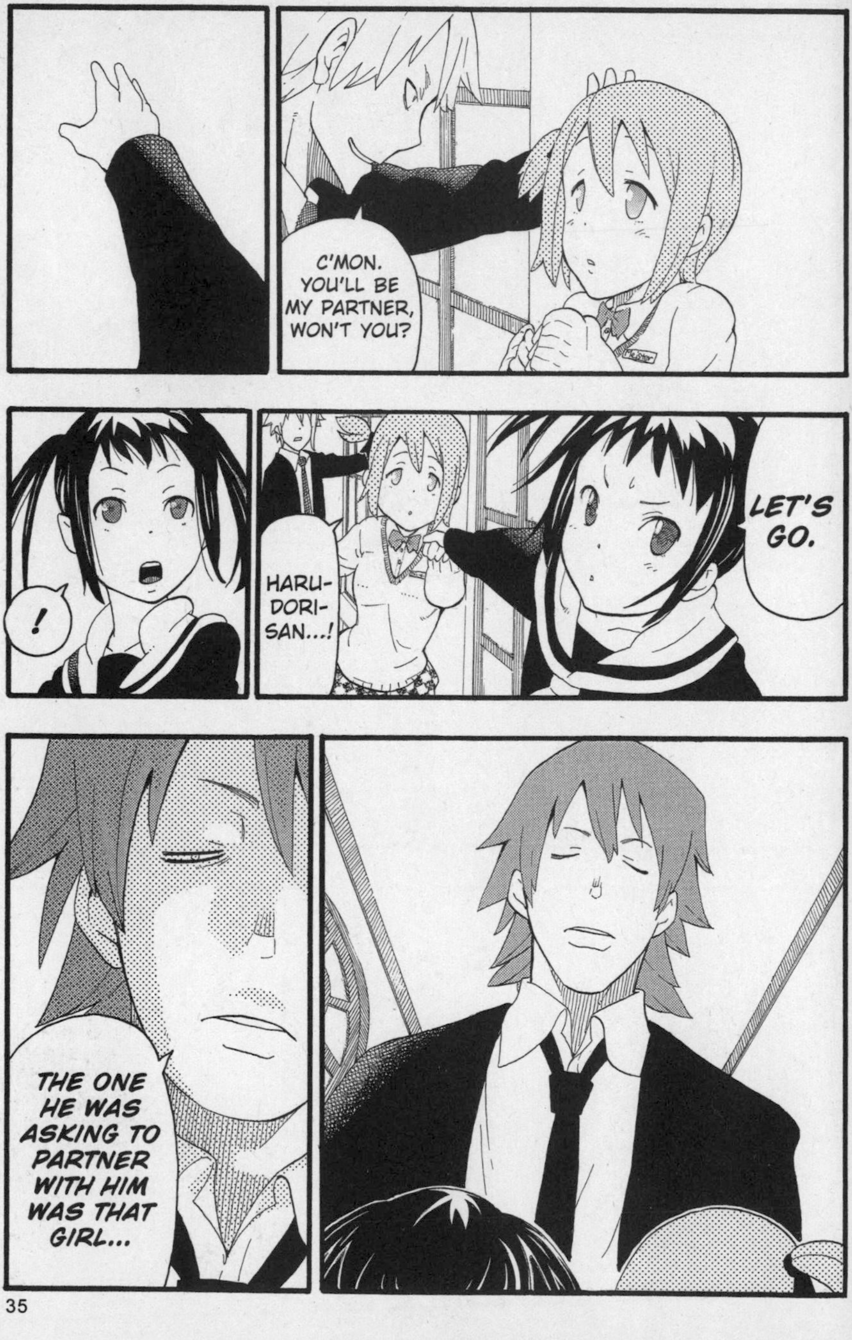
C'MON. YOU'LL BE MY PARTNER, WON'T YOU?
LET'S GO.
HARU-DORI-SAN...!
!
THE ONE HE WAS ASKING TO PARTNER WITH HIM WAS THAT GIRL...

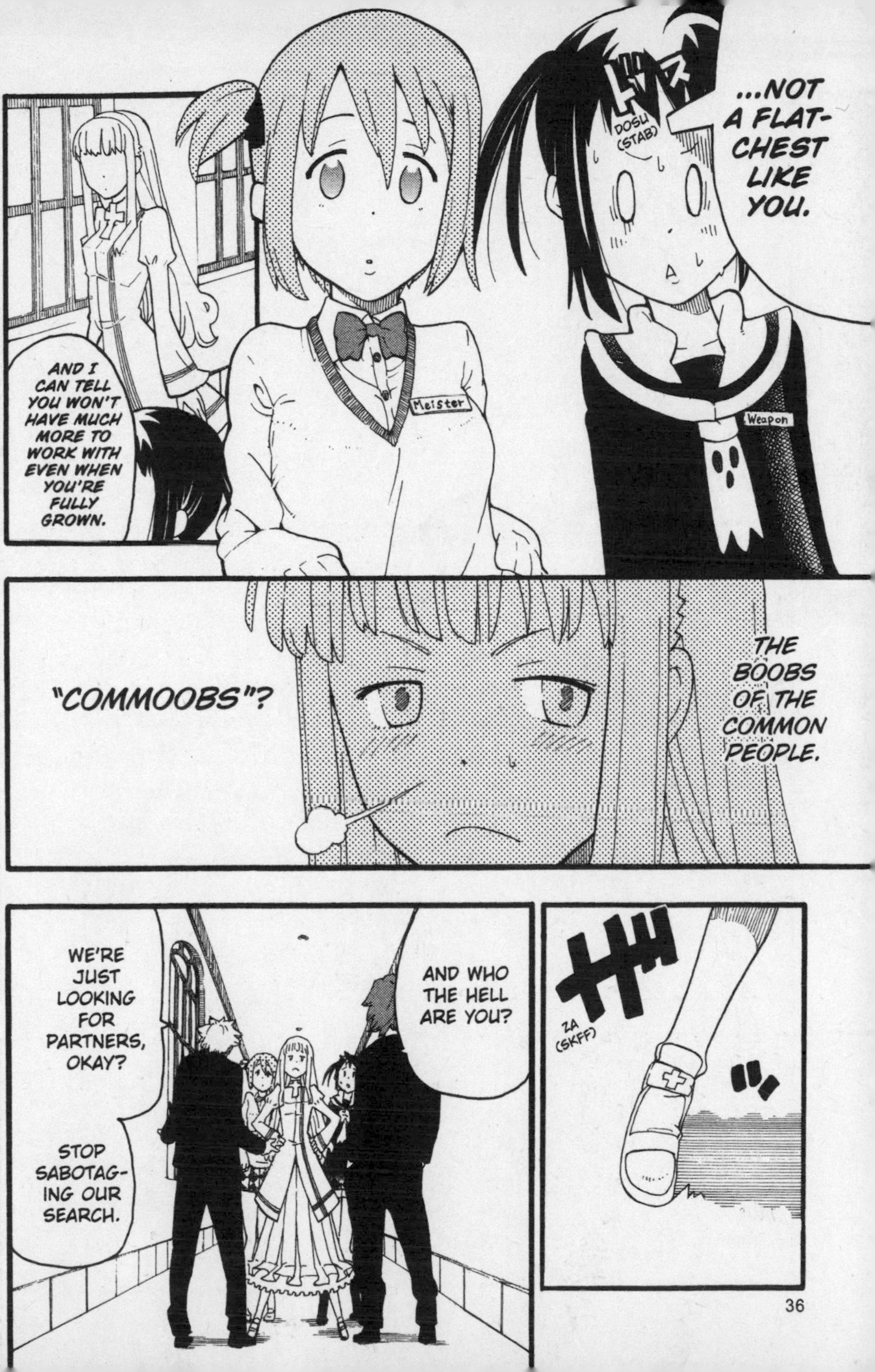

DOSU (STAB)
...NOT A FLAT-CHEST LIKE YOU.
Weapon
Meister
AND I CAN TELL YOU WON'T HAVE MUCH MORE TO WORK WITH EVEN WHEN YOU'RE FULLY GROWN.
THE BOOBS OF THE COMMON PEOPLE.
"COMMOOBS"?
ZA (SKFF)
AND WHO THE HELL ARE YOU?
WE'RE JUST LOOKING FOR PARTNERS, OKAY?
STOP SABOTAGING OUR SEARCH.

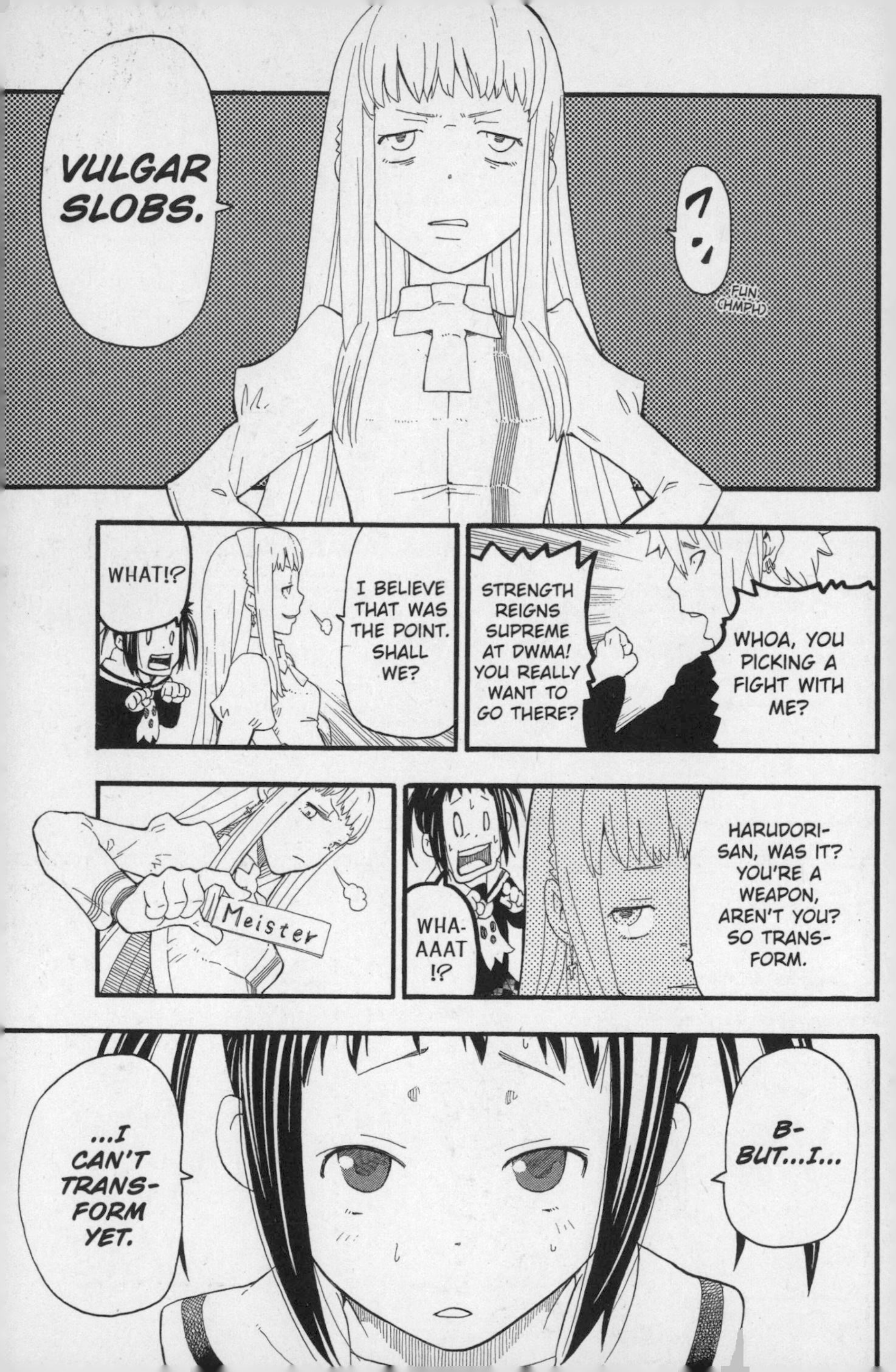
FUN (HMPH)
VULGAR SLOBS.
WHOA, YOU PICKING A FIGHT WITH ME?
STRENGTH REIGNS SUPREME AT DWMA! YOU REALLY WANT TO GO THERE?
I BELIEVE THAT WAS THE POINT. SHALL WE?
WHAT!?
HARUDORI-SAN, WAS IT? YOU'RE A WEAPON, AREN'T YOU? SO TRANS-FORM.
WHA-AAAT !?
Meister
B-BUT...I...
...I CAN'T TRANS-FORM YET.

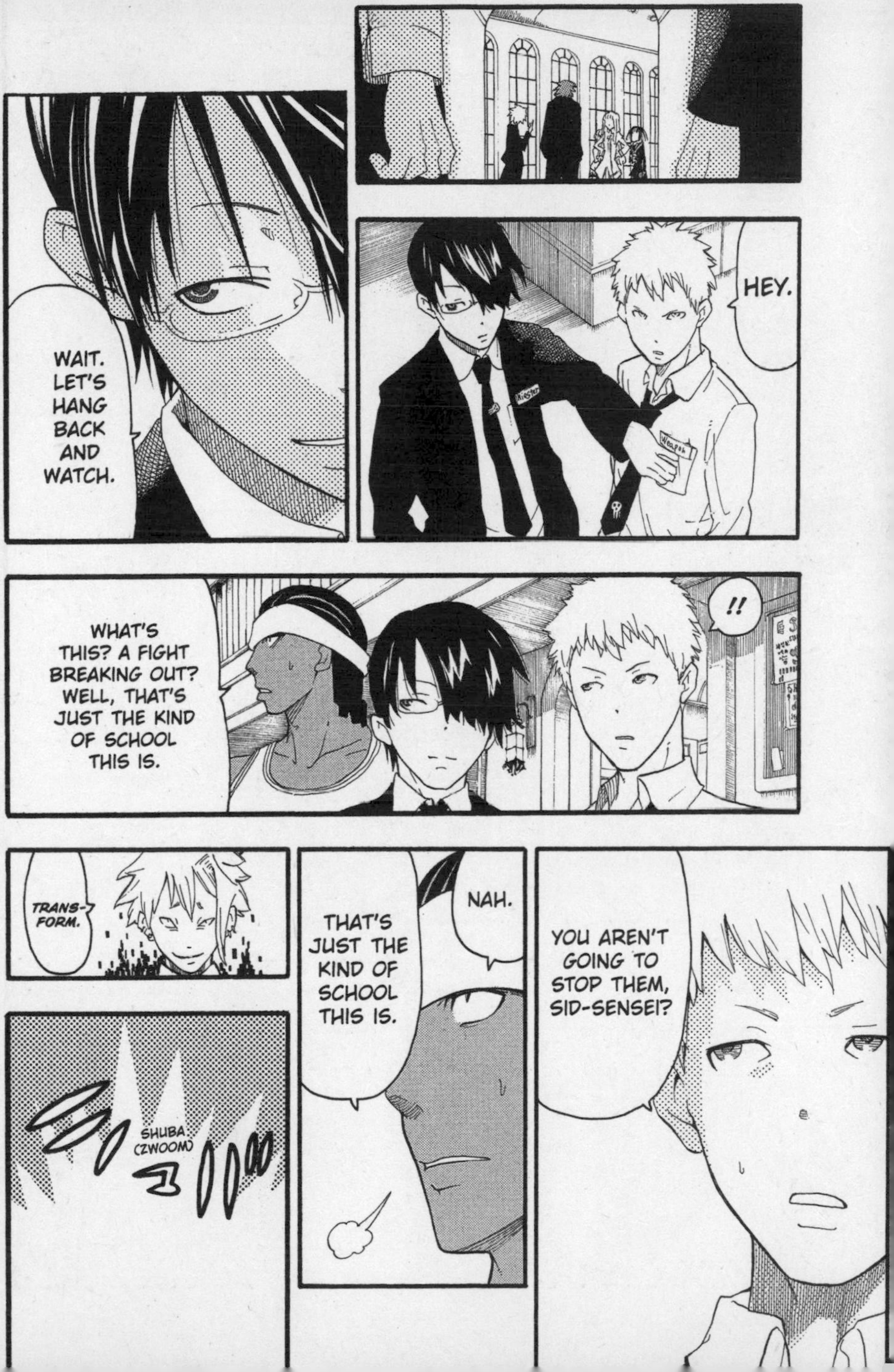
HEY.
WAIT. LET'S HANG BACK AND WATCH.
!!
WHAT'S THIS? A FIGHT BREAKING OUT? WELL, THAT'S JUST THE KIND OF SCHOOL THIS IS.
YOU AREN'T GOING TO STOP THEM, SID-SENSEI?
NAH.
THAT'S JUST THE KIND OF SCHOOL THIS IS.
TRANS-FORM.
SHUBA (ZWOOM)

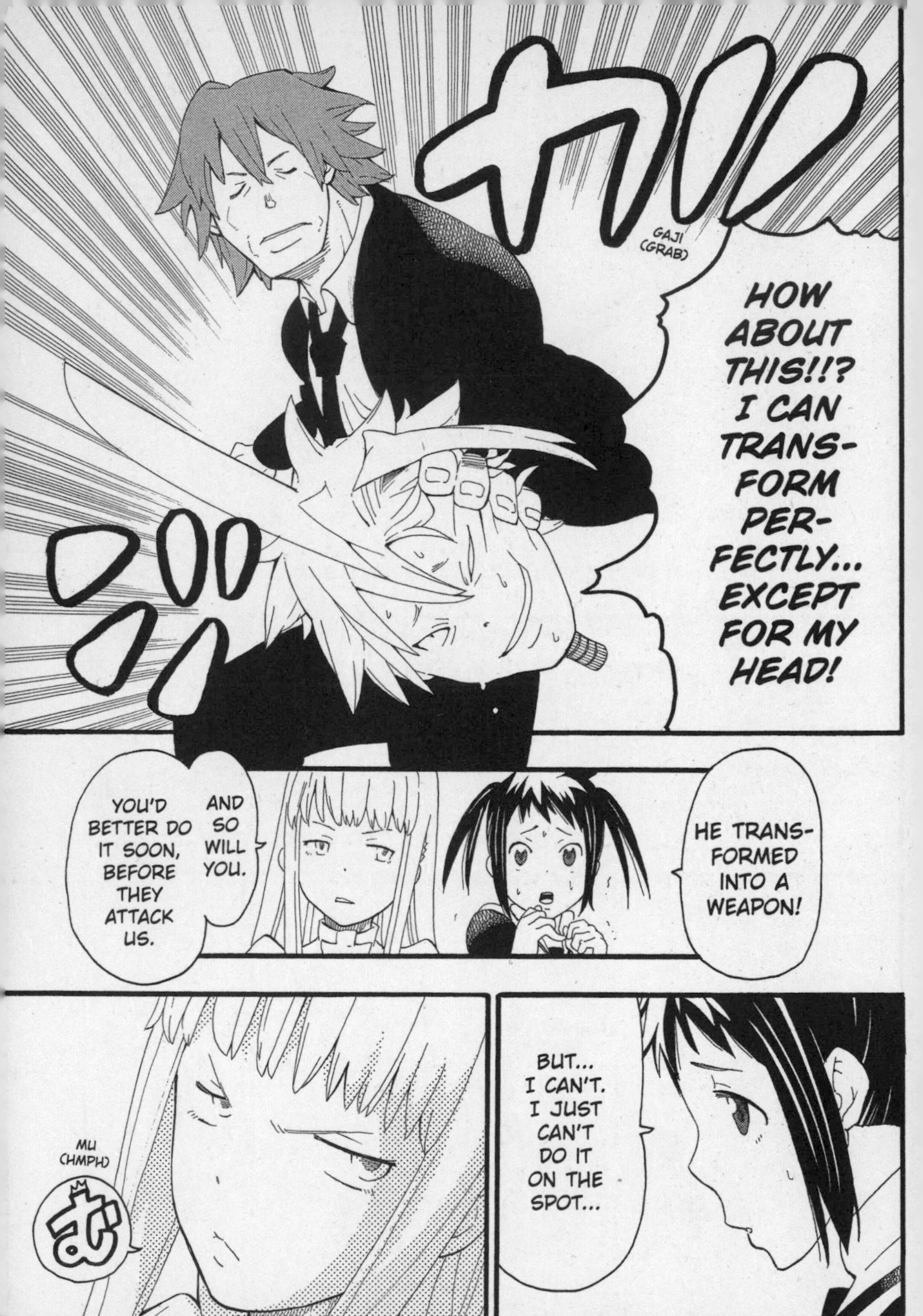
GAJI (GRAB)
HOW ABOUT THIS!!? I CAN TRANS-FORM PER-FECTLY... EXCEPT FOR MY HEAD!
HE TRANS-FORMED INTO A WEAPON!
AND SO WILL YOU.
YOU'D BETTER DO IT SOON, BEFORE THEY ATTACK US.
BUT... I CAN'T. I JUST CAN'T DO IT ON THE SPOT...
MU (HMPH)

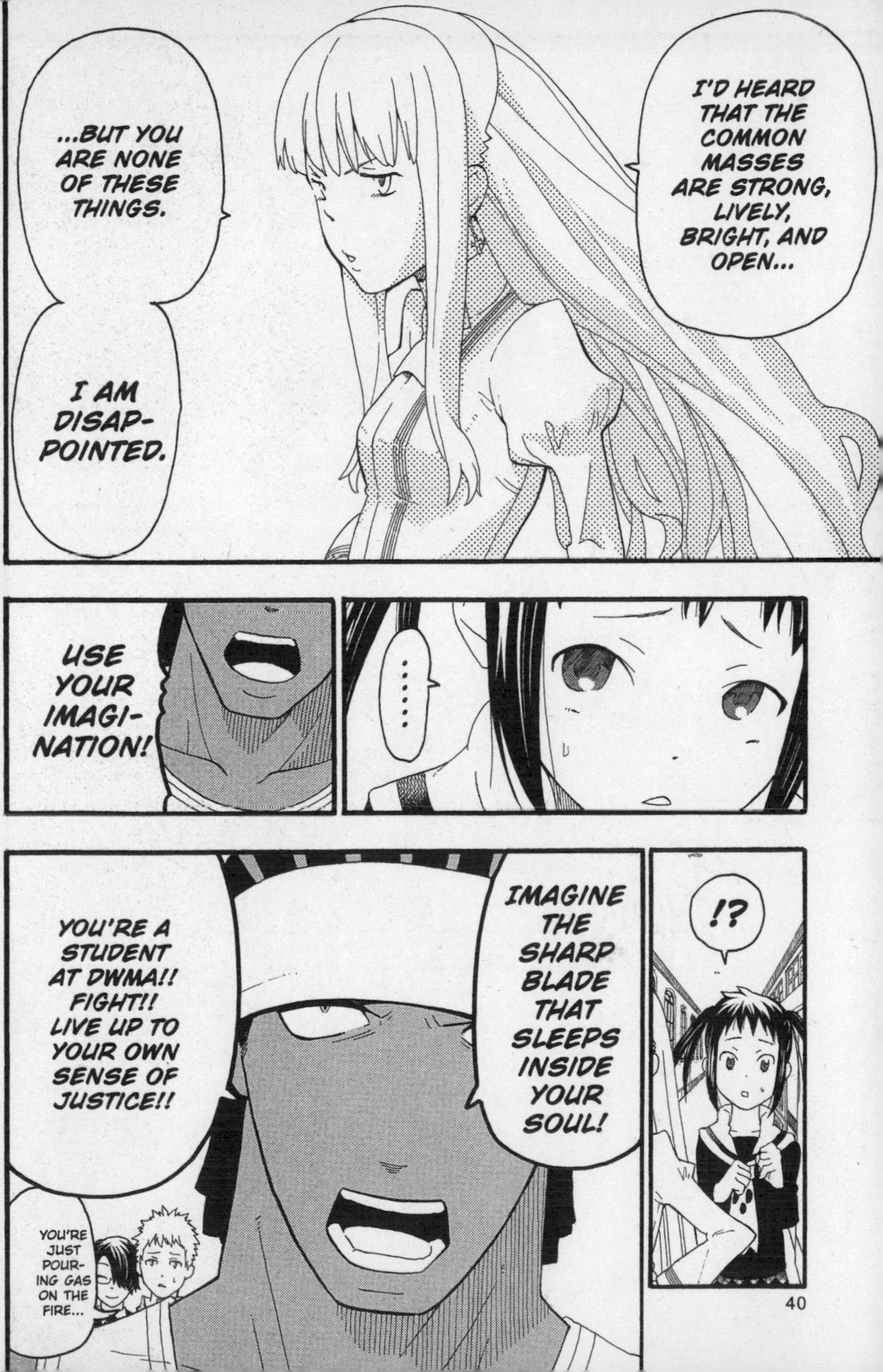
I'D HEARD THAT THE COMMON MASSES ARE STRONG, LIVELY, BRIGHT, AND OPEN...
...BUT YOU ARE NONE OF THESE THINGS.
I AM DISAP-POINTED.
......
USE YOUR IMAGI-NATION!
!?
IMAGINE THE SHARP BLADE THAT SLEEPS INSIDE YOUR SOUL!
YOU'RE A STUDENT AT DWMA!! FIGHT!! LIVE UP TO YOUR OWN SENSE OF JUSTICE!!
YOU'RE JUST POUR-ING GAS ON THE FIRE...

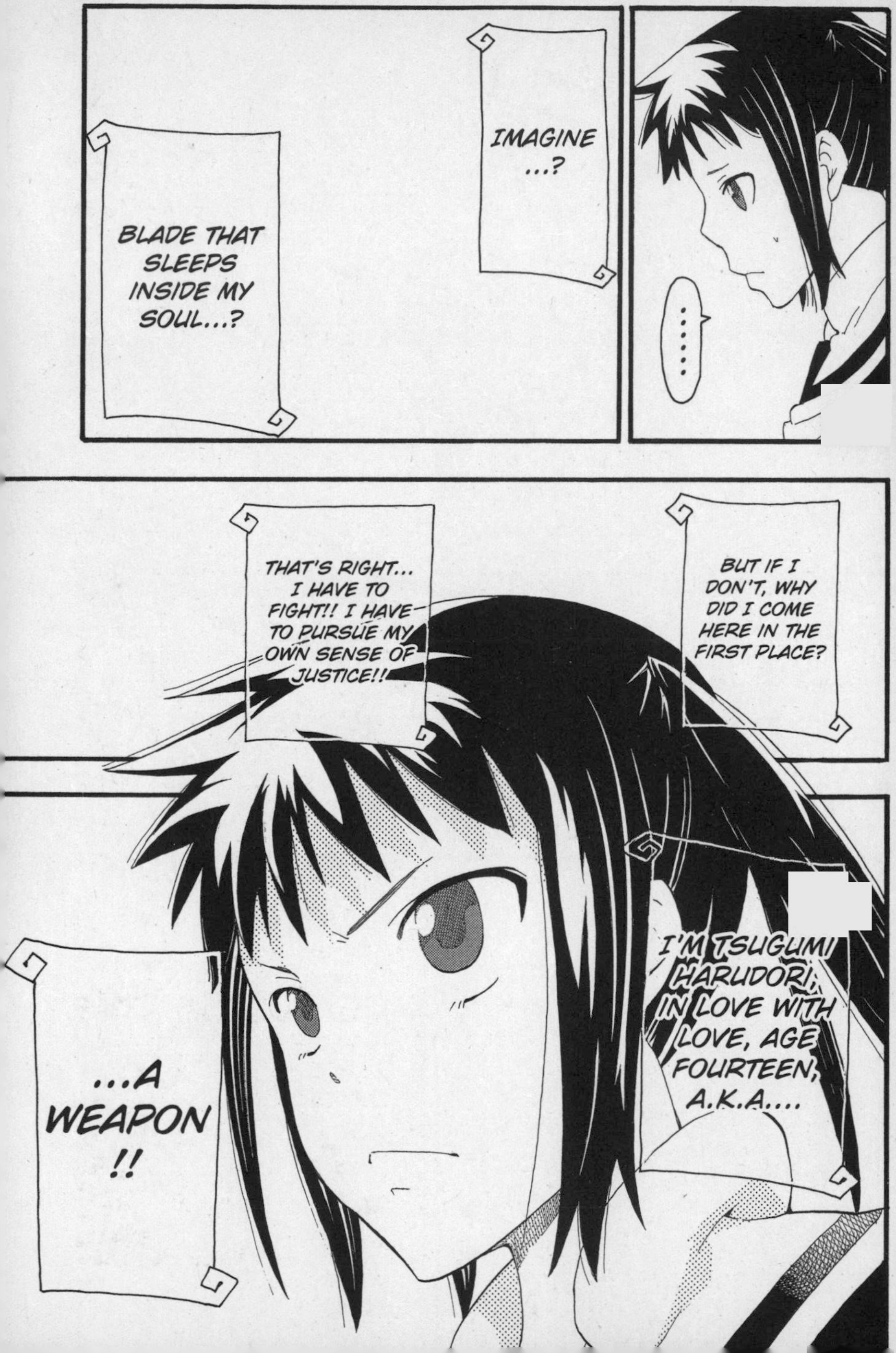

......
IMAGINE ...?
BLADE THAT SLEEPS INSIDE MY SOUL...?
BUT IF I DON'T, WHY DID I COME HERE IN THE FIRST PLACE?
THAT'S RIGHT... I HAVE TO FIGHT!! I HAVE TO PURSUE MY OWN SENSE OF JUSTICE!!
I'M TSUGUMI HARUDORI, IN LOVE WITH LOVE, AGE FOURTEEN, A.K.A....
...A WEAPON!!

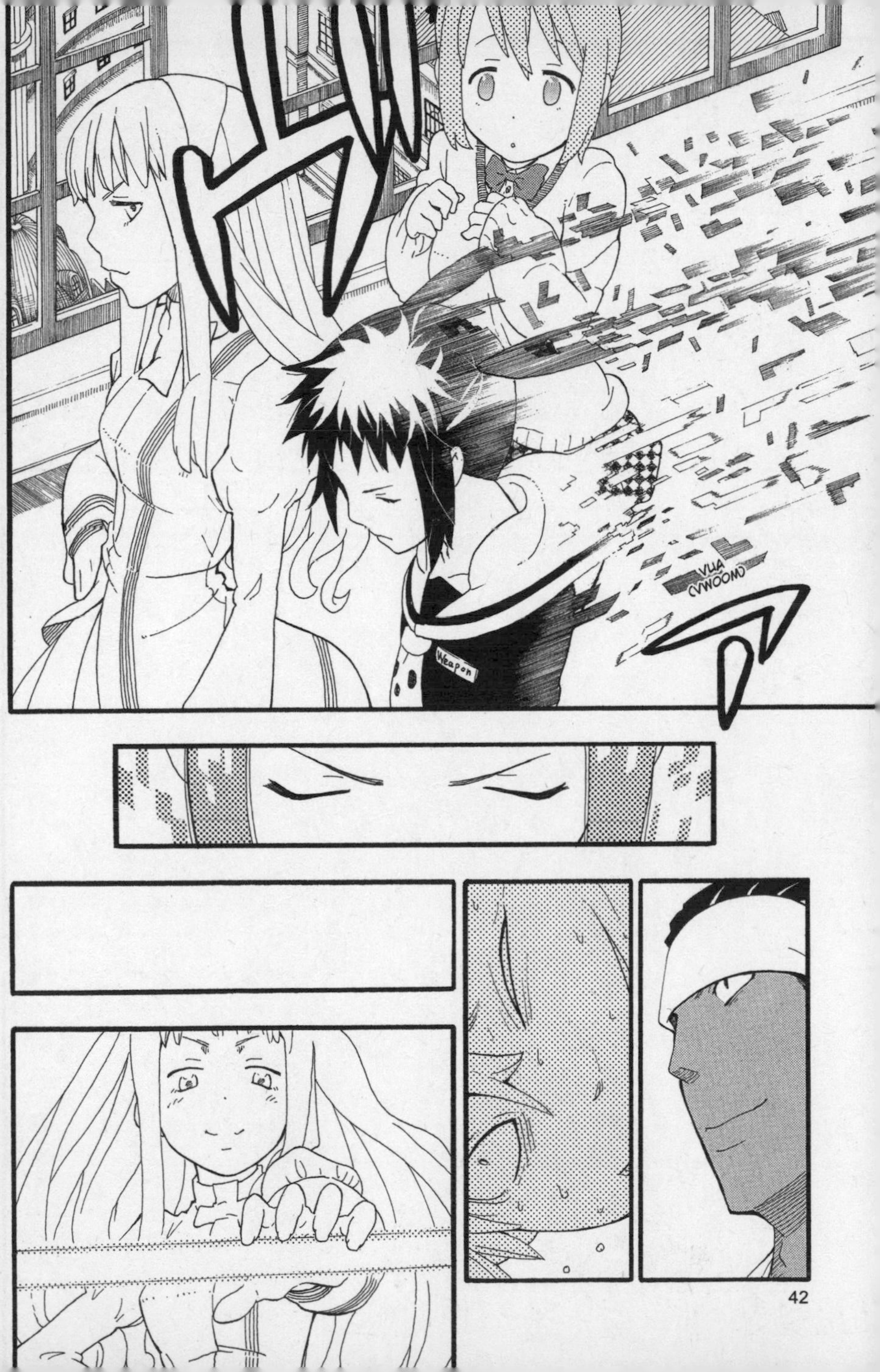
VUA
(VWOOM)
Weapon

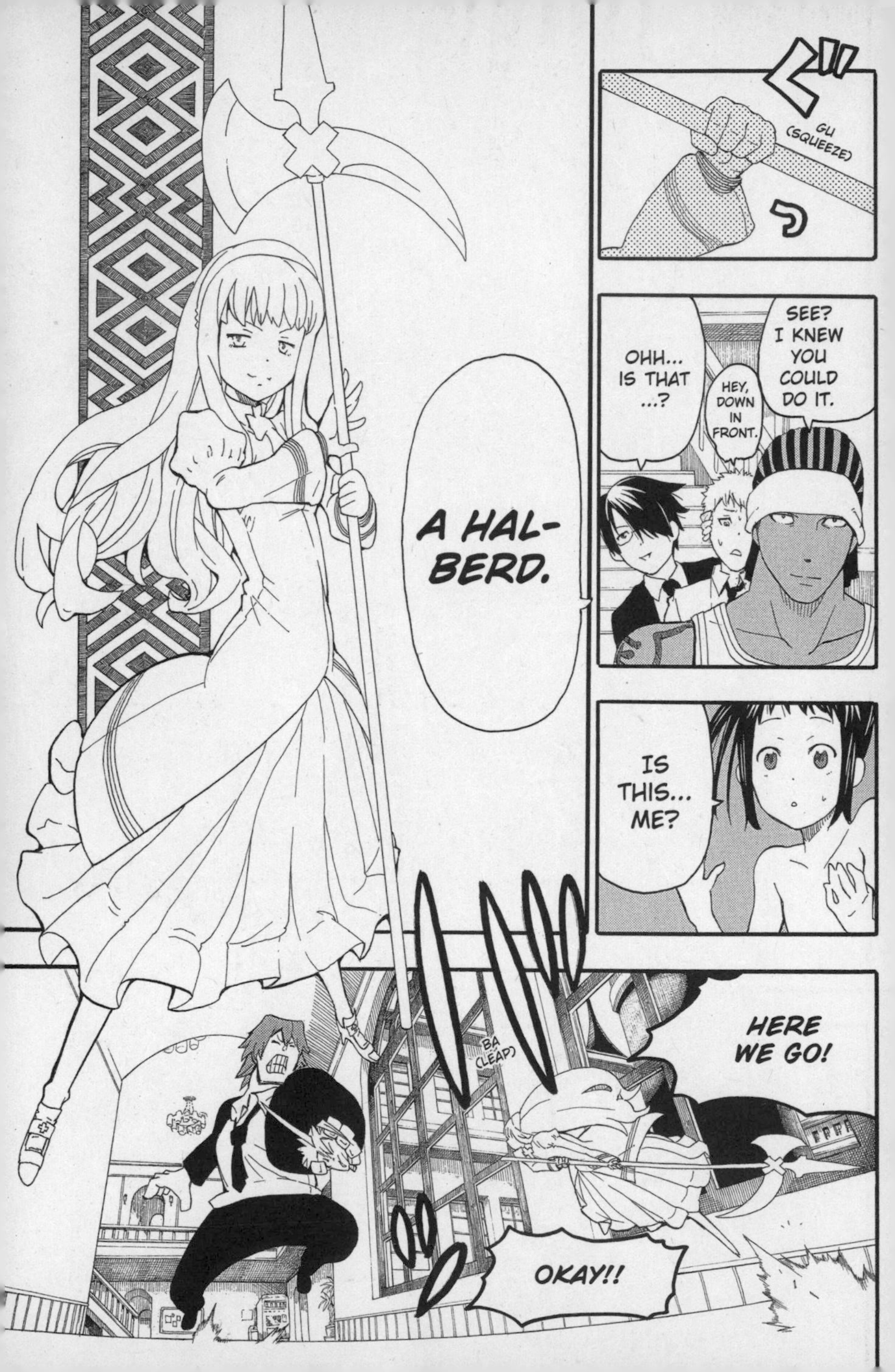
GU (SQUEEZE)
SEE? I KNEW YOU COULD DO IT.
HEY, DOWN IN FRONT.
OHH... IS THAT ...?
IS THIS... ME?
A HAL-BERD.
HERE WE GO!
BA (LEAP)
OKAY!!

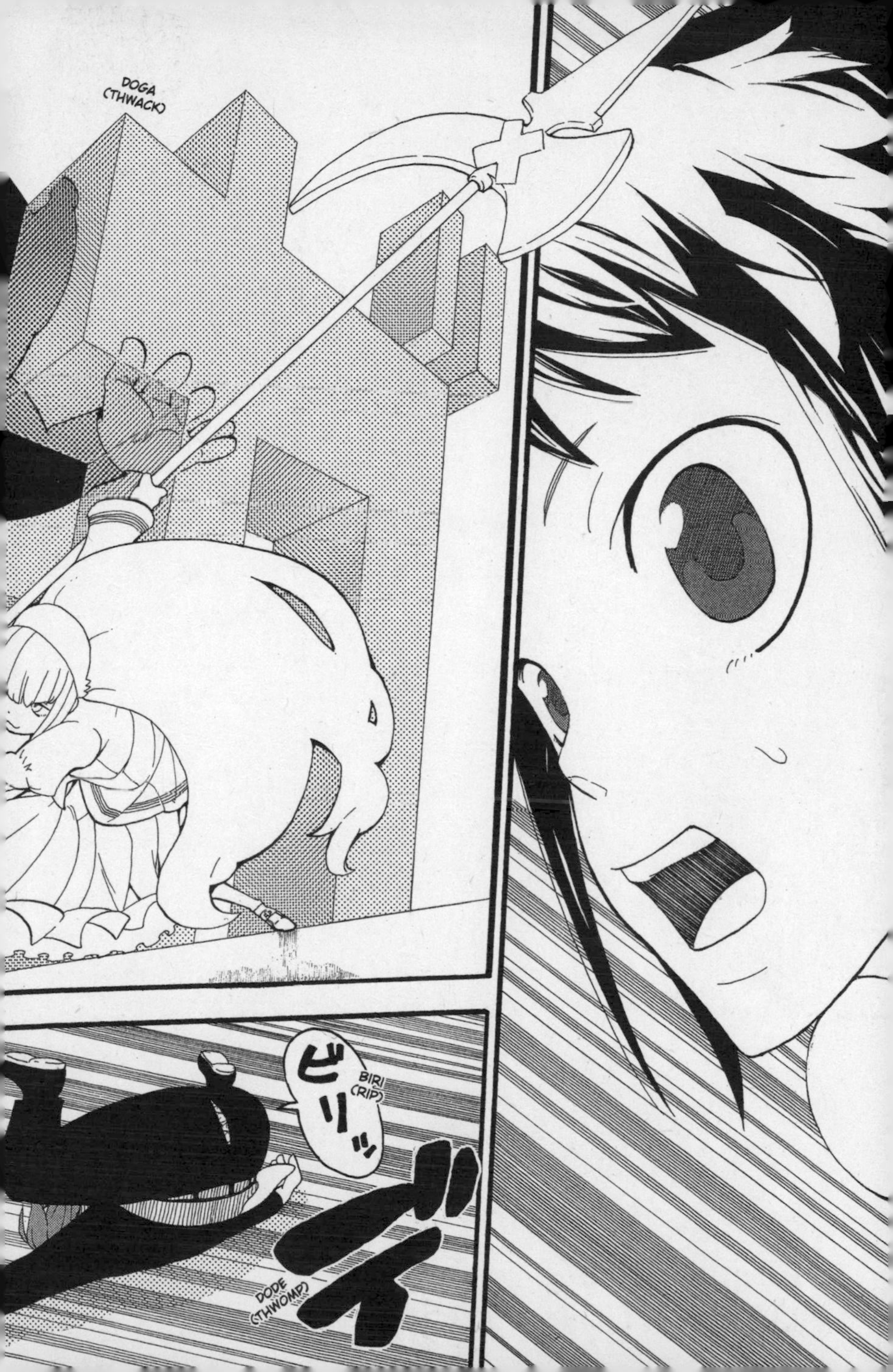
DOGA (THWACK)
ビリッ
BIRI (RIP)
DODE (THWOMP)

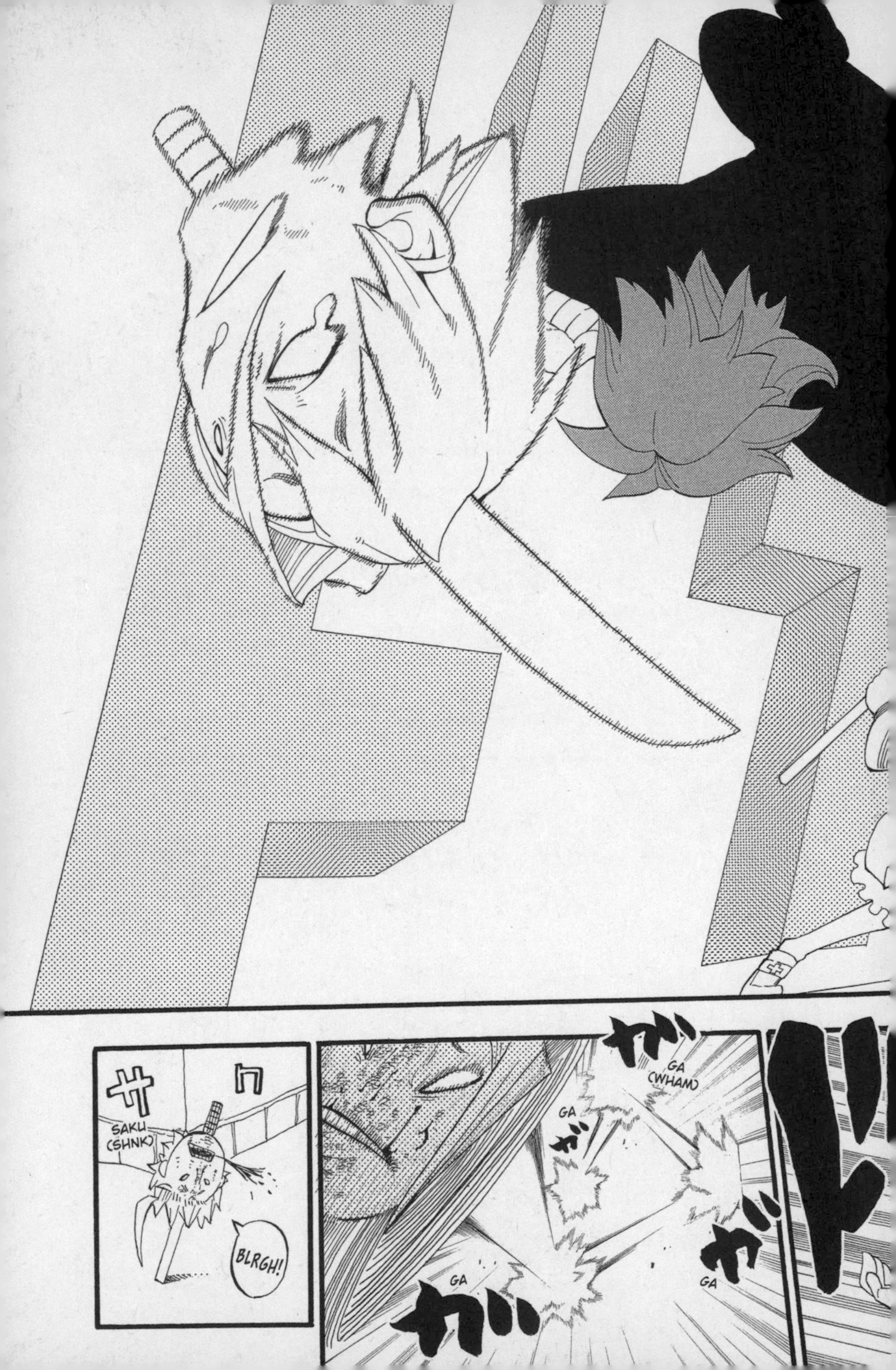
GA
(WHAM)
GA
GA
GA
SAKU
(SHNK)
BLRGH!

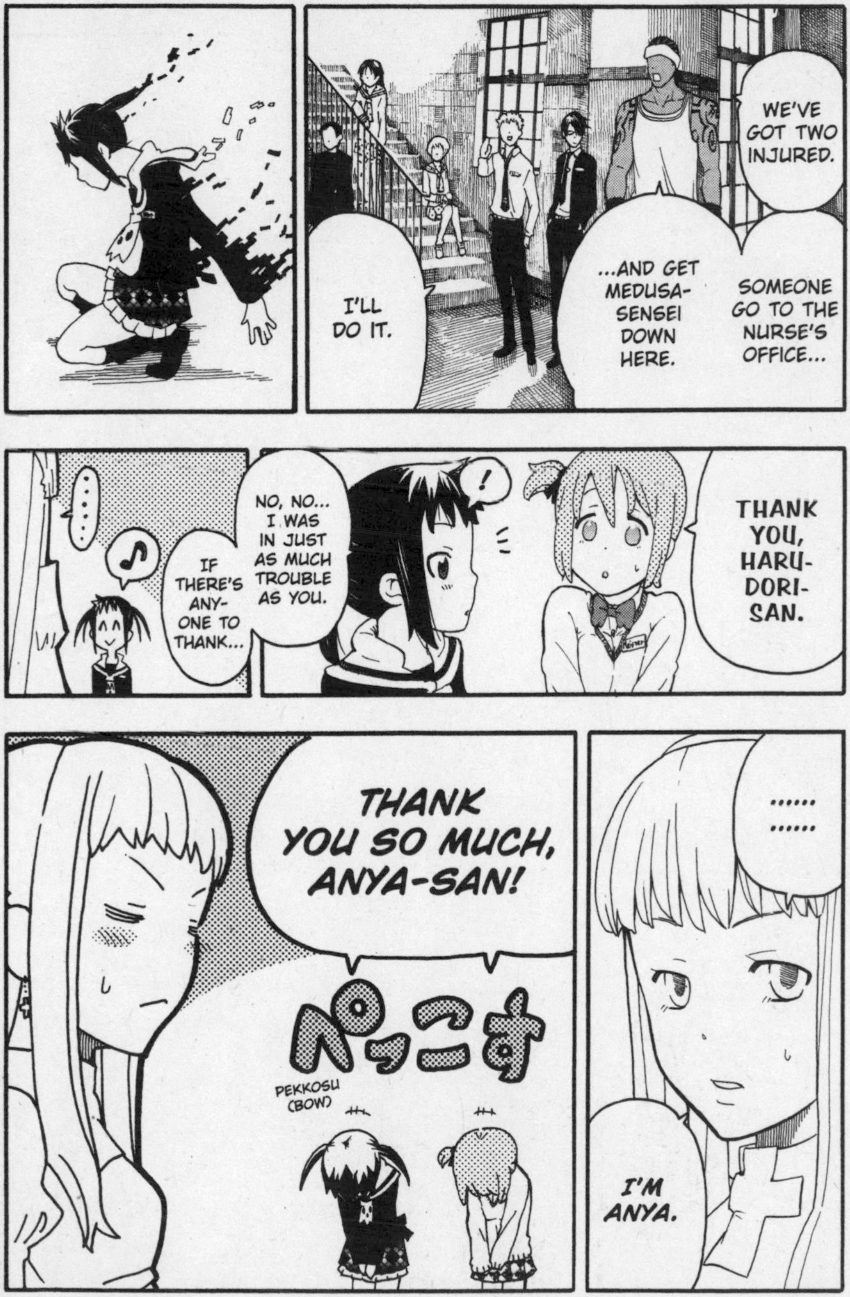
WE'VE GOT TWO INJURED.
SOMEONE GO TO THE NURSE'S OFFICE...
...AND GET MEDUSA-SENSEI DOWN HERE.
I'LL DO IT.
THANK YOU, HARU-DORI-SAN.
!
NO, NO... I WAS IN JUST AS MUCH TROUBLE AS YOU.
IF THERE'S ANY-ONE TO THANK...
♪
....
......
......
I'M ANYA.
THANK YOU SO MUCH, ANYA-SAN!
ぺっこす
PEKKOSU (BOW)

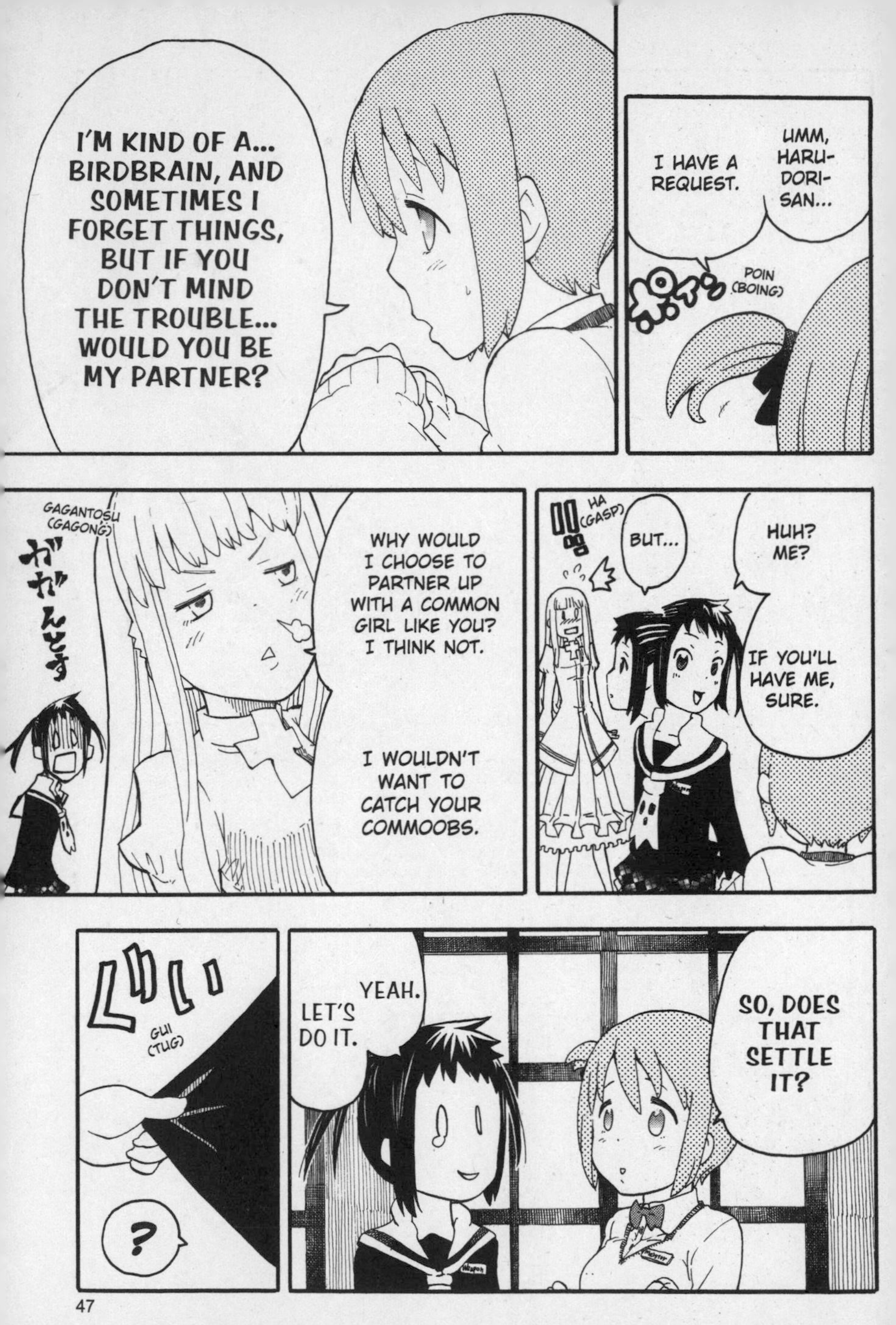
UMM, HARU-DORI-SAN...
I HAVE A REQUEST.
POIN (BOING)
I'M KIND OF A... BIRDBRAIN, AND SOMETIMES I FORGET THINGS, BUT IF YOU DON'T MIND THE TROUBLE... WOULD YOU BE MY PARTNER?
HUH? ME?
IF YOU'LL HAVE ME, SURE.
HA (GASP)
BUT...
WHY WOULD I CHOOSE TO PARTNER UP WITH A COMMON GIRL LIKE YOU? I THINK NOT.
I WOULDN'T WANT TO CATCH YOUR COMMOOBS.
GAGANTOSU (GAGONG)
SO, DOES THAT SETTLE IT?
YEAH.
LET'S DO IT.
GUI (TUG)
?

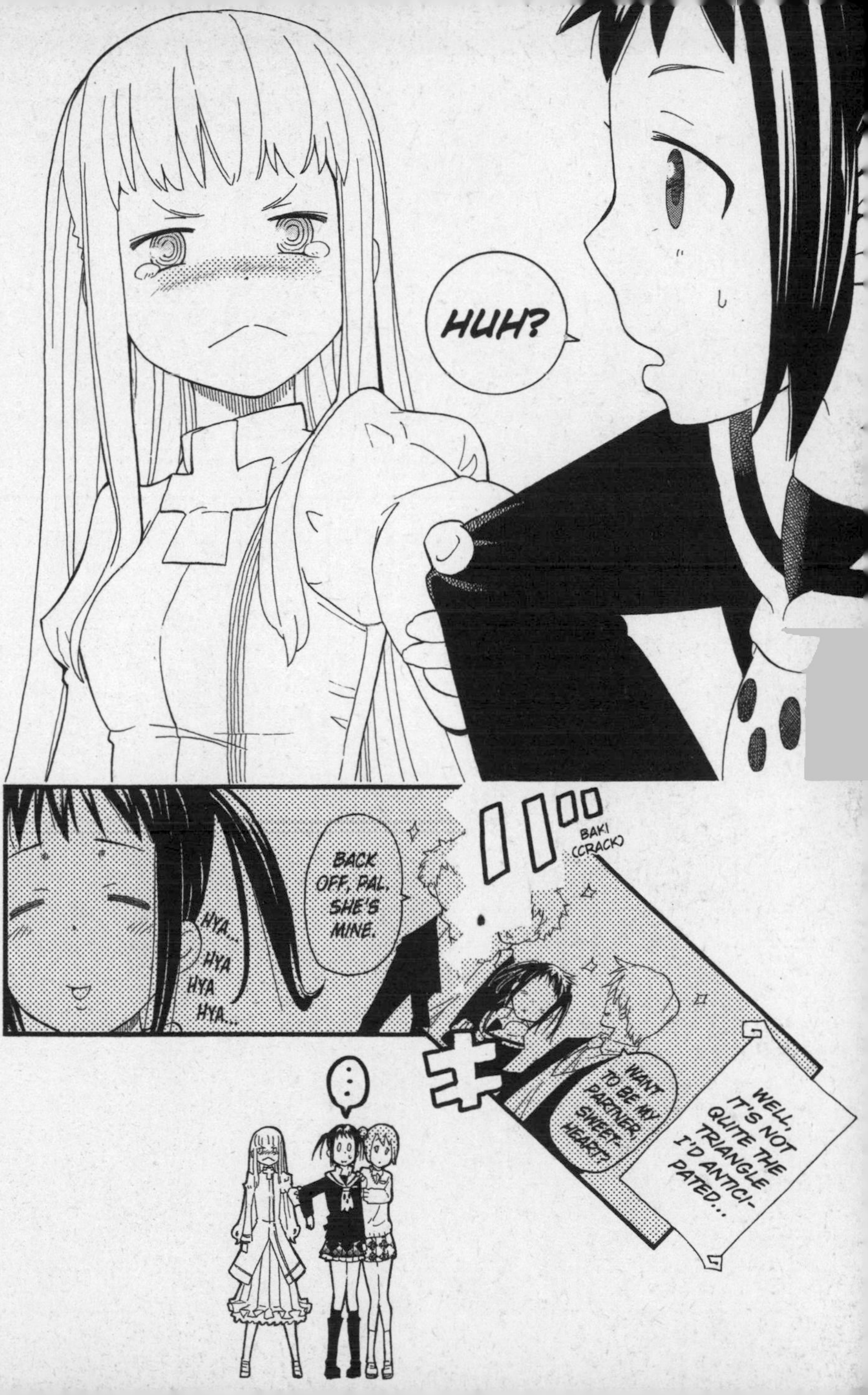
HUH?
BAKI (CRACK)
BACK OFF, PAL, SHE'S MINE.
HYA... HYA HYA HYA...
WELL, IT'S NOT QUITE THE TRIANGLE I'D ANTICI-PATED...
WANT TO BE MY PARTNER, SWEET-HEART?
...

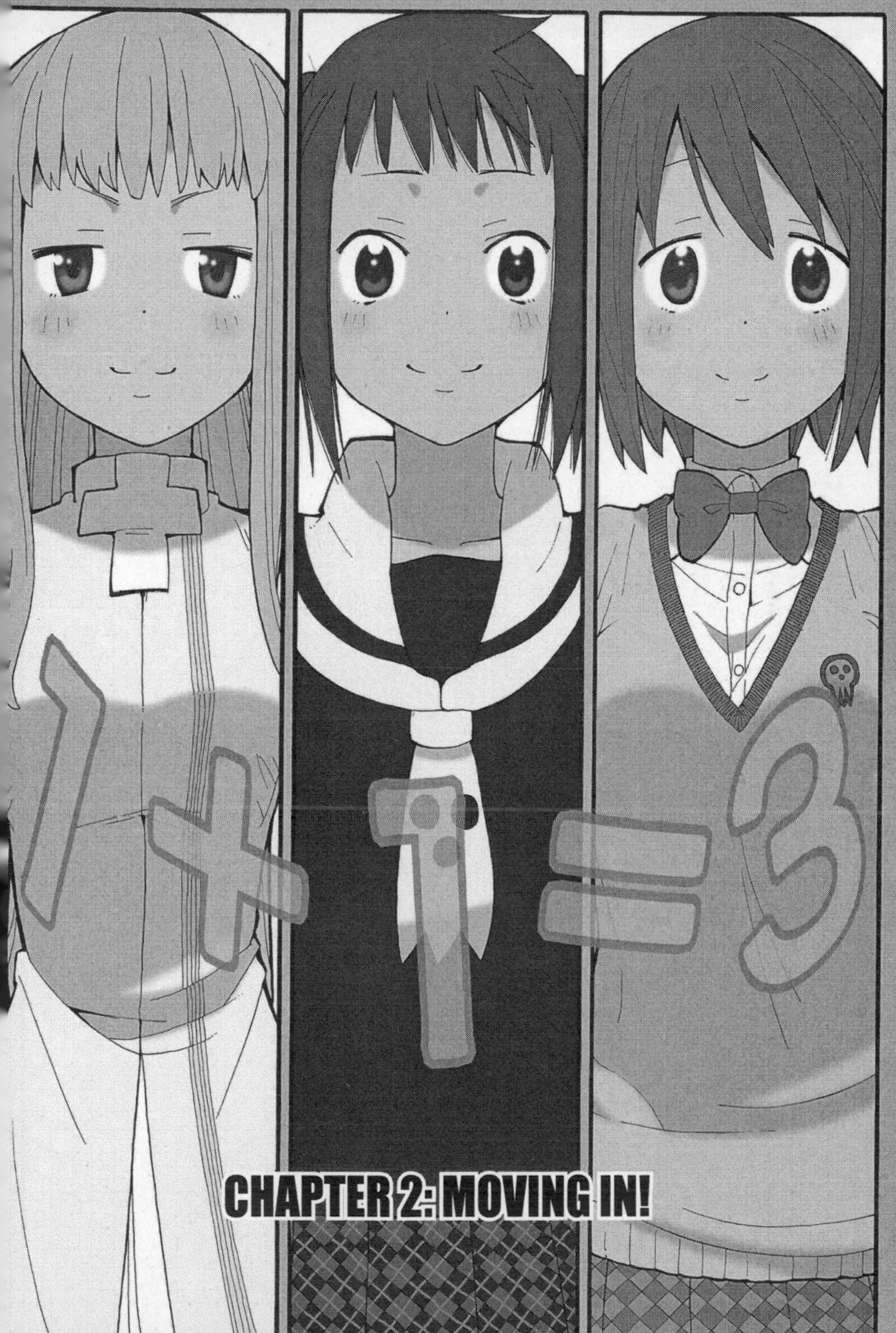
1+1=3
CHAPTER 2: MOVING IN!

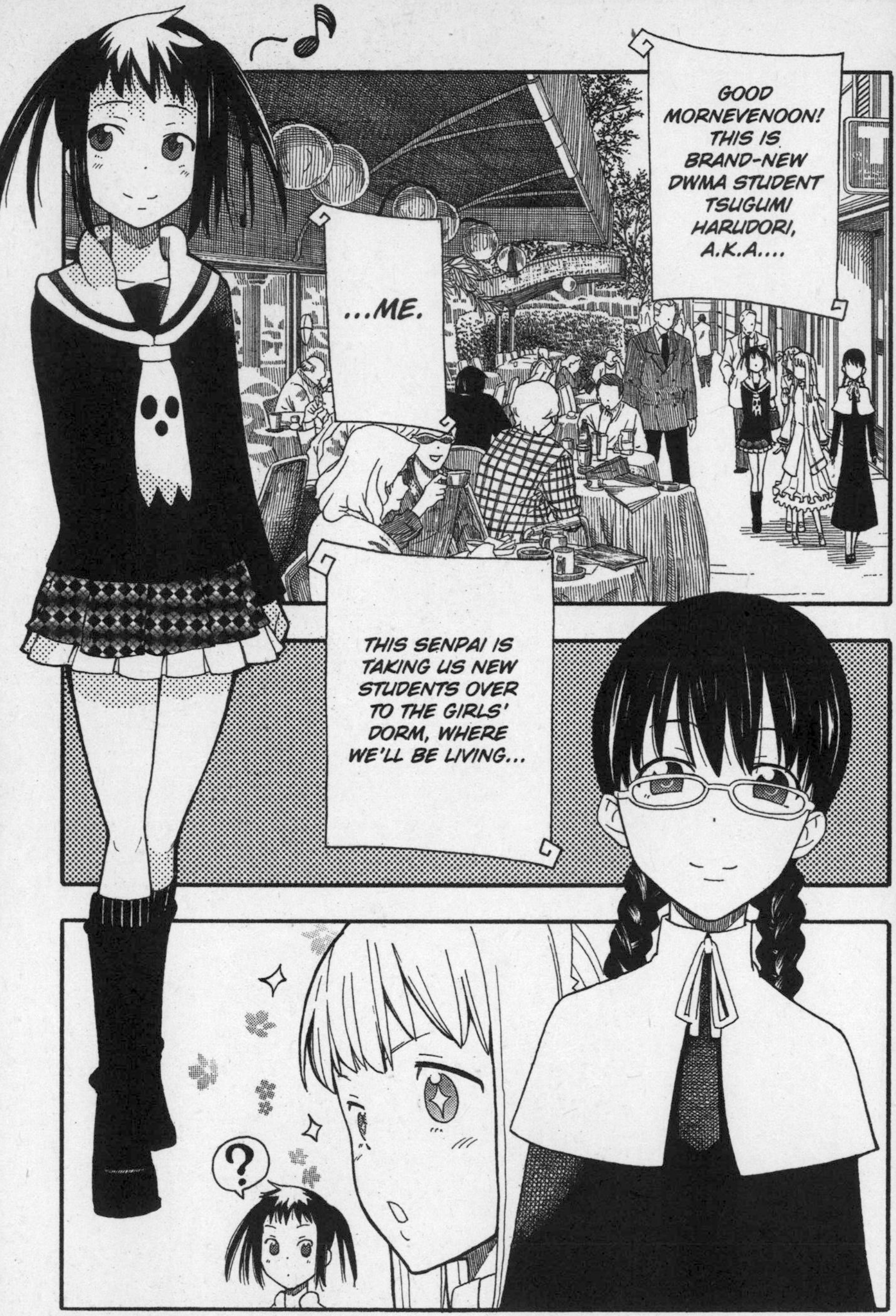
GOOD MORNEVENOON! THIS IS BRAND-NEW DWMA STUDENT TSUGUMI HARUDORI, A.K.A....
...ME.
THIS SENPAI IS TAKING US NEW STUDENTS OVER TO THE GIRLS' DORM, WHERE WE'LL BE LIVING...
?

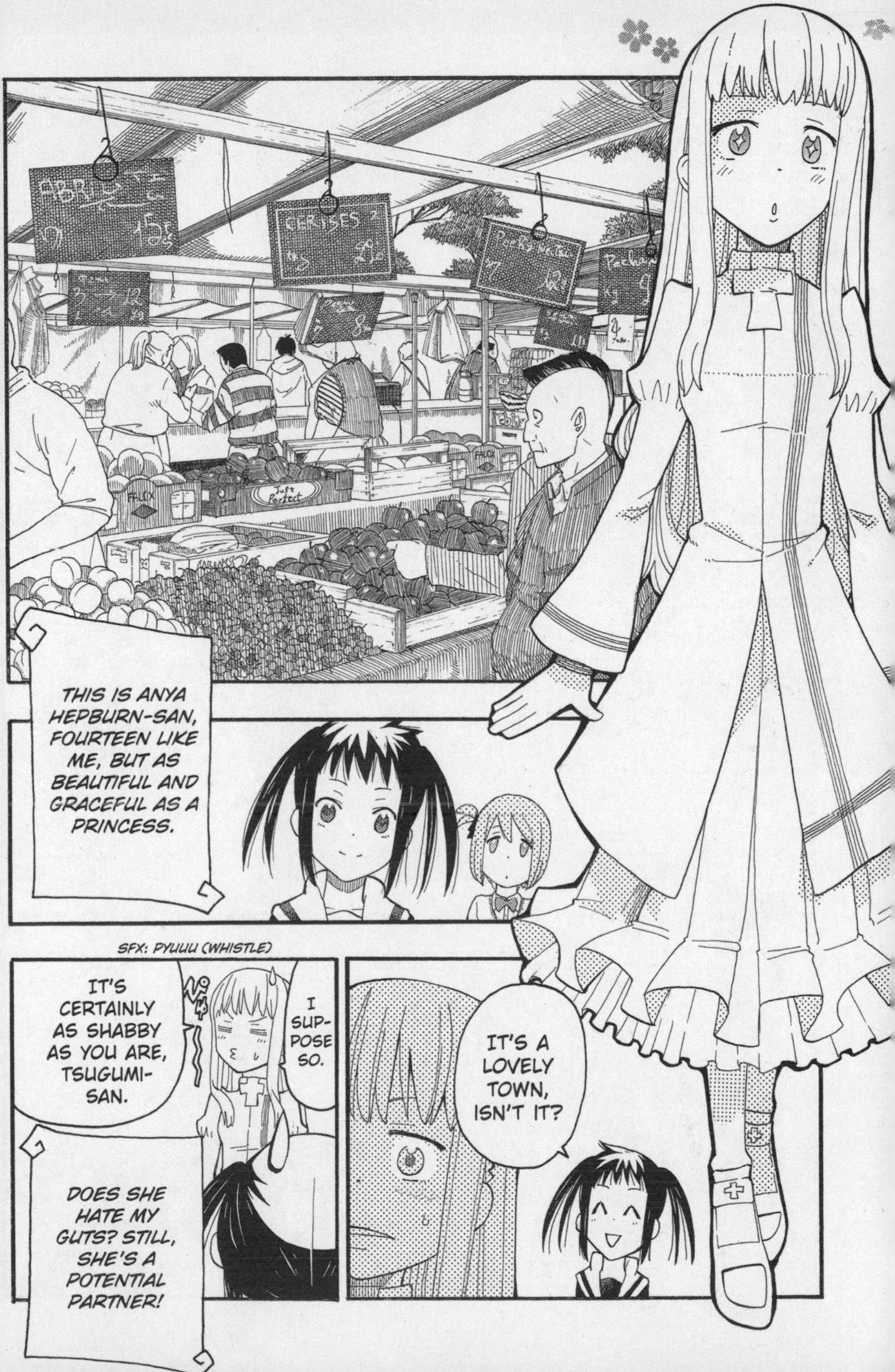
CERISES
Just Perfect
THIS IS ANYA HEPBURN-SAN, FOURTEEN LIKE ME, BUT AS BEAUTIFUL AND GRACEFUL AS A PRINCESS.
IT'S A LOVELY TOWN, ISN'T IT?
SFX: PYUUU (WHISTLE)
I SUPPOSE SO.
IT'S CERTAINLY AS SHABBY AS YOU ARE, TSUGUMI-SAN.
DOES SHE HATE MY GUTS? STILL, SHE'S A POTENTIAL PARTNER!

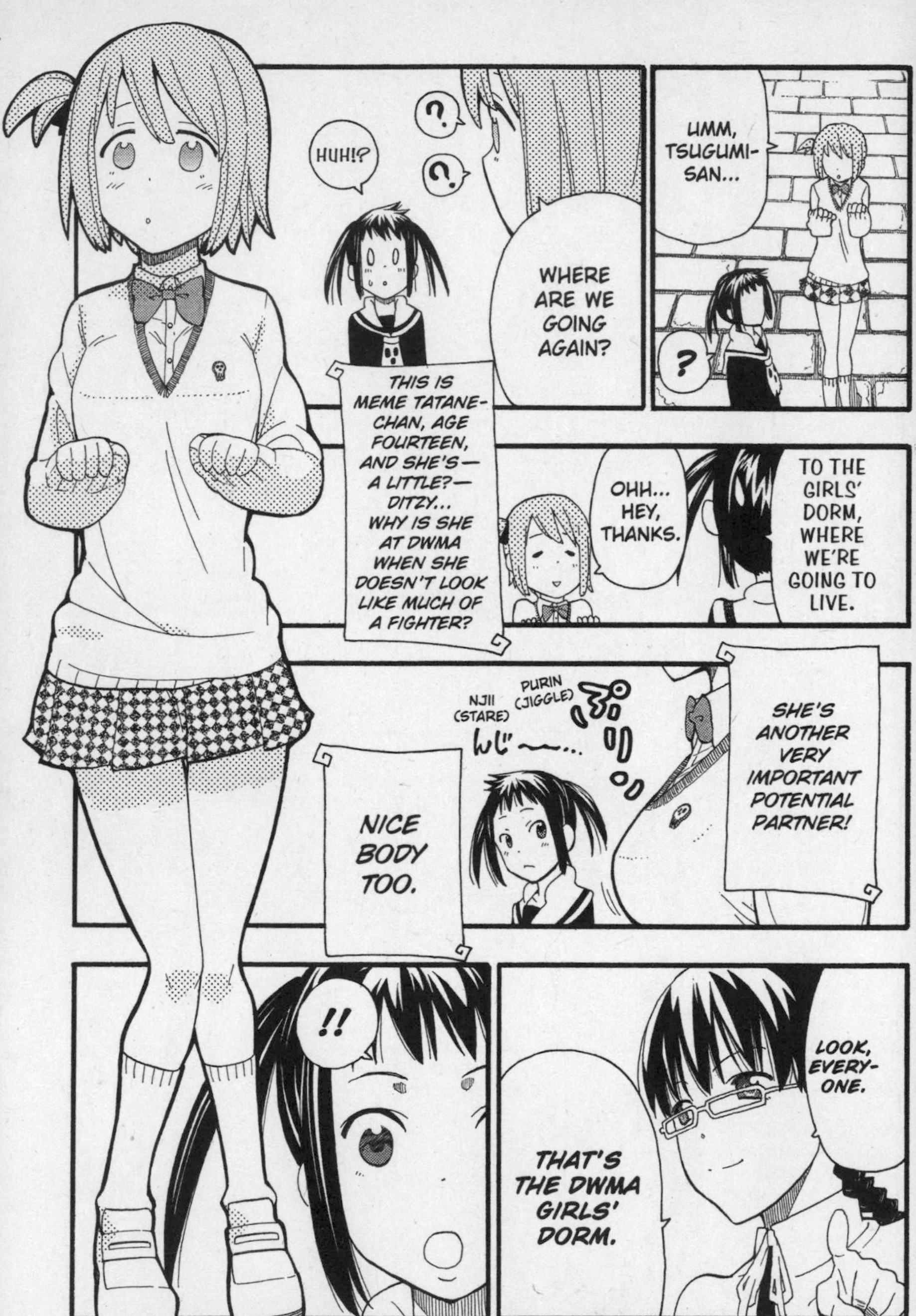

UMM, TSUGUMI-SAN...
?
WHERE ARE WE GOING AGAIN?
?
?
HUH!?
THIS IS MEME TATANE-CHAN, AGE FOURTEEN, AND SHE'S—A LITTLE?—DITZY... WHY IS SHE AT DWMA WHEN SHE DOESN'T LOOK LIKE MUCH OF A FIGHTER?
TO THE GIRLS' DORM, WHERE WE'RE GOING TO LIVE.
OHH... HEY, THANKS.
SHE'S ANOTHER VERY IMPORTANT POTENTIAL PARTNER!
PURIN (JIGGLE)
NJII (STARE)
んじ~~...
NICE BODY TOO.
LOOK, EVERY-ONE.
THAT'S THE DWMA GIRLS' DORM.
!!

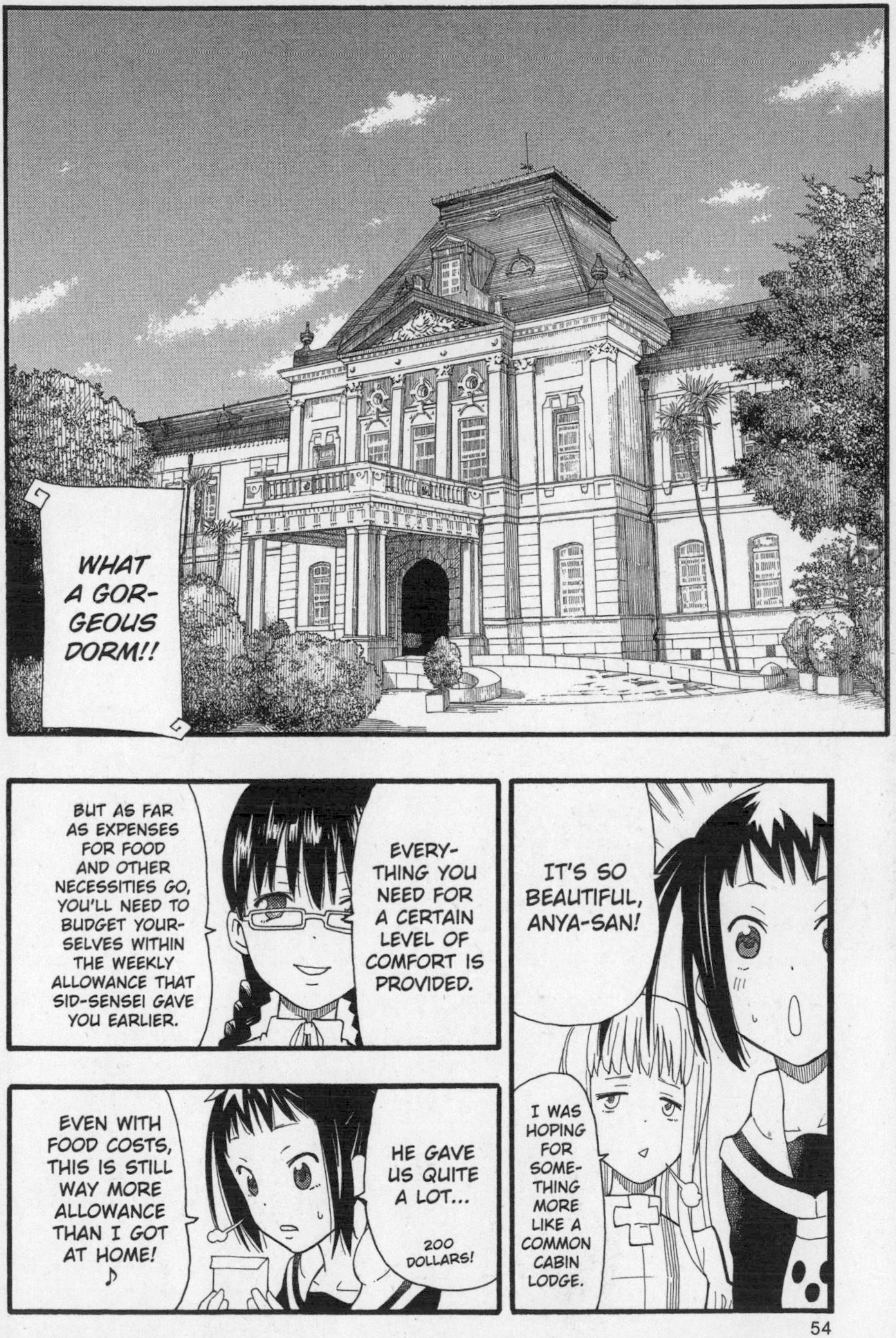

WHAT A GOR-GEOUS DORM!!
IT'S SO BEAUTIFUL, ANYA-SAN!
I WAS HOPING FOR SOME-THING MORE LIKE A COMMON CABIN LODGE.
EVERY-THING YOU NEED FOR A CERTAIN LEVEL OF COMFORT IS PROVIDED.
BUT AS FAR AS EXPENSES FOR FOOD AND OTHER NECESSITIES GO, YOU'LL NEED TO BUDGET YOUR-SELVES WITHIN THE WEEKLY ALLOWANCE THAT SID-SENSEI GAVE YOU EARLIER.
HE GAVE US QUITE A LOT...
200 DOLLARS!
EVEN WITH FOOD COSTS, THIS IS STILL WAY MORE ALLOWANCE THAN I GOT AT HOME! ♪

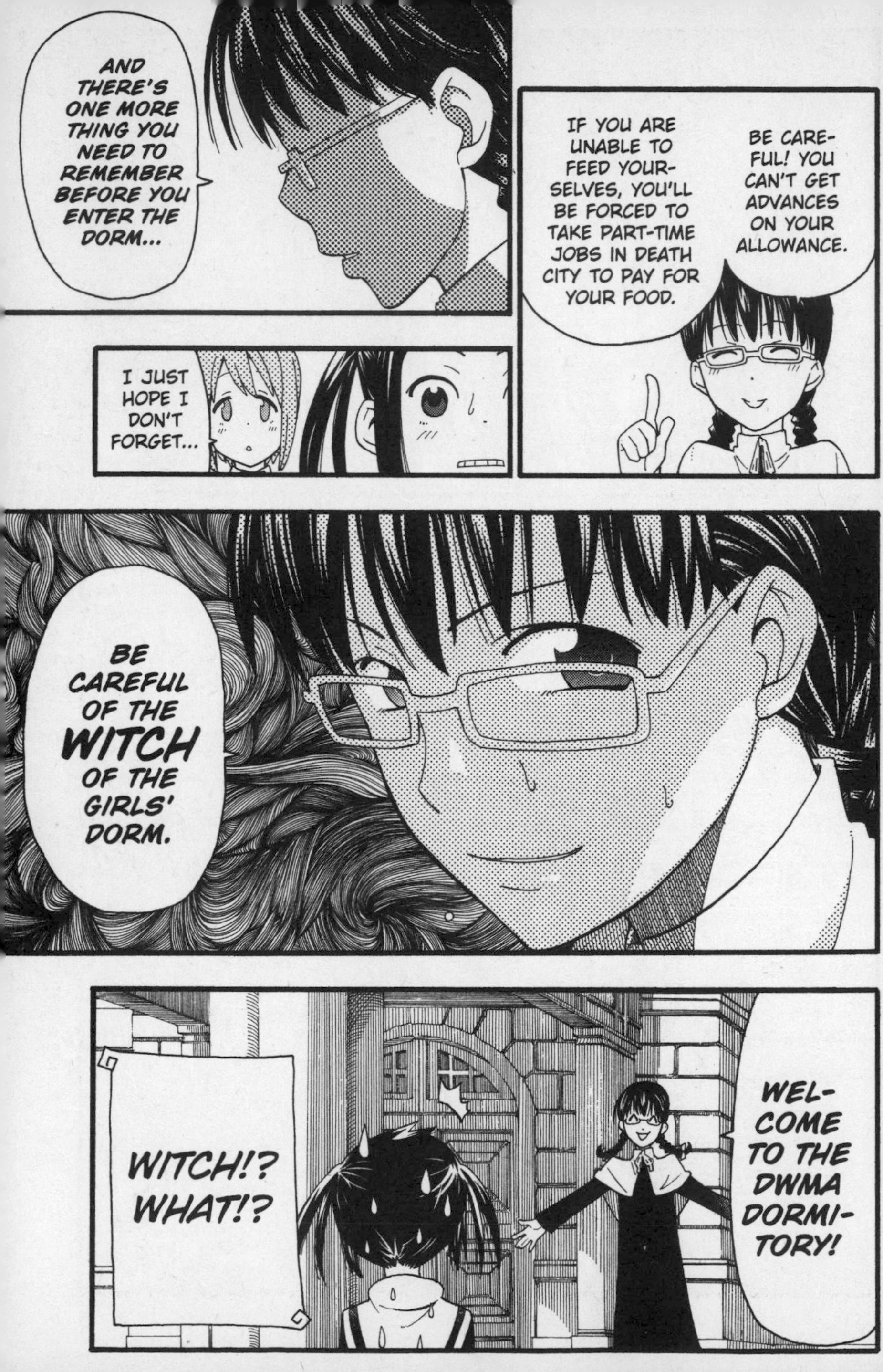

BE CAREFUL! YOU CAN'T GET ADVANCES ON YOUR ALLOWANCE.
IF YOU ARE UNABLE TO FEED YOURSELVES, YOU'LL BE FORCED TO TAKE PART-TIME JOBS IN DEATH CITY TO PAY FOR YOUR FOOD.
AND THERE'S ONE MORE THING YOU NEED TO REMEMBER BEFORE YOU ENTER THE DORM...
I JUST HOPE I DON'T FORGET...
BE CAREFUL OF THE WITCH OF THE GIRLS' DORM.
WELCOME TO THE DWMA DORMITORY!
WITCH!? WHAT!?

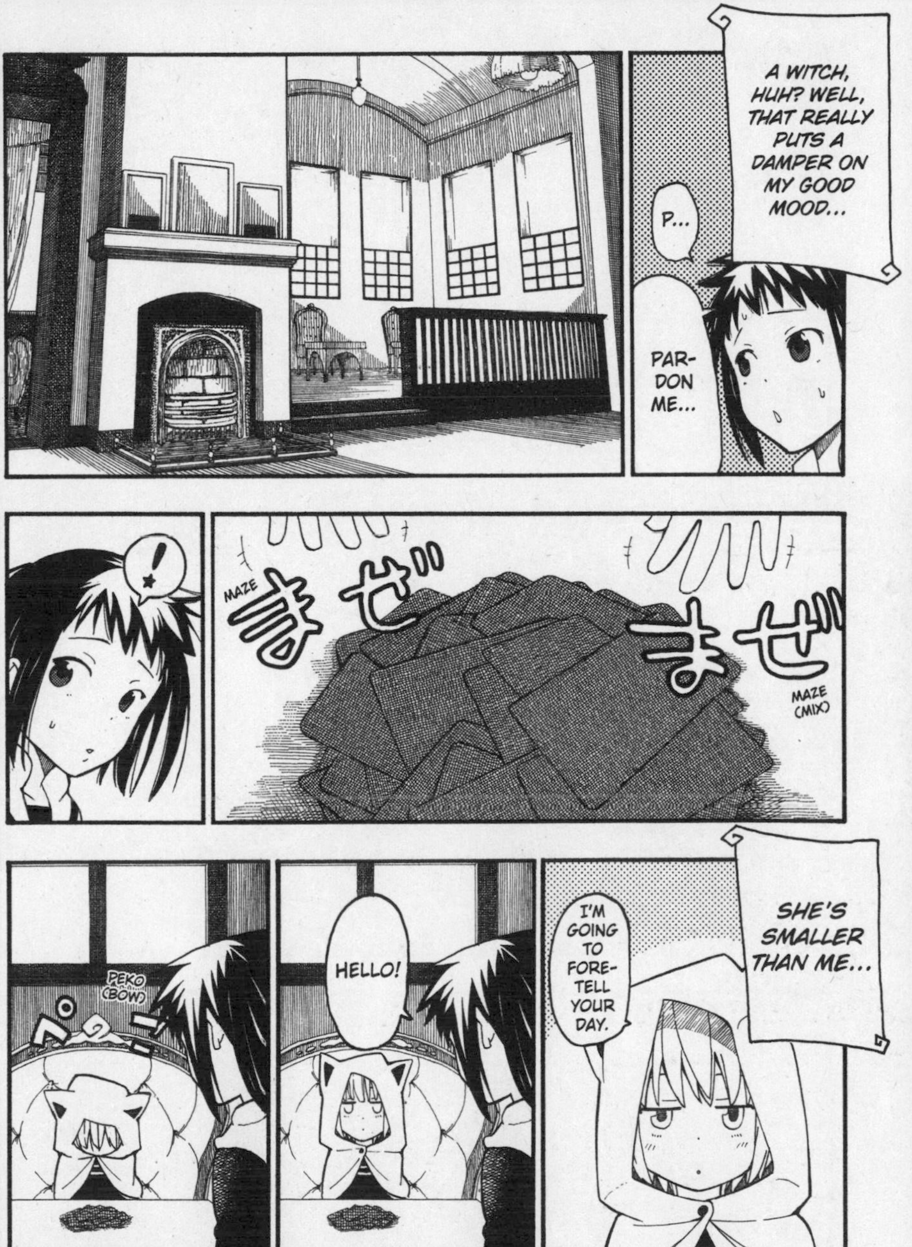
A WITCH, HUH? WELL, THAT REALLY PUTS A DAMPER ON MY GOOD MOOD...
P...
PAR-DON ME...
まぜ
MAZE (MIX)
MAZE
まぜ
!
SHE'S SMALLER THAN ME...
I'M GOING TO FORE-TELL YOUR DAY.
HELLO!
PEKO (BOW)

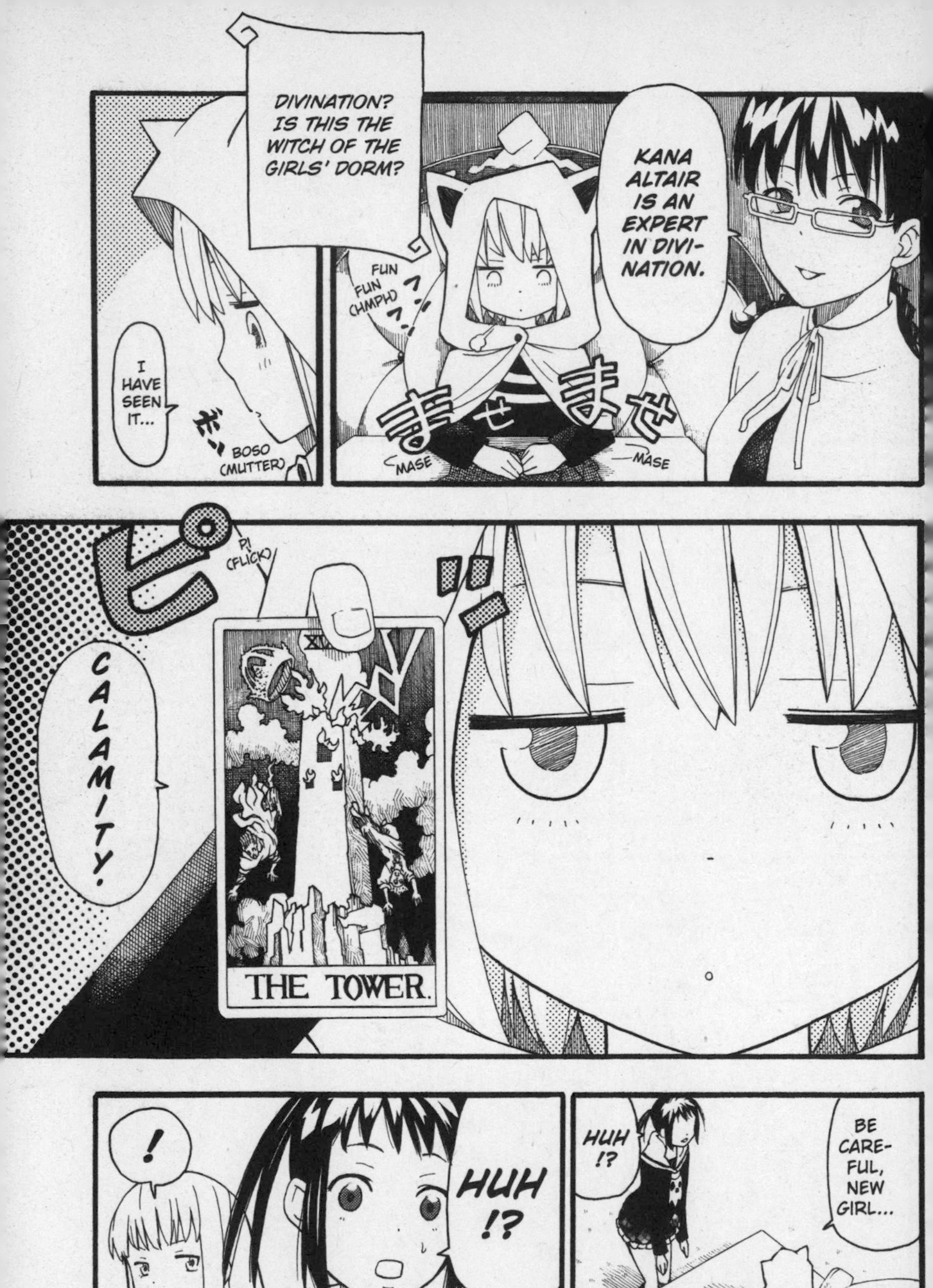
KANA ALTAIR IS AN EXPERT IN DIVINATION.
FUN FUN (HMPH)
MASE
MASE
DIVINATION? IS THIS THE WITCH OF THE GIRLS' DORM?
I HAVE SEEN IT...
BOSO (MUTTER)
PI (FLICK)
THE TOWER.
CALAMITY.
BE CAREFUL, NEW GIRL...
HUH!?
HUH!?
!

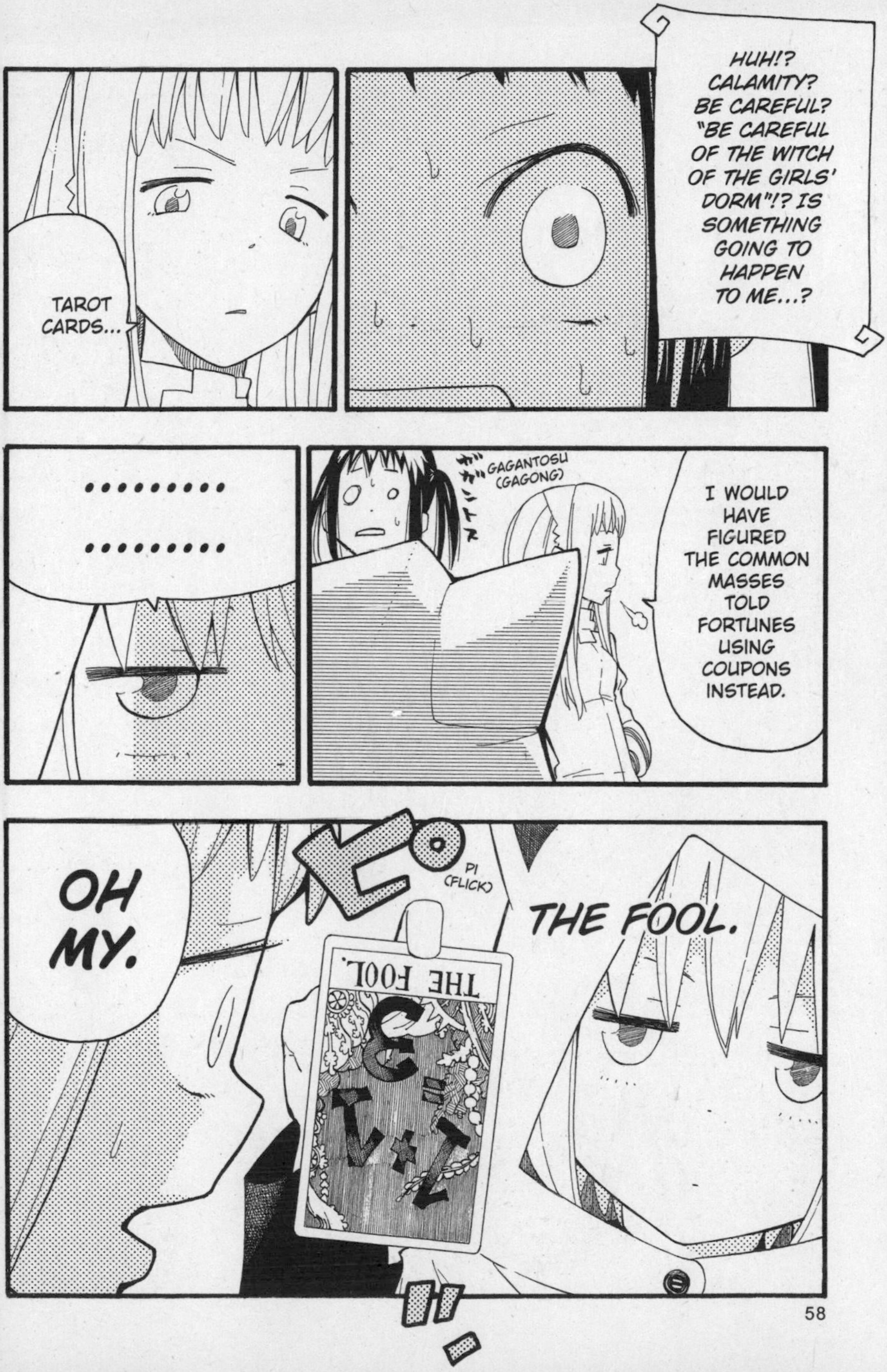
HUH!? CALAMITY? BE CAREFUL? "BE CAREFUL OF THE WITCH OF THE GIRLS' DORM"!? IS SOMETHING GOING TO HAPPEN TO ME...?
TAROT CARDS...
I WOULD HAVE FIGURED THE COMMON MASSES TOLD FORTUNES USING COUPONS INSTEAD.
GAGANTOSU (GAGONG)
....
....
PI (FLICK)
THE FOOL.
THE FOOL.
OH MY.

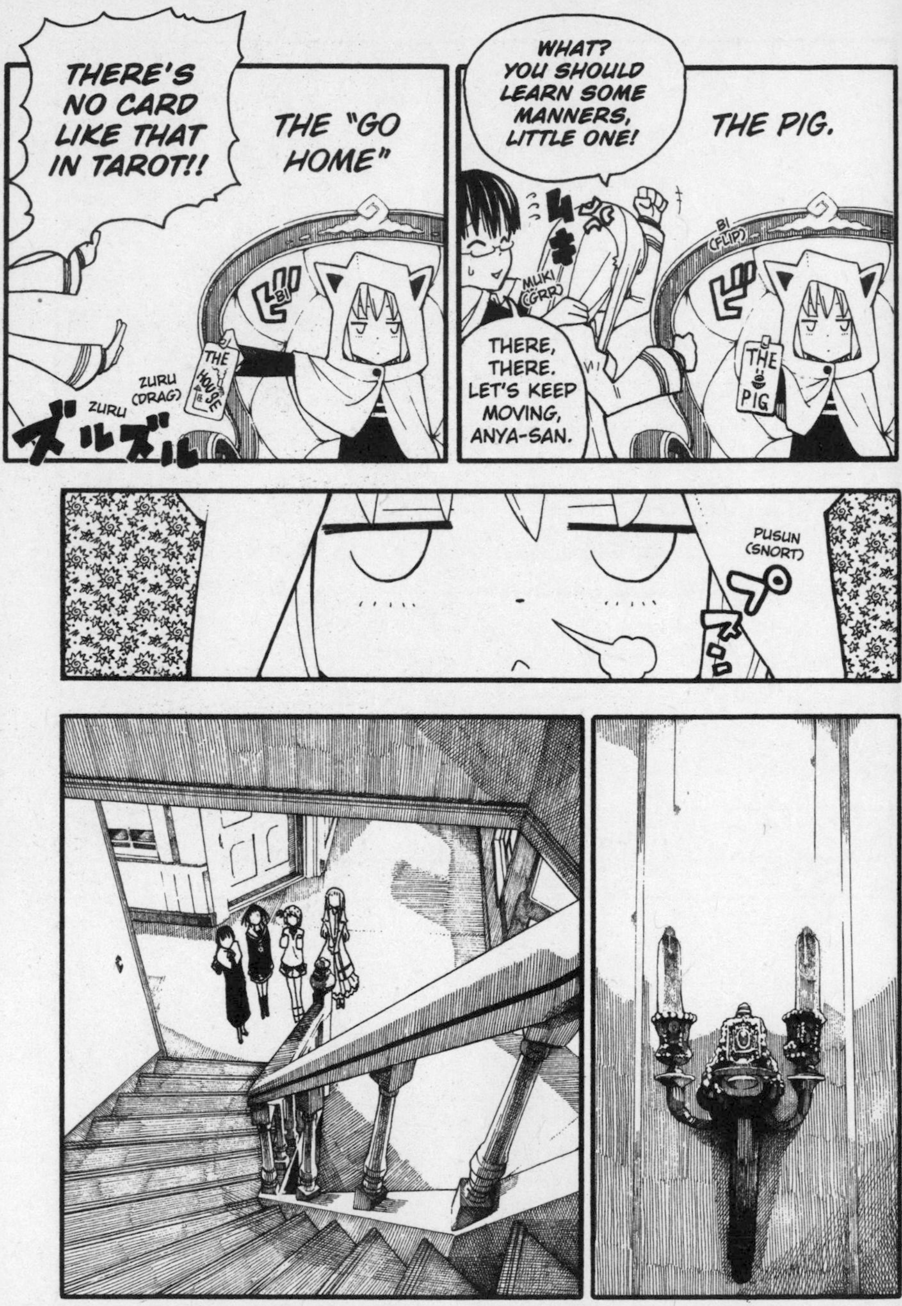
THE PIG.
WHAT? YOU SHOULD LEARN SOME MANNERS, LITTLE ONE!
BI (FLIP)
THE PIG
MUKI (GRR)
THERE, THERE. LET'S KEEP MOVING, ANYA-SAN.
THE "GO HOME"
THERE'S NO CARD LIKE THAT IN TAROT!!
THE HOUSE
ZURU (DRAG)
ZURU
PUSUN (SNORT)

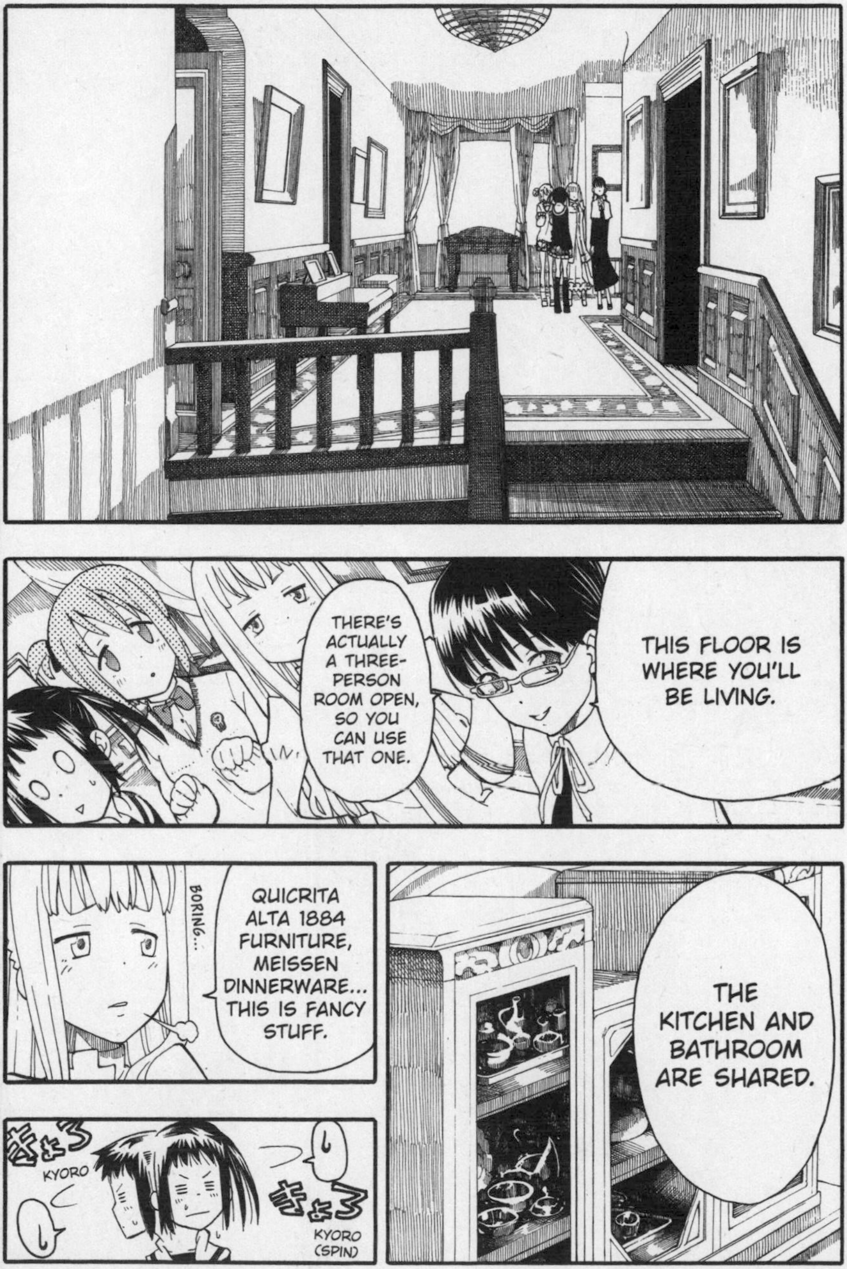
THIS FLOOR IS WHERE YOU'LL BE LIVING.
THERE'S ACTUALLY A THREE-PERSON ROOM OPEN, SO YOU CAN USE THAT ONE.
THE KITCHEN AND BATHROOM ARE SHARED.
QUICRITA ALTA 1884 FURNITURE, MEISSEN DINNERWARE... THIS IS FANCY STUFF.
BORING...
KYORO (SPIN)
KYORO

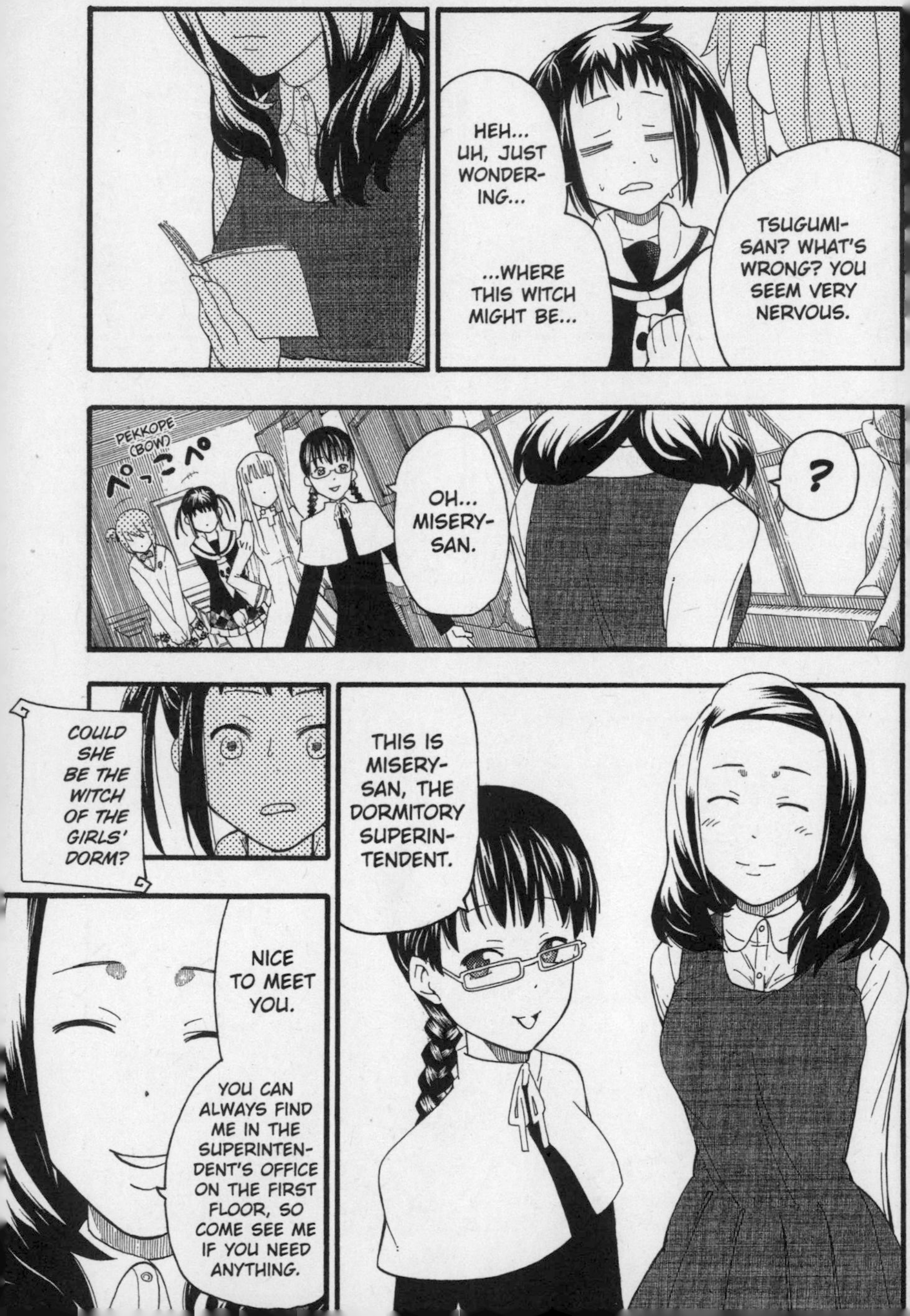
TSUGUMI-SAN? WHAT'S WRONG? YOU SEEM VERY NERVOUS.
HEH... UH, JUST WONDERING...
...WHERE THIS WITCH MIGHT BE...
?
OH... MISERY-SAN.
PEKKOPE (BOW)
ぺっこぺ
THIS IS MISERY-SAN, THE DORMITORY SUPERINTENDENT.
COULD SHE BE THE WITCH OF THE GIRLS' DORM?
NICE TO MEET YOU.
YOU CAN ALWAYS FIND ME IN THE SUPERINTENDENT'S OFFICE ON THE FIRST FLOOR, SO COME SEE ME IF YOU NEED ANYTHING.

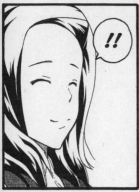

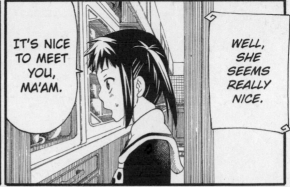

WELL, SHE SEEMS REALLY NICE.
IT'S NICE TO MEET YOU, MA'AM.
!!
ペラ ペラ
PERA
PERA (FLIP)
……
チラリ
CHIRARI (PEEK)
?
WHY, SHE'S MARY SMITH, PROTAGONIST OF THE COMMONERS OF FLANDERS, MY VERY FAVORITE NOVEL... SHE IS THE VERY IMAGE OF MARY SMITH THAT I SEE IN MY MIND!
BWA HEH HEH!
SHE'S CERTAINLY A FAR CRY FROM THAT HORRENDOUS HADE KILABIYA AND HER FLAM-BOYANT PERFORMANCE IN THAT STUPID MOVIE ADAPTATION! I REFUSE TO ACKNOWLEDGE THAT FARCE, BUT THIS GIRL'S THE REAL THING, IF YOU ASK ME...

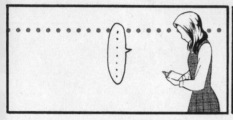

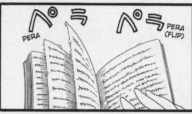

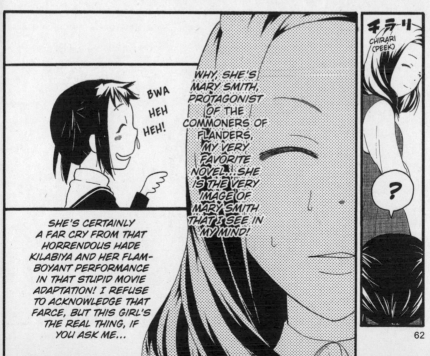

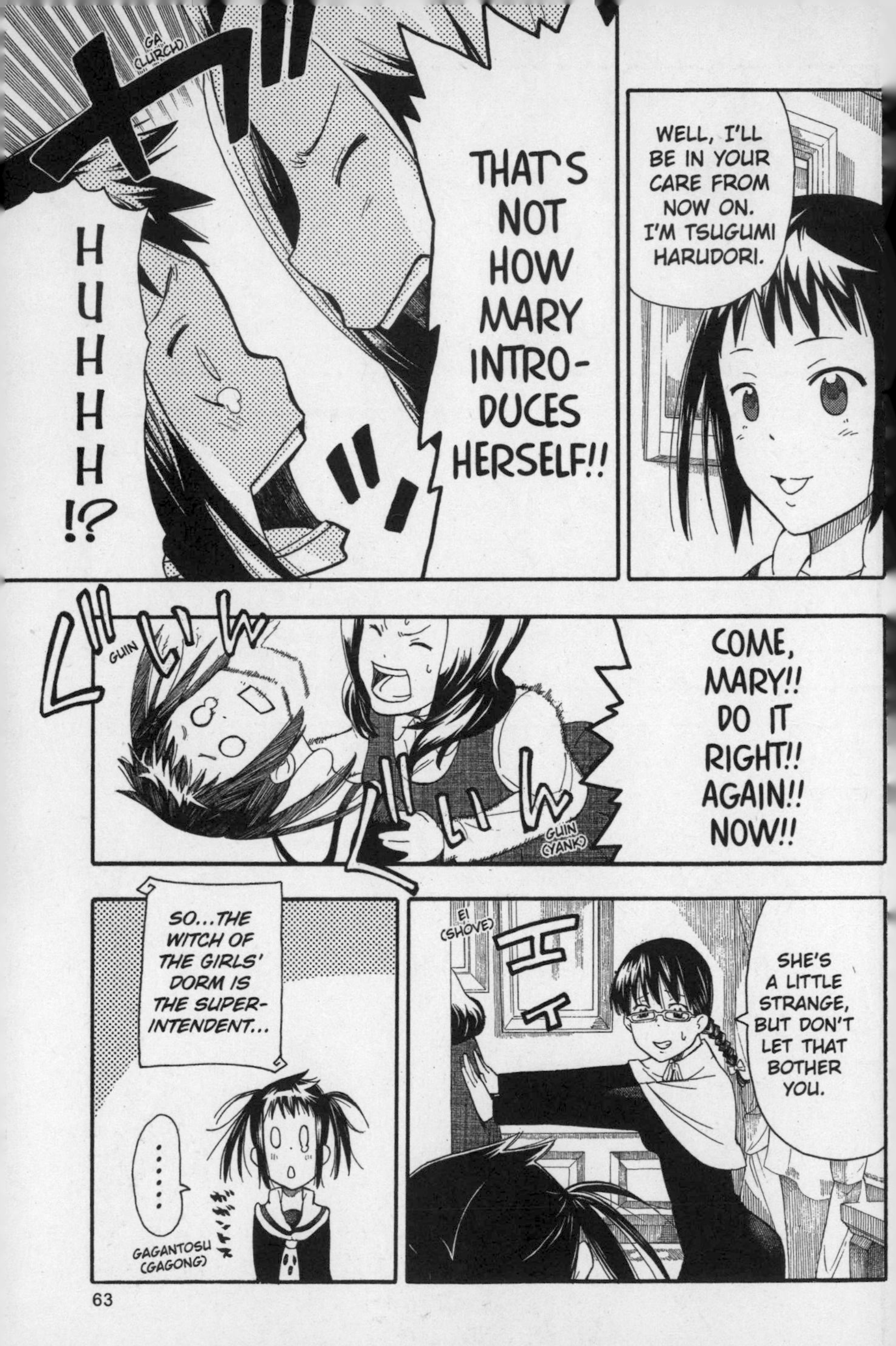
WELL, I'LL BE IN YOUR CARE FROM NOW ON. I'M TSUGUMI HARUDORI.
THAT'S NOT HOW MARY INTRO-DUCES HERSELF!!
GA (LURCH)
HUHHHH!?
COME, MARY!! DO IT RIGHT!! AGAIN!! NOW!!
GUIN
GUIN (YANK)
SHE'S A LITTLE STRANGE, BUT DON'T LET THAT BOTHER YOU.
EI (SHOVE)
SO...THE WITCH OF THE GIRLS' DORM IS THE SUPER-INTENDENT...
......
GAGANTOSU (GAGONG)

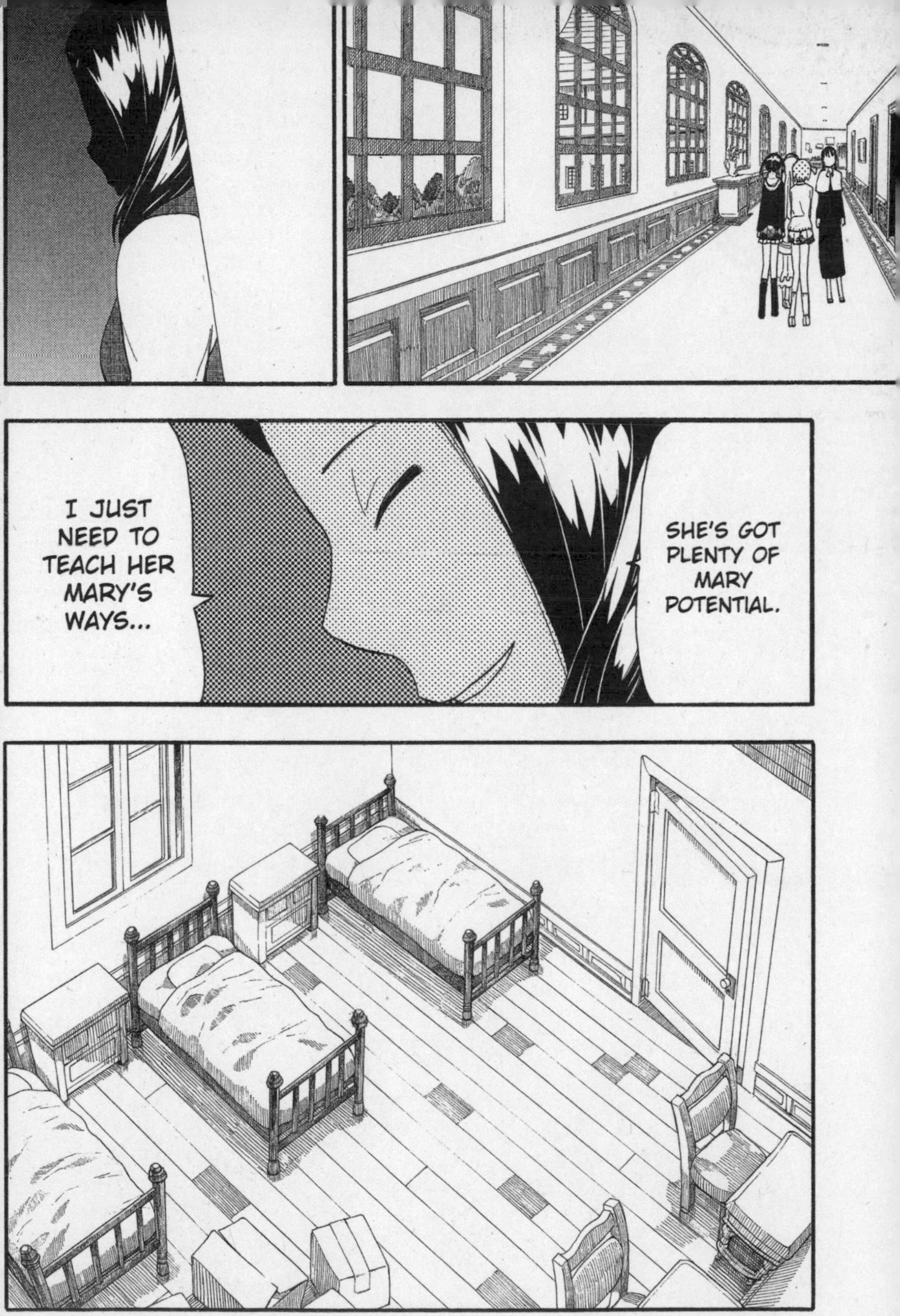
SHE'S GOT PLENTY OF MARY POTENTIAL.
I JUST NEED TO TEACH HER MARY'S WAYS...

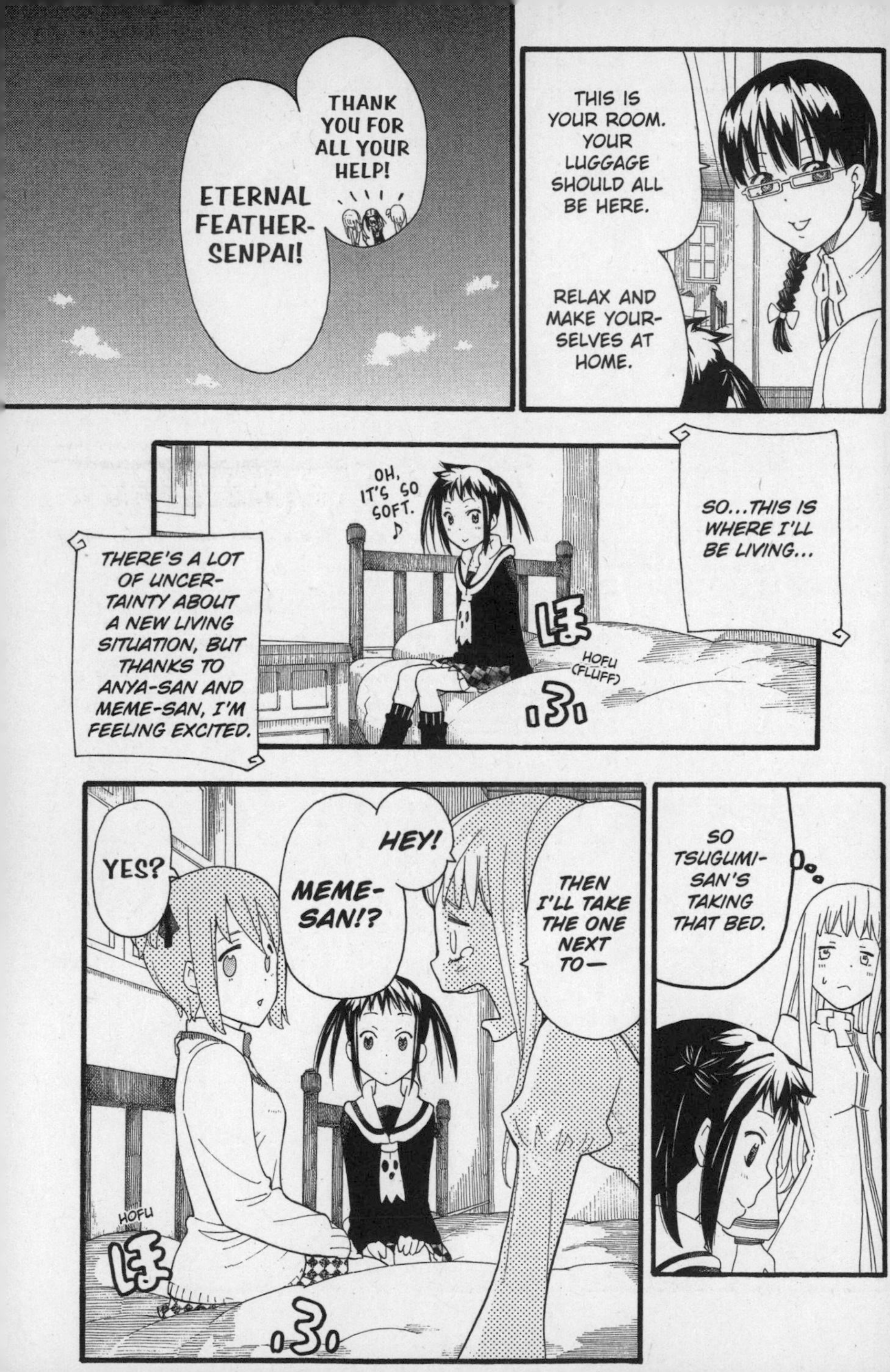
THIS IS YOUR ROOM. YOUR LUGGAGE SHOULD ALL BE HERE.
RELAX AND MAKE YOURSELVES AT HOME.
THANK YOU FOR ALL YOUR HELP! ETERNAL FEATHER-SENPAI!
SO...THIS IS WHERE I'LL BE LIVING...
OH, IT'S SO SOFT. ♪
ほ
ふ
HOFU (FLUFF)
THERE'S A LOT OF UNCERTAINTY ABOUT A NEW LIVING SITUATION, BUT THANKS TO ANYA-SAN AND MEME-SAN, I'M FEELING EXCITED.
SO TSUGUMI-SAN'S TAKING THAT BED.
THEN I'LL TAKE THE ONE NEXT TO—
HEY! MEME-SAN!?
YES?
ほ
ふ
HOFU

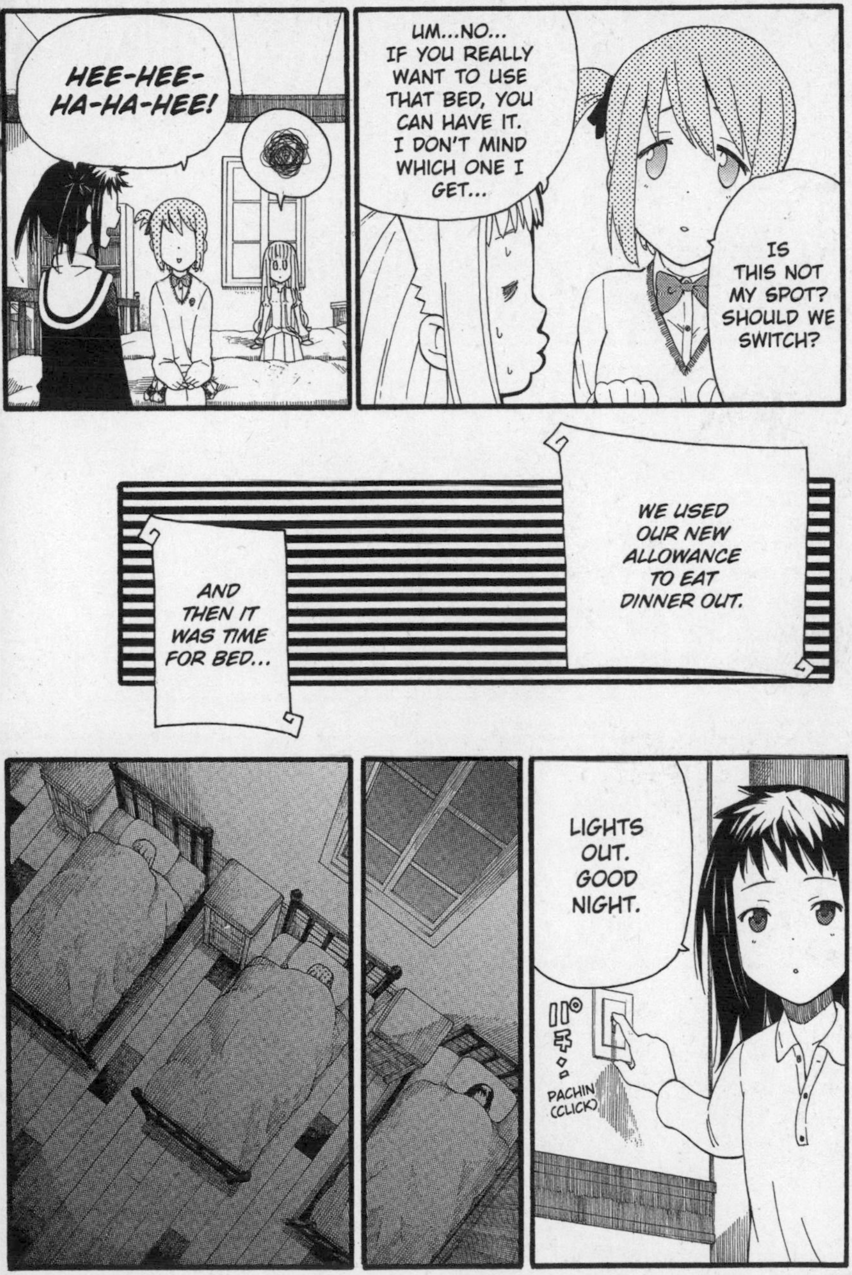
IS THIS NOT MY SPOT? SHOULD WE SWITCH?
UM...NO... IF YOU REALLY WANT TO USE THAT BED, YOU CAN HAVE IT. I DON'T MIND WHICH ONE I GET...
HEE-HEE-HA-HA-HEE!
WE USED OUR NEW ALLOWANCE TO EAT DINNER OUT.
AND THEN IT WAS TIME FOR BED...
LIGHTS OUT. GOOD NIGHT.
PACHIN (CLICK)

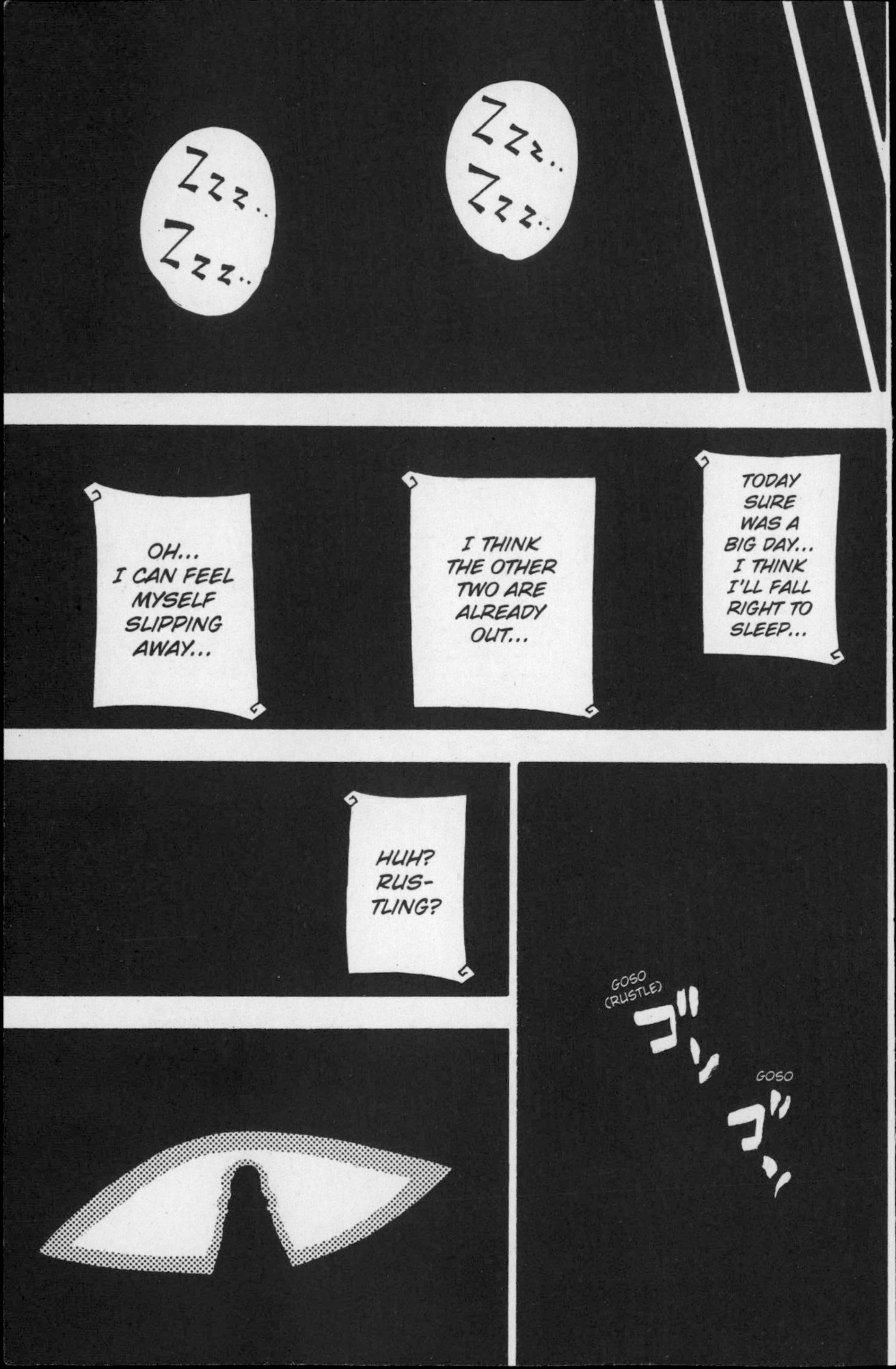
Zzz... Zzz...
Zzz... Zzz...
TODAY SURE WAS A BIG DAY... I THINK I'LL FALL RIGHT TO SLEEP...
I THINK THE OTHER TWO ARE ALREADY OUT...
OH... I CAN FEEL MYSELF SLIPPING AWAY...
GOSO (RUSTLE)
GOSO
HUH? RUS-TLING?

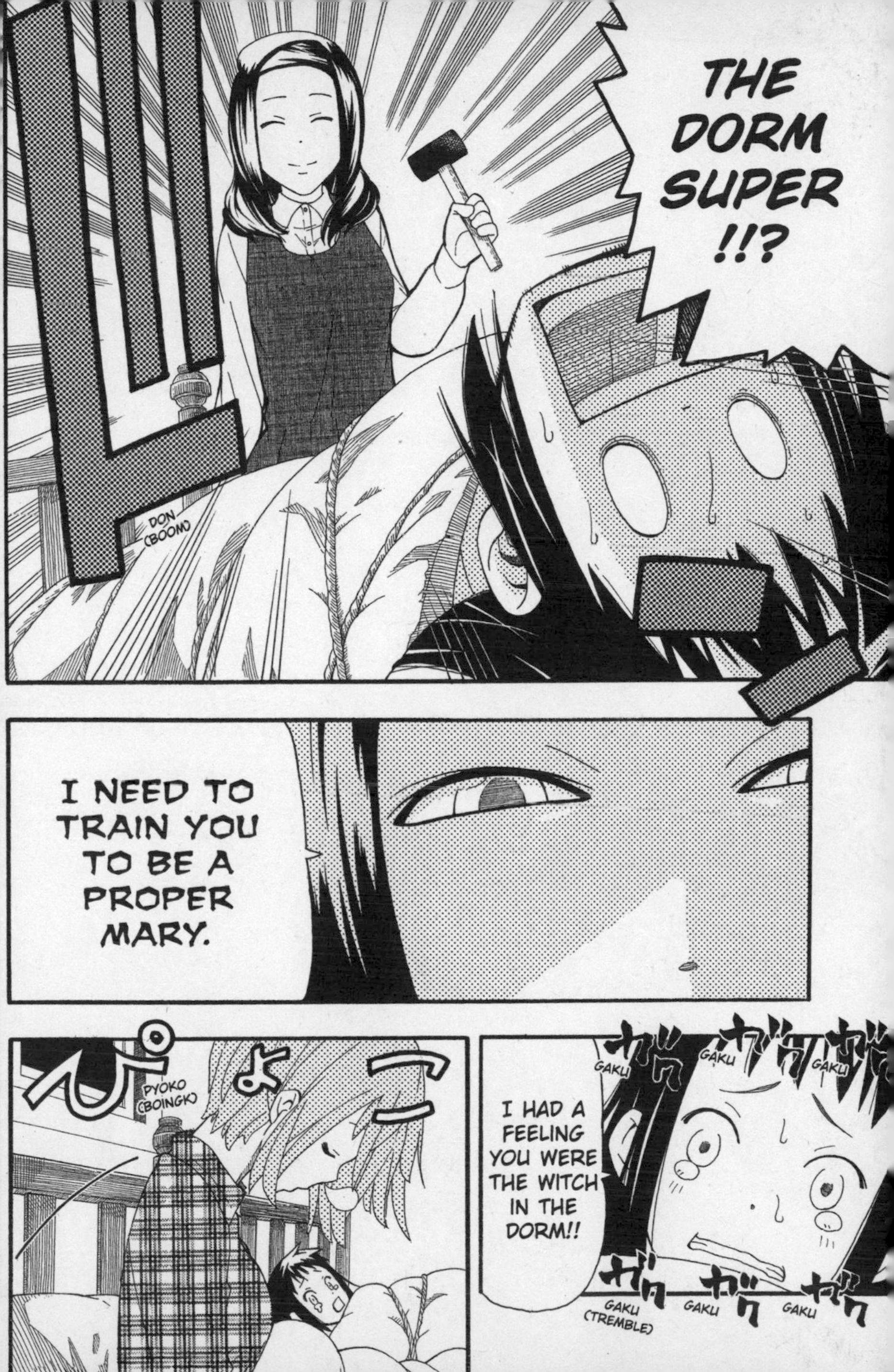
THE DORM SUPER !!?
DON (BOOM)
I NEED TO TRAIN YOU TO BE A PROPER MARY.
GAKU
GAKU
GAKU
I HAD A FEELING YOU WERE THE WITCH IN THE DORM!!
GAKU
GAKU
GAKU (TREMBLE)
PYOKO (BOINGK)

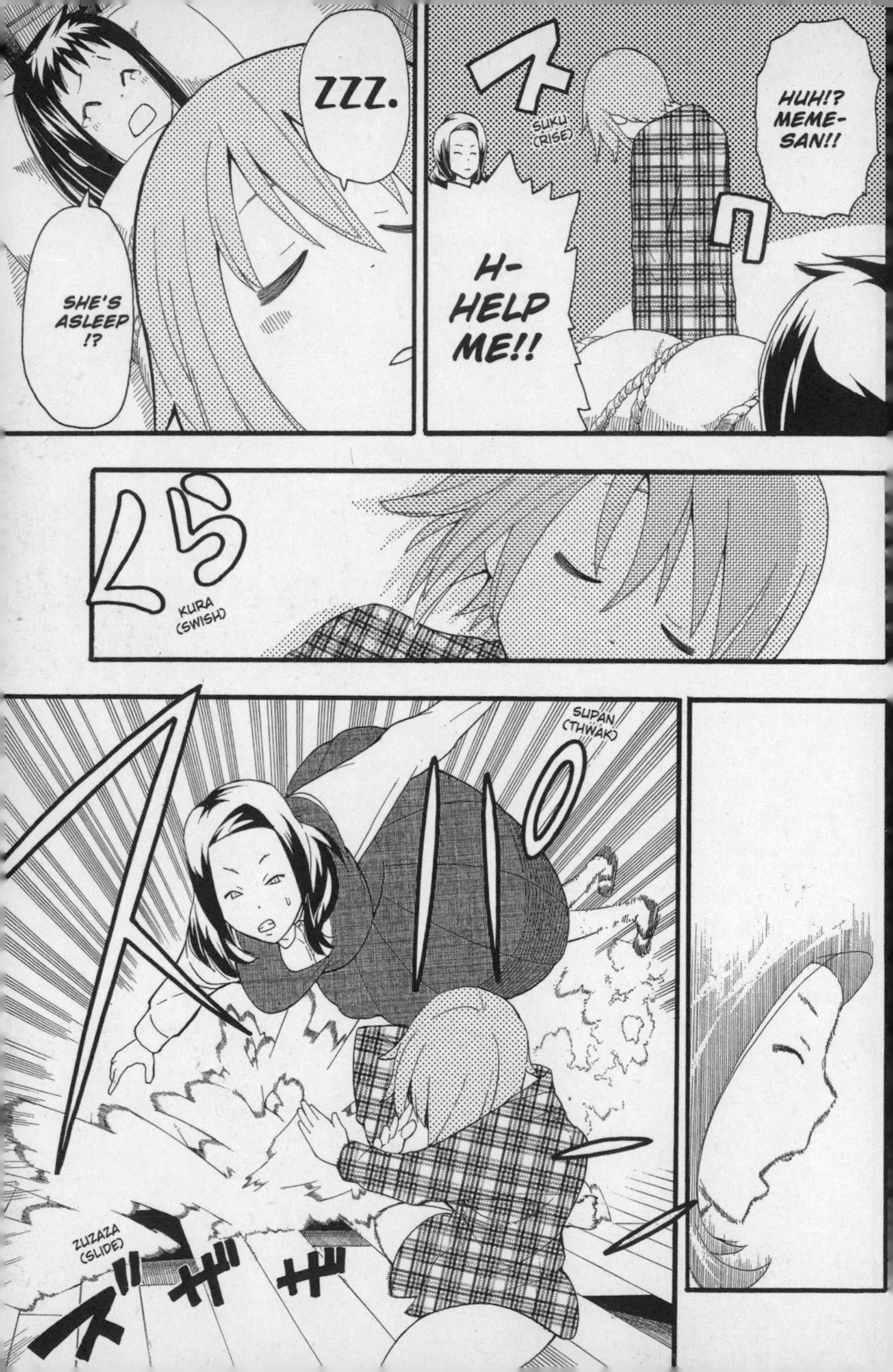
HUH!? MEME-SAN!!
SUKU (RISE)
H-HELP ME!!
ZZZ.
SHE'S ASLEEP!?
KURA (SWISH)
SUPAN (THWAK)
ZUZAZA (SLIDE)

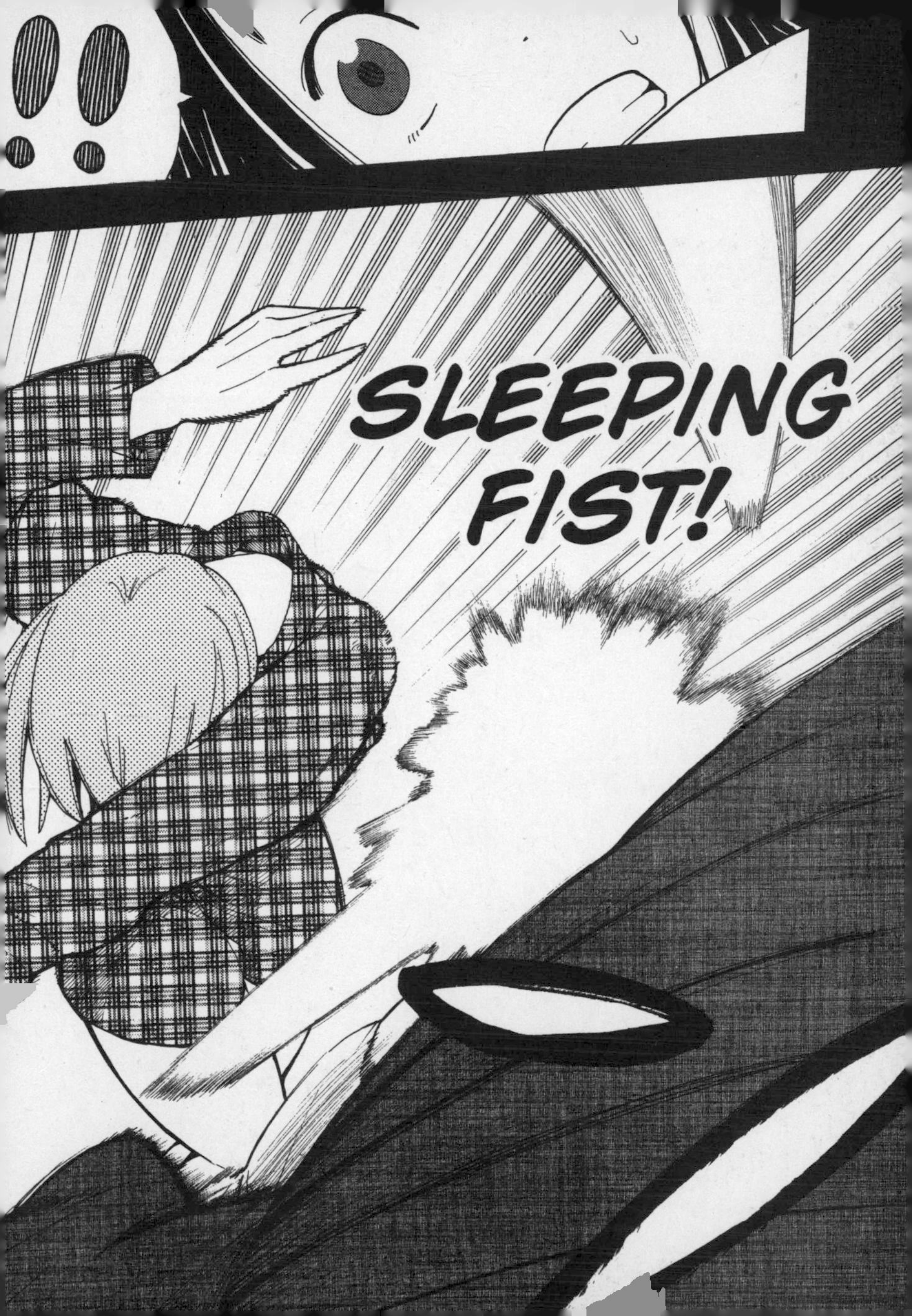
!!
SLEEPING FIST!

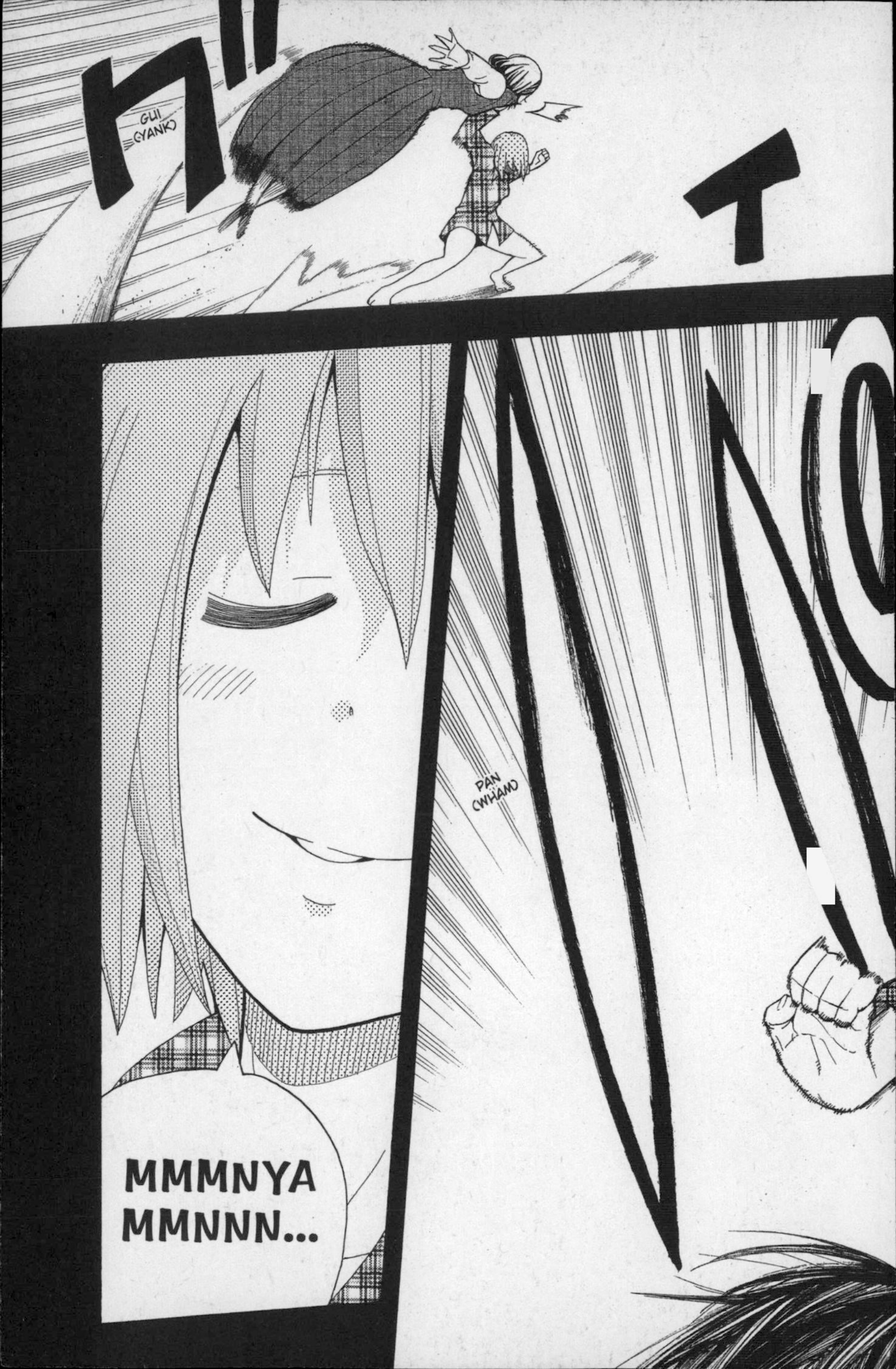
GUI (YANK)
PAN (WHAM)
MMMNYA MMNNN...

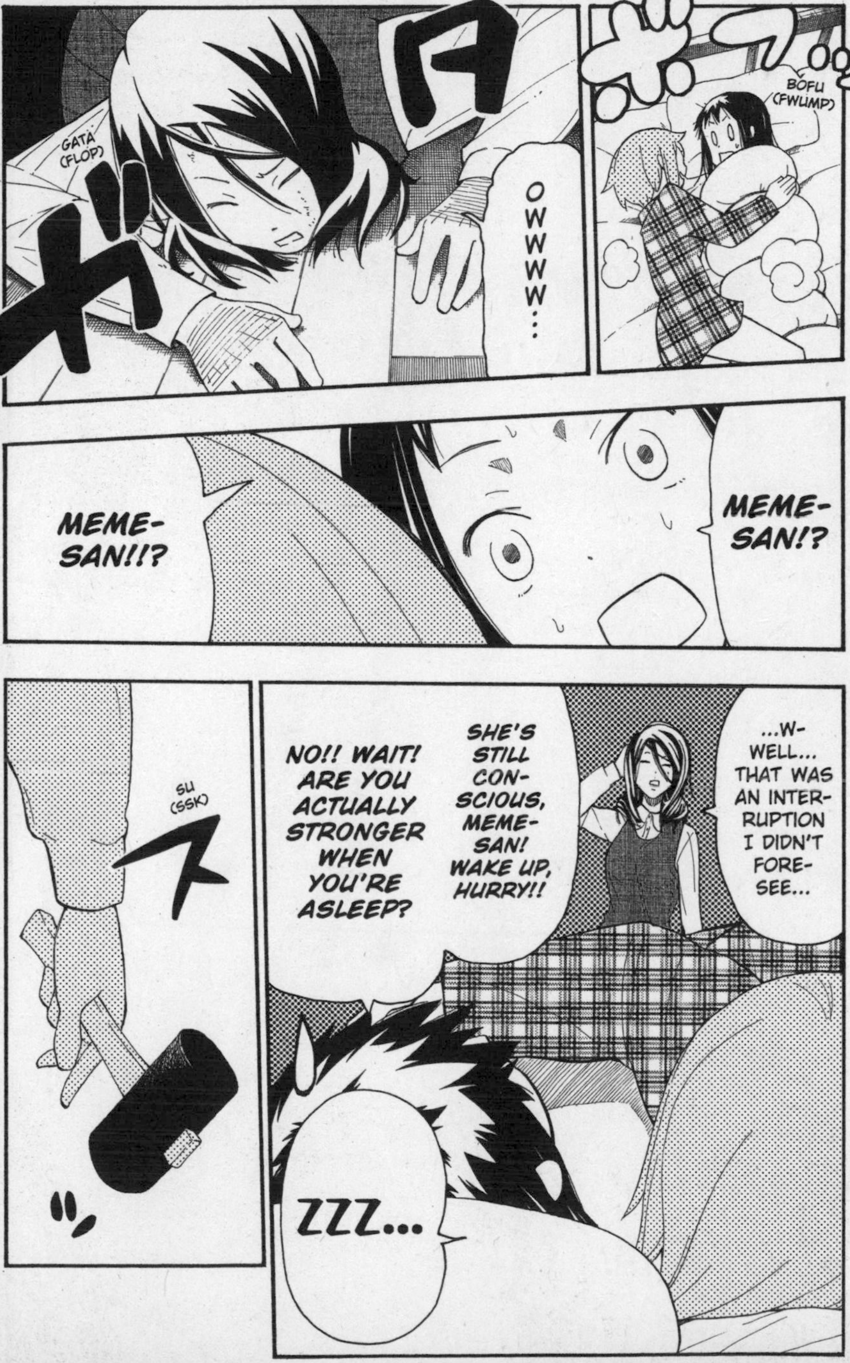
BOFU (FWUMP)
GATA (FLOP)
OWWWWW...
MEME-SAN!?
MEME-SAN!!?
...W-WELL... THAT WAS AN INTERRUPTION I DIDN'T FORESEE...
SHE'S STILL CONSCIOUS, MEME-SAN! WAKE UP, HURRY!!
NO!! WAIT! ARE YOU ACTUALLY STRONGER WHEN YOU'RE ASLEEP?
ZZZ...
SU (SSK)

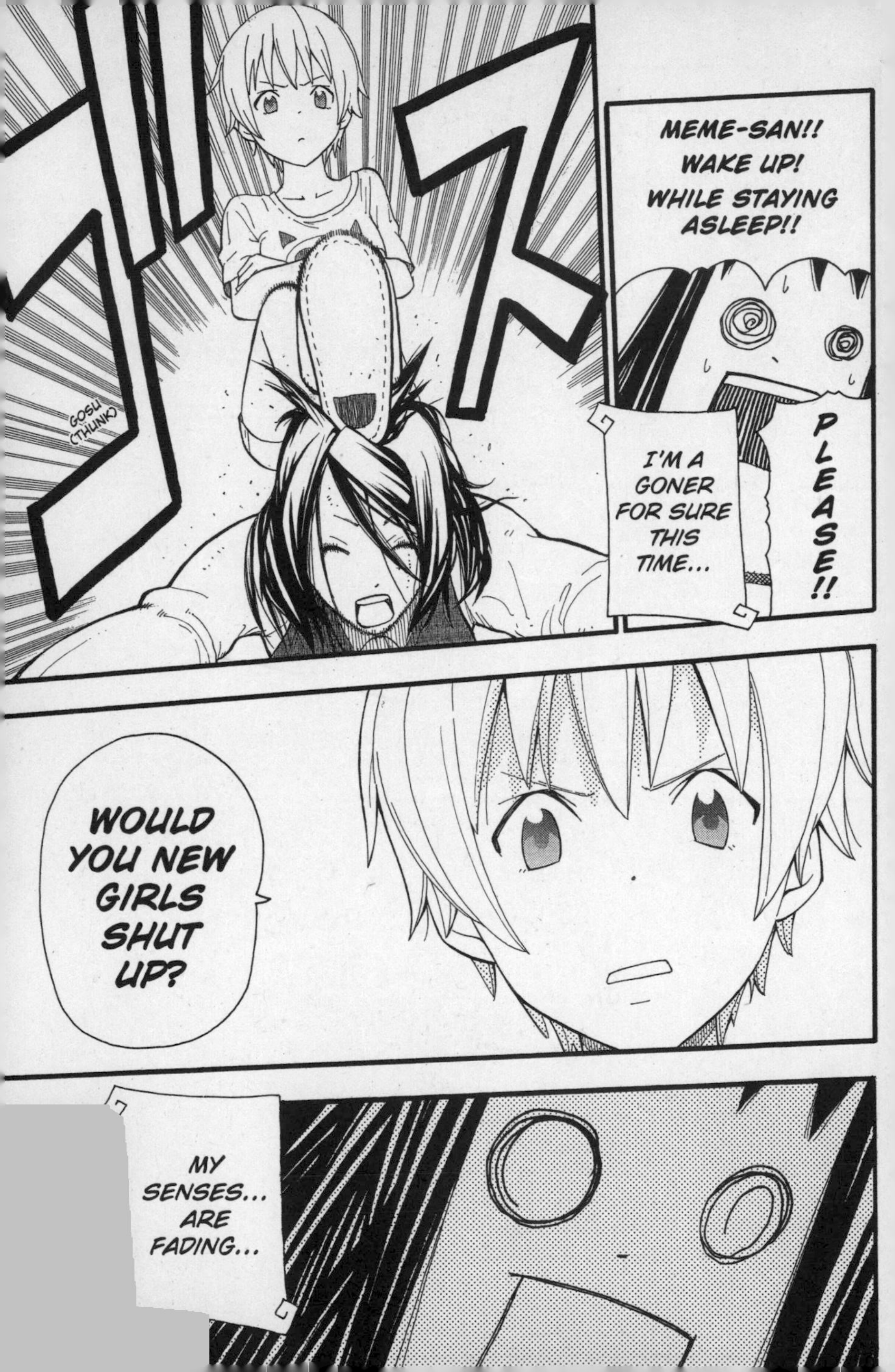
MEME-SAN!! WAKE UP! WHILE STAYING ASLEEP!!
PLEASE!!
I'M A GONER FOR SURE THIS TIME...
GOSU (THUNK)
WOULD YOU NEW GIRLS SHUT UP?
MY SENSES... ARE FADING...

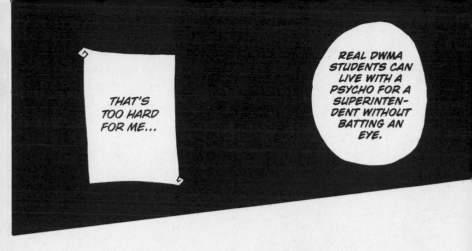

REAL DWMA STUDENTS CAN LIVE WITH A PSYCHO FOR A SUPERINTENDENT WITHOUT BATTING AN EYE.

THAT'S TOO HARD FOR ME...

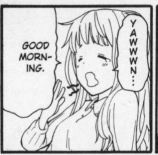

GOOD MORNING.

YAWWWN...

CHUN (CHIRP)

ちゅん ちゅん CHUN

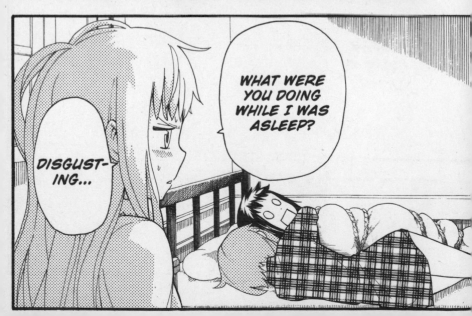

WHAT WERE YOU DOING WHILE I WAS ASLEEP?

DISGUSTING...

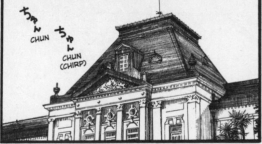

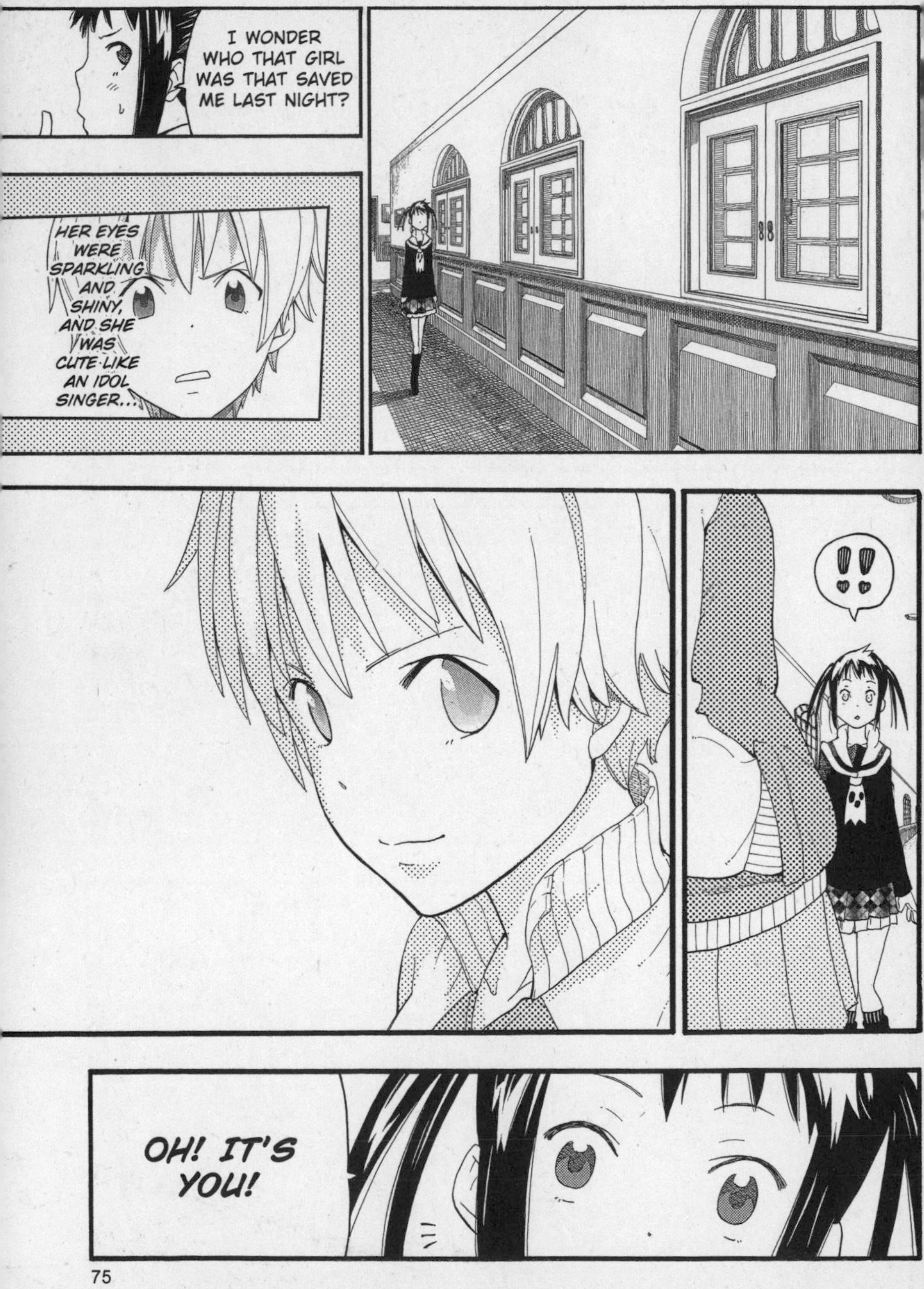
I WONDER WHO THAT GIRL WAS THAT SAVED ME LAST NIGHT?
HER EYES WERE SPARKLING AND SHINY, AND SHE WAS CUTE LIKE AN IDOL SINGER...
!!
OH! IT'S YOU!

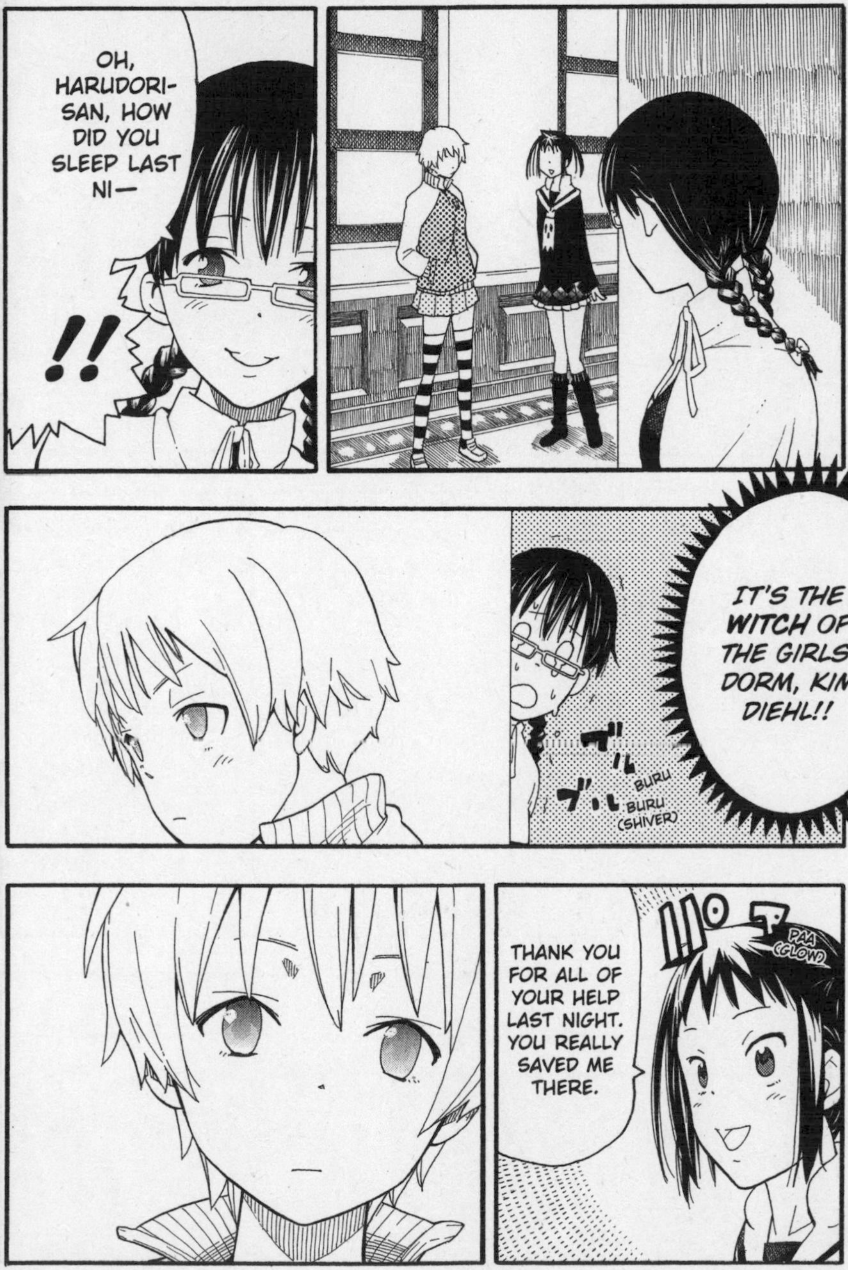
OH, HARUDORI-SAN, HOW DID YOU SLEEP LAST NI—
!!
IT'S THE WITCH OF THE GIRLS' DORM, KIM DIEHL!!
BURU BURU (SHIVER)
PAA (GLOW)
THANK YOU FOR ALL OF YOUR HELP LAST NIGHT. YOU REALLY SAVED ME THERE.

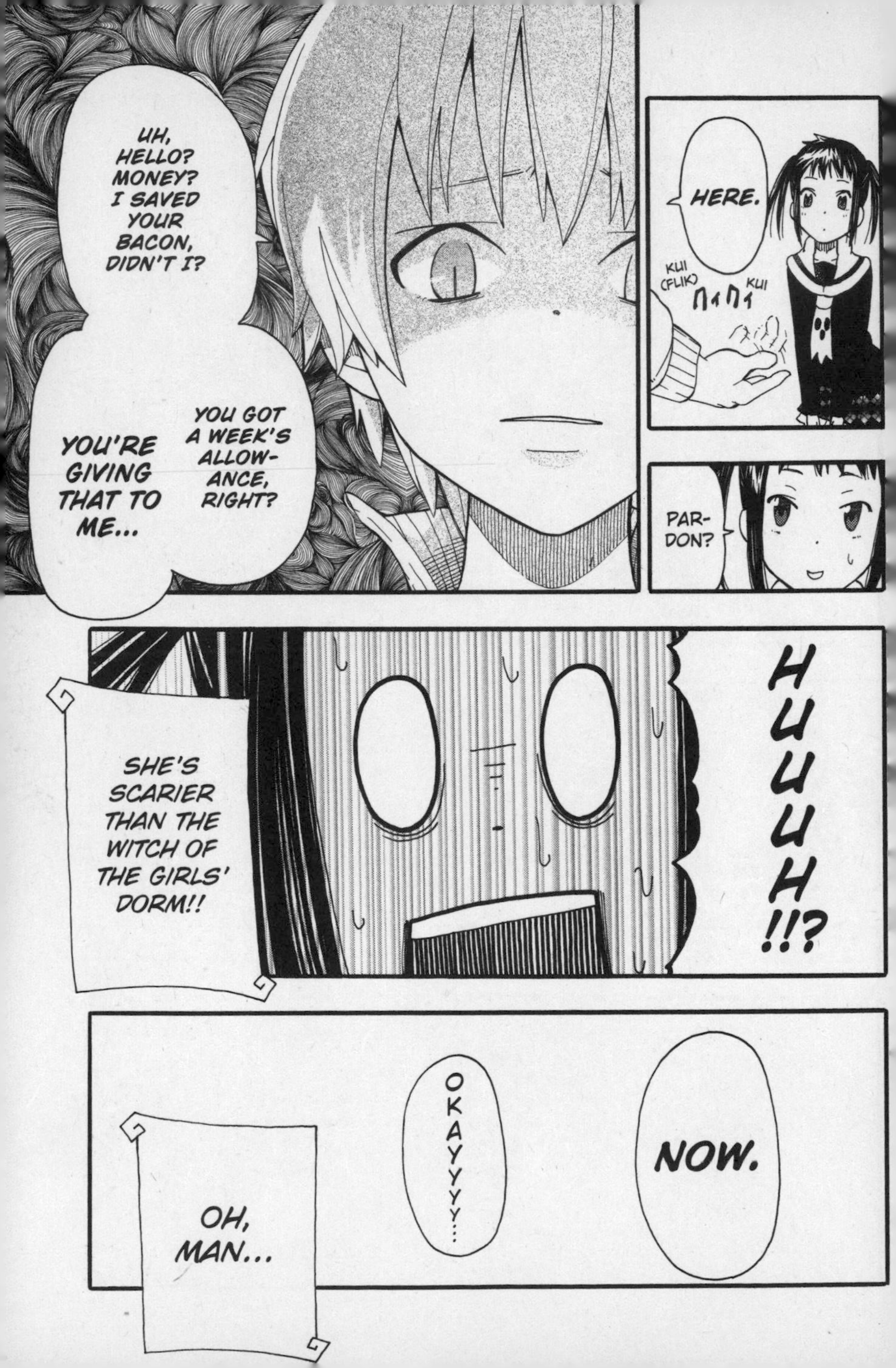
HERE.
KUI (FLIK) KUI
PARDON?
UH, HELLO? MONEY? I SAVED YOUR BACON, DIDN'T I?
YOU GOT A WEEK'S ALLOW-ANCE, RIGHT?
YOU'RE GIVING THAT TO ME...
HUUUH!!?
SHE'S SCARIER THAN THE WITCH OF THE GIRLS' DORM!!
NOW.
OKAYYYY...
OH, MAN...

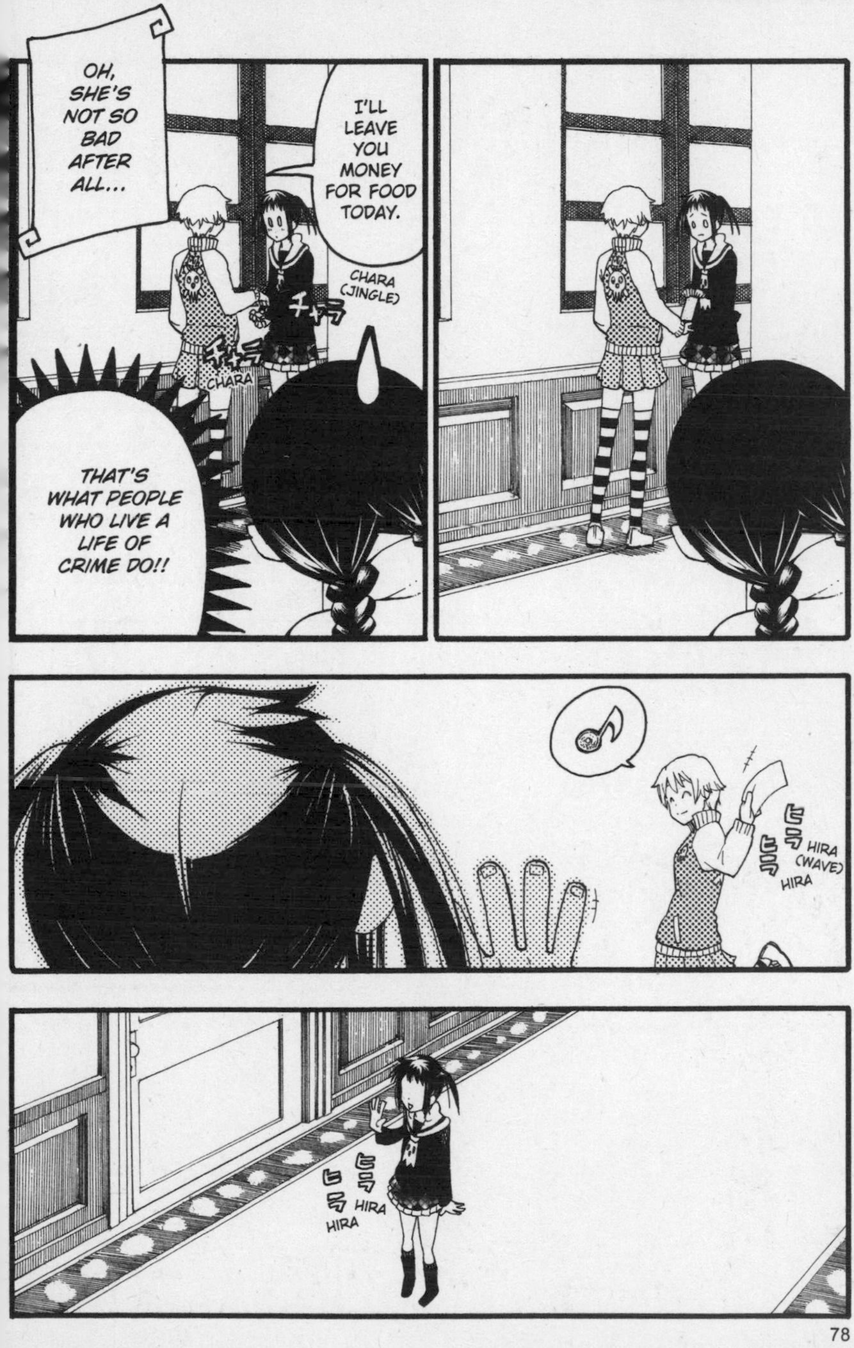
I'LL LEAVE YOU MONEY FOR FOOD TODAY.
チャラ
CHARA (JINGLE)
OH, SHE'S NOT SO BAD AFTER ALL...
チャラ
CHARA
THAT'S WHAT PEOPLE WHO LIVE A LIFE OF CRIME DO!!
ヒラ
HIRA (WAVE)
ヒラ
HIRA
ヒラ
HIRA
ヒラ
HIRA

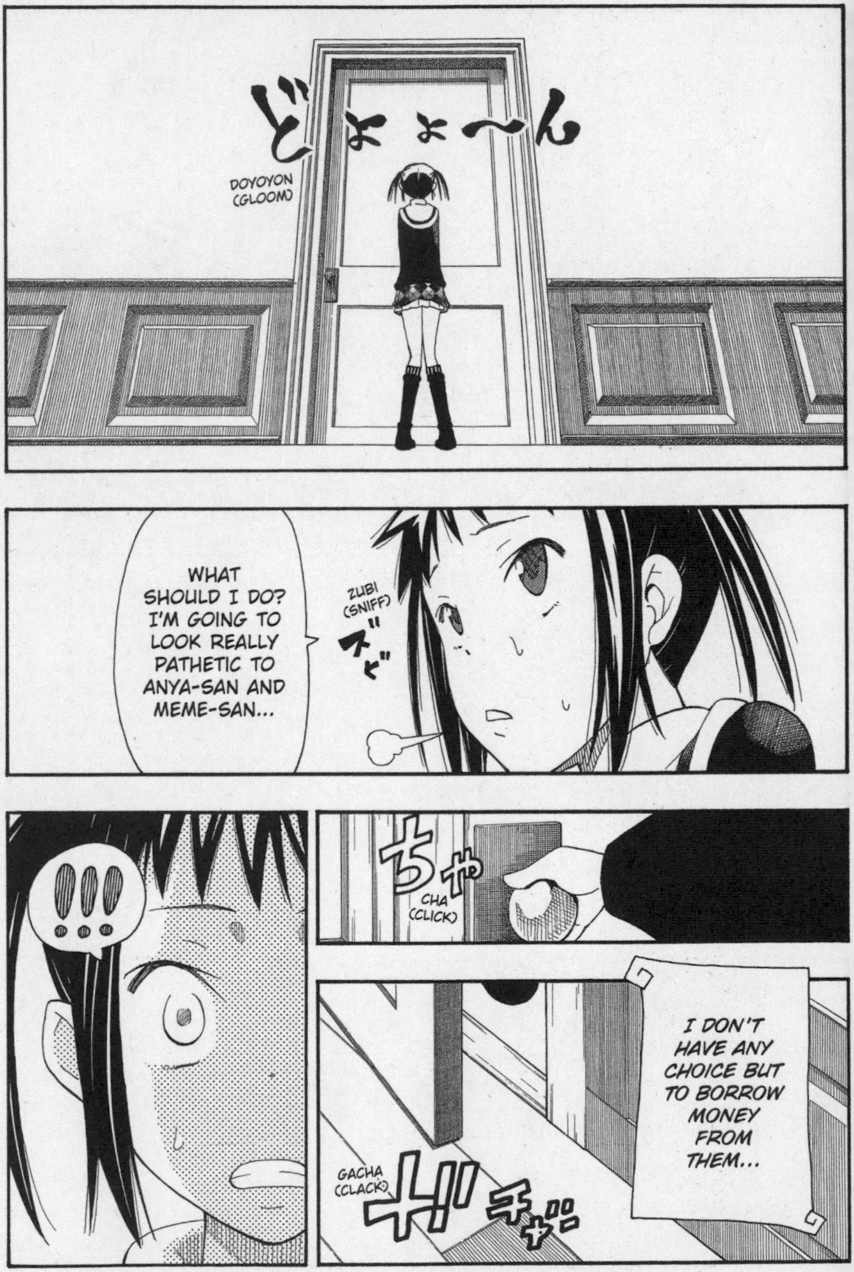

どよょ〜ん
DOYOYON (GLOOM)
ズビ
ZUBI (SNIFF)
WHAT SHOULD I DO? I'M GOING TO LOOK REALLY PATHETIC TO ANYA-SAN AND MEME-SAN...
ちゃ
CHA (CLICK)
I DON'T HAVE ANY CHOICE BUT TO BORROW MONEY FROM THEM...
ガチャ
GACHA (CLACK)
!!!

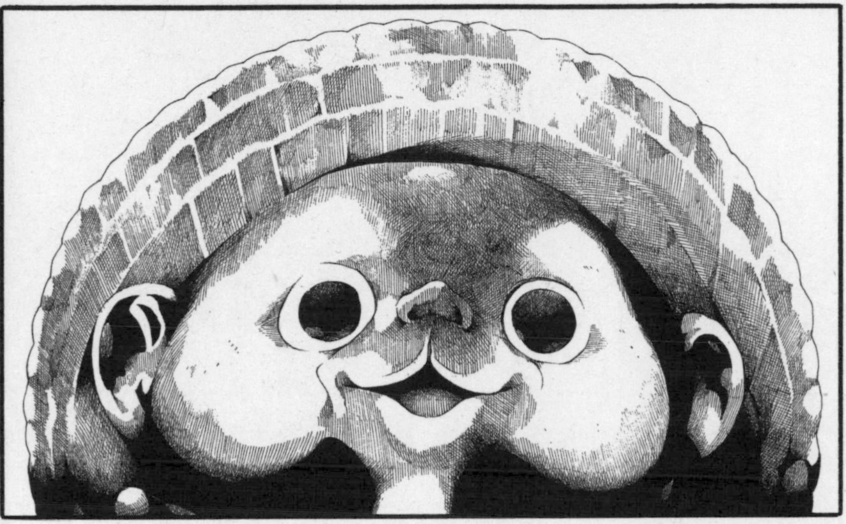

LANTERN: DWMA, BANNER: PLACE OF DEATH

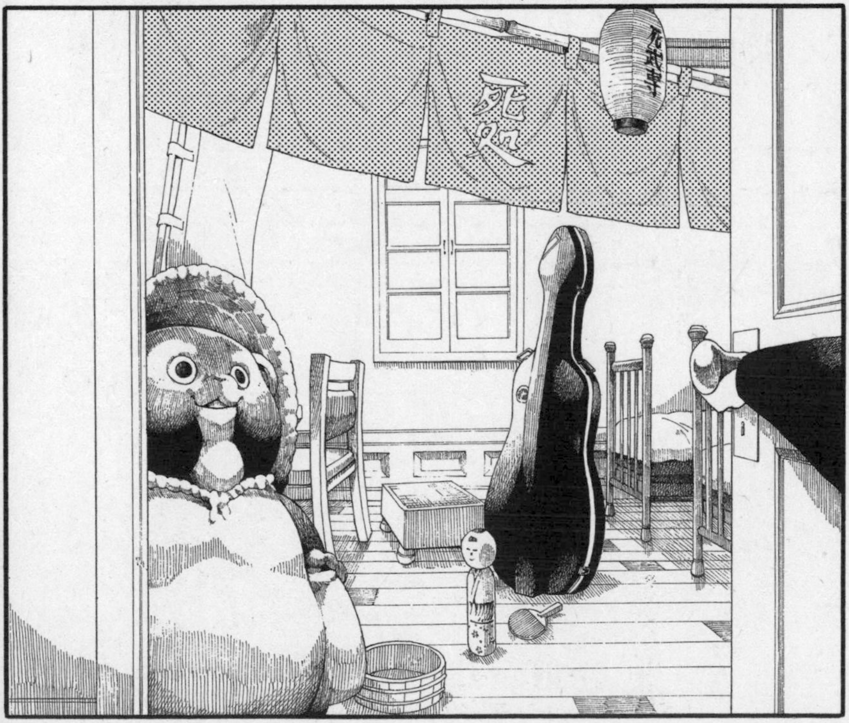
死処

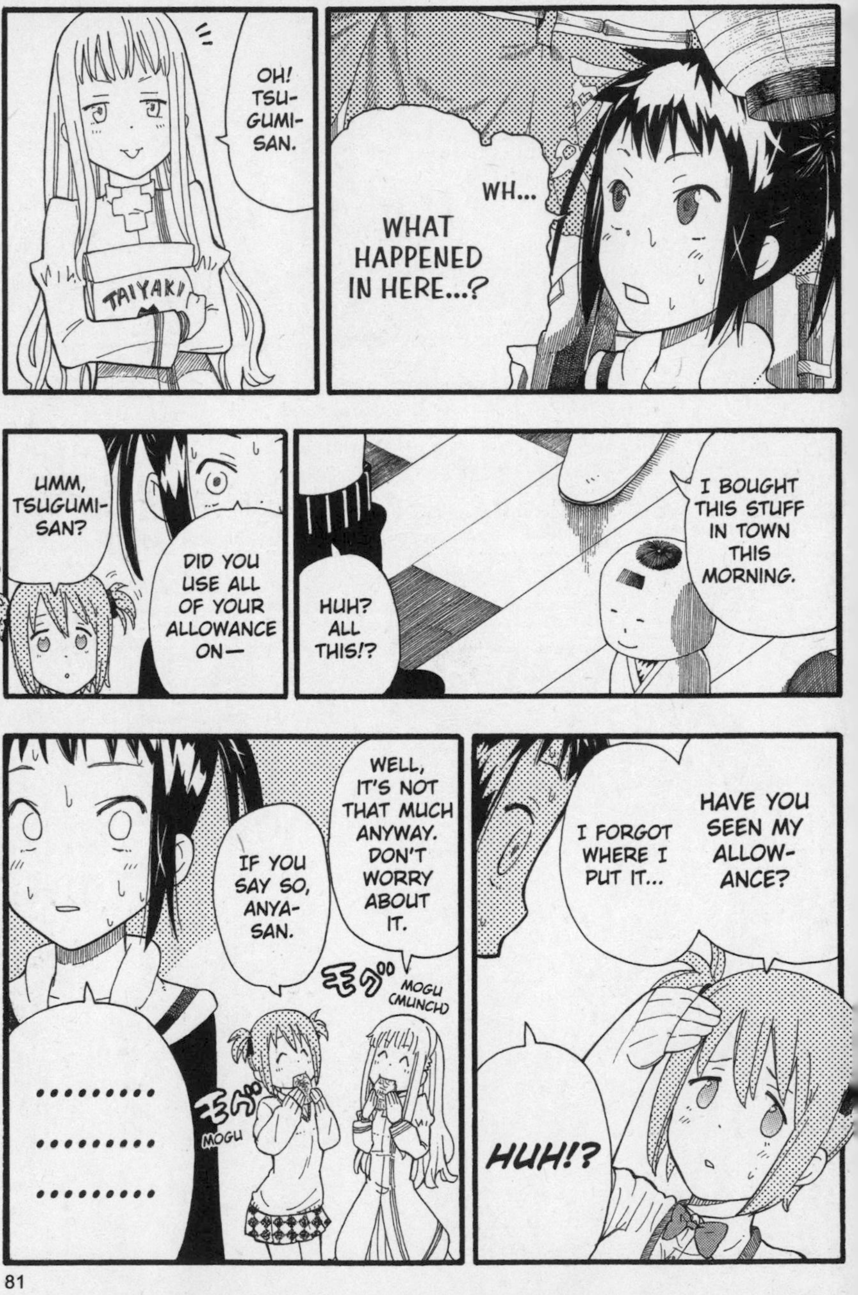
WH...
WHAT HAPPENED IN HERE...?
OH! TSUGUMI-SAN.
TAIYAKI
I BOUGHT THIS STUFF IN TOWN THIS MORNING.
HUH? ALL THIS!?
DID YOU USE ALL OF YOUR ALLOWANCE ON—
POIN (BOING)
UMM, TSUGUMI-SAN?
HAVE YOU SEEN MY ALLOWANCE?
I FORGOT WHERE I PUT IT...
HUH!?
WELL, IT'S NOT THAT MUCH ANYWAY. DON'T WORRY ABOUT IT.
MOGU (MUNCH)
IF YOU SAY SO, ANYA-SAN.
MOGU
....
....
....

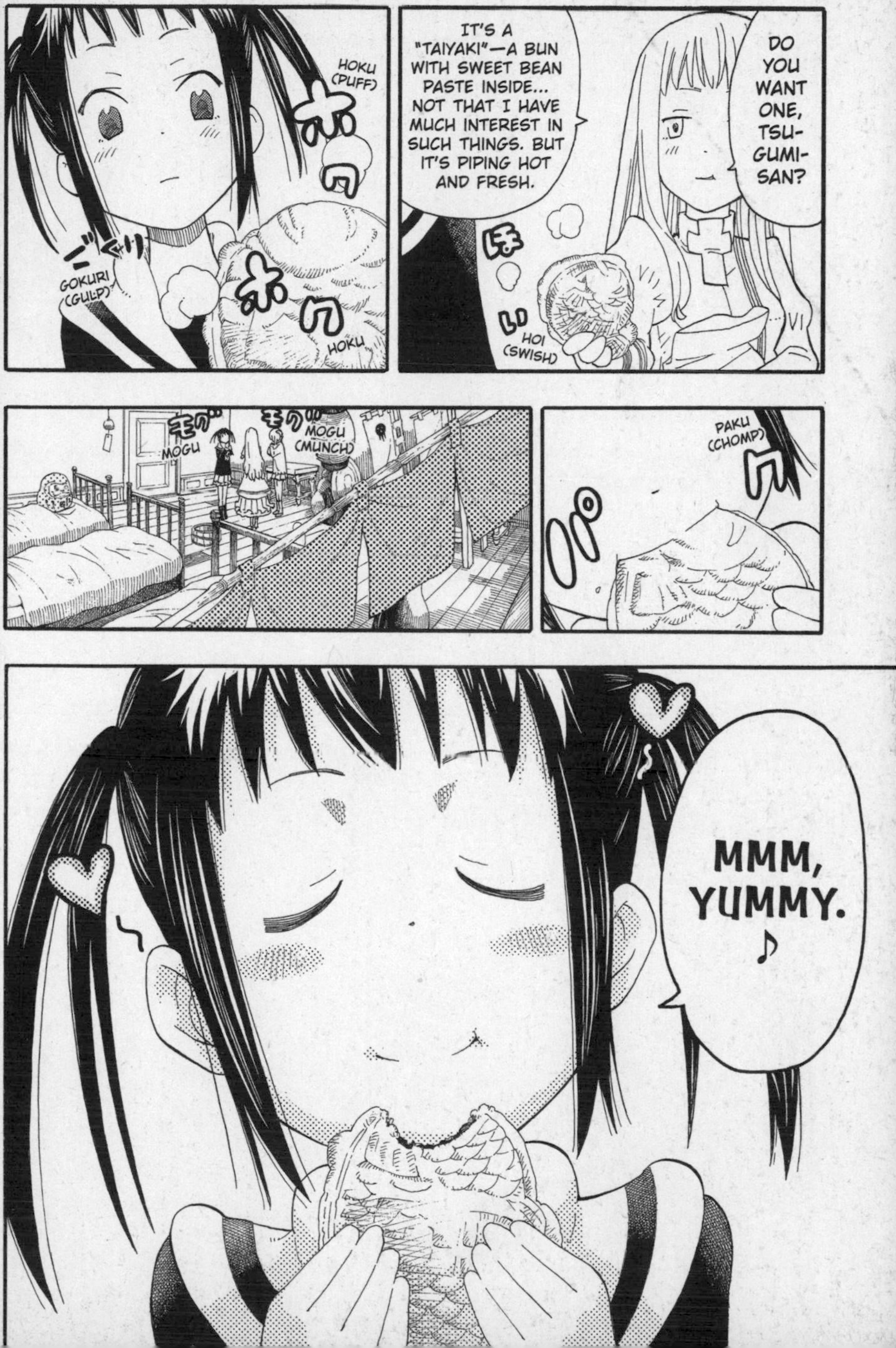
DO YOU WANT ONE, TSUGUMI-SAN?
IT'S A "TAIYAKI"—A BUN WITH SWEET BEAN PASTE INSIDE... NOT THAT I HAVE MUCH INTEREST IN SUCH THINGS. BUT IT'S PIPING HOT AND FRESH.
HOI (SWISH)
HOKU (PUFF)
GOKURI (GULP)
HOKU
PAKU (CHOMP)
MOGU (MUNCH)
MOGU
MMM, YUMMY. ♪

SOUL EATER NOT!

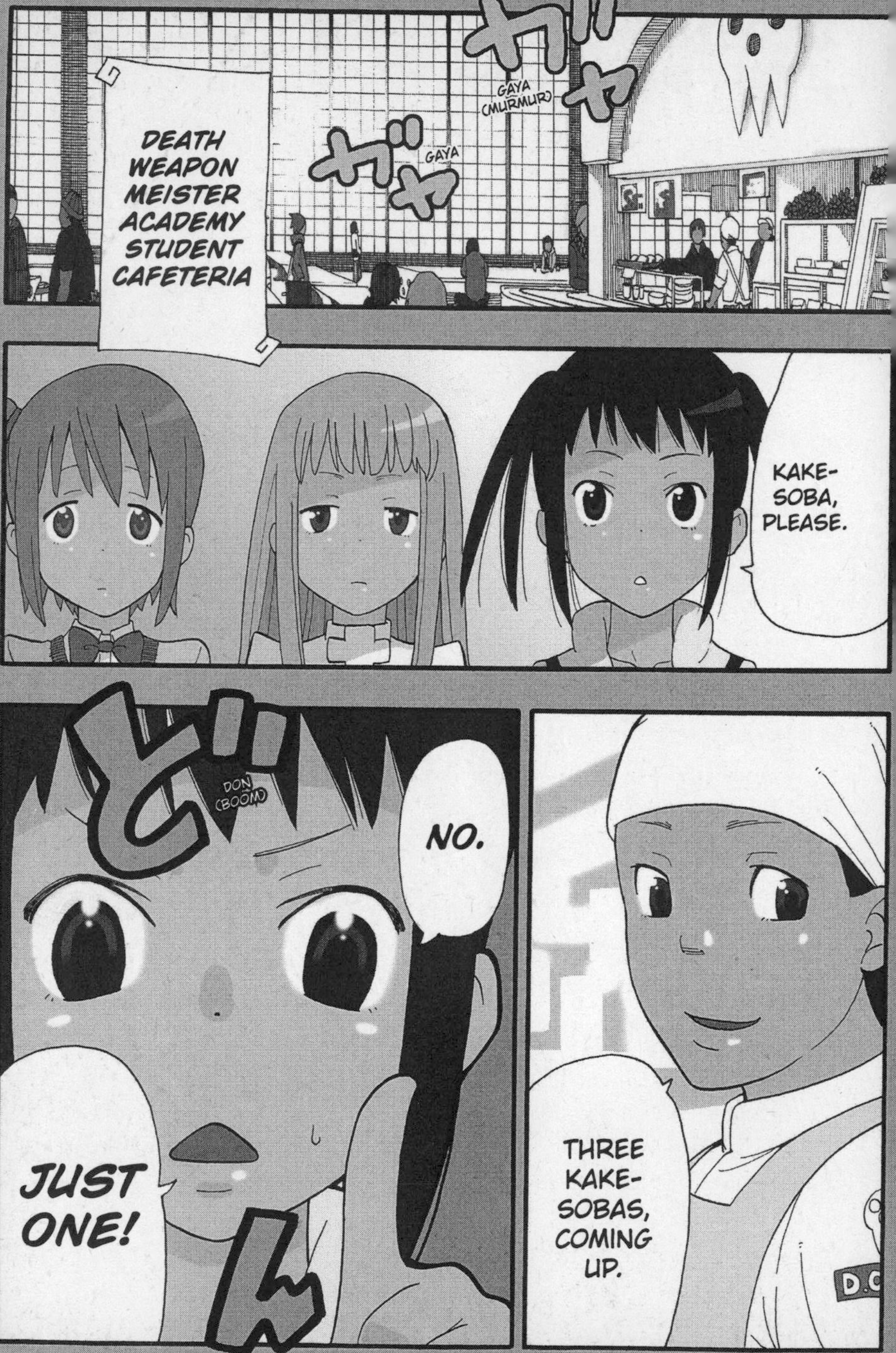
GAYA (MURMUR)
GAYA
DEATH WEAPON MEISTER ACADEMY STUDENT CAFETERIA
KAKE-SOBA, PLEASE.
THREE KAKE-SOBAS, COMING UP.
DON (BOOM)
NO.
JUST ONE!

CHAPTER 3: $$$! MONEY, MONEY, MONEY!

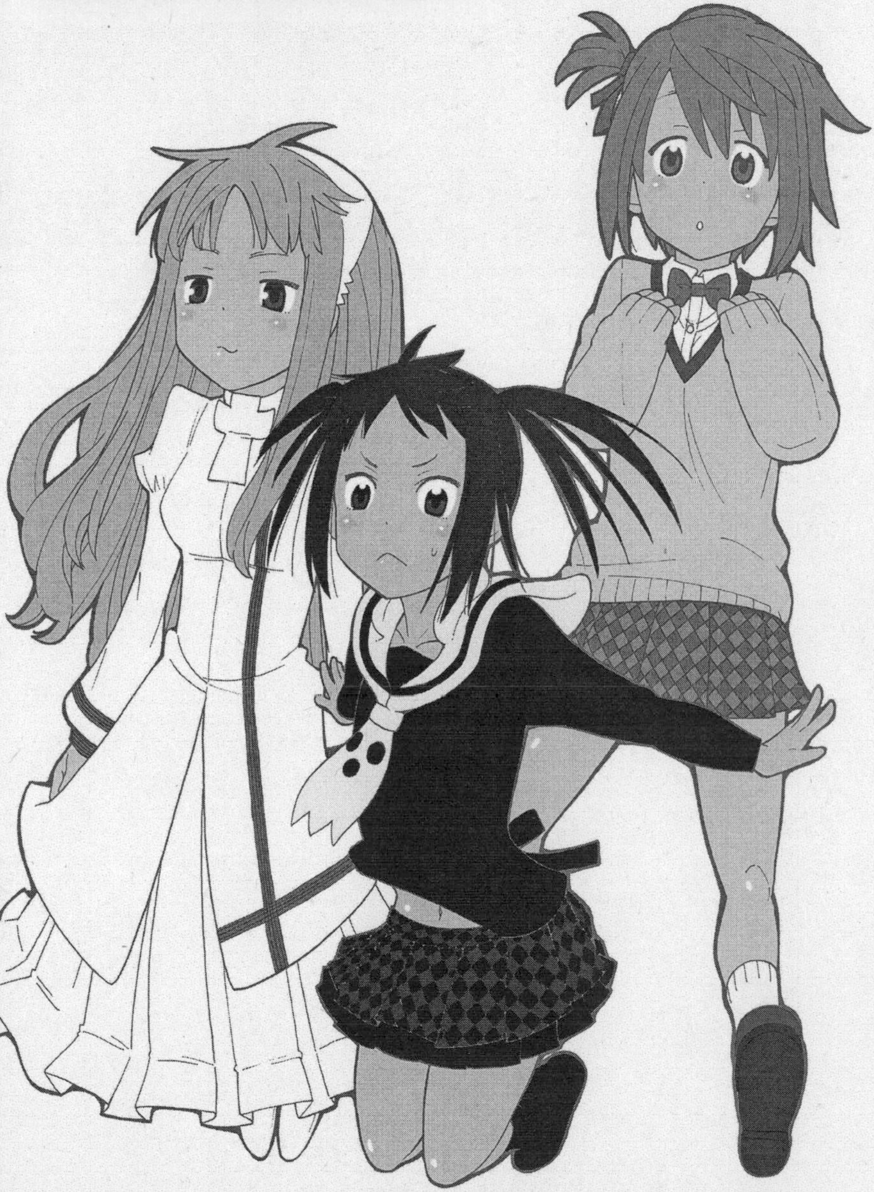

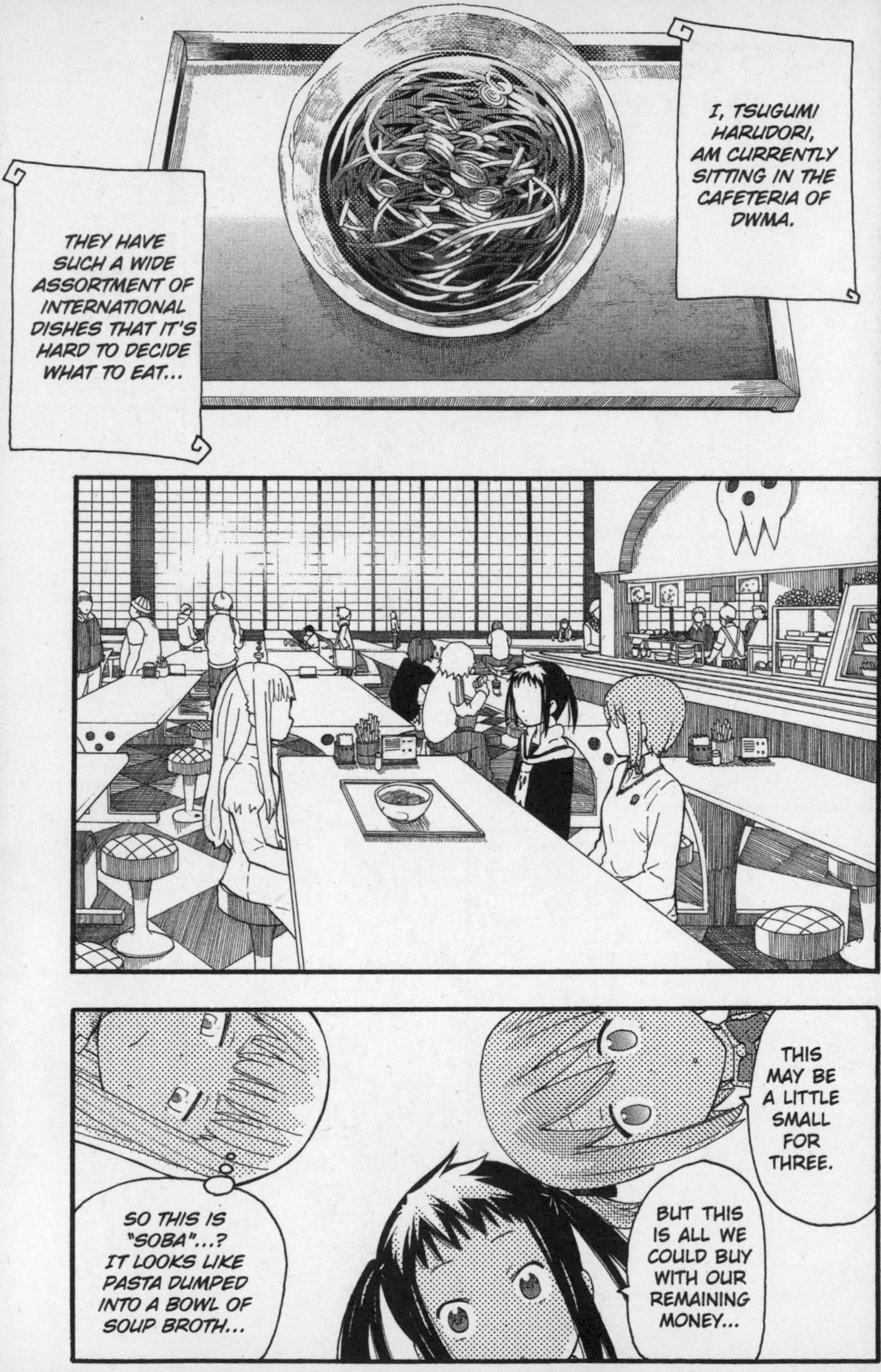
I, TSUGUMI HARUDORI, AM CURRENTLY SITTING IN THE CAFETERIA OF DWMA.
THEY HAVE SUCH A WIDE ASSORTMENT OF INTERNATIONAL DISHES THAT IT'S HARD TO DECIDE WHAT TO EAT...
THIS MAY BE A LITTLE SMALL FOR THREE.
BUT THIS IS ALL WE COULD BUY WITH OUR REMAINING MONEY...
SO THIS IS "SOBA"...? IT LOOKS LIKE PASTA DUMPED INTO A BOWL OF SOUP BROTH...

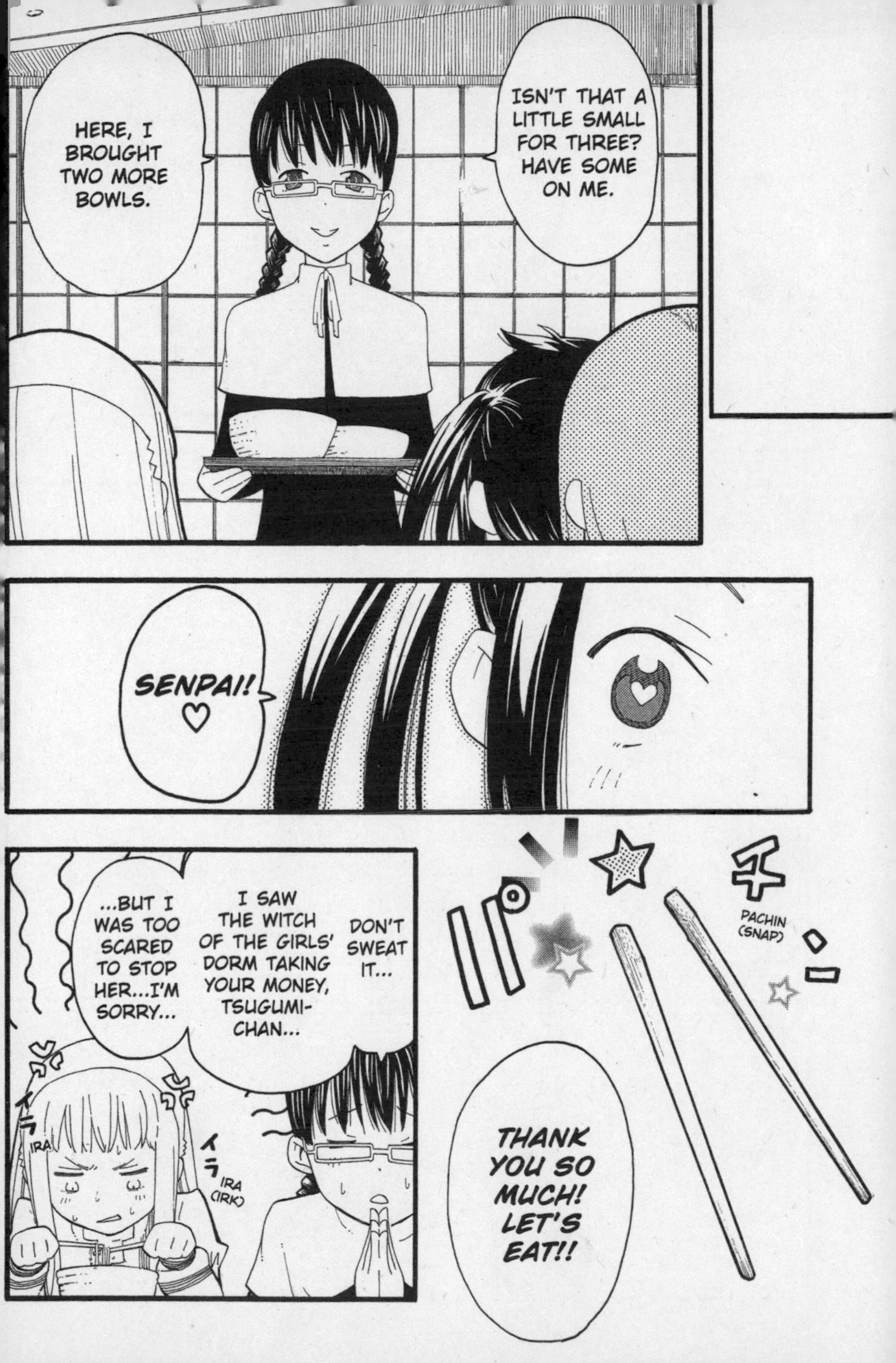

ISN'T THAT A LITTLE SMALL FOR THREE? HAVE SOME ON ME.
HERE, I BROUGHT TWO MORE BOWLS.
SENPAI! ♡
PACHIN (SNAP)
THANK YOU SO MUCH! LET'S EAT!!
DON'T SWEAT IT...
I SAW THE WITCH OF THE GIRLS' DORM TAKING YOUR MONEY, TSUGUMI-CHAN...
...BUT I WAS TOO SCARED TO STOP HER...I'M SORRY...
IRA (IRK)
IRA

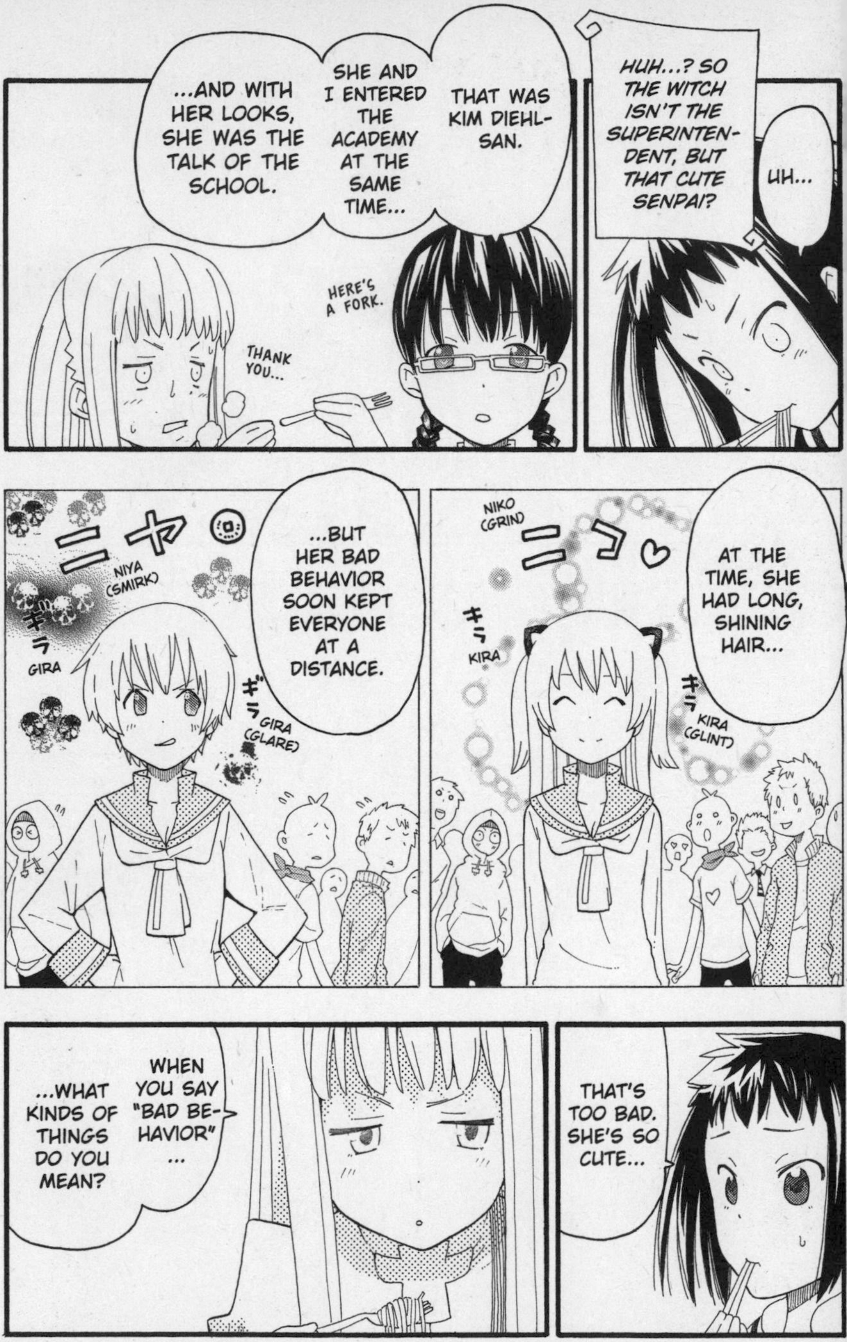
HUH...? SO THE WITCH ISN'T THE SUPERINTENDENT, BUT THAT CUTE SENPAI?
UH...
THAT WAS KIM DIEHL-SAN.
SHE AND I ENTERED THE ACADEMY AT THE SAME TIME...
...AND WITH HER LOOKS, SHE WAS THE TALK OF THE SCHOOL.
HERE'S A FORK.
THANK YOU...
AT THE TIME, SHE HAD LONG, SHINING HAIR...
ニコ
NIKO (GRIN)
キラ
KIRA (GLINT)
キラ
KIRA
...BUT HER BAD BEHAVIOR SOON KEPT EVERYONE AT A DISTANCE.
ニヤ
NIYA (SMIRK)
ギラ
GIRA (GLARE)
ギラ
GIRA
THAT'S TOO BAD. SHE'S SO CUTE...
WHEN YOU SAY "BAD BEHAVIOR"...
...WHAT KINDS OF THINGS DO YOU MEAN?

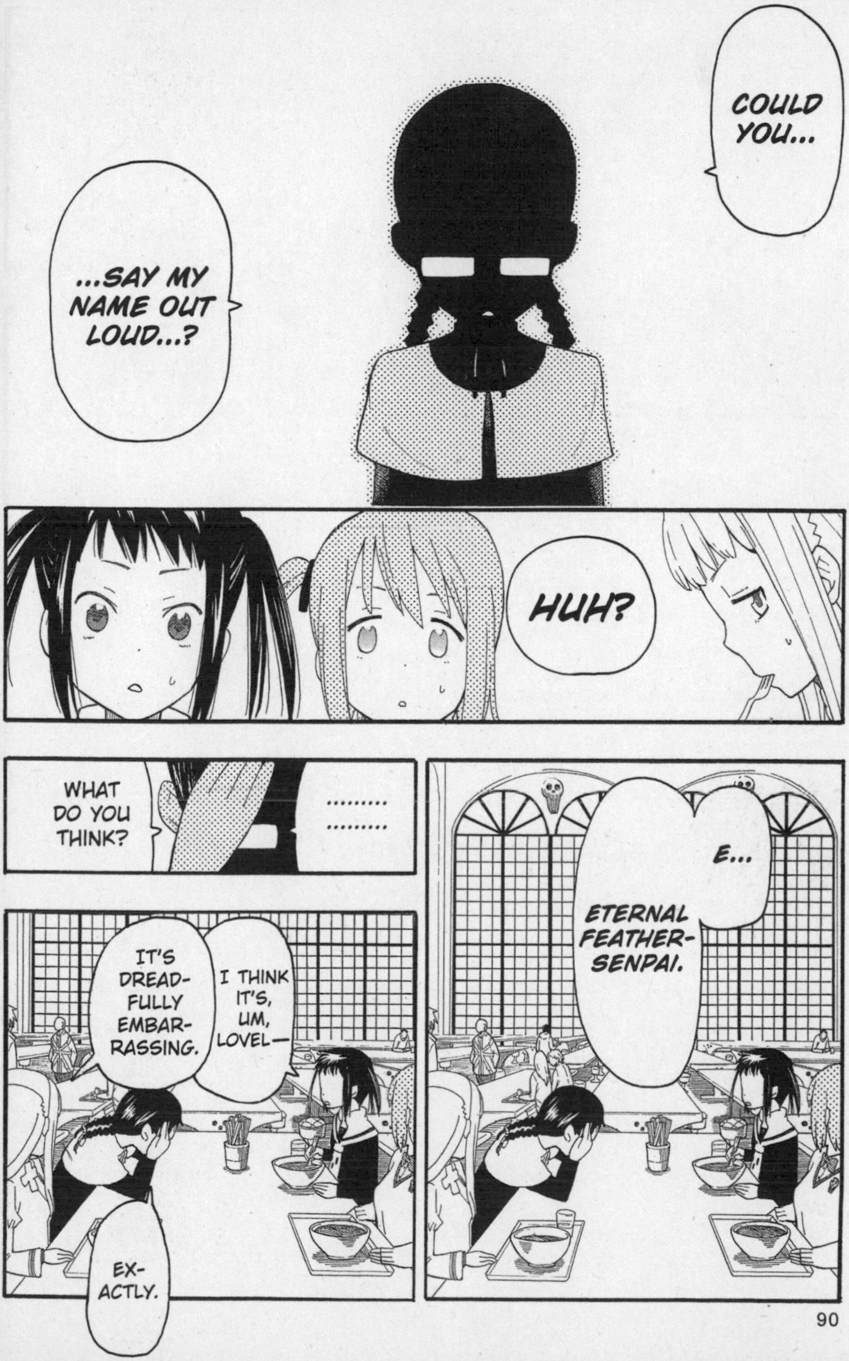

COULD YOU...
...SAY MY NAME OUT LOUD...?
HUH?
E...
ETERNAL FEATHER-SENPAI.
....
....
WHAT DO YOU THINK?
I THINK IT'S, UM, LOVEL—
IT'S DREADFULLY EMBARRASSING.
EXACTLY.

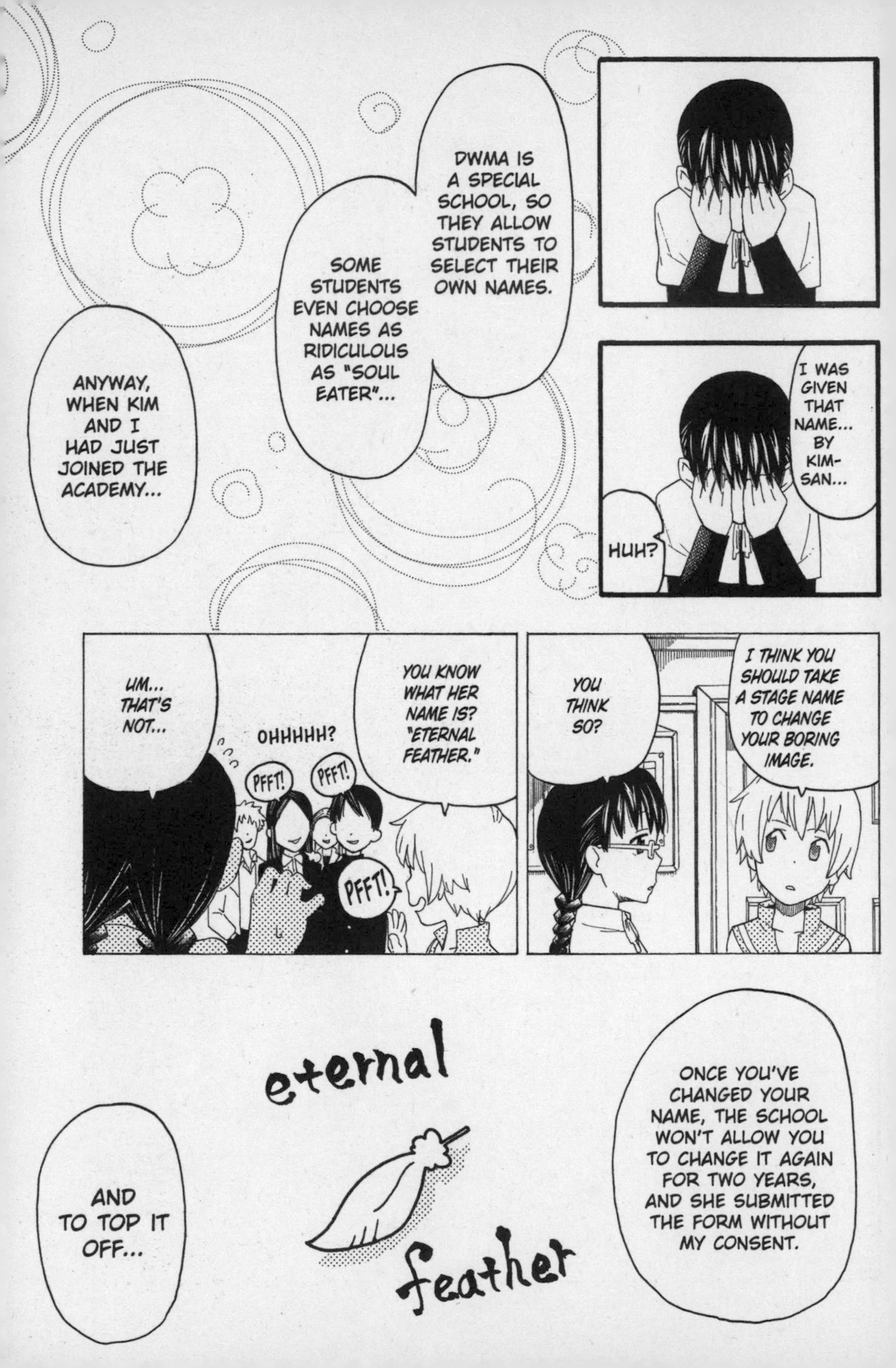
I WAS GIVEN THAT NAME... BY KIM-SAN...
HUH?
DWMA IS A SPECIAL SCHOOL, SO THEY ALLOW STUDENTS TO SELECT THEIR OWN NAMES.
SOME STUDENTS EVEN CHOOSE NAMES AS RIDICULOUS AS "SOUL EATER"...
ANYWAY, WHEN KIM AND I HAD JUST JOINED THE ACADEMY...
I THINK YOU SHOULD TAKE A STAGE NAME TO CHANGE YOUR BORING IMAGE.
YOU THINK SO?
YOU KNOW WHAT HER NAME IS? "ETERNAL FEATHER."
PFFT!
PFFT!
PFFT!
OHHHHH?
UM... THAT'S NOT...
ONCE YOU'VE CHANGED YOUR NAME, THE SCHOOL WON'T ALLOW YOU TO CHANGE IT AGAIN FOR TWO YEARS, AND SHE SUBMITTED THE FORM WITHOUT MY CONSENT.
eternal feather
AND TO TOP IT OFF...

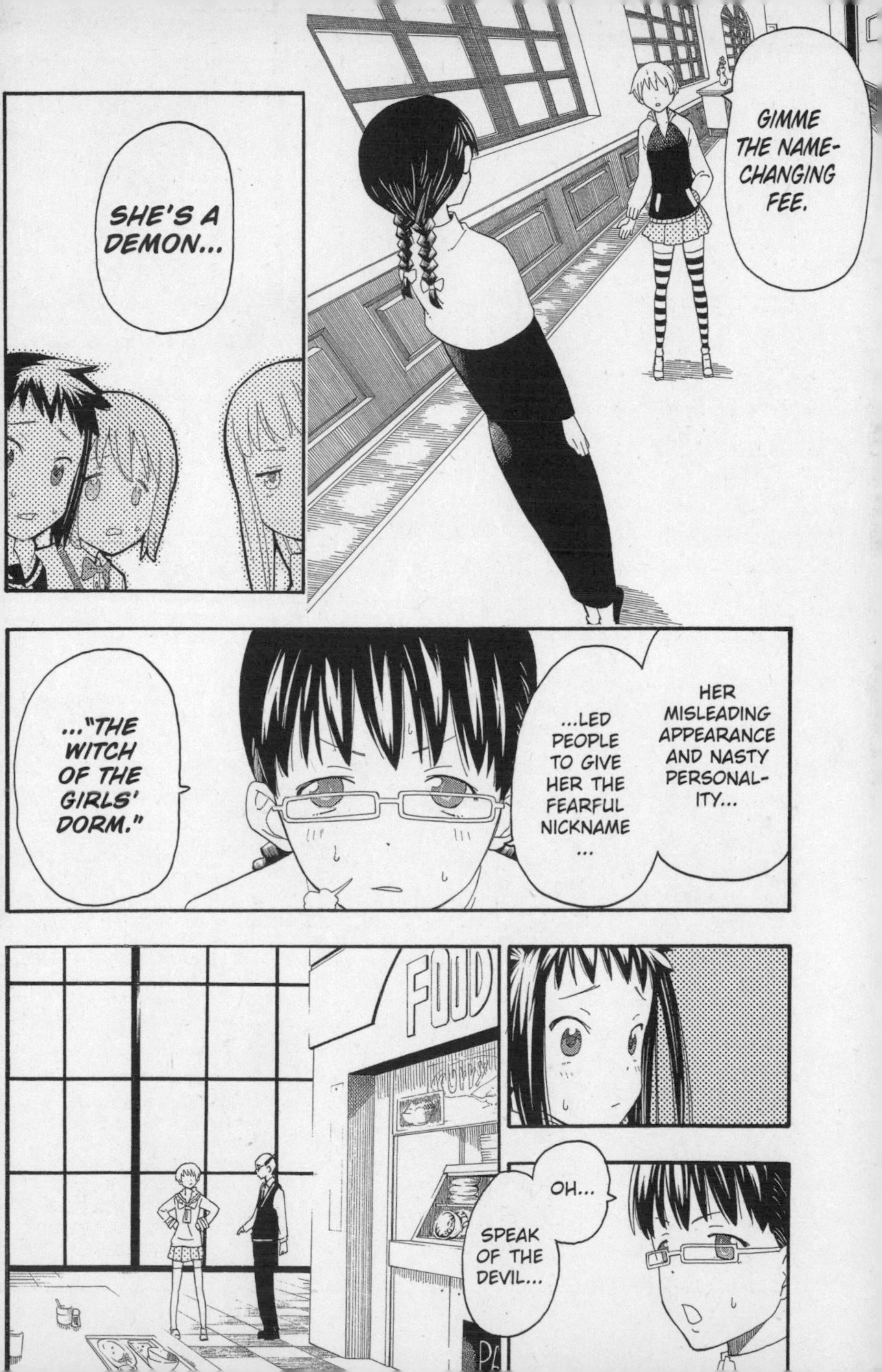
GIMME THE NAME-CHANGING FEE.
SHE'S A DEMON...
HER MISLEADING APPEARANCE AND NASTY PERSONAL-ITY...
...LED PEOPLE TO GIVE HER THE FEARFUL NICKNAME ...
..."THE WITCH OF THE GIRLS' DORM."
OH...
SPEAK OF THE DEVIL...
FOOD

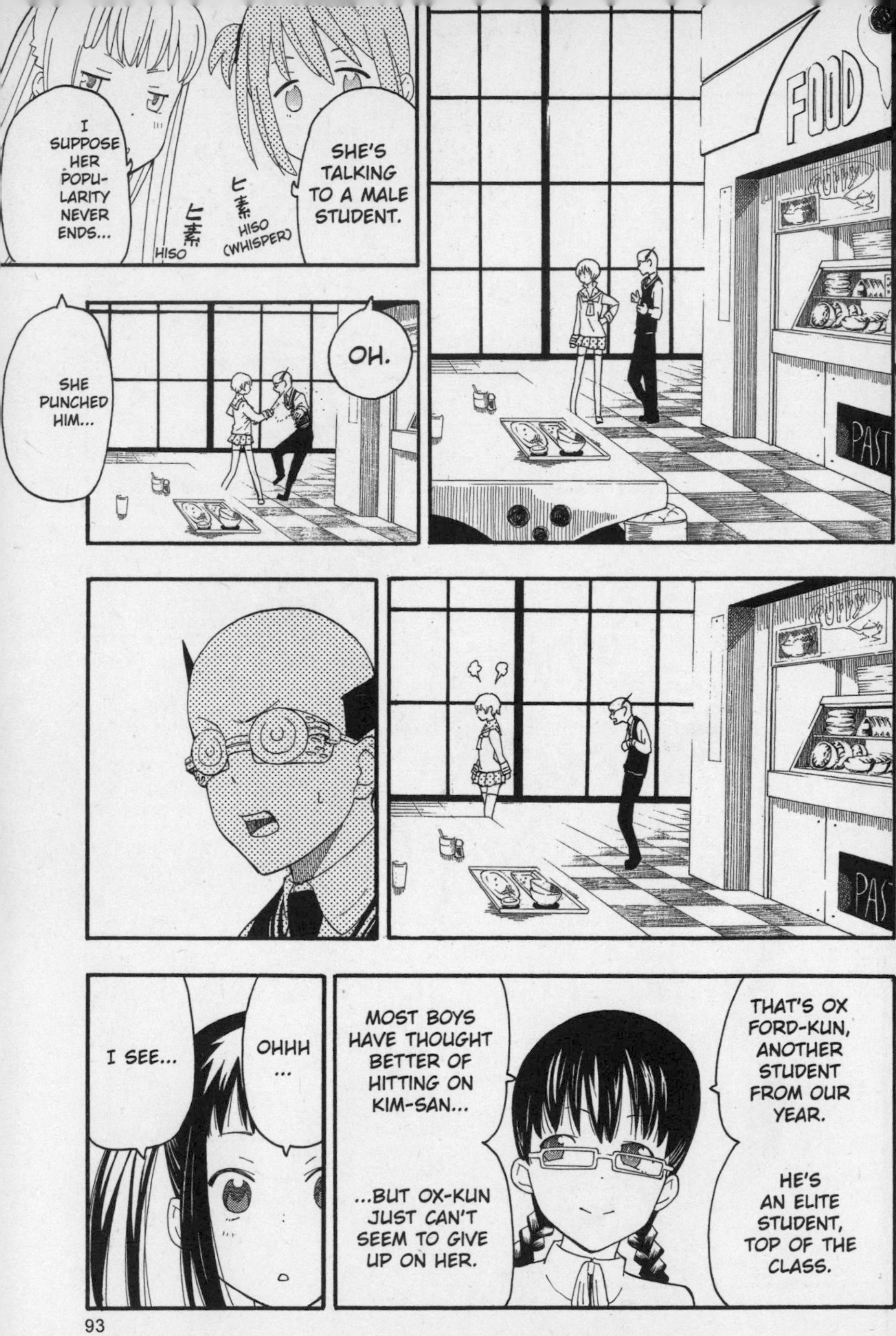
FOOD
PAST
SHE'S TALKING TO A MALE STUDENT.
ヒ素 HISO (WHISPER)
ヒ素 HISO
I SUPPOSE HER POPU-LARITY NEVER ENDS...
OH.
SHE PUNCHED HIM...
PAST
THAT'S OX FORD-KUN, ANOTHER STUDENT FROM OUR YEAR.
HE'S AN ELITE STUDENT, TOP OF THE CLASS.
MOST BOYS HAVE THOUGHT BETTER OF HITTING ON KIM-SAN...
...BUT OX-KUN JUST CAN'T SEEM TO GIVE UP ON HER.
OHHH ...
I SEE...

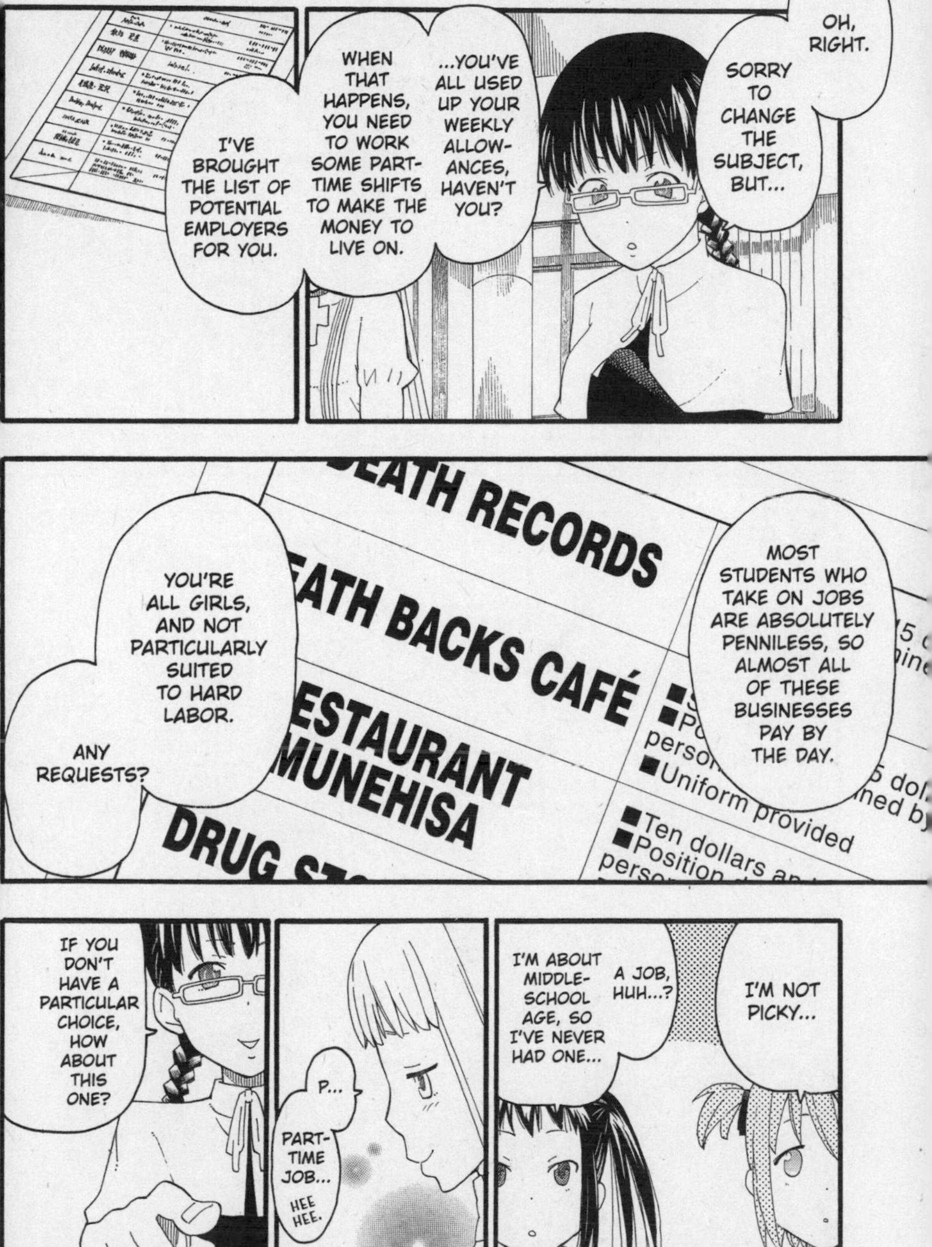
OH, RIGHT.
SORRY TO CHANGE THE SUBJECT, BUT...
...YOU'VE ALL USED UP YOUR WEEKLY ALLOWANCES, HAVEN'T YOU?
WHEN THAT HAPPENS, YOU NEED TO WORK SOME PART-TIME SHIFTS TO MAKE THE MONEY TO LIVE ON.
I'VE BROUGHT THE LIST OF POTENTIAL EMPLOYERS FOR YOU.
MOST STUDENTS WHO TAKE ON JOBS ARE ABSOLUTELY PENNILESS, SO ALMOST ALL OF THESE BUSINESSES PAY BY THE DAY.
DEATH RECORDS
EATH BACKS CAFÉ
ESTAURANT MUNEHISA
Uniform provided
YOU'RE ALL GIRLS, AND NOT PARTICULARLY SUITED TO HARD LABOR.
ANY REQUESTS?
I'M NOT PICKY...
A JOB, HUH...?
I'M ABOUT MIDDLE-SCHOOL AGE, SO I'VE NEVER HAD ONE...
P...
PART-TIME JOB...
HEE HEE.
IF YOU DON'T HAVE A PARTICULAR CHOICE, HOW ABOUT THIS ONE?

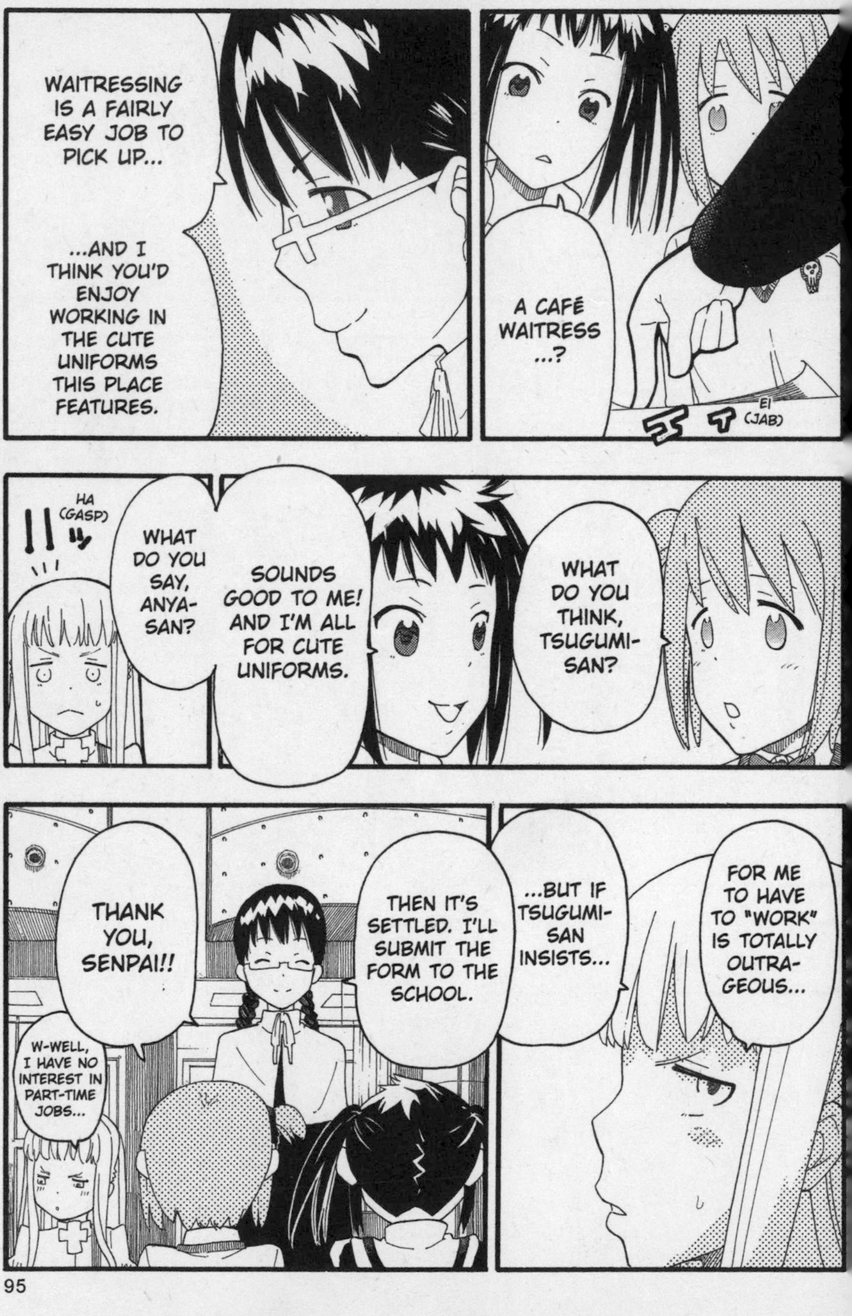
A CAFÉ WAITRESS ...?
EI (JAB)
WAITRESSING IS A FAIRLY EASY JOB TO PICK UP...
...AND I THINK YOU'D ENJOY WORKING IN THE CUTE UNIFORMS THIS PLACE FEATURES.
WHAT DO YOU THINK, TSUGUMI-SAN?
SOUNDS GOOD TO ME! AND I'M ALL FOR CUTE UNIFORMS.
WHAT DO YOU SAY, ANYA-SAN?
HA (GASP)
FOR ME TO HAVE TO "WORK" IS TOTALLY OUTRA-GEOUS...
...BUT IF TSUGUMI-SAN INSISTS...
THEN IT'S SETTLED. I'LL SUBMIT THE FORM TO THE SCHOOL.
THANK YOU, SENPAI!!
W-WELL, I HAVE NO INTEREST IN PART-TIME JOBS...

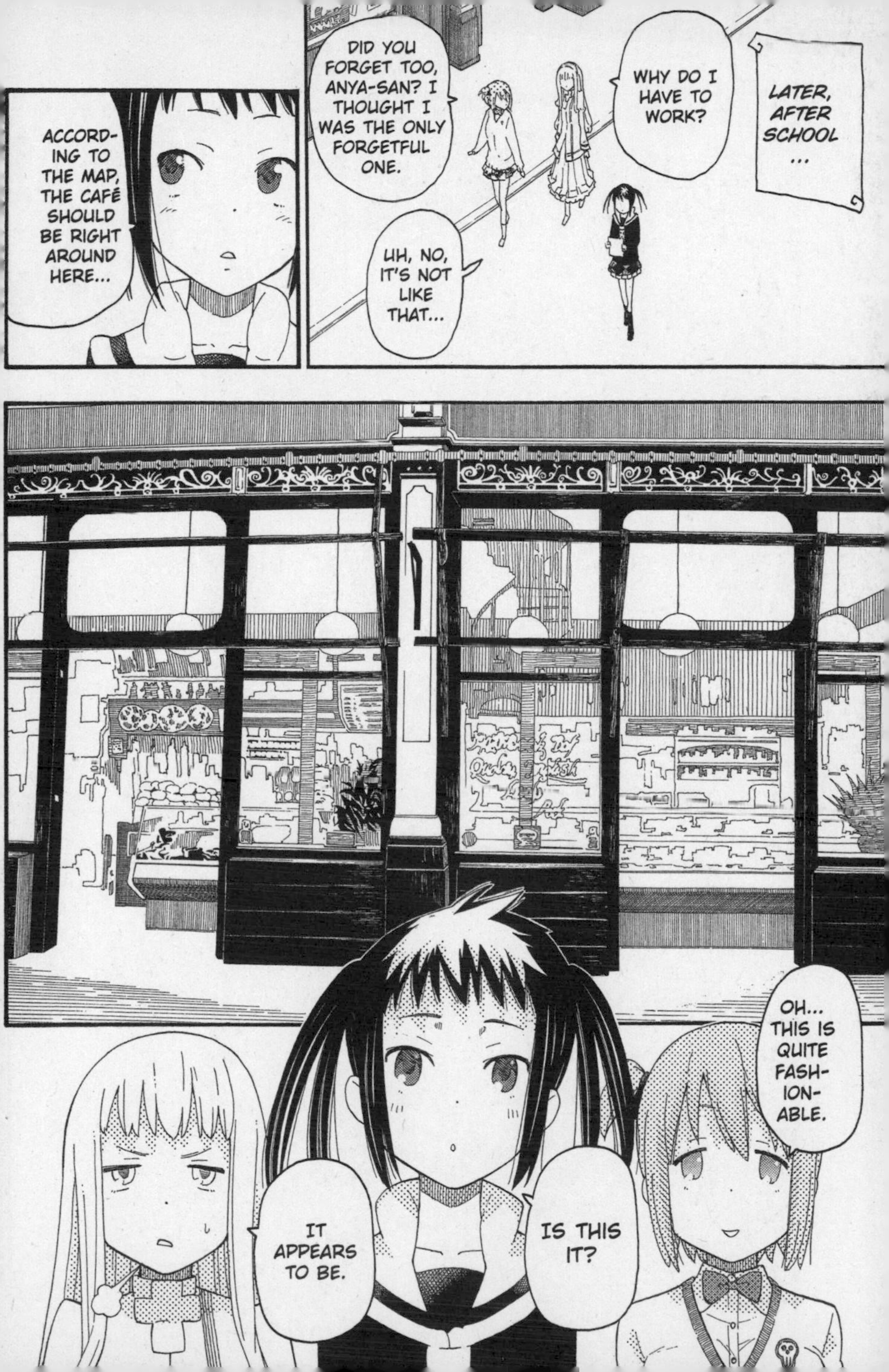
LATER, AFTER SCHOOL ...
WHY DO I HAVE TO WORK?
DID YOU FORGET TOO, ANYA-SAN? I THOUGHT I WAS THE ONLY FORGETFUL ONE.
UH, NO, IT'S NOT LIKE THAT...
ACCORDING TO THE MAP, THE CAFÉ SHOULD BE RIGHT AROUND HERE...
OH... THIS IS QUITE FASHIONABLE.
IS THIS IT?
IT APPEARS TO BE.

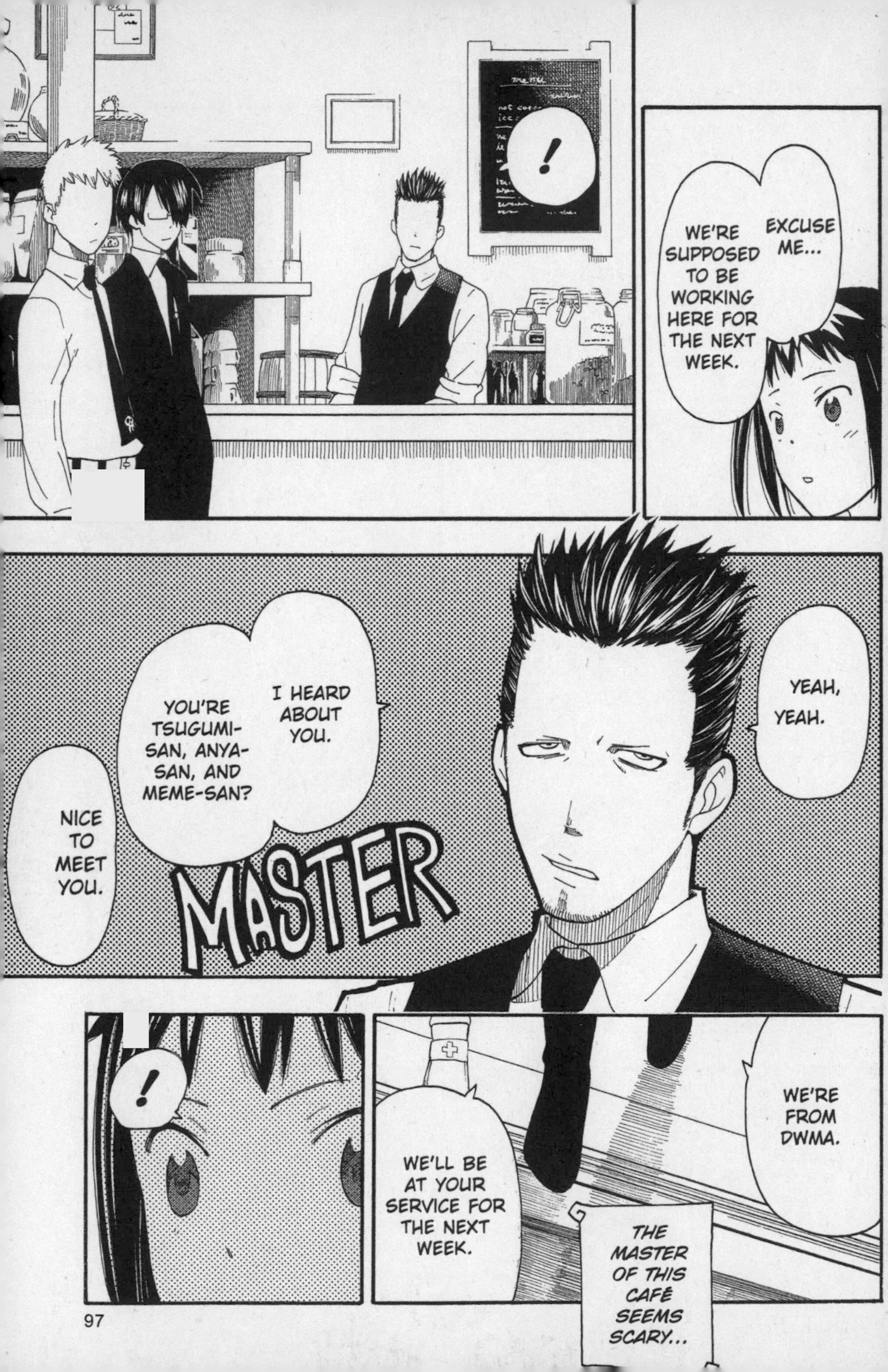
EXCUSE ME...
WE'RE SUPPOSED TO BE WORKING HERE FOR THE NEXT WEEK.
!
YEAH, YEAH.
I HEARD ABOUT YOU.
YOU'RE TSUGUMI-SAN, ANYA-SAN, AND MEME-SAN?
NICE TO MEET YOU.
MASTER
WE'RE FROM DWMA.
WE'LL BE AT YOUR SERVICE FOR THE NEXT WEEK.
THE MASTER OF THIS CAFÉ SEEMS SCARY...
!

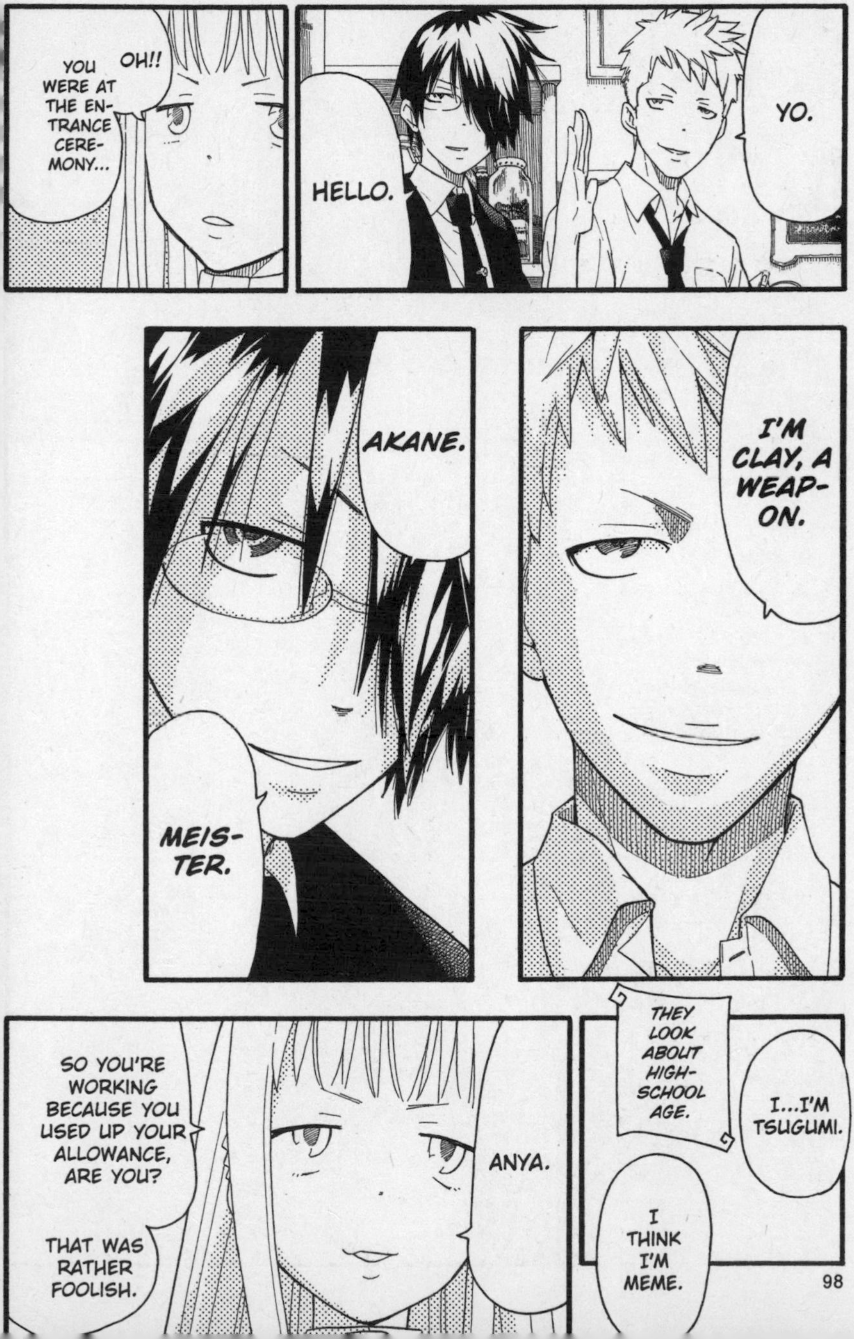
YO.
HELLO.
OH!!
YOU WERE AT THE EN-TRANCE CERE-MONY...
I'M CLAY, A WEAP-ON.
AKANE.
MEIS-TER.
THEY LOOK ABOUT HIGH-SCHOOL AGE.
I...I'M TSUGUMI.
I THINK I'M MEME.
ANYA.
SO YOU'RE WORKING BECAUSE YOU USED UP YOUR ALLOWANCE, ARE YOU?
THAT WAS RATHER FOOLISH.

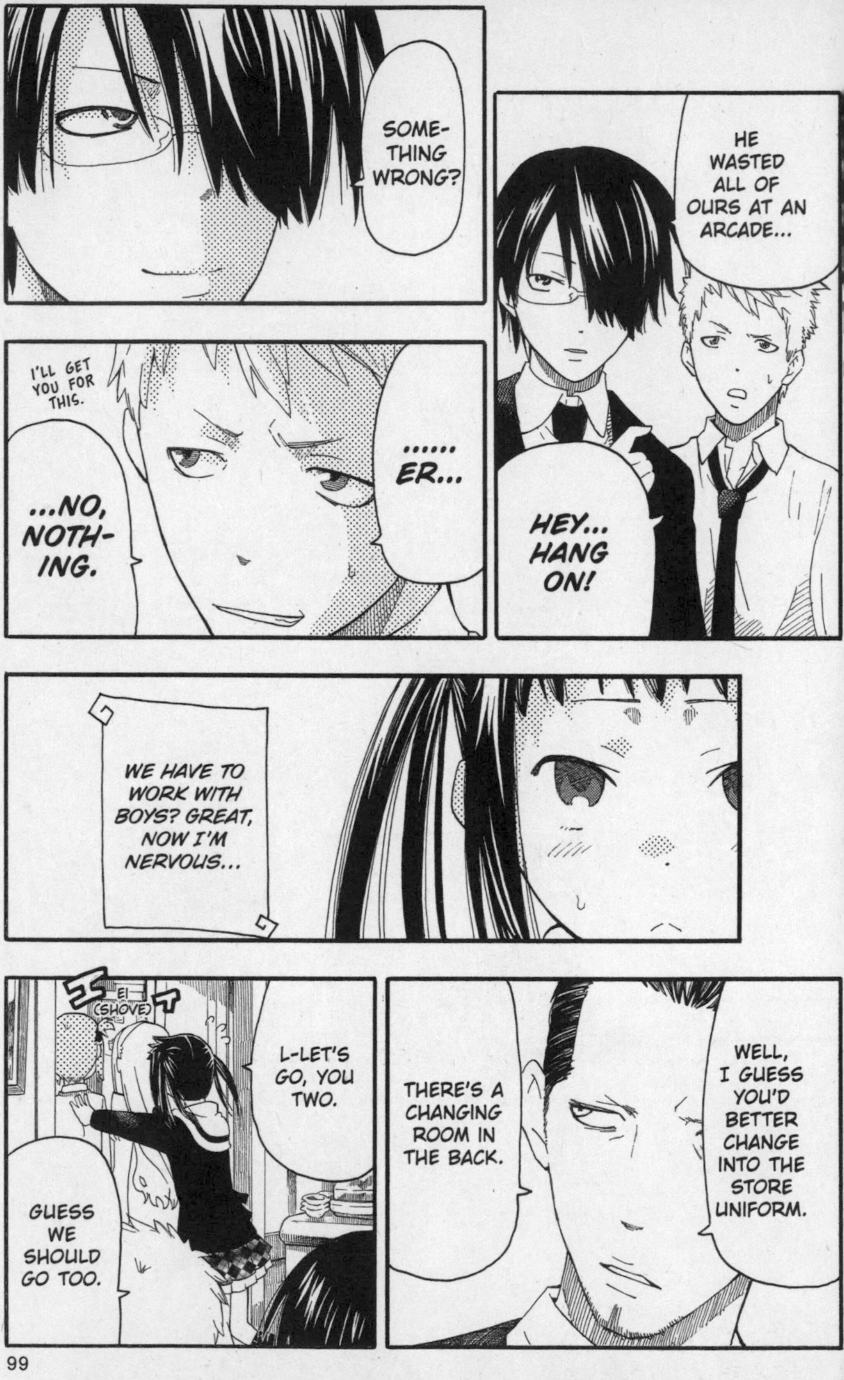
HE WASTED ALL OF OURS AT AN ARCADE...
HEY... HANG ON!
SOME-THING WRONG?
......ER...
I'LL GET YOU FOR THIS.
...NO, NOTH-ING.
WE HAVE TO WORK WITH BOYS? GREAT, NOW I'M NERVOUS...
WELL, I GUESS YOU'D BETTER CHANGE INTO THE STORE UNIFORM.
THERE'S A CHANGING ROOM IN THE BACK.
L-LET'S GO, YOU TWO.
EI (SHOVE)
GUESS WE SHOULD GO TOO.

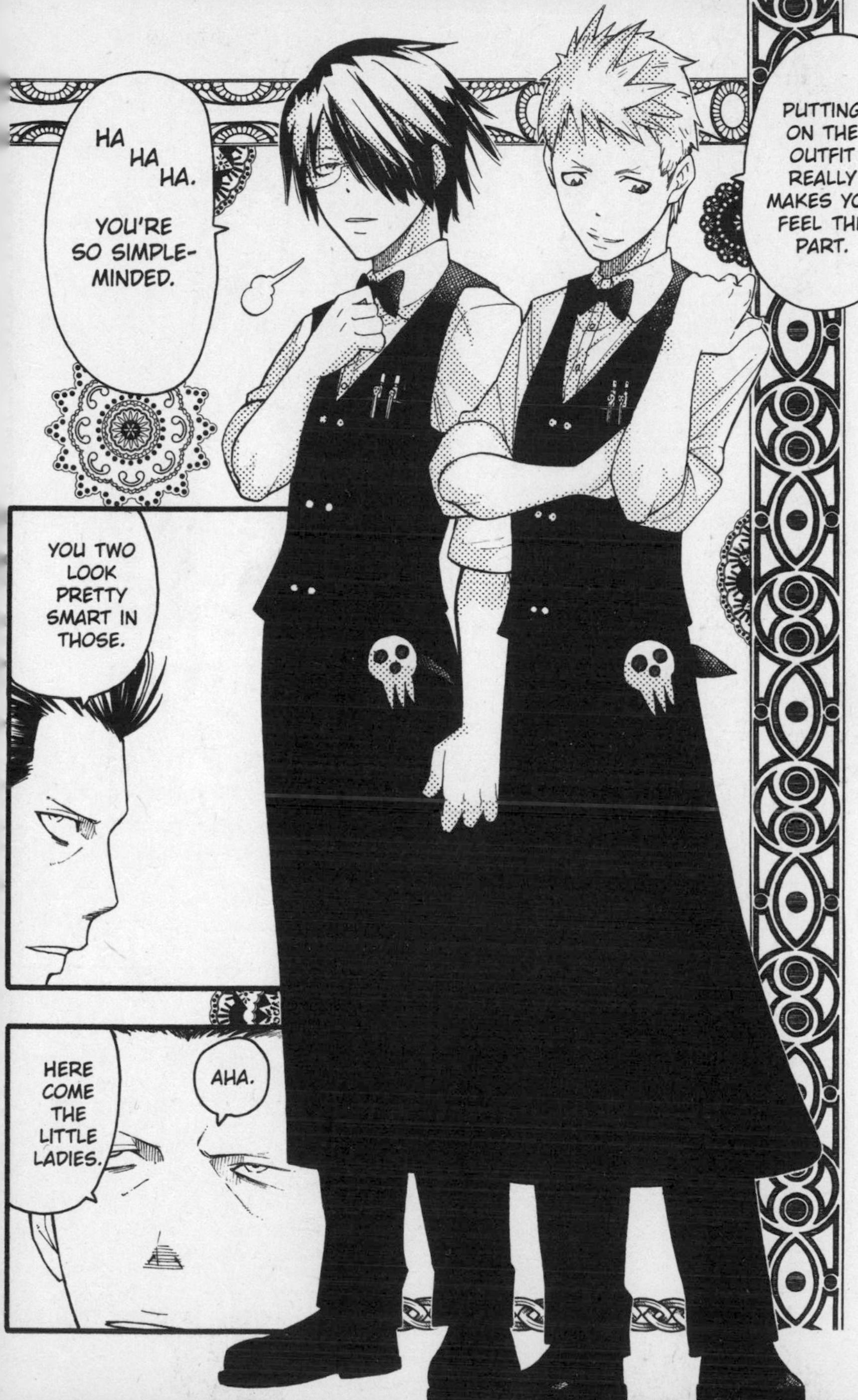
PUTTING ON THE OUTFIT REALLY MAKES YOU FEEL THE PART.
HA HA HA. YOU'RE SO SIMPLE-MINDED.
YOU TWO LOOK PRETTY SMART IN THOSE.
AHA.
HERE COME THE LITTLE LADIES.

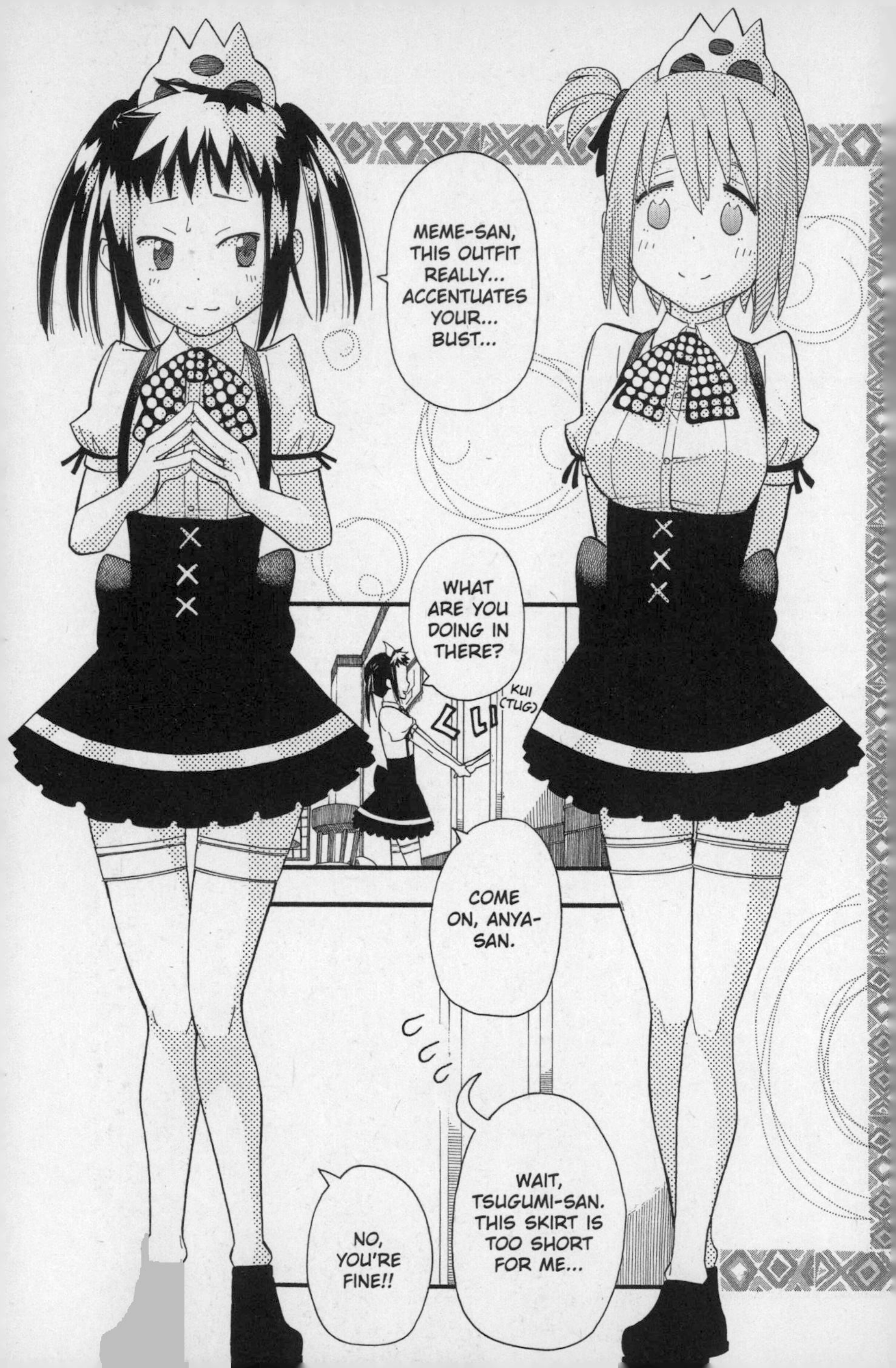
MEME-SAN, THIS OUTFIT REALLY... ACCENTUATES YOUR... BUST...
WHAT ARE YOU DOING IN THERE?
KUI (TUG)
COME ON, ANYA-SAN.
WAIT, TSUGUMI-SAN. THIS SKIRT IS TOO SHORT FOR ME...
NO, YOU'RE FINE!!

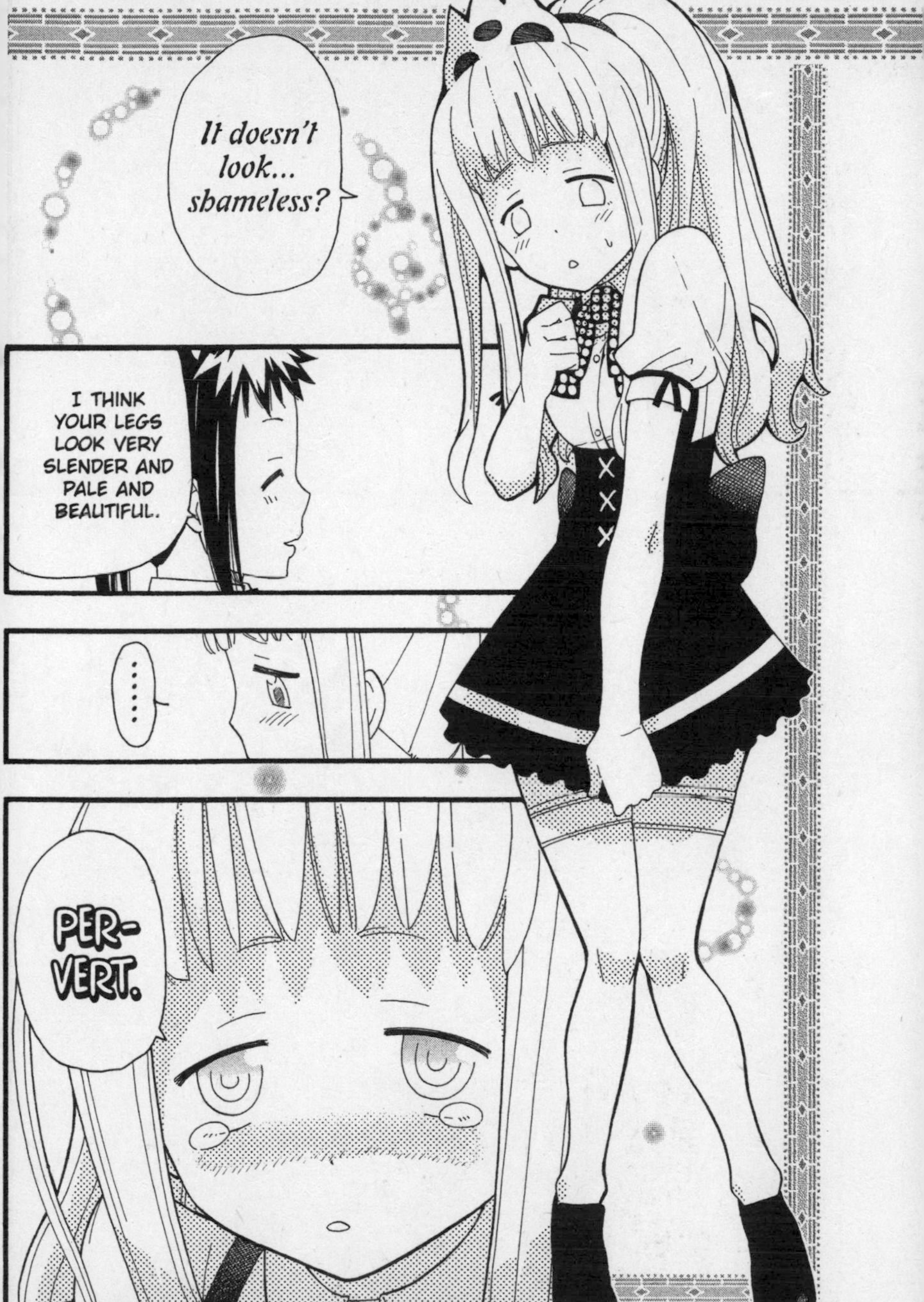
It doesn't look... shameless?
I THINK YOUR LEGS LOOK VERY SLENDER AND PALE AND BEAUTIFUL.
......
PER-VERT.

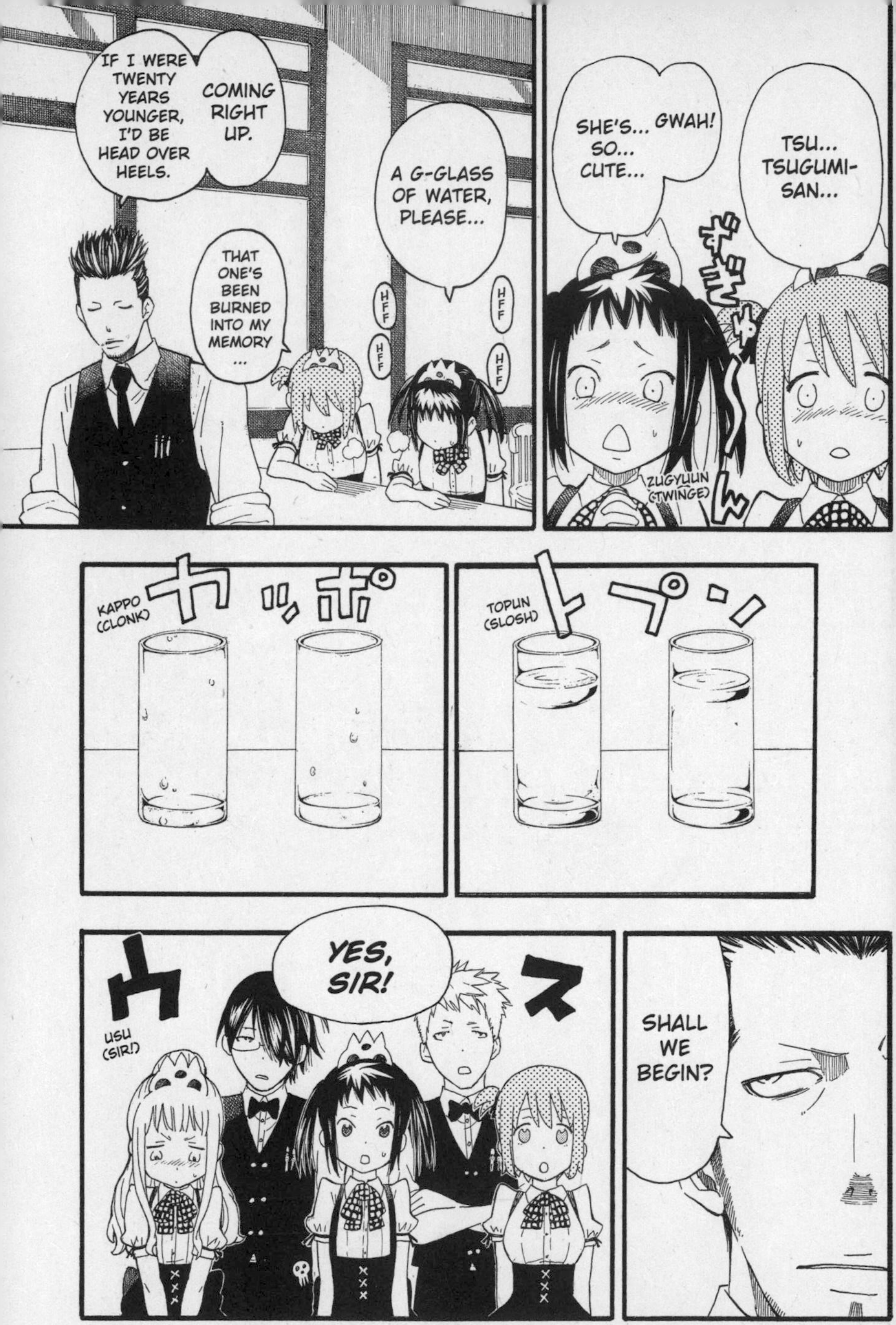

TSU... TSUGUMI-SAN...
GWAH!
SHE'S... SO... CUTE...
ZUGYUUN (TWINGE)
A G-GLASS OF WATER, PLEASE...
HFF HFF
HFF HFF
COMING RIGHT UP.
IF I WERE TWENTY YEARS YOUNGER, I'D BE HEAD OVER HEELS.
THAT ONE'S BEEN BURNED INTO MY MEMORY...
TOPUN (SLOSH)
KAPPO (CLONK)
SHALL WE BEGIN?
YES, SIR!
USU (SIR!)

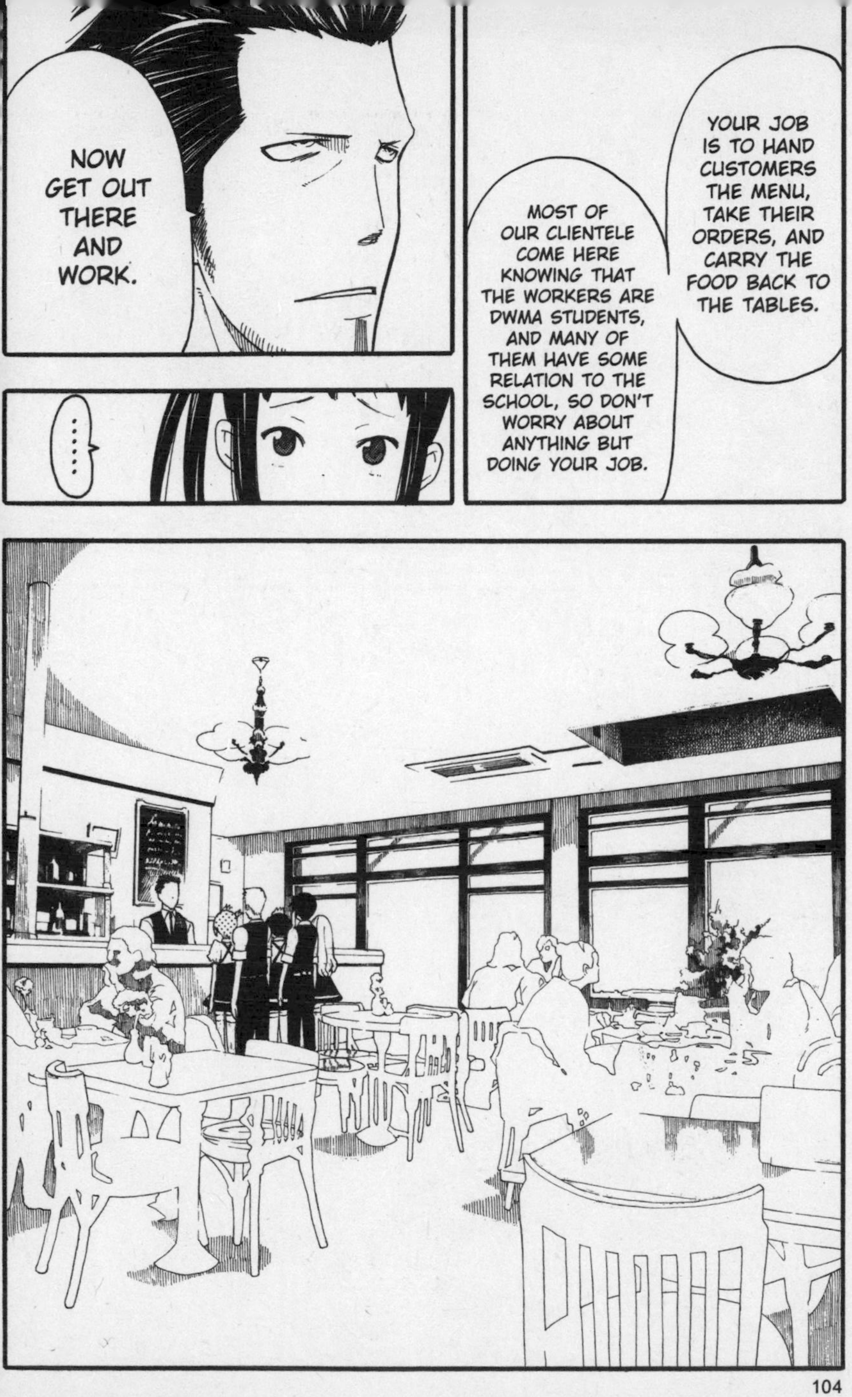
YOUR JOB IS TO HAND CUSTOMERS THE MENU, TAKE THEIR ORDERS, AND CARRY THE FOOD BACK TO THE TABLES.
MOST OF OUR CLIENTELE COME HERE KNOWING THAT THE WORKERS ARE DWMA STUDENTS, AND MANY OF THEM HAVE SOME RELATION TO THE SCHOOL, SO DON'T WORRY ABOUT ANYTHING BUT DOING YOUR JOB.
NOW GET OUT THERE AND WORK.
......

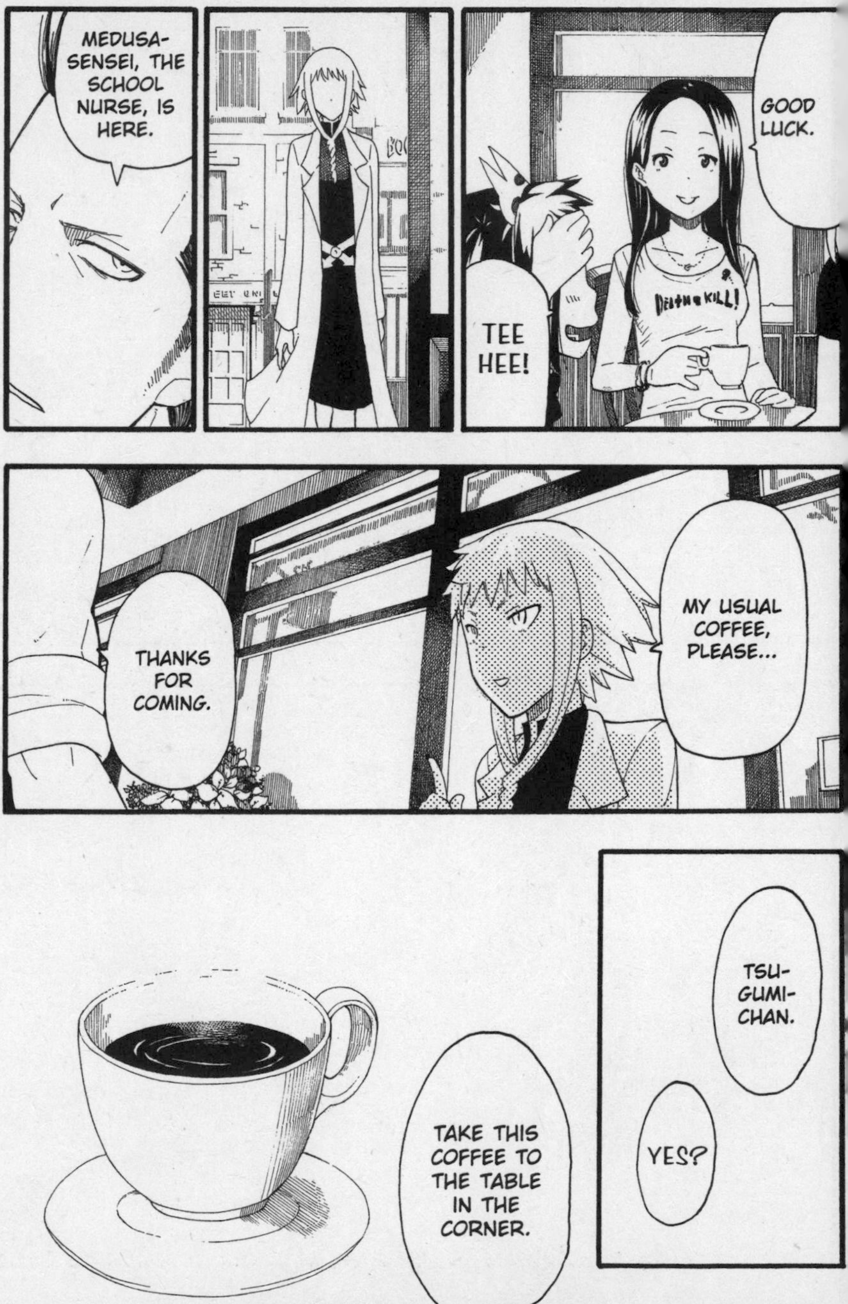
GOOD LUCK.
TEE HEE!
MEDUSA-SENSEI, THE SCHOOL NURSE, IS HERE.
MY USUAL COFFEE, PLEASE...
THANKS FOR COMING.
TSU-GUMI-CHAN.
YES?
TAKE THIS COFFEE TO THE TABLE IN THE CORNER.

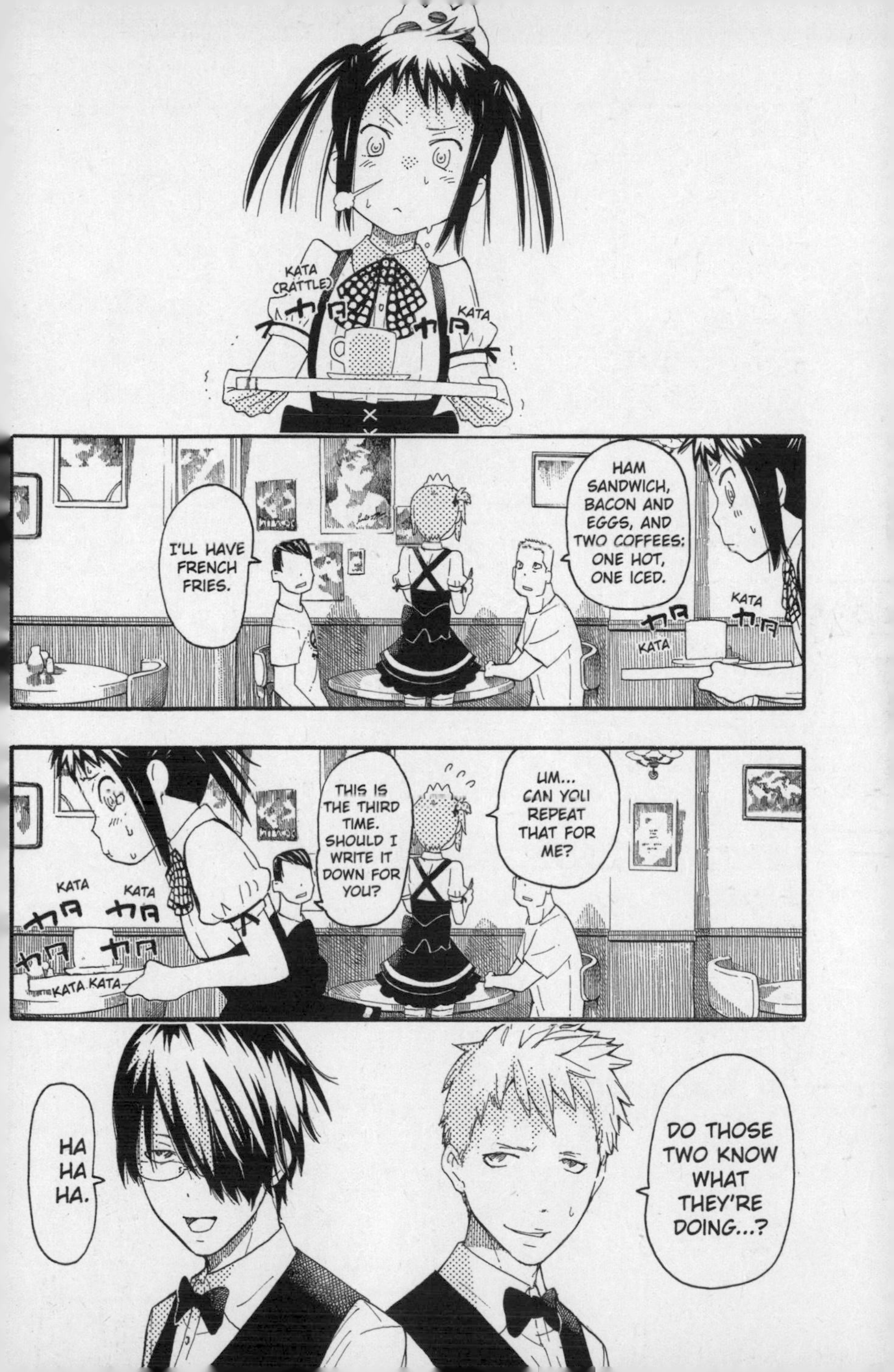
KATA (RATTLE)
カタ
KATA
カタ
HAM SANDWICH, BACON AND EGGS, AND TWO COFFEES: ONE HOT, ONE ICED.
KATA
カタ
KATA
カタ
I'LL HAVE FRENCH FRIES.
UM... CAN YOU REPEAT THAT FOR ME?
THIS IS THE THIRD TIME. SHOULD I WRITE IT DOWN FOR YOU?
KATA
カタ
KATA
カタ
カタ
カタ
KATA KATA
DO THOSE TWO KNOW WHAT THEY'RE DOING...?
HA HA HA.

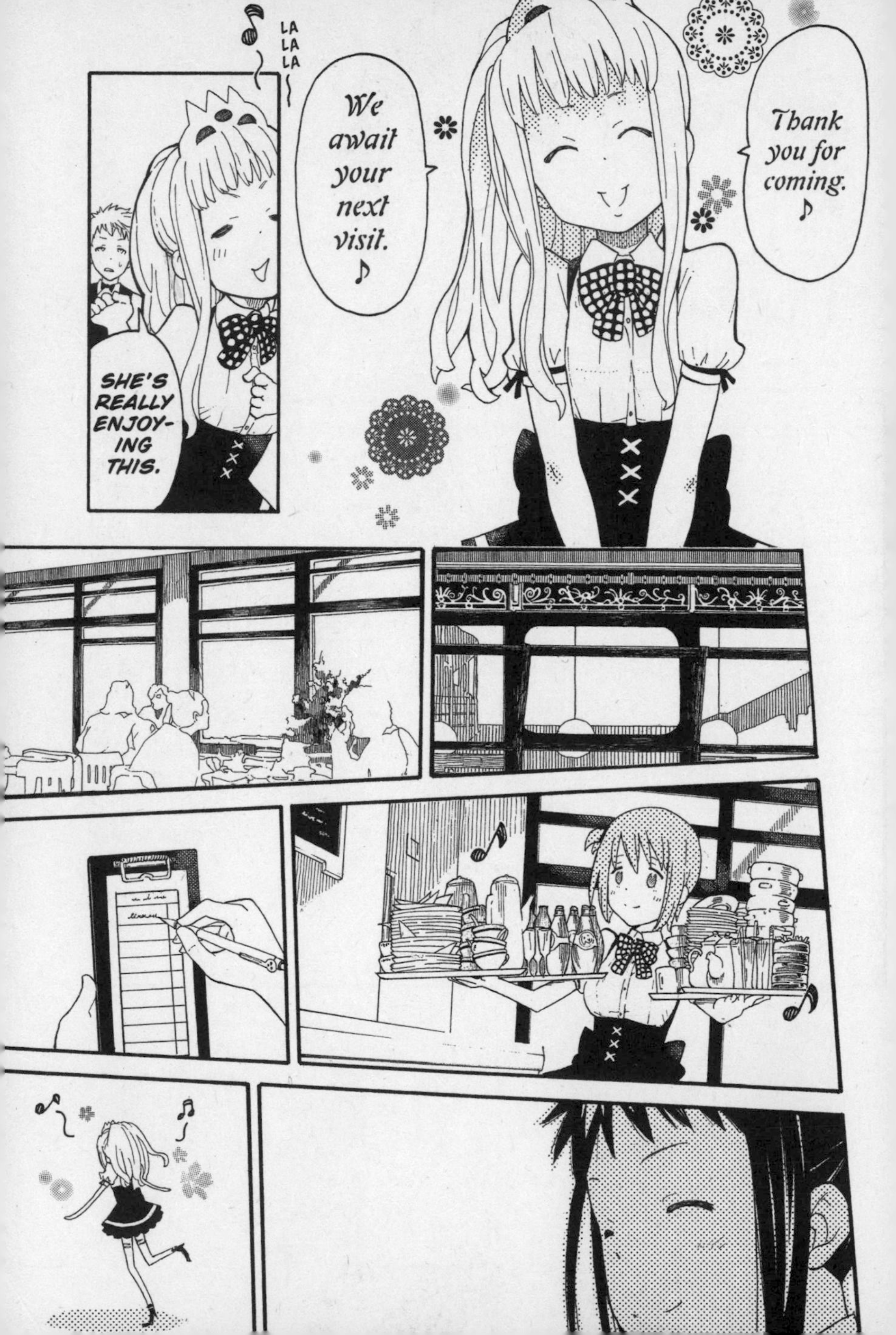
Thank you for coming. ♪
We await your next visit. ♪
LA LA LA~
SHE'S REALLY ENJOYING THIS.

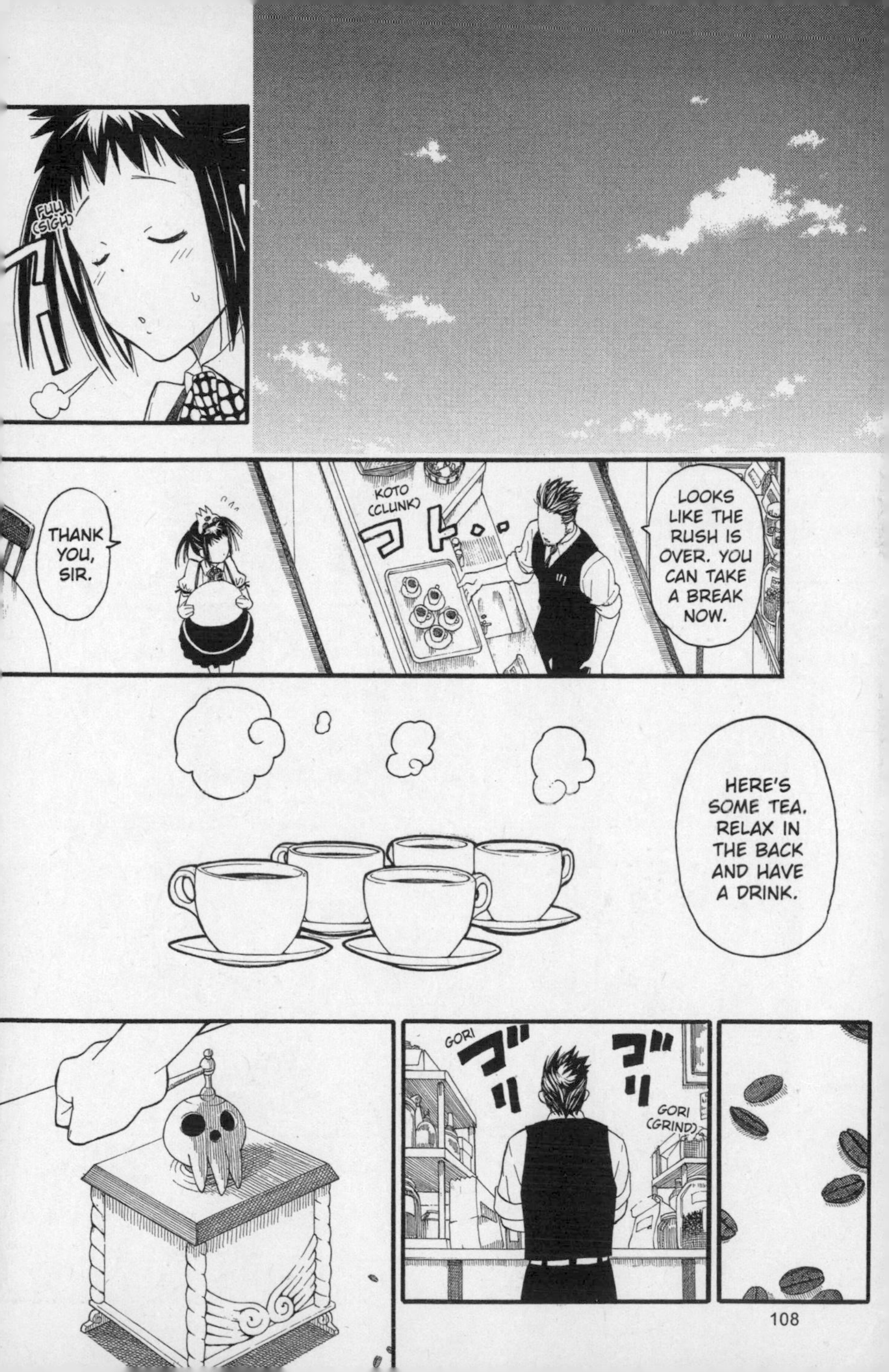
FUU (SIGH)
LOOKS LIKE THE RUSH IS OVER. YOU CAN TAKE A BREAK NOW.
KOTO (CLUNK)
THANK YOU, SIR.
HERE'S SOME TEA. RELAX IN THE BACK AND HAVE A DRINK.
GORI
GORI (GRIND)

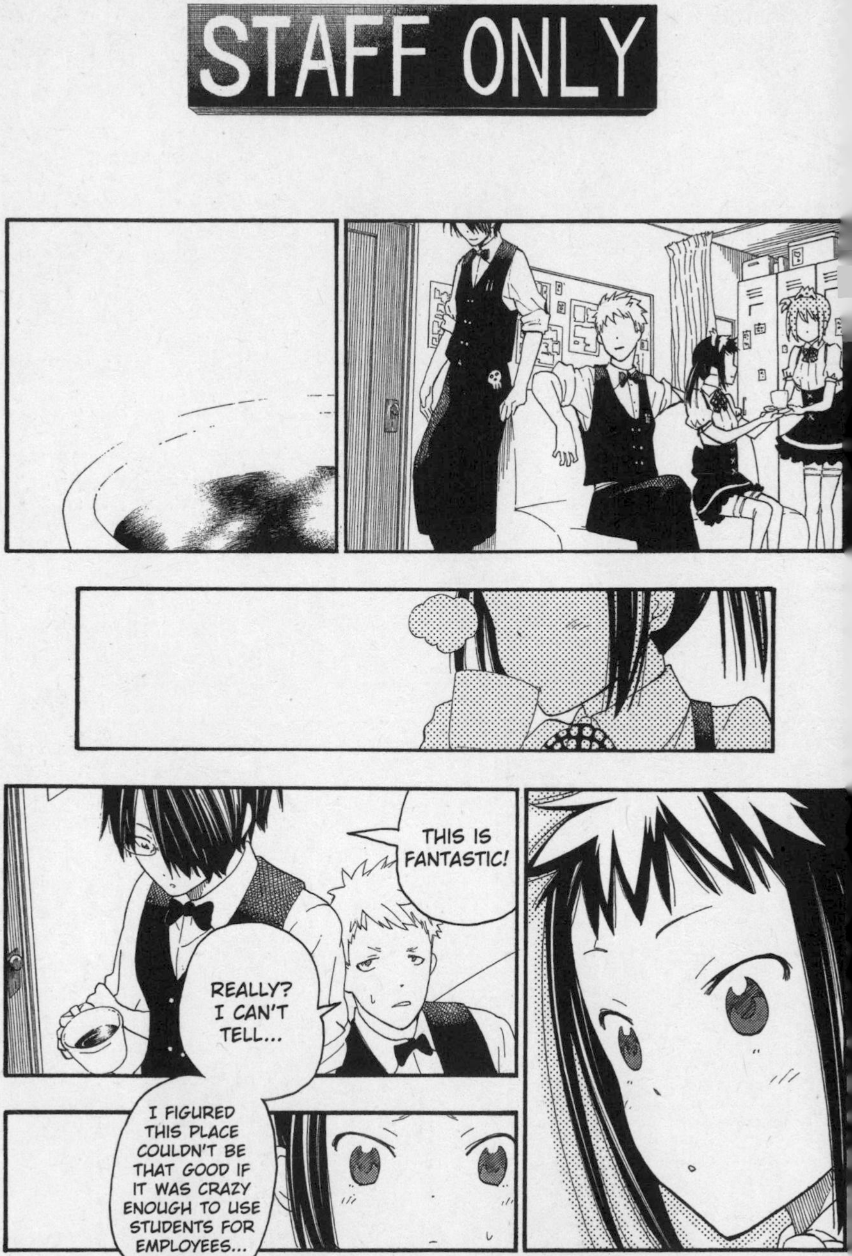
STAFF ONLY
THIS IS FANTASTIC!
REALLY? I CAN'T TELL...
I FIGURED THIS PLACE COULDN'T BE THAT GOOD IF IT WAS CRAZY ENOUGH TO USE STUDENTS FOR EMPLOYEES...

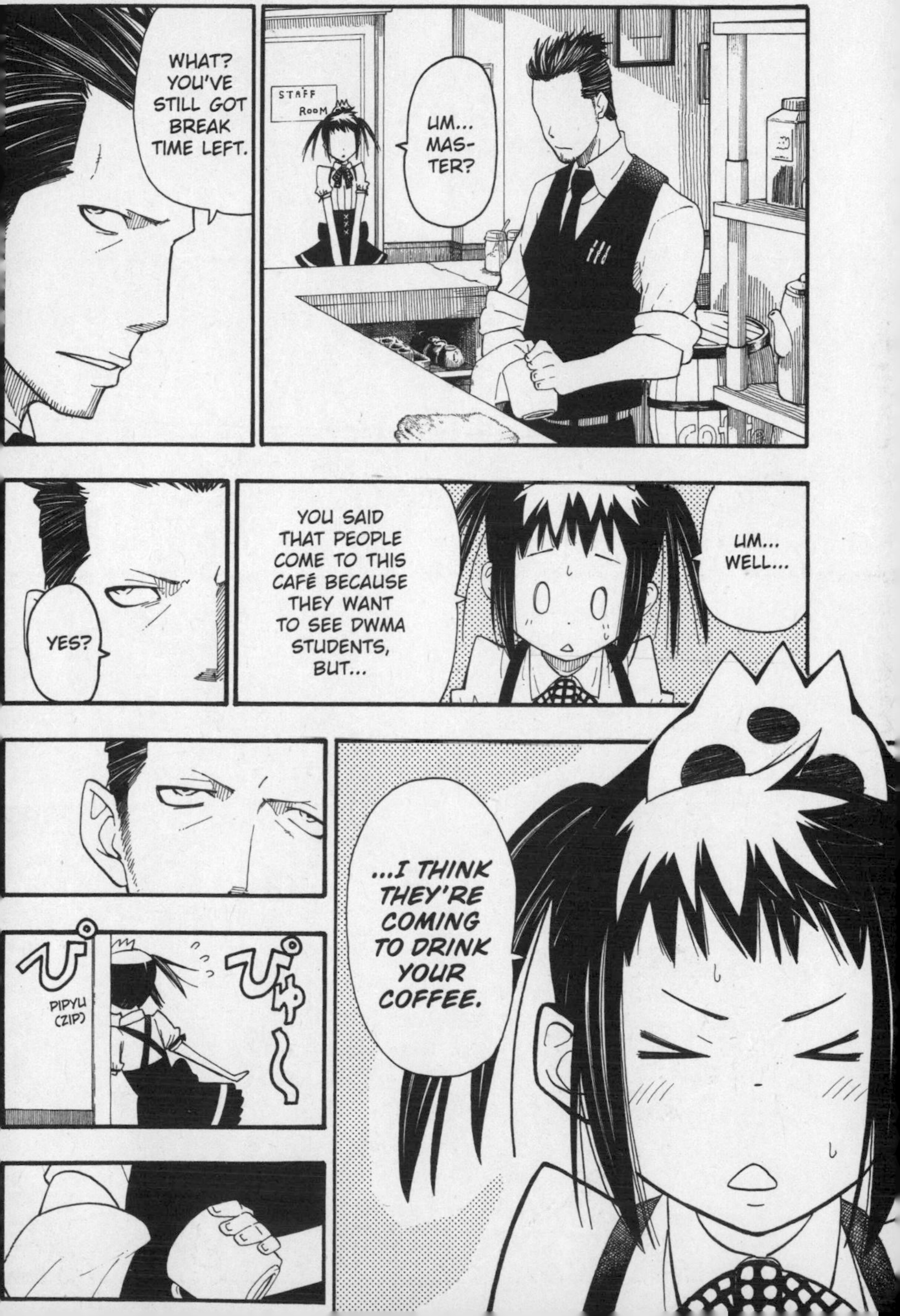
STAFF ROOM
UM... MAS-TER?
WHAT? YOU'VE STILL GOT BREAK TIME LEFT.
UM... WELL...
YOU SAID THAT PEOPLE COME TO THIS CAFÉ BECAUSE THEY WANT TO SEE DWMA STUDENTS, BUT...
YES?
...I THINK THEY'RE COMING TO DRINK YOUR COFFEE.
ぴぴゅ〜
PIPYU (ZIP)

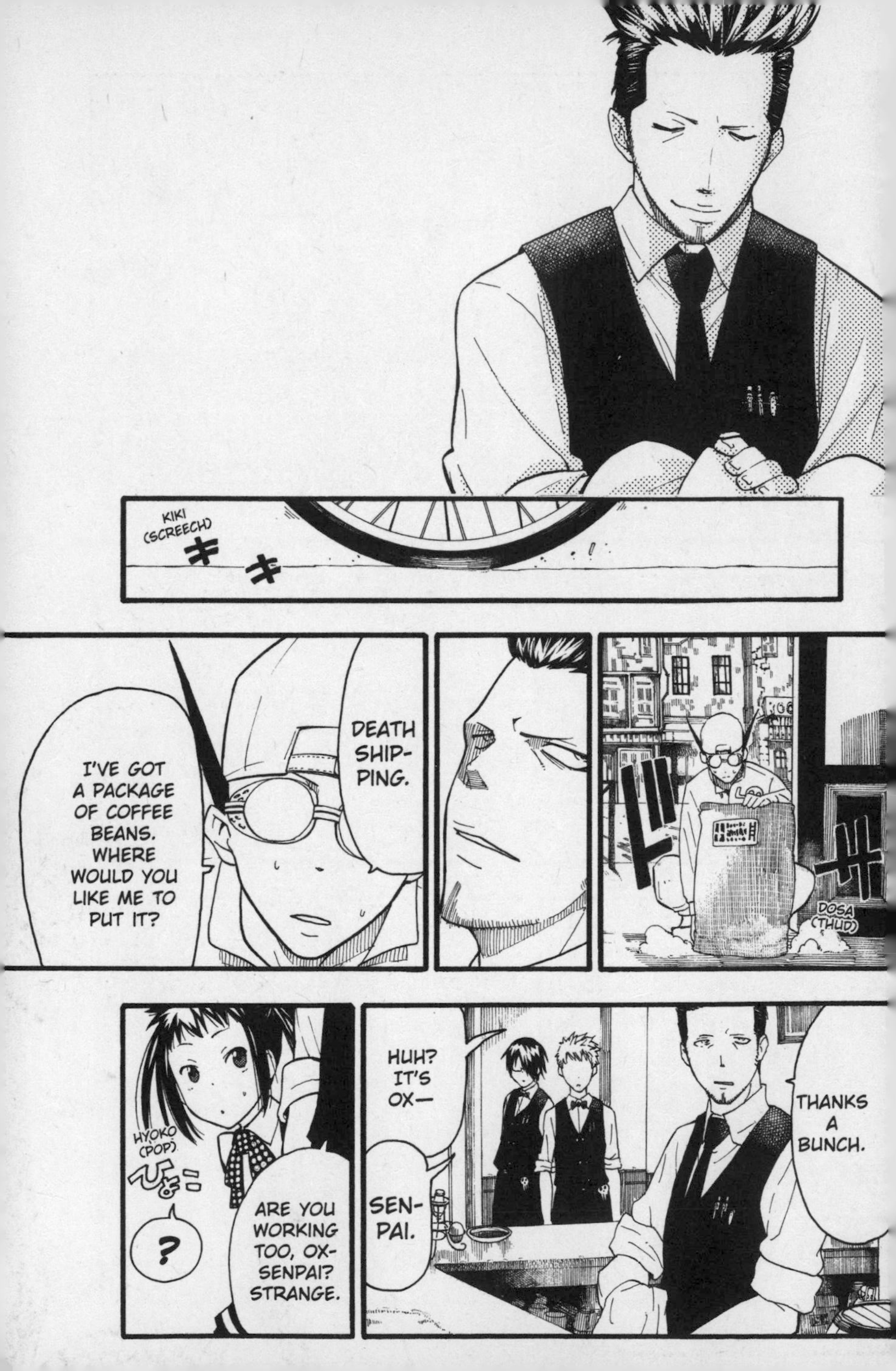
KIKI (SCREECH)
キ キ
ドサ
DOSA (THUD)
DEATH SHIPPING.
I'VE GOT A PACKAGE OF COFFEE BEANS. WHERE WOULD YOU LIKE ME TO PUT IT?
THANKS A BUNCH.
HUH? IT'S OX—
SEN-PAI.
ARE YOU WORKING TOO, OX-SENPAI? STRANGE.
HYOKO (POP)
?

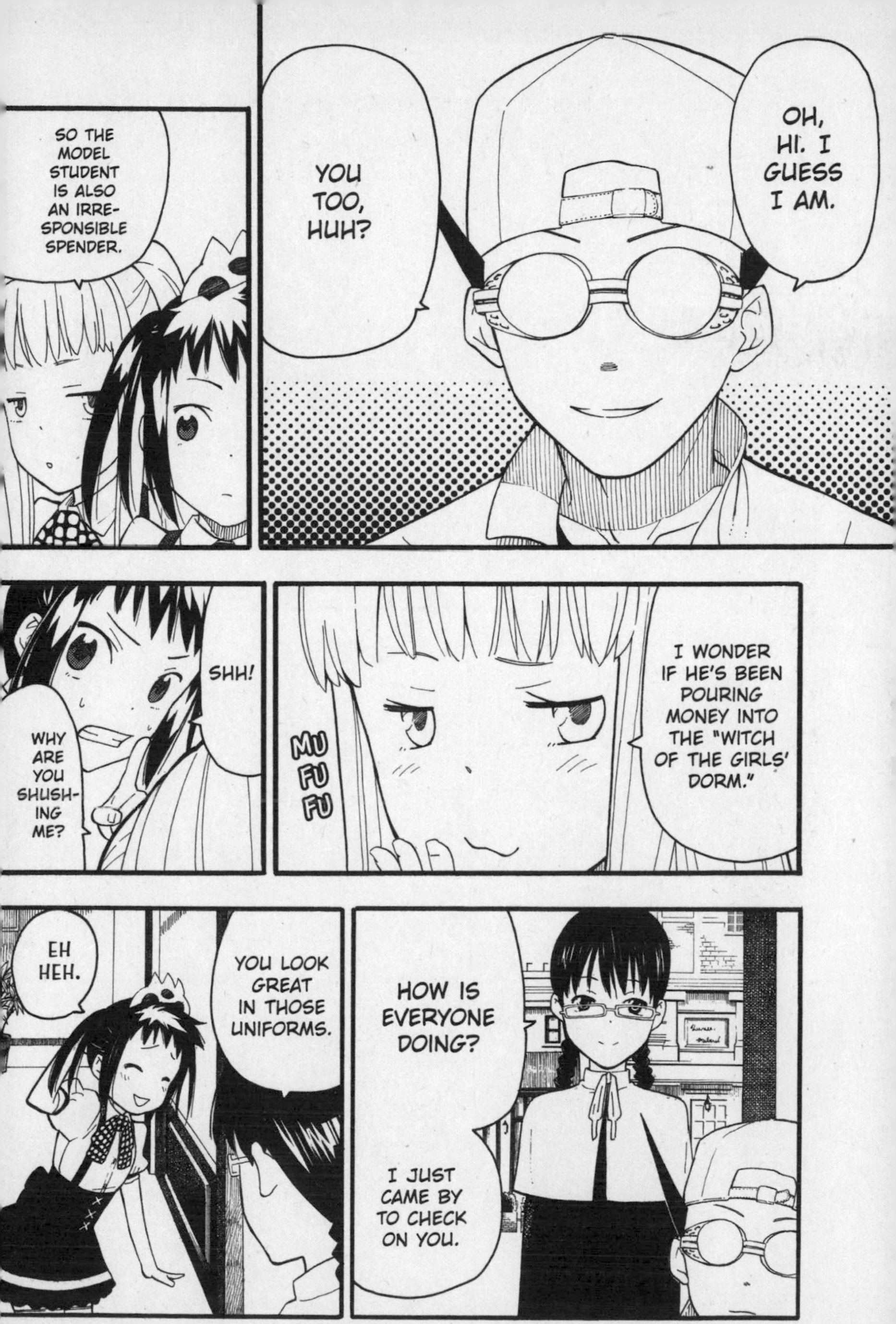
OH, HI. I GUESS I AM.
YOU TOO, HUH?
SO THE MODEL STUDENT IS ALSO AN IRRE-SPONSIBLE SPENDER.
I WONDER IF HE'S BEEN POURING MONEY INTO THE "WITCH OF THE GIRLS' DORM."
MU FU FU
SHH!
WHY ARE YOU SHUSHING ME?
HOW IS EVERYONE DOING?
I JUST CAME BY TO CHECK ON YOU.
YOU LOOK GREAT IN THOSE UNIFORMS.
EH HEH.

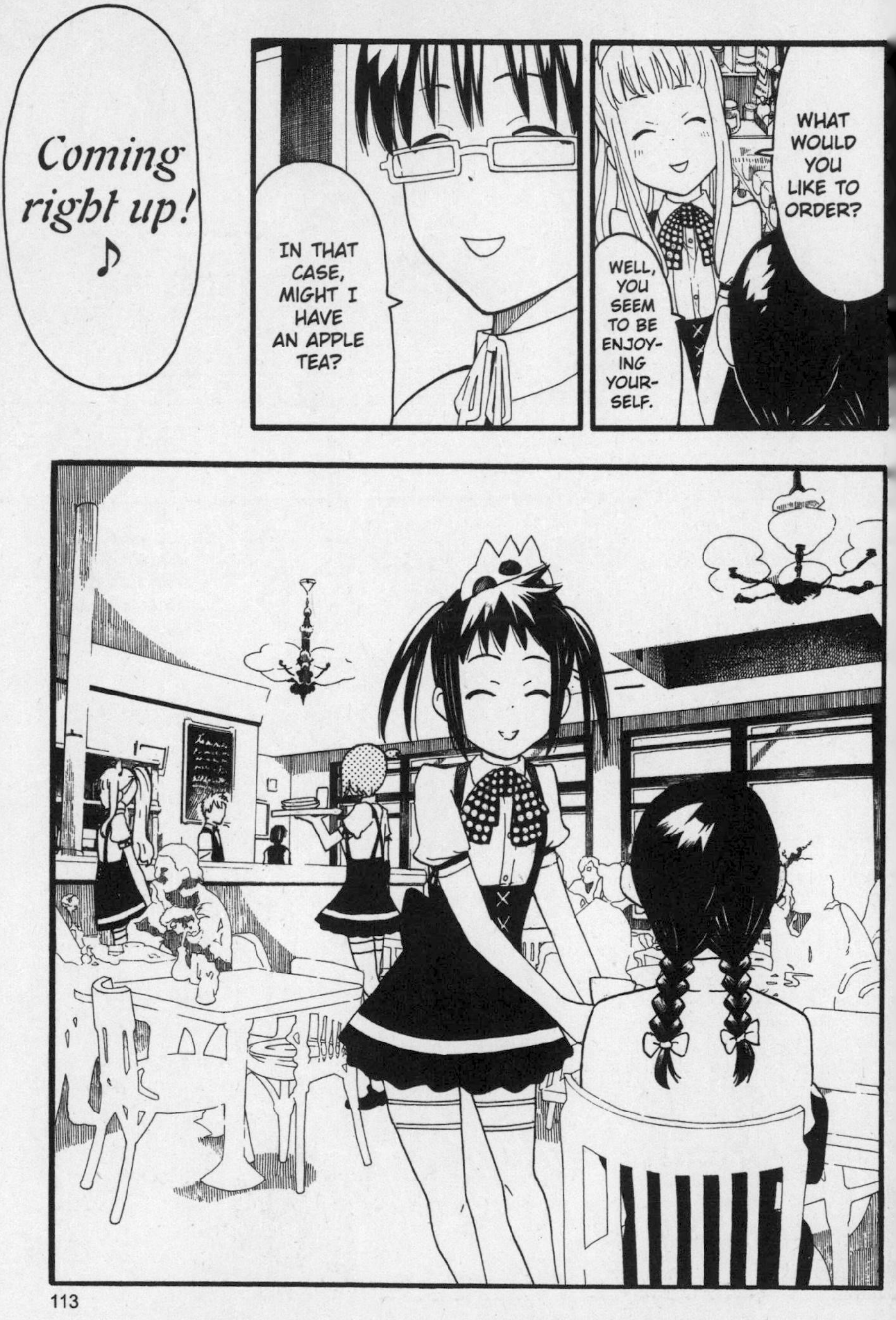
WHAT WOULD YOU LIKE TO ORDER?
WELL, YOU SEEM TO BE ENJOYING YOURSELF.
IN THAT CASE, MIGHT I HAVE AN APPLE TEA?
Coming right up! ♪

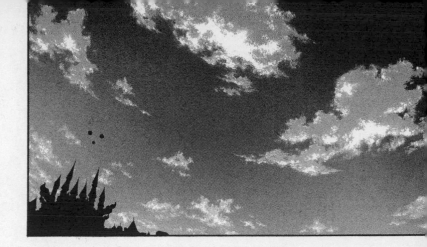

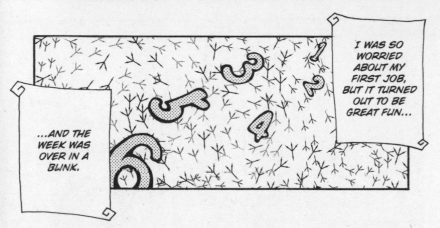

I WAS SO WORRIED ABOUT MY FIRST JOB, BUT IT TURNED OUT TO BE GREAT FUN...

...AND THE WEEK WAS OVER IN A BLINK.

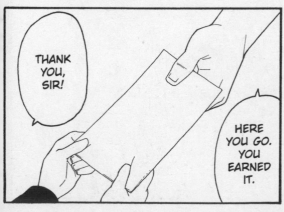

THANK YOU, SIR!

HERE YOU GO. YOU EARNED IT.

AND THEN...

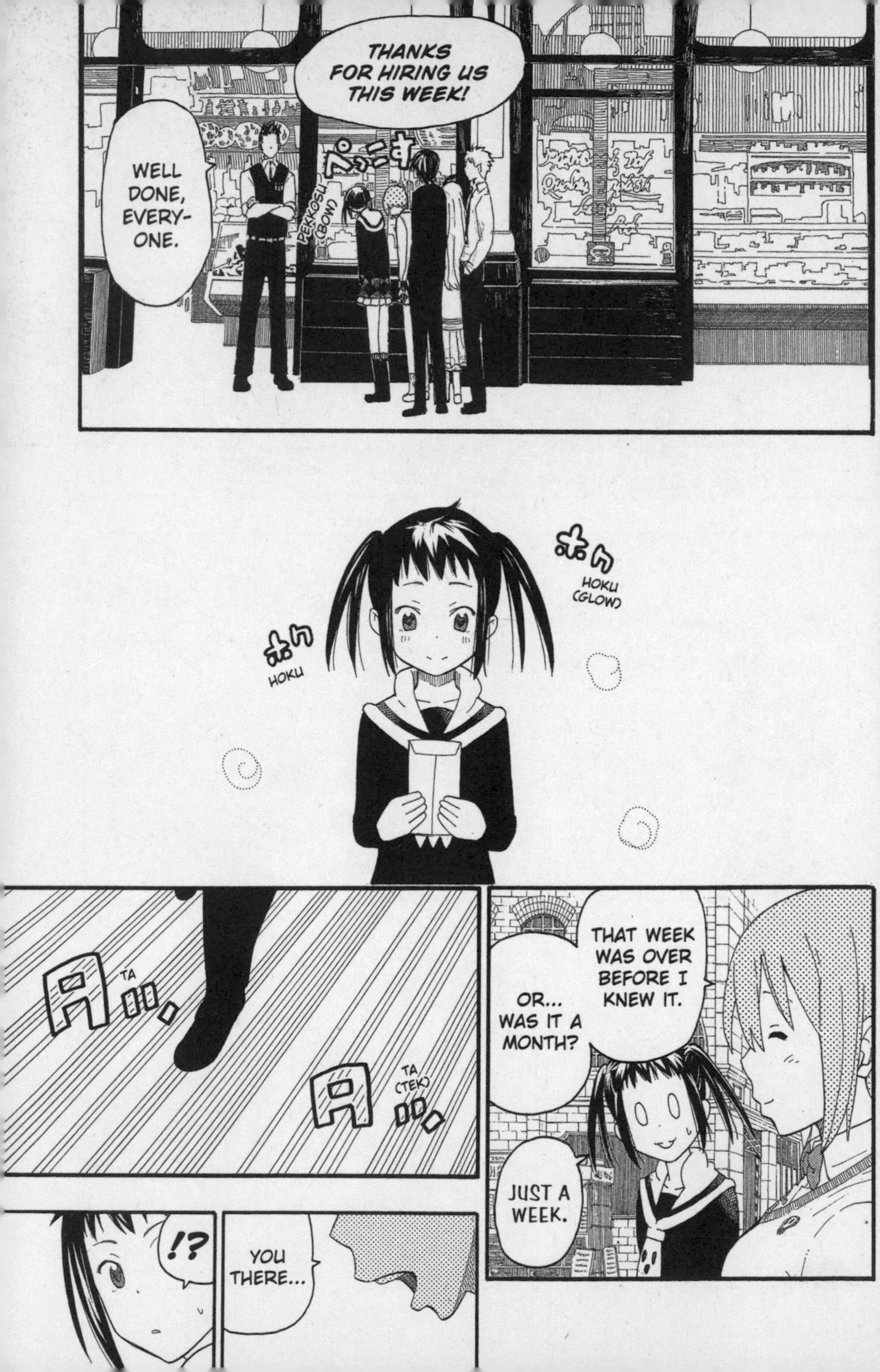

THANKS FOR HIRING US THIS WEEK!
PEKKOSU (BOW)
WELL DONE, EVERY-ONE.
HOKU (GLOW)
HOKU
THAT WEEK WAS OVER BEFORE I KNEW IT.
OR... WAS IT A MONTH?
JUST A WEEK.
TA
TA (TEK)
YOU THERE...
!?

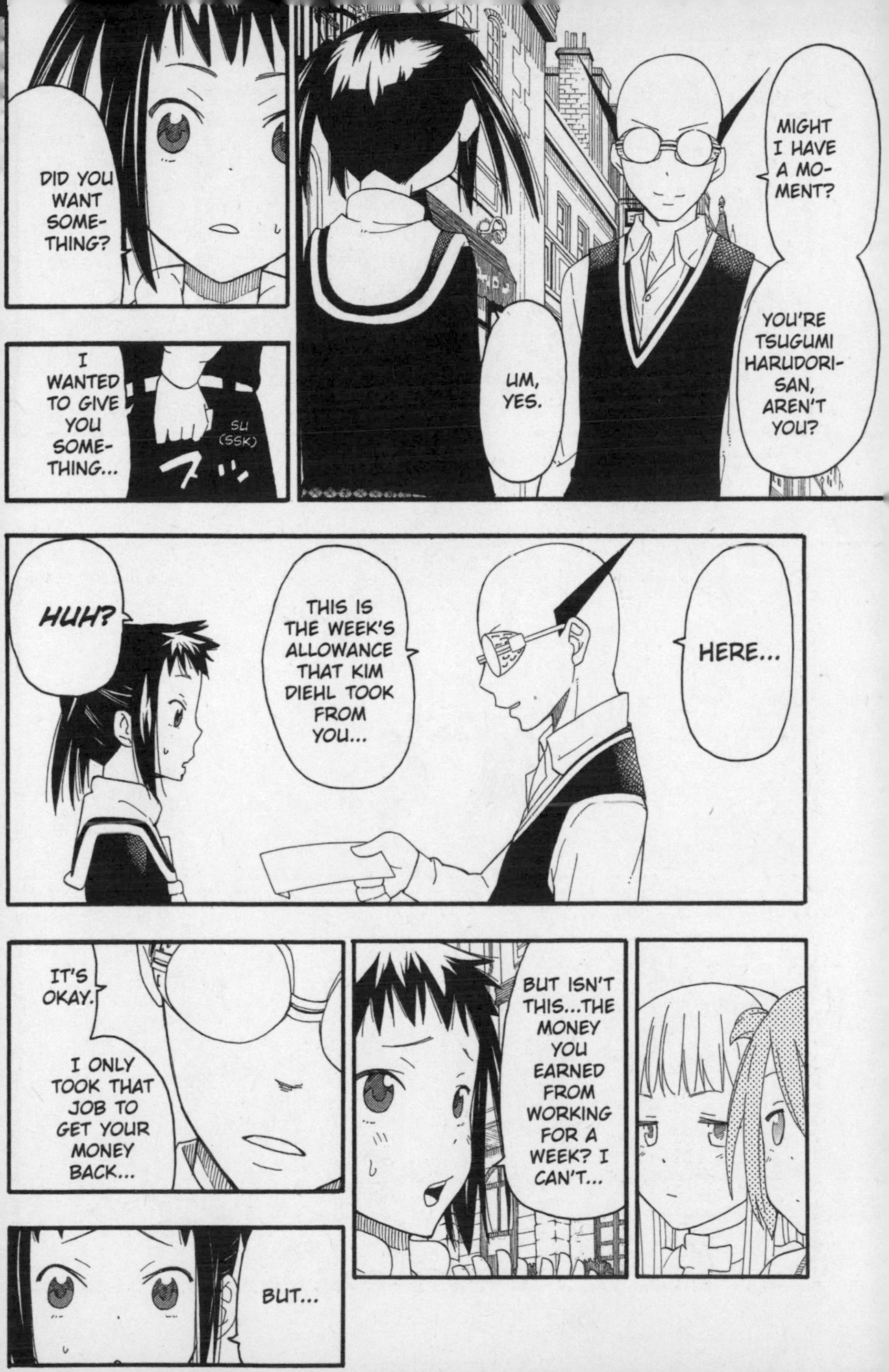
MIGHT I HAVE A MO-MENT?
YOU'RE TSUGUMI HARUDORI-SAN, AREN'T YOU?
UM, YES.
DID YOU WANT SOME-THING?
I WANTED TO GIVE YOU SOME-THING...
SU (SSK)
HERE...
THIS IS THE WEEK'S ALLOWANCE THAT KIM DIEHL TOOK FROM YOU...
HUH?
BUT ISN'T THIS...THE MONEY YOU EARNED FROM WORKING FOR A WEEK? I CAN'T...
IT'S OKAY.
I ONLY TOOK THAT JOB TO GET YOUR MONEY BACK...
BUT...

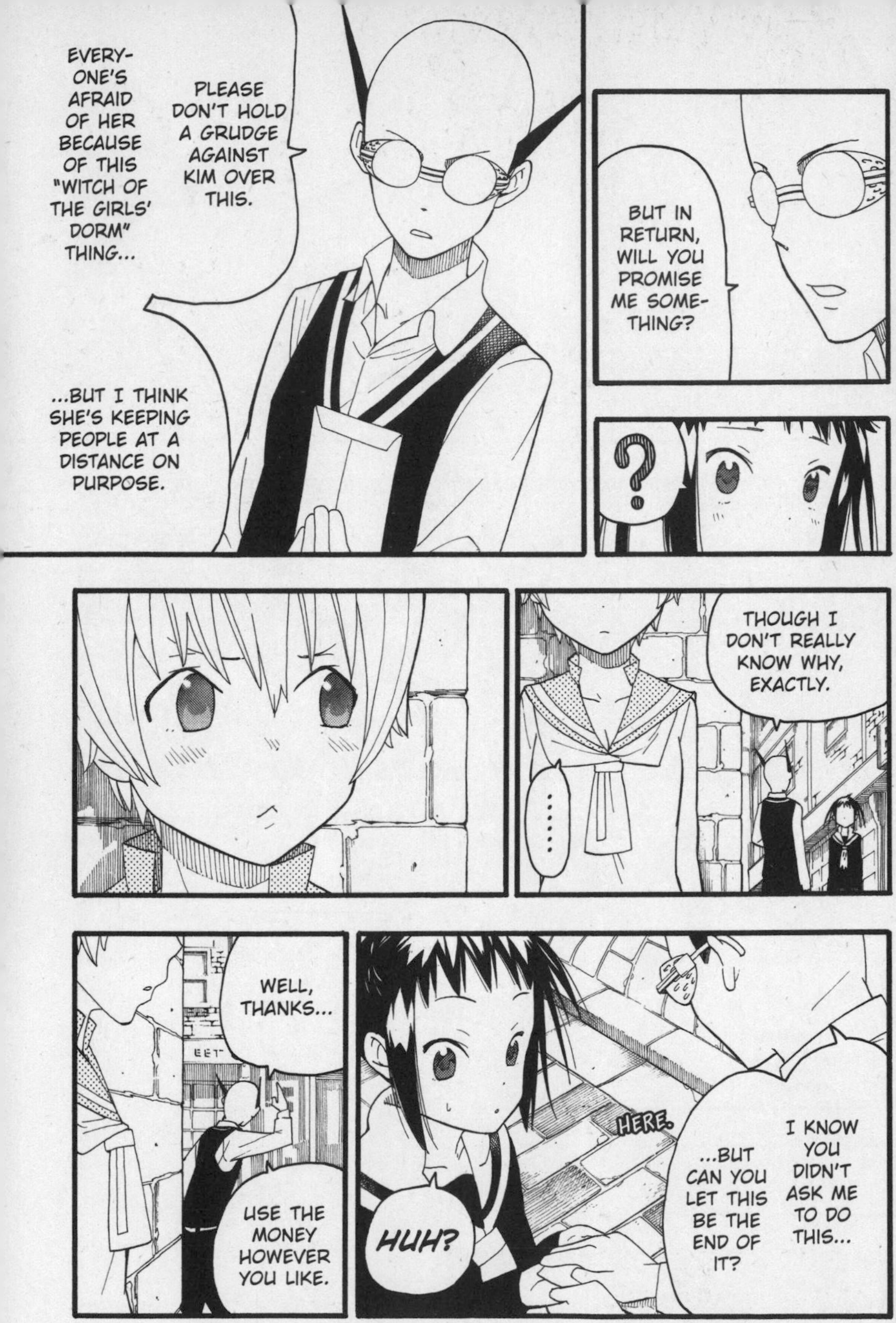
BUT IN RETURN, WILL YOU PROMISE ME SOME-THING?
?
PLEASE DON'T HOLD A GRUDGE AGAINST KIM OVER THIS.
EVERY-ONE'S AFRAID OF HER BECAUSE OF THIS "WITCH OF THE GIRLS' DORM" THING...
...BUT I THINK SHE'S KEEPING PEOPLE AT A DISTANCE ON PURPOSE.
THOUGH I DON'T REALLY KNOW WHY, EXACTLY.
......
I KNOW YOU DIDN'T ASK ME TO DO THIS...
...BUT CAN YOU LET THIS BE THE END OF IT?
HERE.
HUH?
WELL, THANKS...
USE THE MONEY HOWEVER YOU LIKE.

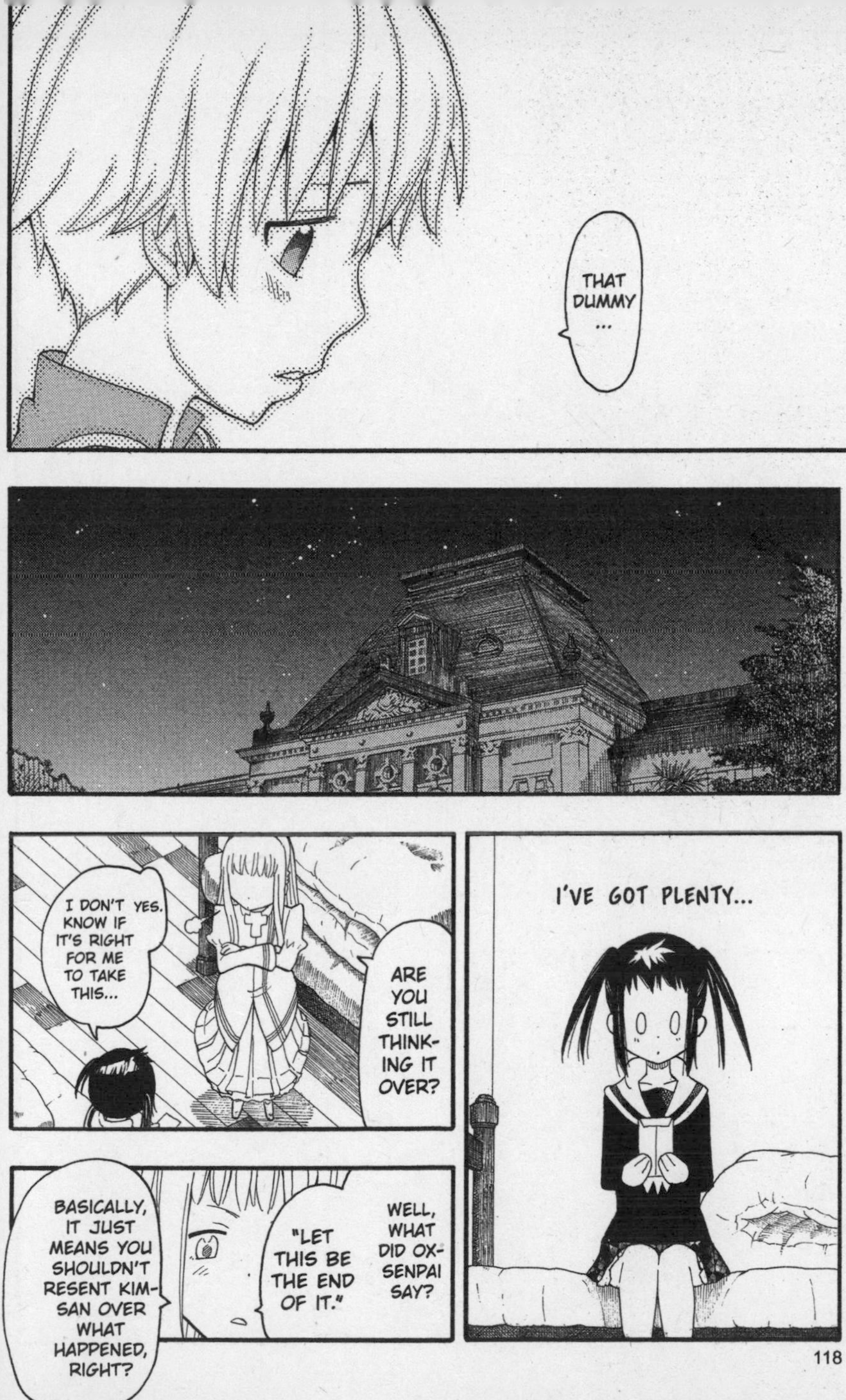
THAT DUMMY ...
I'VE GOT PLENTY...
ARE YOU STILL THINKING IT OVER?
YES.
I DON'T KNOW IF IT'S RIGHT FOR ME TO TAKE THIS...
WELL, WHAT DID OX-SENPAI SAY?
"LET THIS BE THE END OF IT."
BASICALLY, IT JUST MEANS YOU SHOULDN'T RESENT KIM-SAN OVER WHAT HAPPENED, RIGHT?

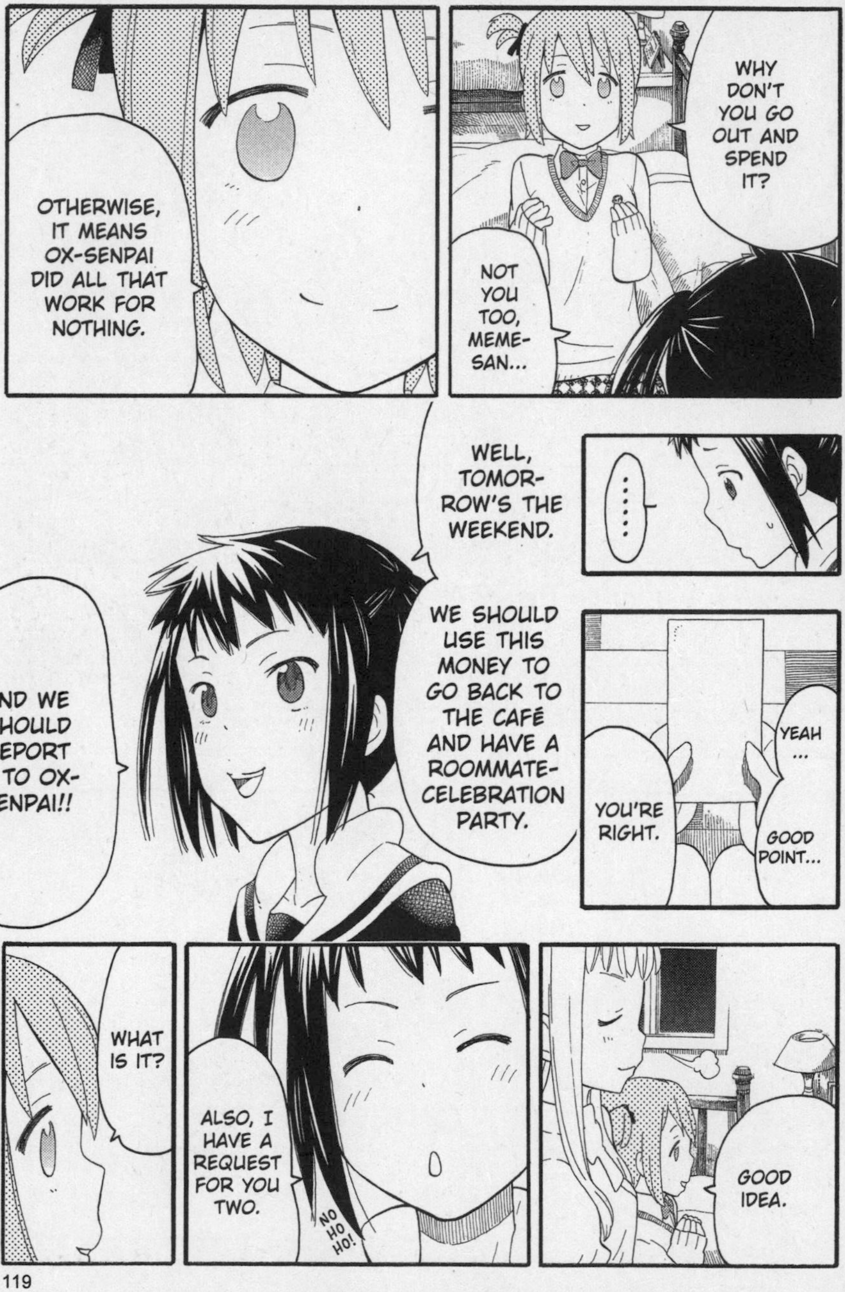
WHY DON'T YOU GO OUT AND SPEND IT?
NOT YOU TOO, MEME-SAN...
OTHERWISE, IT MEANS OX-SENPAI DID ALL THAT WORK FOR NOTHING.
......
YEAH ...
YOU'RE RIGHT.
GOOD POINT...
WELL, TOMOR-ROW'S THE WEEKEND.
WE SHOULD USE THIS MONEY TO GO BACK TO THE CAFÉ AND HAVE A ROOMMATE-CELEBRATION PARTY.
AND WE SHOULD REPORT IT TO OX-SENPAI!!
GOOD IDEA.
ALSO, I HAVE A REQUEST FOR YOU TWO.
NO HO HO!
WHAT IS IT?

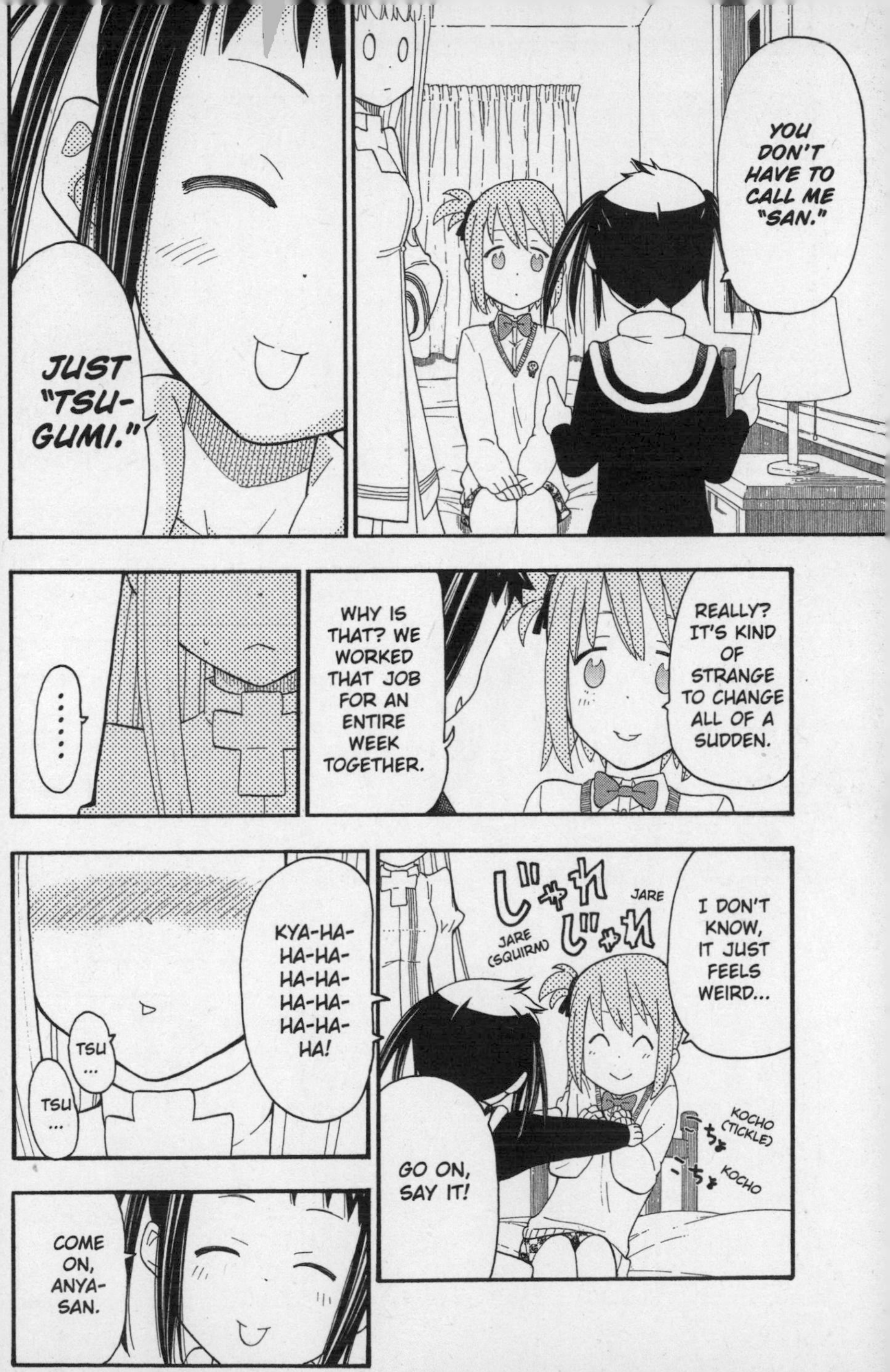
YOU DON'T HAVE TO CALL ME "SAN."
JUST "TSU-GUMI."
REALLY? IT'S KIND OF STRANGE TO CHANGE ALL OF A SUDDEN.
WHY IS THAT? WE WORKED THAT JOB FOR AN ENTIRE WEEK TOGETHER.
......
I DON'T KNOW, IT JUST FEELS WEIRD...
じゃれ
JARE
じゃれ
JARE (SQUIRM)
こちょ
KOCHO (TICKLE)
こちょ
KOCHO
GO ON, SAY IT!
KYA-HA-HA-HA-HA-HA-HA-HA-HA-HA-HA!
TSU...
TSU...
COME ON, ANYA-SAN.

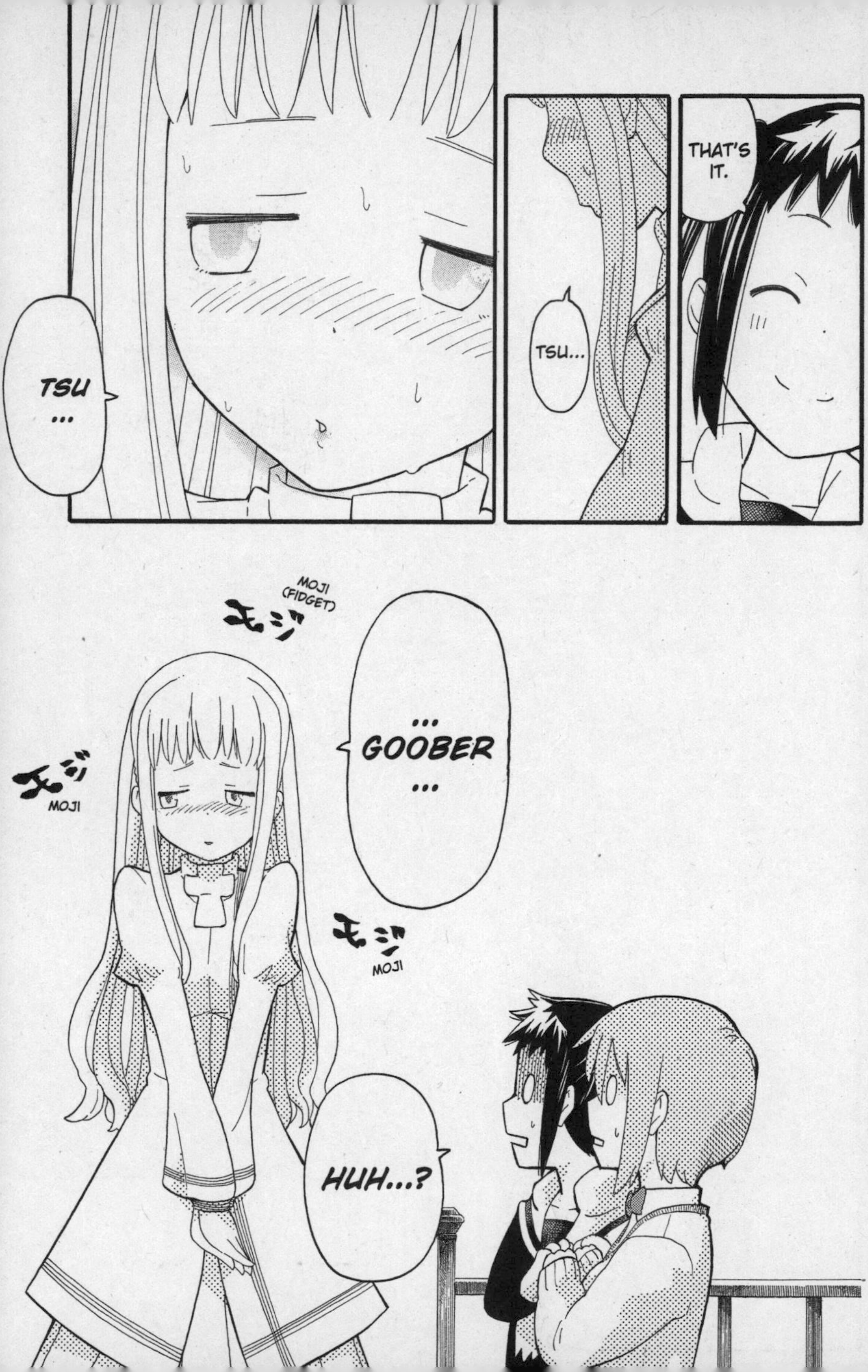
THAT'S IT.
TSU...
TSU ...
モジ MOJI (FIDGET)
... GOOBER ...
モジ MOJI
モジ MOJI
HUH...?

SOUL EATER NOT!

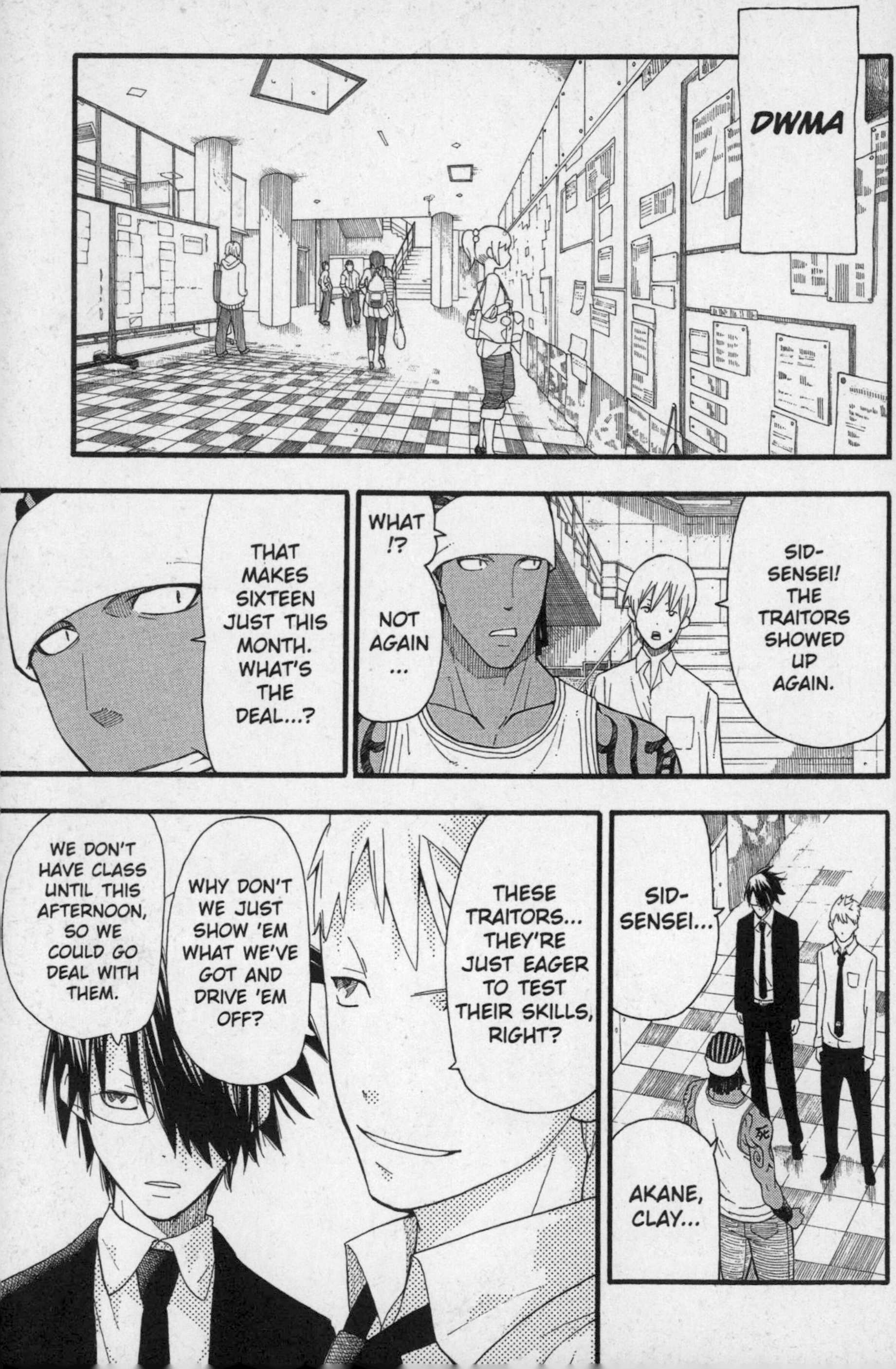
DWMA
SID-SENSEI! THE TRAITORS SHOWED UP AGAIN.
WHAT!?
NOT AGAIN...
THAT MAKES SIXTEEN JUST THIS MONTH. WHAT'S THE DEAL...?
SID-SENSEI...
AKANE, CLAY...
THESE TRAITORS... THEY'RE JUST EAGER TO TEST THEIR SKILLS, RIGHT?
WHY DON'T WE JUST SHOW 'EM WHAT WE'VE GOT AND DRIVE 'EM OFF?
WE DON'T HAVE CLASS UNTIL THIS AFTERNOON, SO WE COULD GO DEAL WITH THEM.

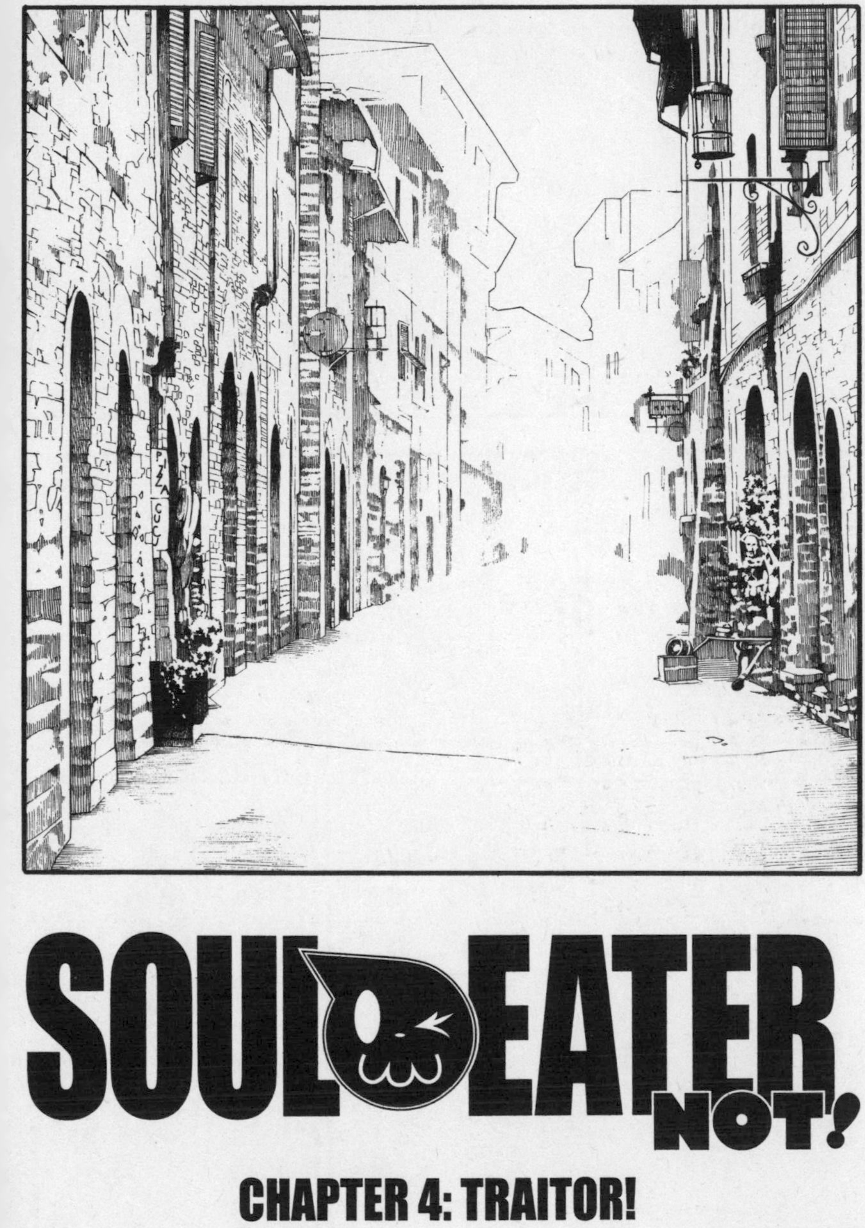

SOUL EATER NOT!

CHAPTER 4: TRAITOR!

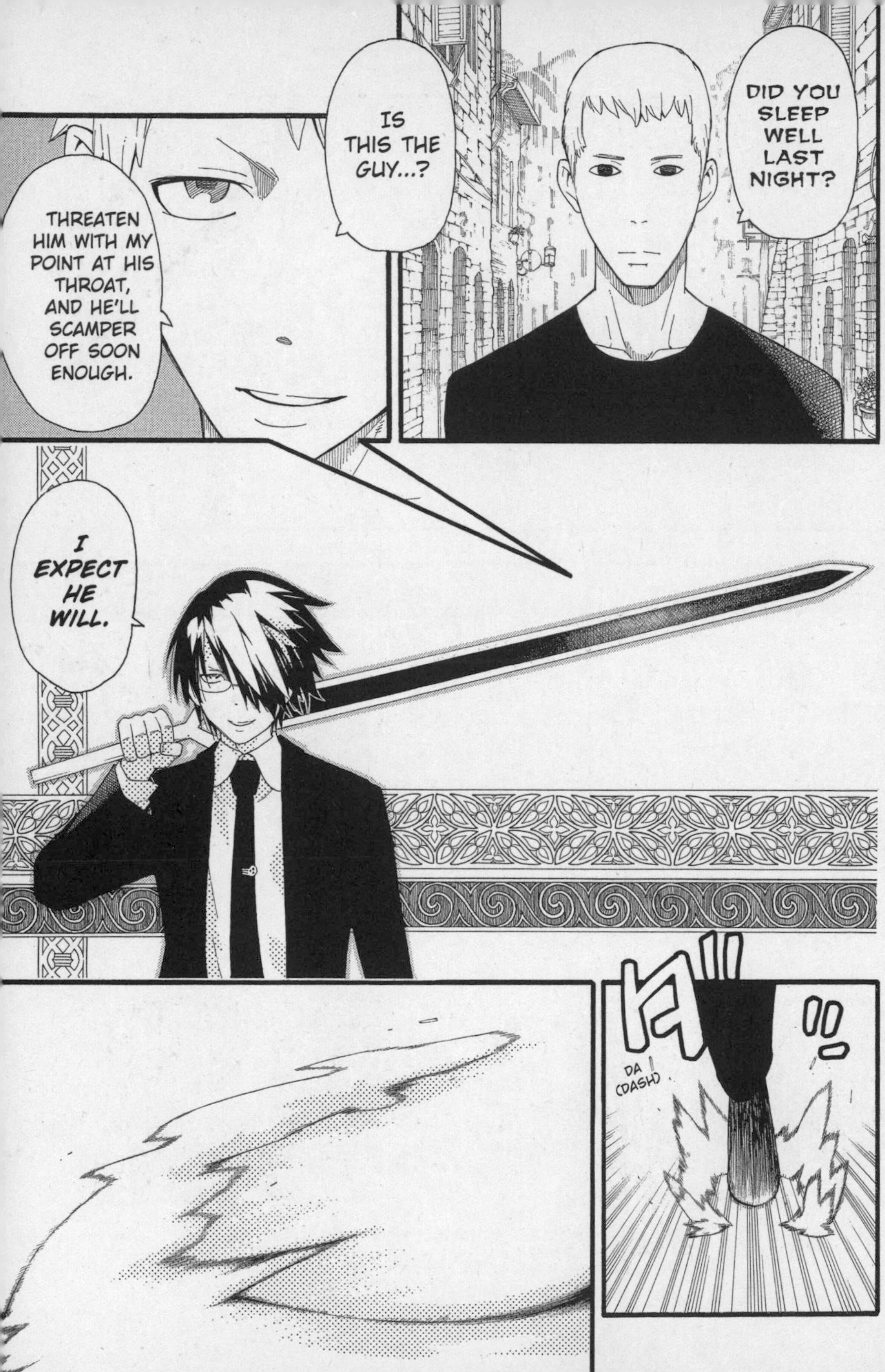
DID YOU SLEEP WELL LAST NIGHT?
IS THIS THE GUY...?
THREATEN HIM WITH MY POINT AT HIS THROAT, AND HE'LL SCAMPER OFF SOON ENOUGH.
I EXPECT HE WILL.
DA (DASH)

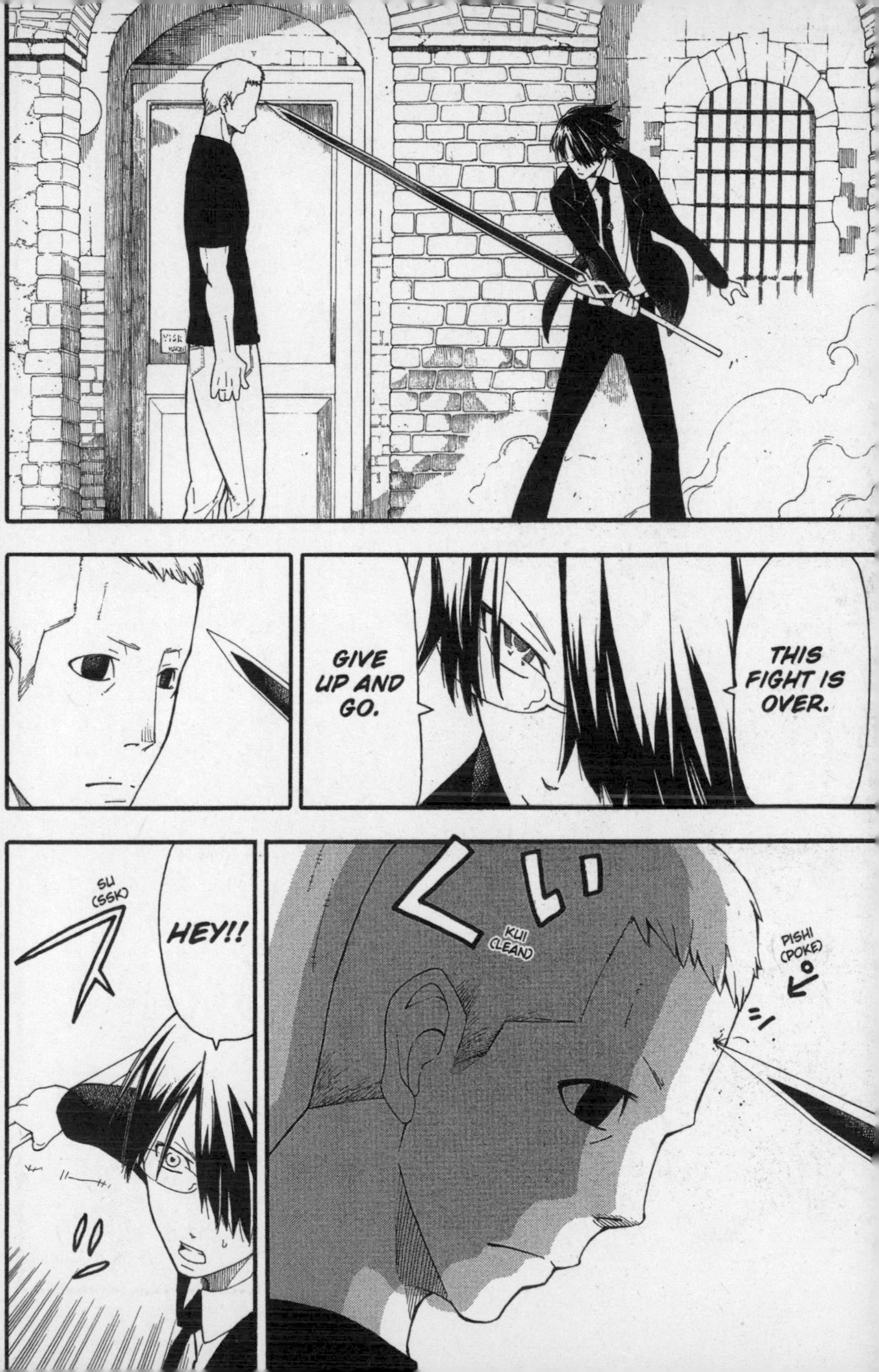
THIS FIGHT IS OVER.
GIVE UP AND GO.
PISHI (POKE)
KUI (CLEAN)
HEY!!
SU (SSK)

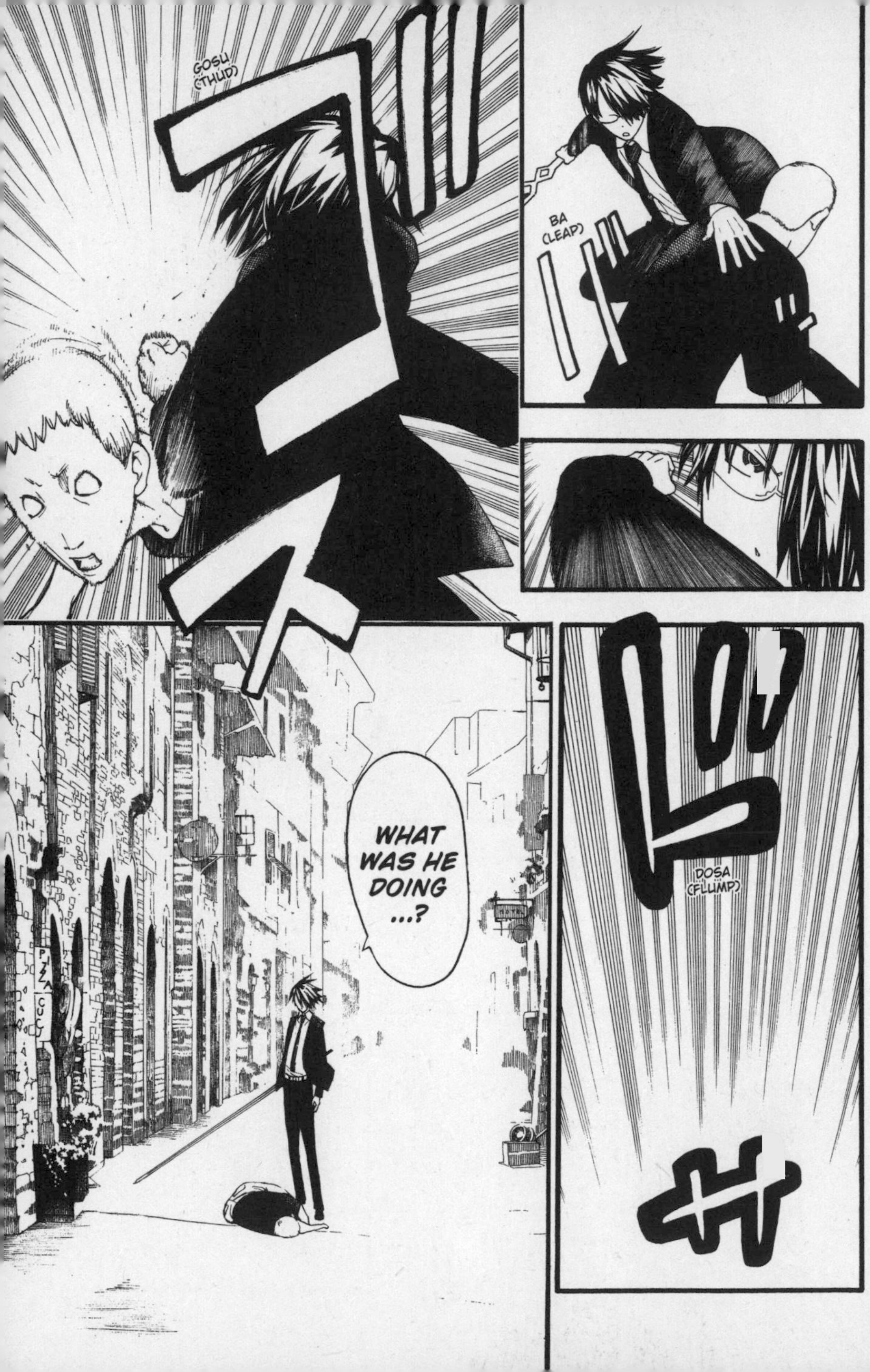
BA (LEAP)
GOSU (THUD)
DOSA (FLUMP)
WHAT WAS HE DOING ...?

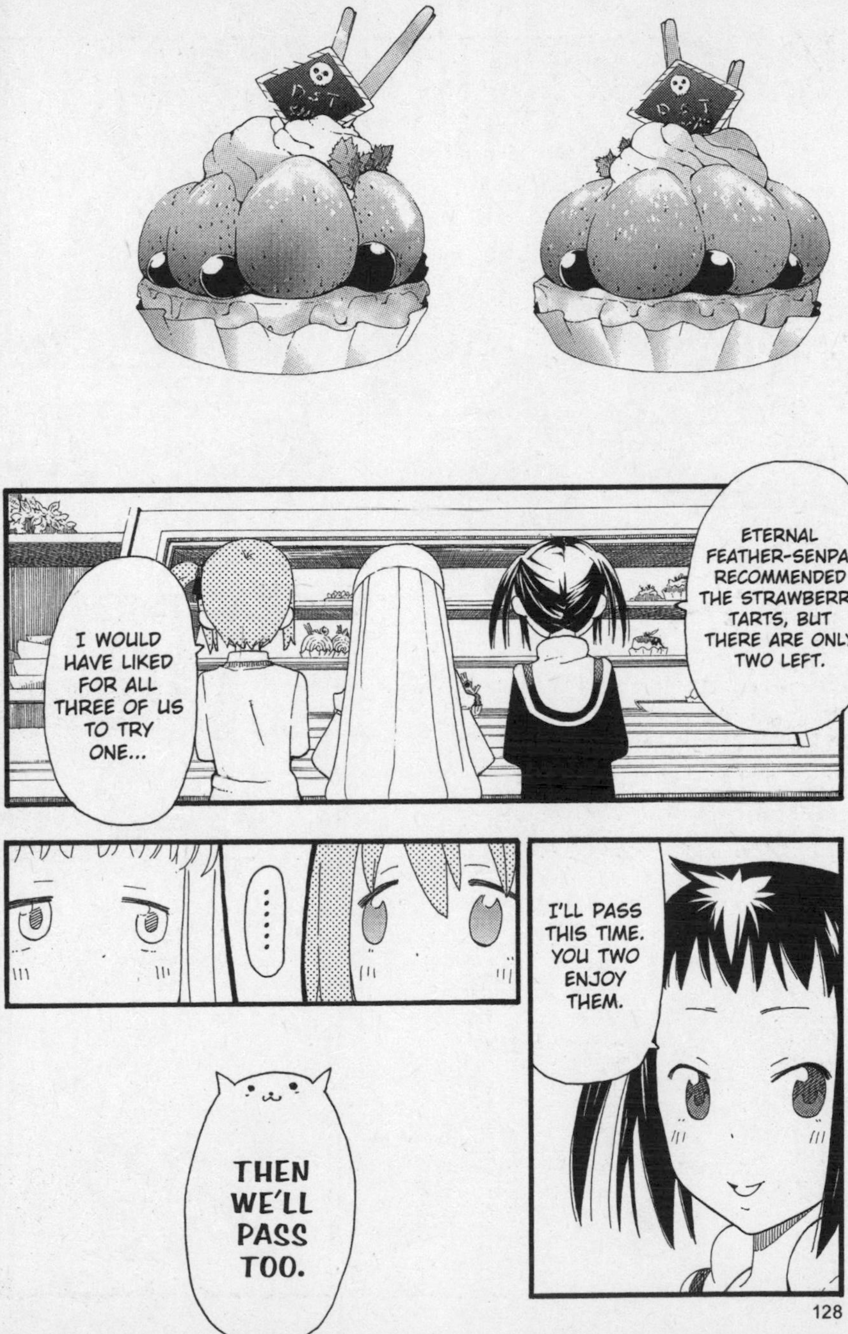
ETERNAL FEATHER-SENPAI RECOMMENDED THE STRAWBERRY TARTS, BUT THERE ARE ONLY TWO LEFT.
I WOULD HAVE LIKED FOR ALL THREE OF US TO TRY ONE...
I'LL PASS THIS TIME. YOU TWO ENJOY THEM.
......
THEN WE'LL PASS TOO.

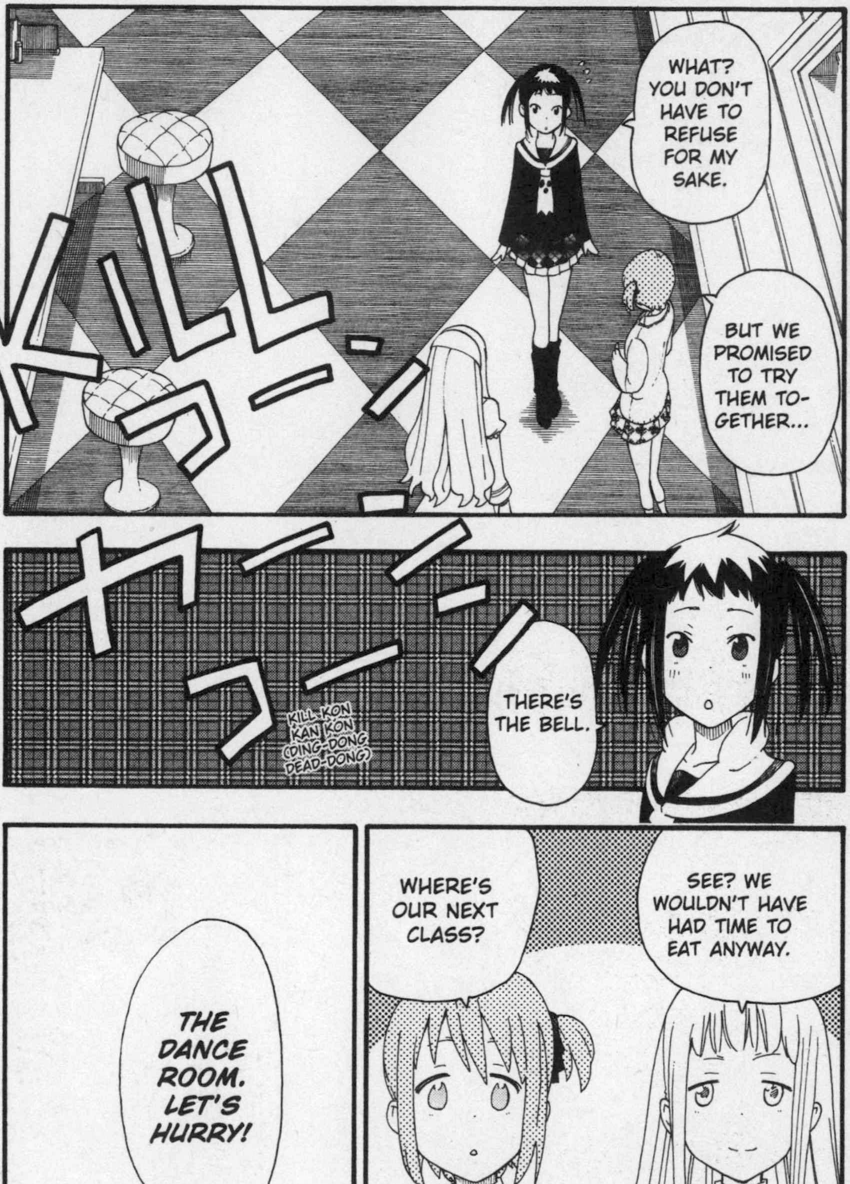

WHAT? YOU DON'T HAVE TO REFUSE FOR MY SAKE.
BUT WE PROMISED TO TRY THEM TOGETHER...
KILL-
THERE'S THE BELL.
KILL KON KAN KON (DING-DONG DEAD-DONG)
SEE? WE WOULDN'T HAVE HAD TIME TO EAT ANYWAY.
WHERE'S OUR NEXT CLASS?
THE DANCE ROOM. LET'S HURRY!

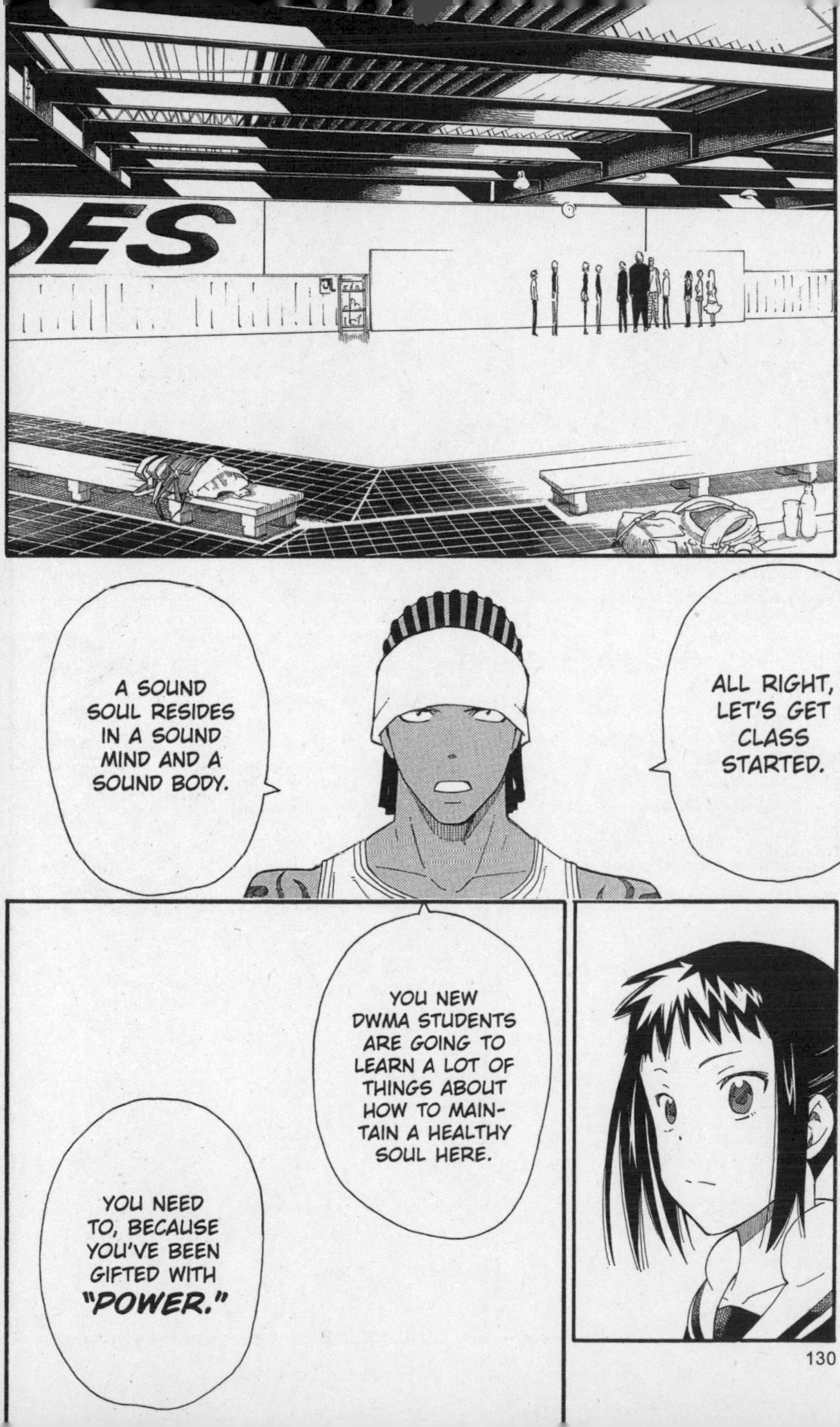
DES
ALL RIGHT, LET'S GET CLASS STARTED.
A SOUND SOUL RESIDES IN A SOUND MIND AND A SOUND BODY.
YOU NEW DWMA STUDENTS ARE GOING TO LEARN A LOT OF THINGS ABOUT HOW TO MAIN-TAIN A HEALTHY SOUL HERE.
YOU NEED TO, BECAUSE YOU'VE BEEN GIFTED WITH "POWER."

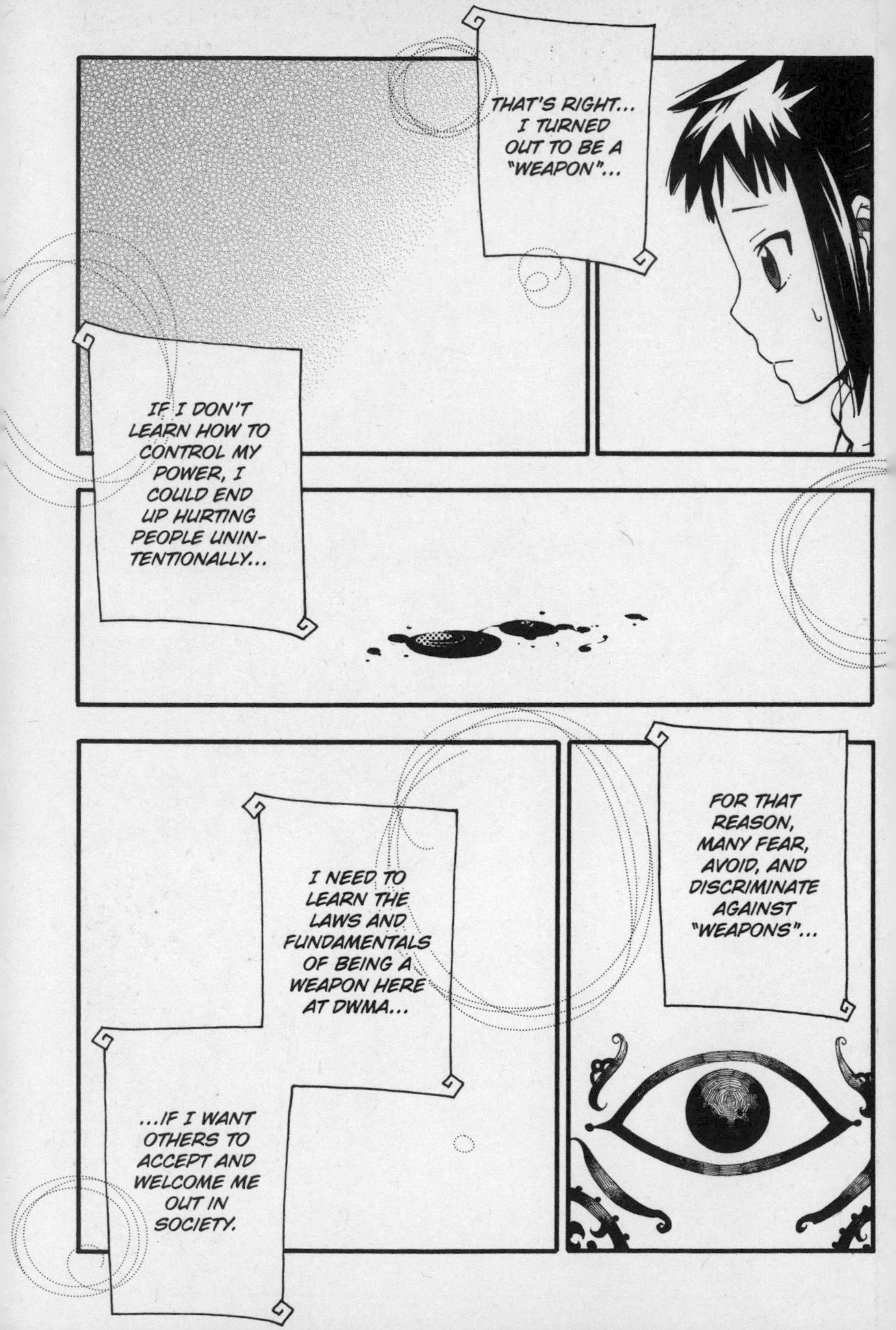
THAT'S RIGHT... I TURNED OUT TO BE A "WEAPON"...
IF I DON'T LEARN HOW TO CONTROL MY POWER, I COULD END UP HURTING PEOPLE UNIN-TENTIONALLY...
FOR THAT REASON, MANY FEAR, AVOID, AND DISCRIMINATE AGAINST "WEAPONS"...
I NEED TO LEARN THE LAWS AND FUNDAMENTALS OF BEING A WEAPON HERE AT DWMA...
...IF I WANT OTHERS TO ACCEPT AND WELCOME ME OUT IN SOCIETY.

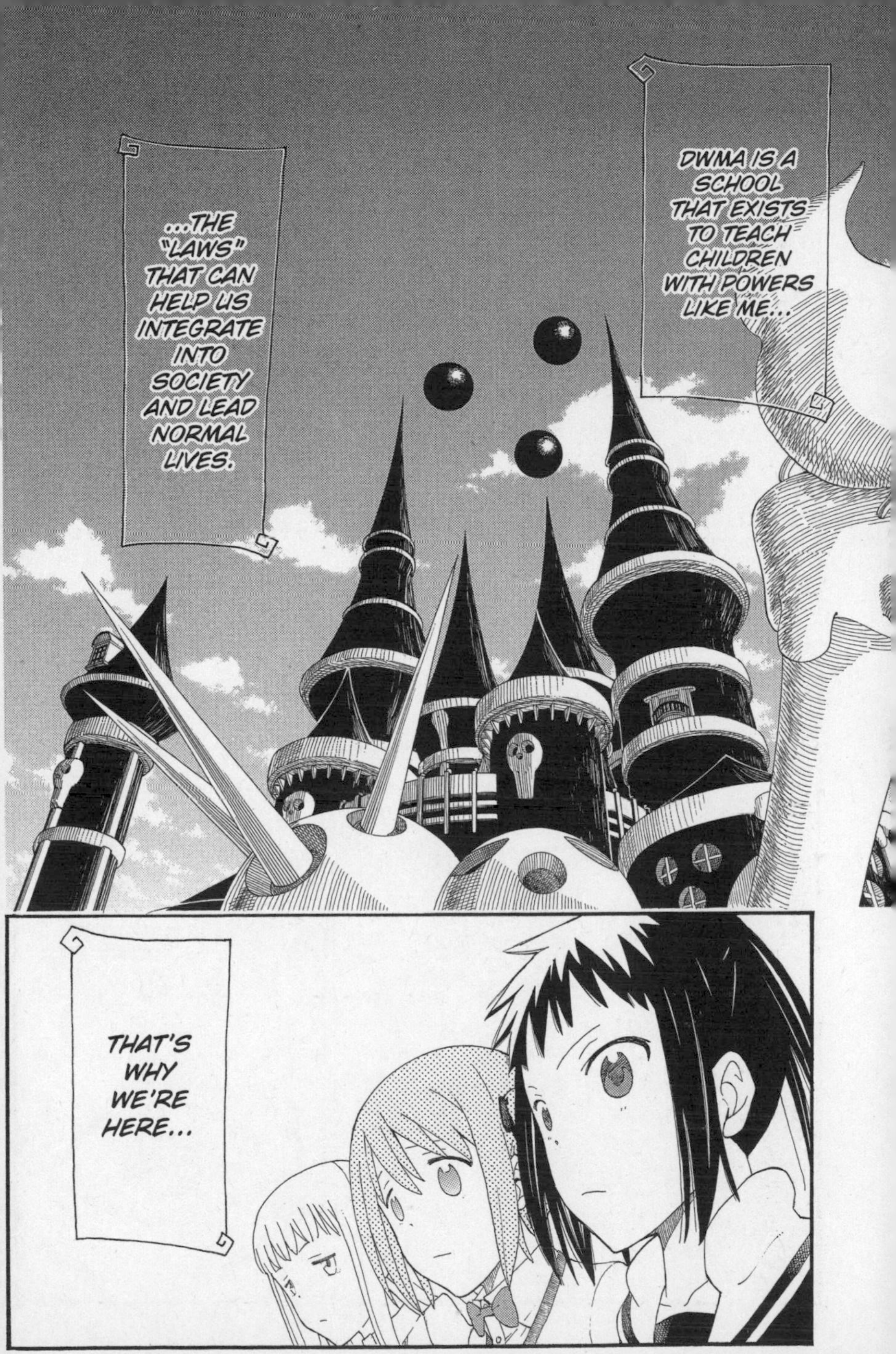
DWMA IS A SCHOOL THAT EXISTS TO TEACH CHILDREN WITH POWERS LIKE ME...
...THE "LAWS" THAT CAN HELP US INTEGRATE INTO SOCIETY AND LEAD NORMAL LIVES.
THAT'S WHY WE'RE HERE...

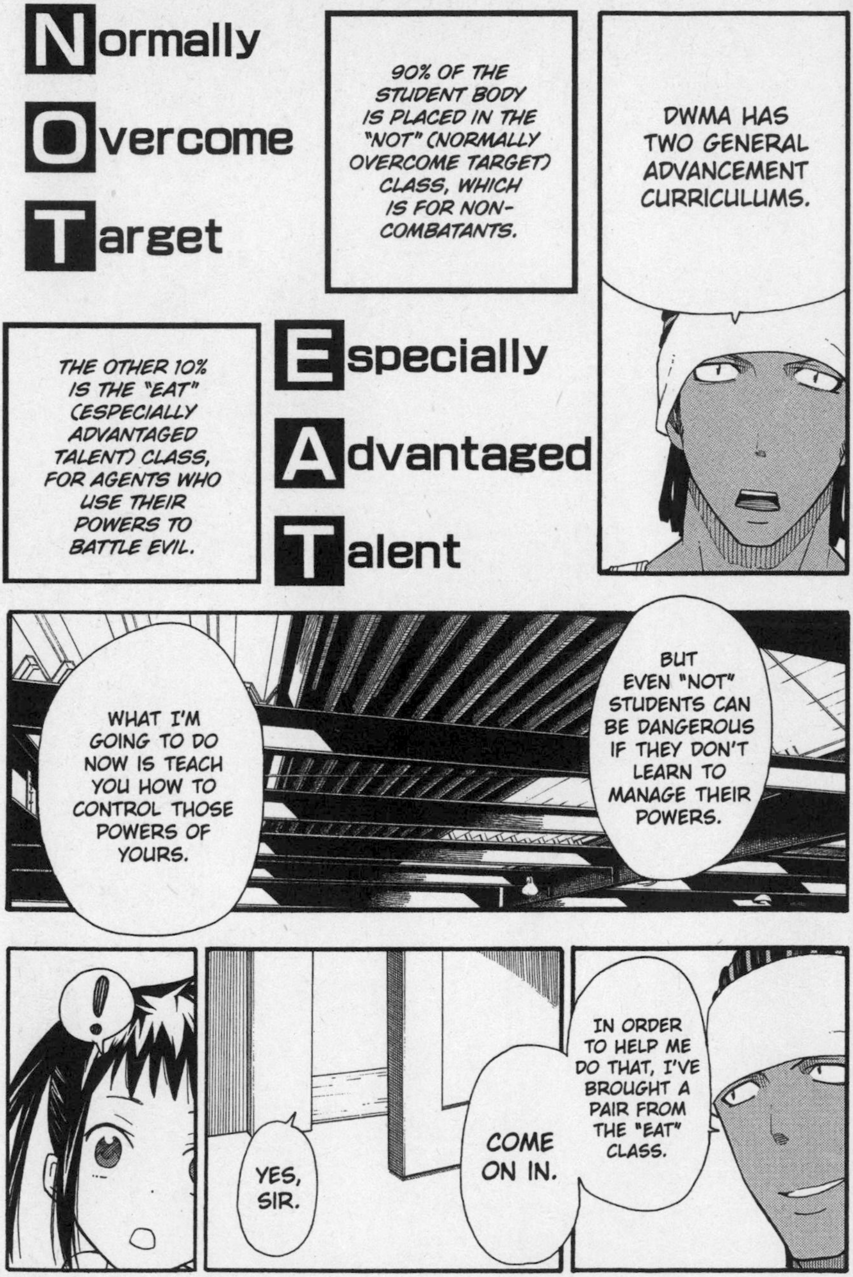
DWMA HAS TWO GENERAL ADVANCEMENT CURRICULUMS.
90% OF THE STUDENT BODY IS PLACED IN THE "NOT" (NORMALLY OVERCOME TARGET) CLASS, WHICH IS FOR NON-COMBATANTS.
Normally Overcome Target
Especially Advantaged Talent
THE OTHER 10% IS THE "EAT" (ESPECIALLY ADVANTAGED TALENT) CLASS, FOR AGENTS WHO USE THEIR POWERS TO BATTLE EVIL.
BUT EVEN "NOT" STUDENTS CAN BE DANGEROUS IF THEY DON'T LEARN TO MANAGE THEIR POWERS.
WHAT I'M GOING TO DO NOW IS TEACH YOU HOW TO CONTROL THOSE POWERS OF YOURS.
IN ORDER TO HELP ME DO THAT, I'VE BROUGHT A PAIR FROM THE "EAT" CLASS.
COME ON IN.
YES, SIR.
!

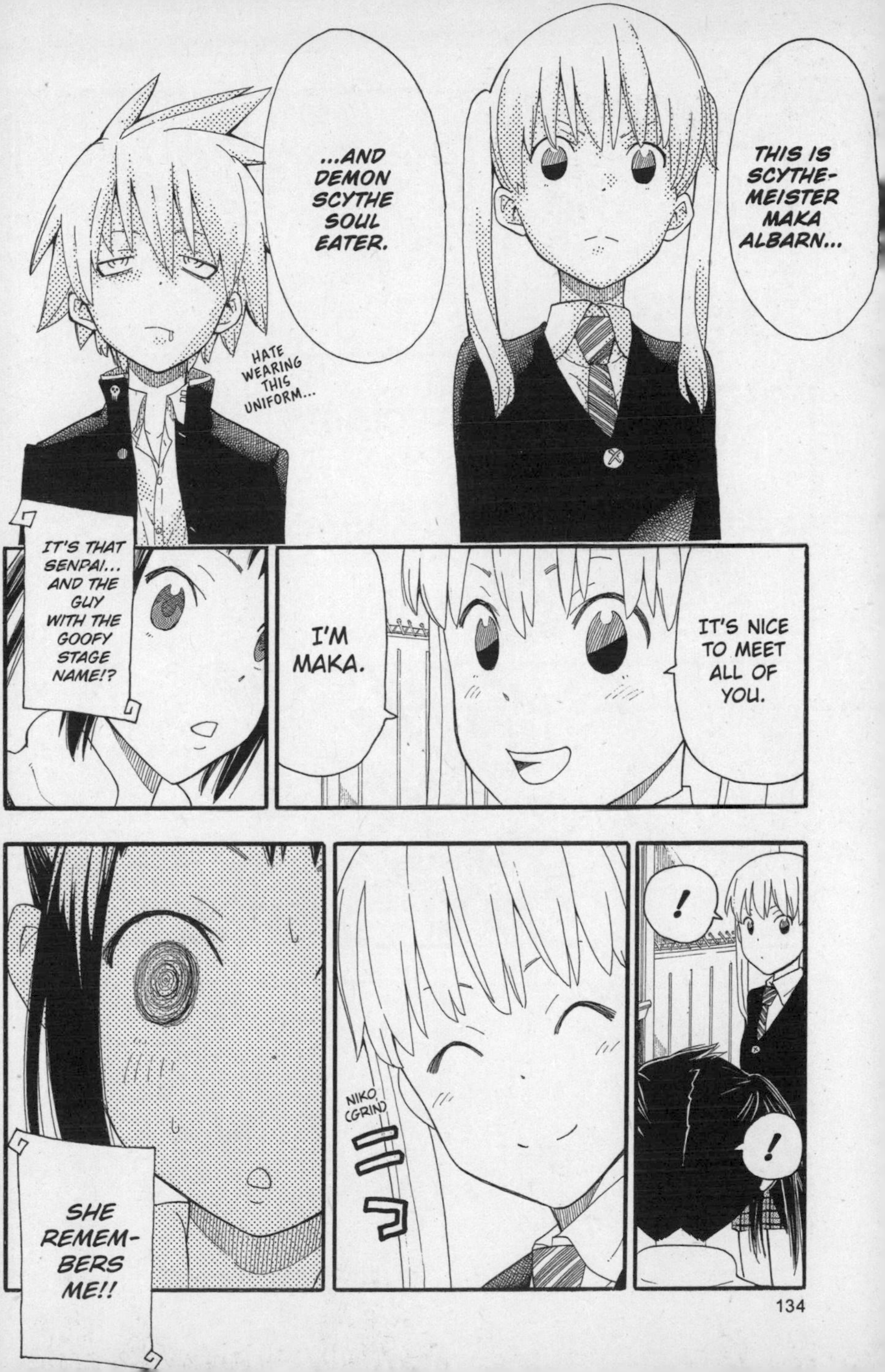
THIS IS SCYTHE-MEISTER MAKA ALBARN...
...AND DEMON SCYTHE SOUL EATER.
HATE WEARING THIS UNIFORM...
IT'S NICE TO MEET ALL OF YOU.
I'M MAKA.
IT'S THAT SENPAI... AND THE GUY WITH THE GOOFY STAGE NAME!?
!
!
NIKO (GRIN)
SHE REMEMBERS ME!!

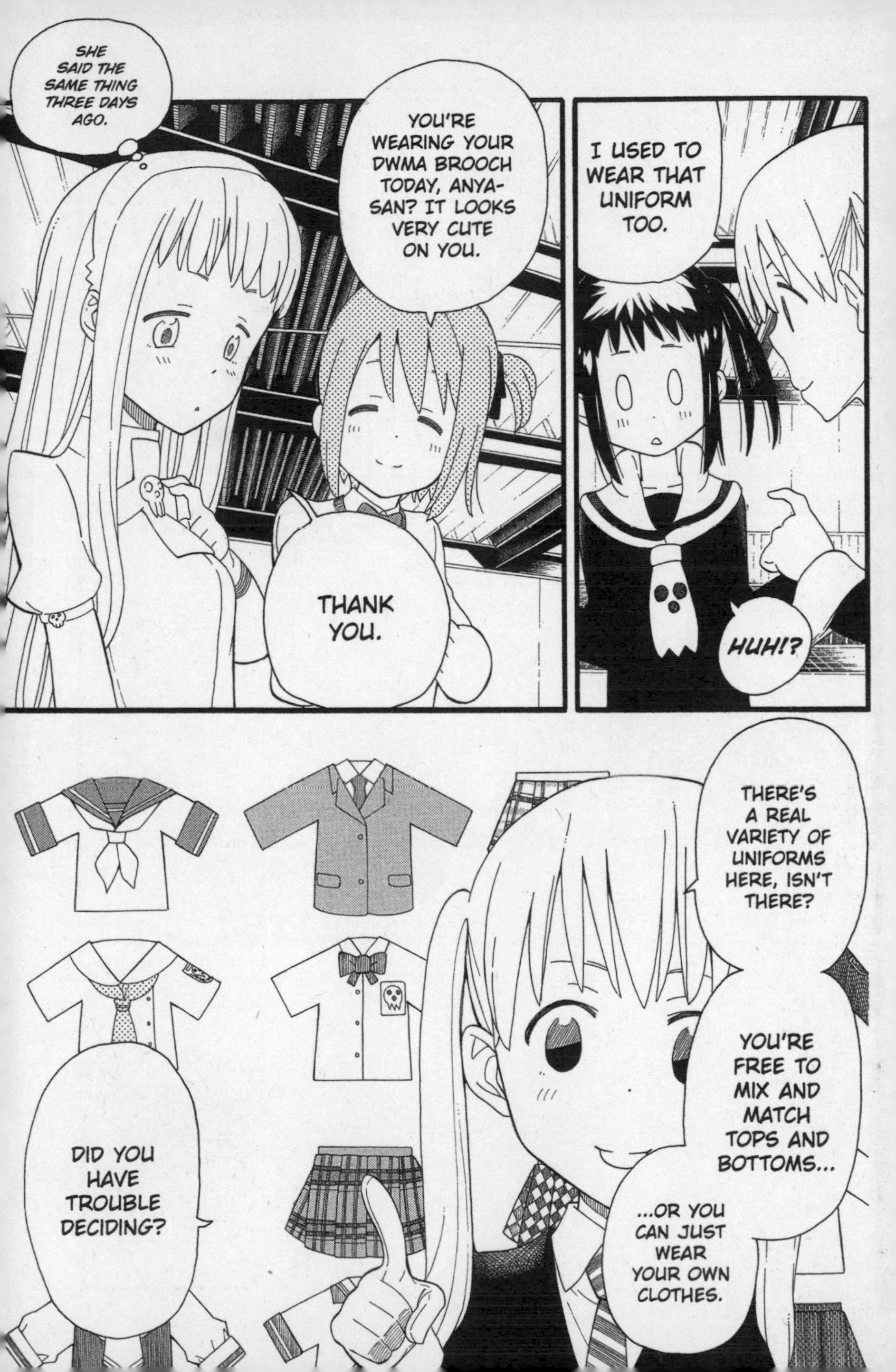
I USED TO WEAR THAT UNIFORM TOO.
HUH!?
YOU'RE WEARING YOUR DWMA BROOCH TODAY, ANYA-SAN? IT LOOKS VERY CUTE ON YOU.
SHE SAID THE SAME THING THREE DAYS AGO.
THANK YOU.
THERE'S A REAL VARIETY OF UNIFORMS HERE, ISN'T THERE?
YOU'RE FREE TO MIX AND MATCH TOPS AND BOTTOMS...
...OR YOU CAN JUST WEAR YOUR OWN CLOTHES.
DID YOU HAVE TROUBLE DECIDING?

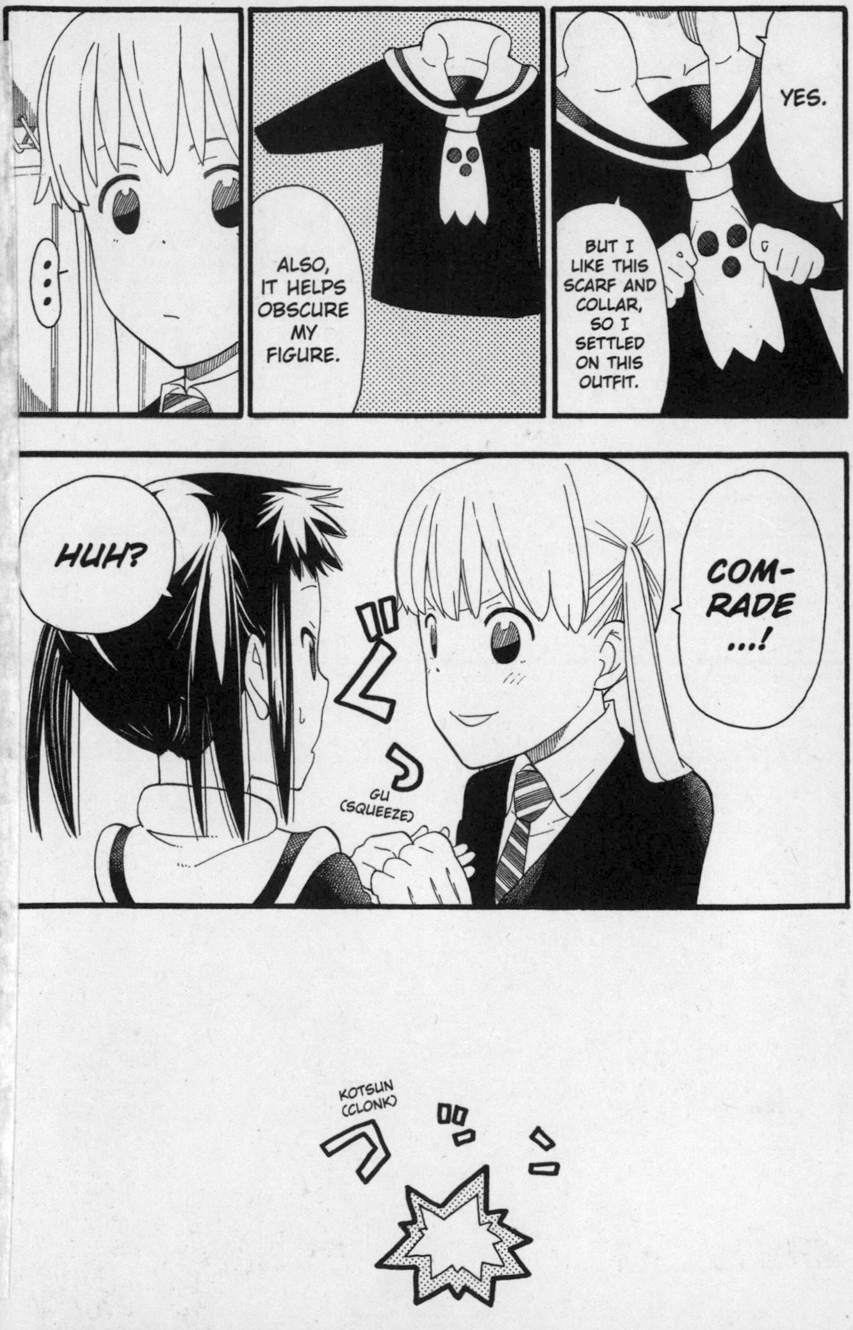
YES.
BUT I LIKE THIS SCARF AND COLLAR, SO I SETTLED ON THIS OUTFIT.
ALSO, IT HELPS OBSCURE MY FIGURE.
...
COM-RADE ...!
GU (SQUEEZE)
HUH?
KOTSUN (CLONK)

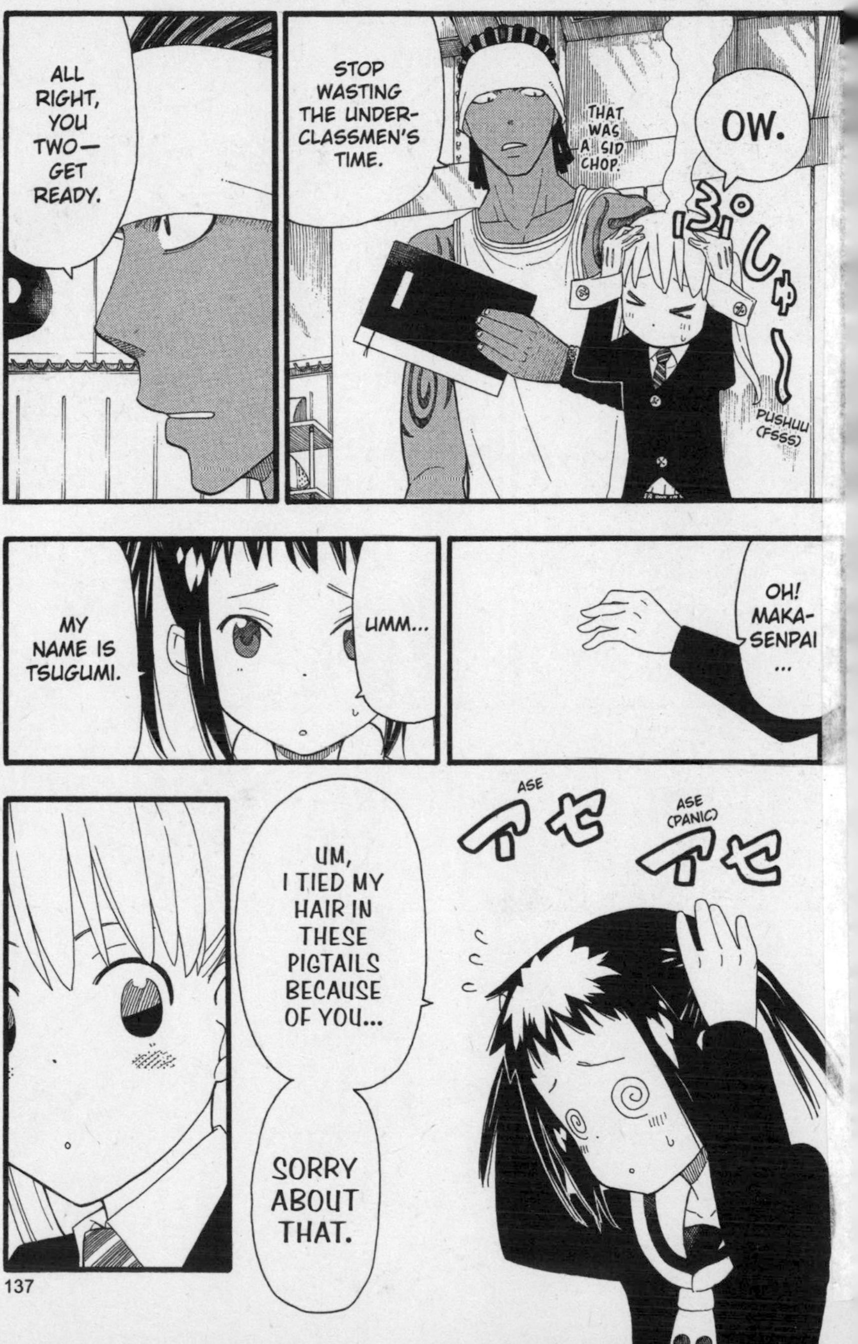
STOP WASTING THE UNDER-CLASSMEN'S TIME.
THAT WAS A SID CHOP.
OW.
ぷしゅ～
PUSHUU (FSSS)
ALL RIGHT, YOU TWO— GET READY.
OH! MAKA-SENPAI ...
UMM...
MY NAME IS TSUGUMI.
ASE
アセ
ASE (PANIC)
アセ
UM, I TIED MY HAIR IN THESE PIGTAILS BECAUSE OF YOU...
SORRY ABOUT THAT.

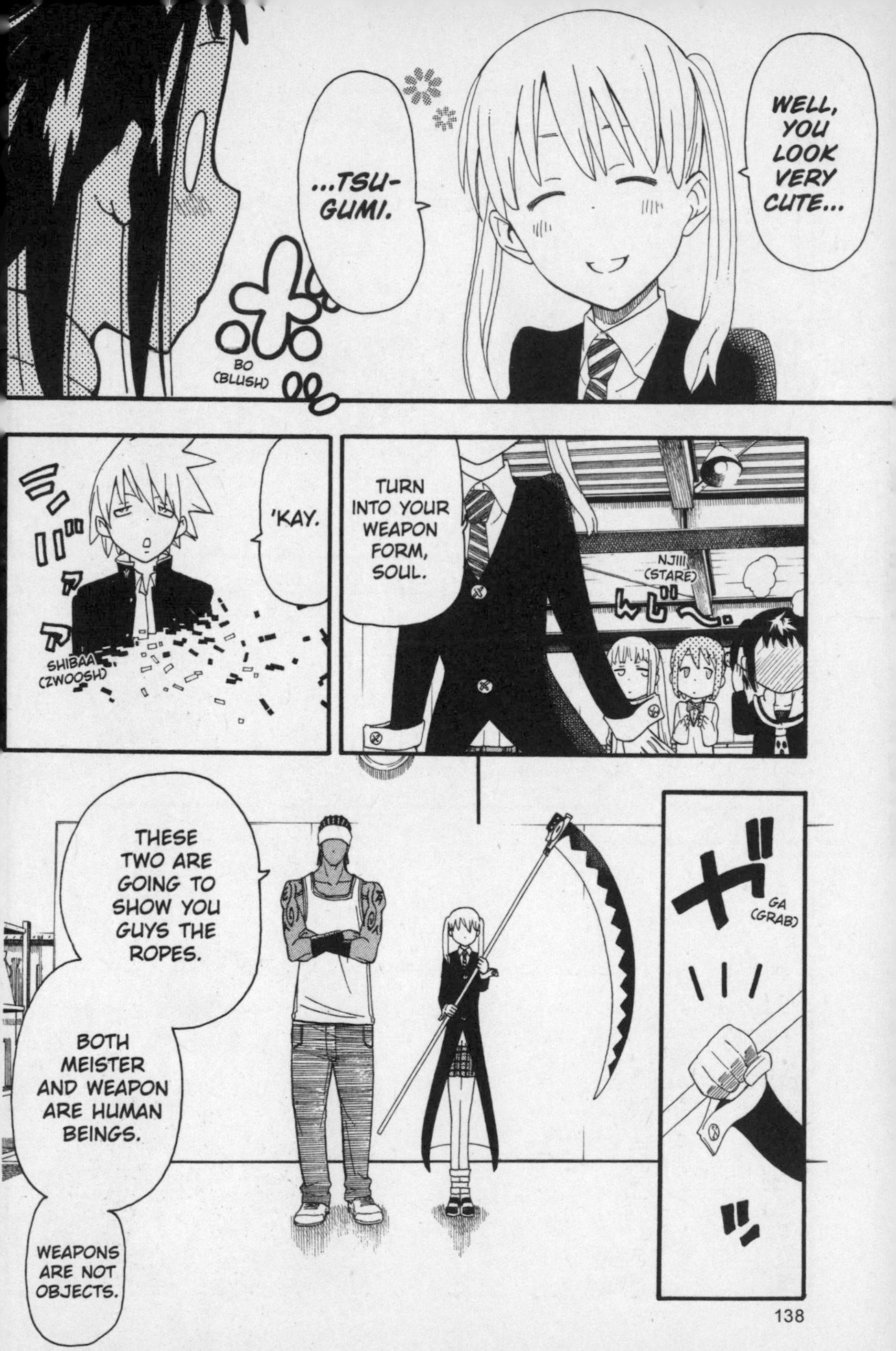
WELL, YOU LOOK VERY CUTE...
...TSU-GUMI.
BO (BLUSH)
TURN INTO YOUR WEAPON FORM, SOUL.
NJIII (STARE)
'KAY.
SHIBAA (ZWOOSH)
GA (GRAB)
THESE TWO ARE GOING TO SHOW YOU GUYS THE ROPES.
BOTH MEISTER AND WEAPON ARE HUMAN BEINGS.
WEAPONS ARE NOT OBJECTS.

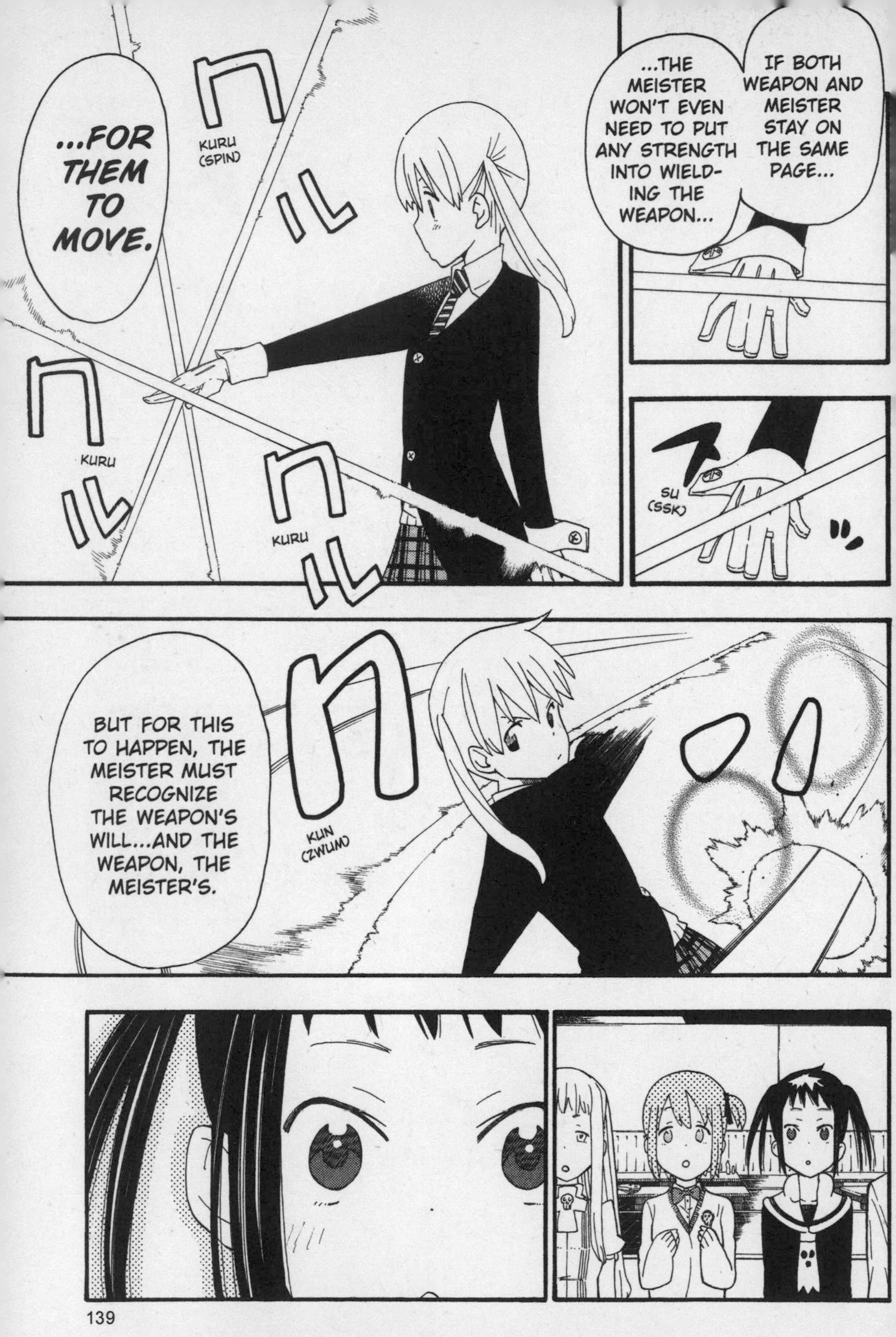
IF BOTH WEAPON AND MEISTER STAY ON THE SAME PAGE...
...THE MEISTER WON'T EVEN NEED TO PUT ANY STRENGTH INTO WIELDING THE WEAPON...
SU (SSK)
KURU (SPIN)
...FOR THEM TO MOVE.
KURU
KURU
KUN (ZWUM)
BUT FOR THIS TO HAPPEN, THE MEISTER MUST RECOGNIZE THE WEAPON'S WILL...AND THE WEAPON, THE MEISTER'S.

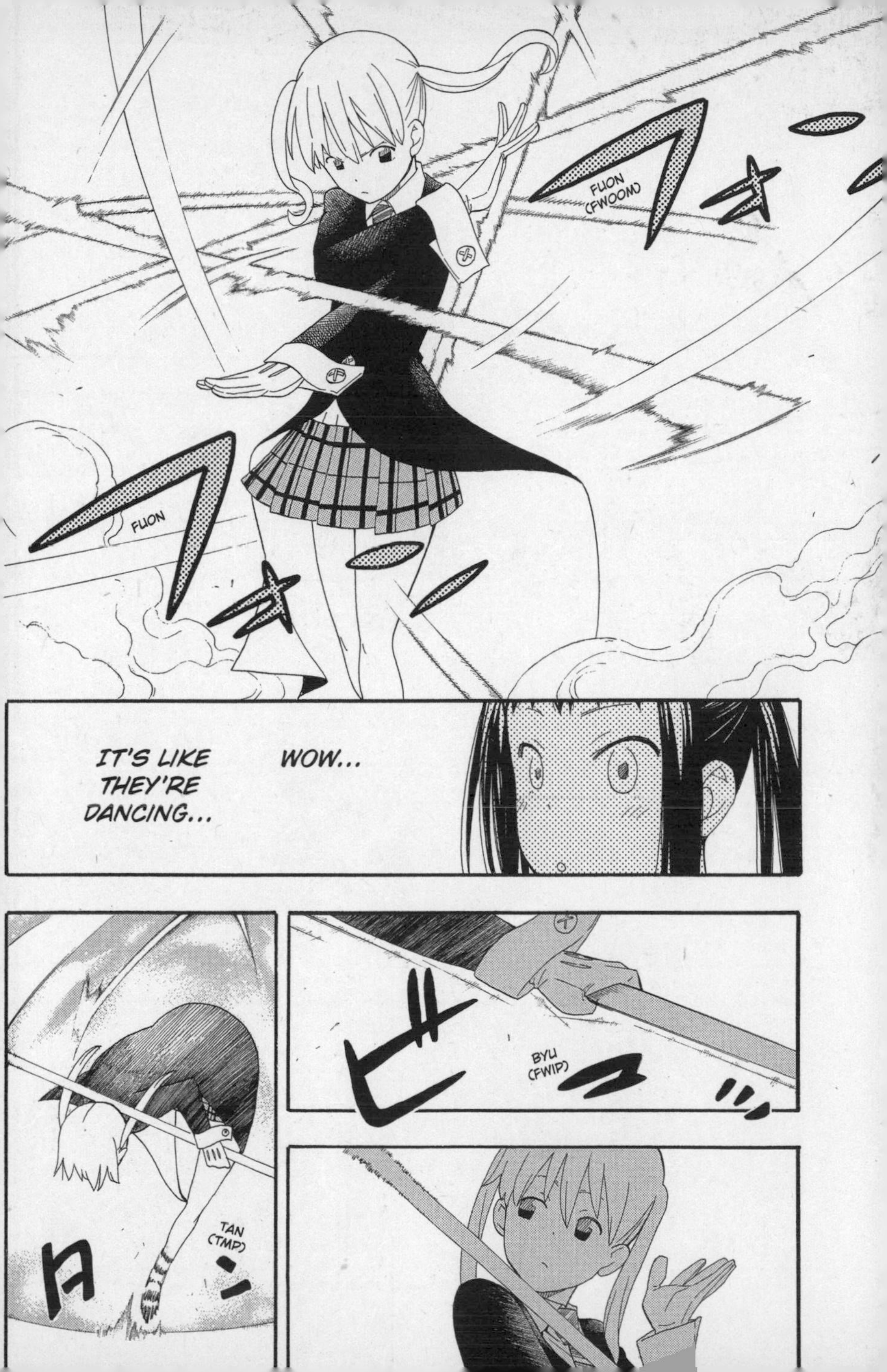
FUON (FWOOM)
FUON
WOW...
IT'S LIKE THEY'RE DANCING...
BYU (FWIP)
TAN (TMP)

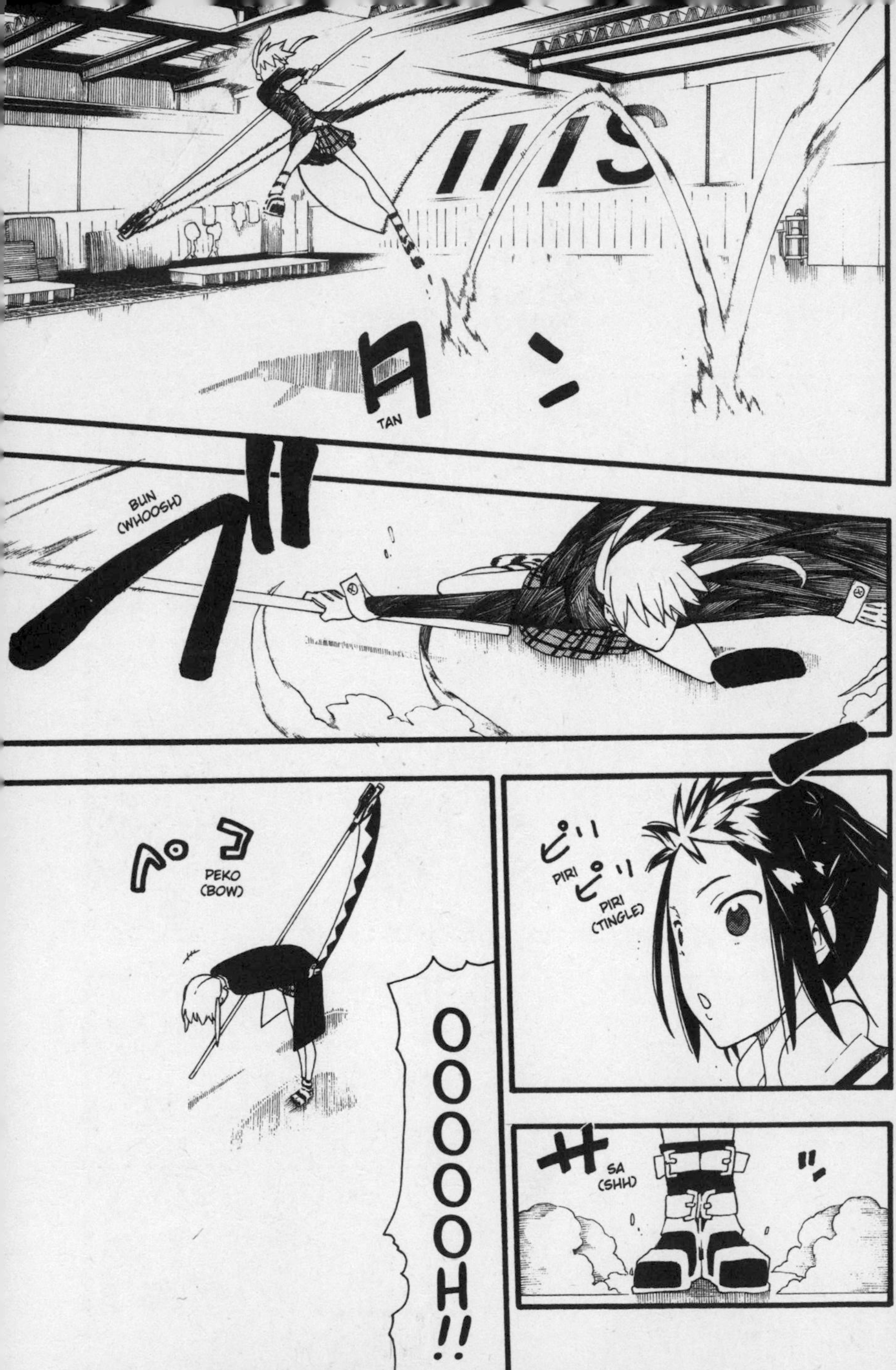
TAN
BUN (WHOOSH)
PIRI PIRI (TINGLE)
SA (SHH)
PEKO (BOW)
OOOOOH!!

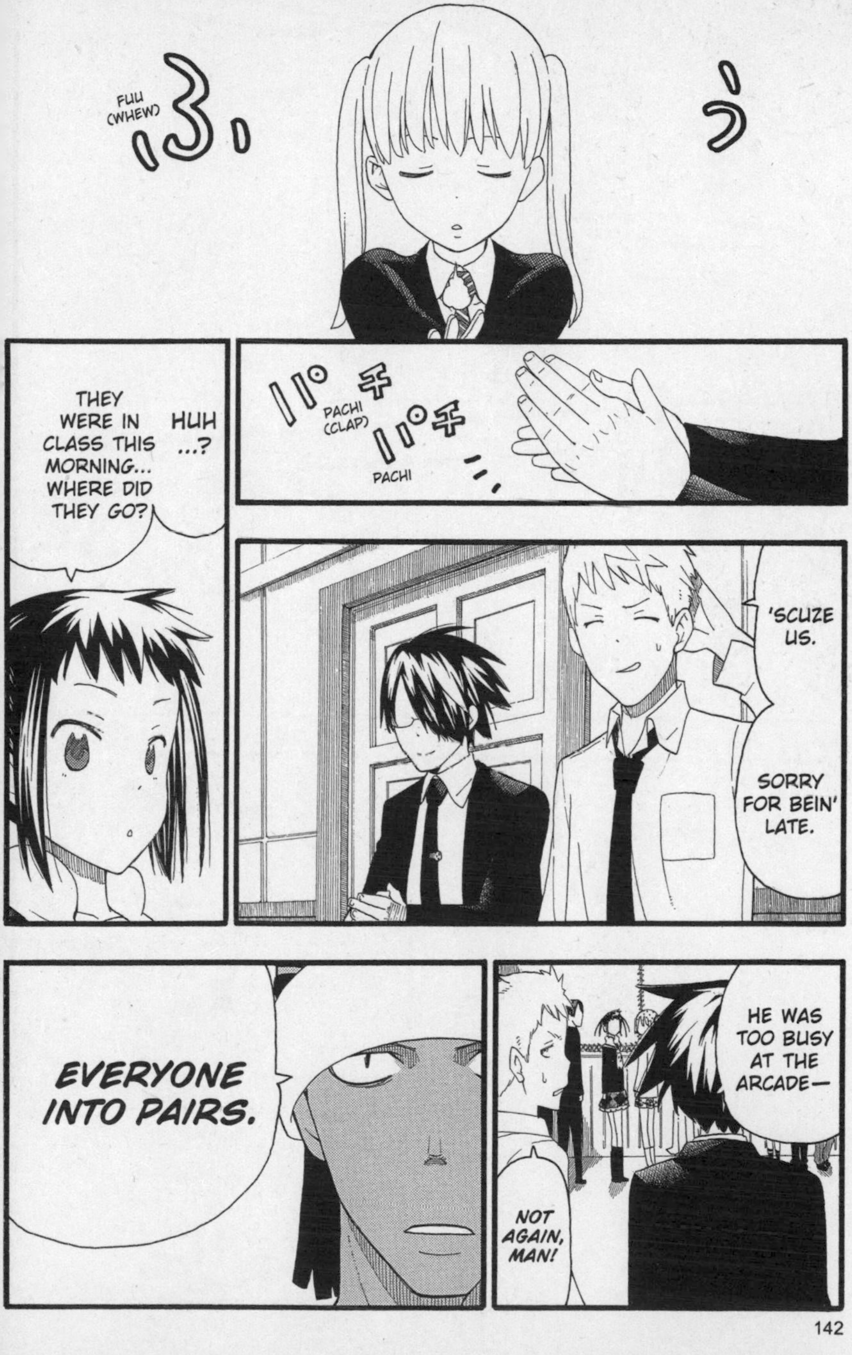
FUU (WHEW)
PACHI (CLAP)
PACHI
'SCUZE US.
SORRY FOR BEIN' LATE.
HUH ...?
THEY WERE IN CLASS THIS MORNING... WHERE DID THEY GO?
HE WAS TOO BUSY AT THE ARCADE—
NOT AGAIN, MAN!
EVERYONE INTO PAIRS.

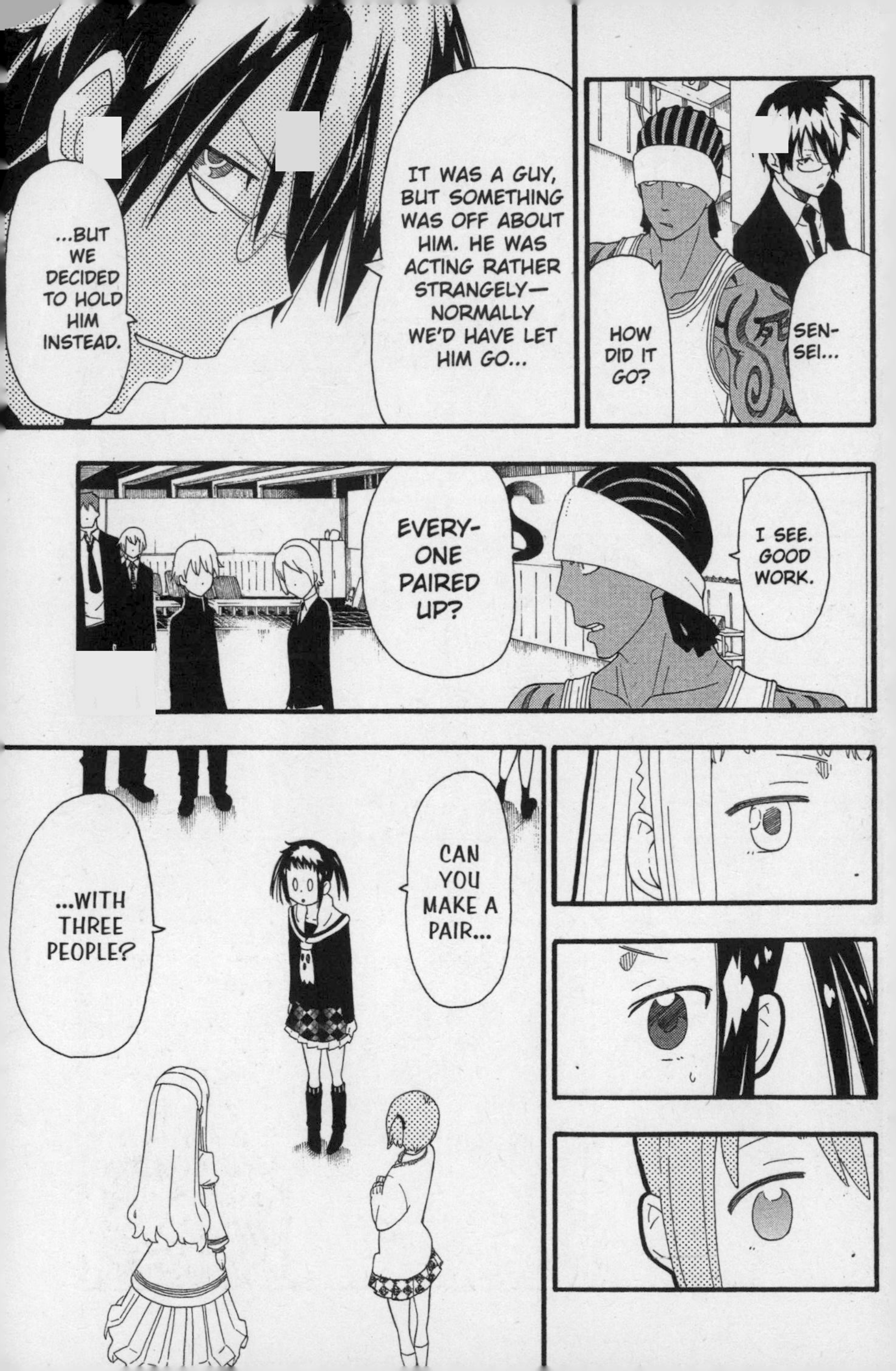
SEN-SEI...
HOW DID IT GO?
IT WAS A GUY, BUT SOMETHING WAS OFF ABOUT HIM. HE WAS ACTING RATHER STRANGELY—NORMALLY WE'D HAVE LET HIM GO...
...BUT WE DECIDED TO HOLD HIM INSTEAD.
I SEE. GOOD WORK.
EVERY-ONE PAIRED UP?
CAN YOU MAKE A PAIR...
...WITH THREE PEOPLE?

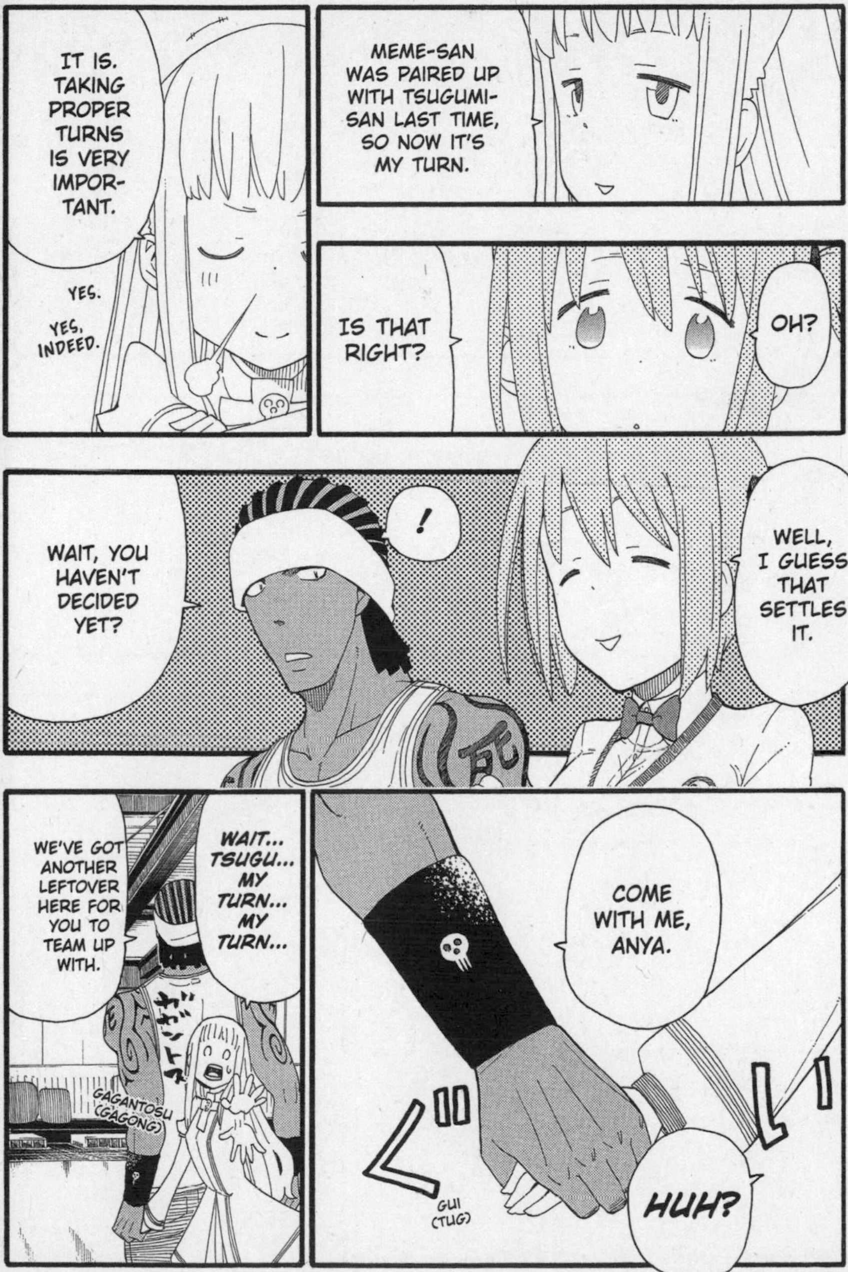
MEME-SAN WAS PAIRED UP WITH TSUGUMI-SAN LAST TIME, SO NOW IT'S MY TURN.
OH?
IS THAT RIGHT?
IT IS. TAKING PROPER TURNS IS VERY IMPORTANT.
YES.
YES, INDEED.
WELL, I GUESS THAT SETTLES IT.
!
WAIT, YOU HAVEN'T DECIDED YET?
COME WITH ME, ANYA.
GUI (TUG)
HUH?
WAIT... TSUGU... MY TURN... MY TURN...
WE'VE GOT ANOTHER LEFTOVER HERE FOR YOU TO TEAM UP WITH.
GAGANTOSU (GAGONG)

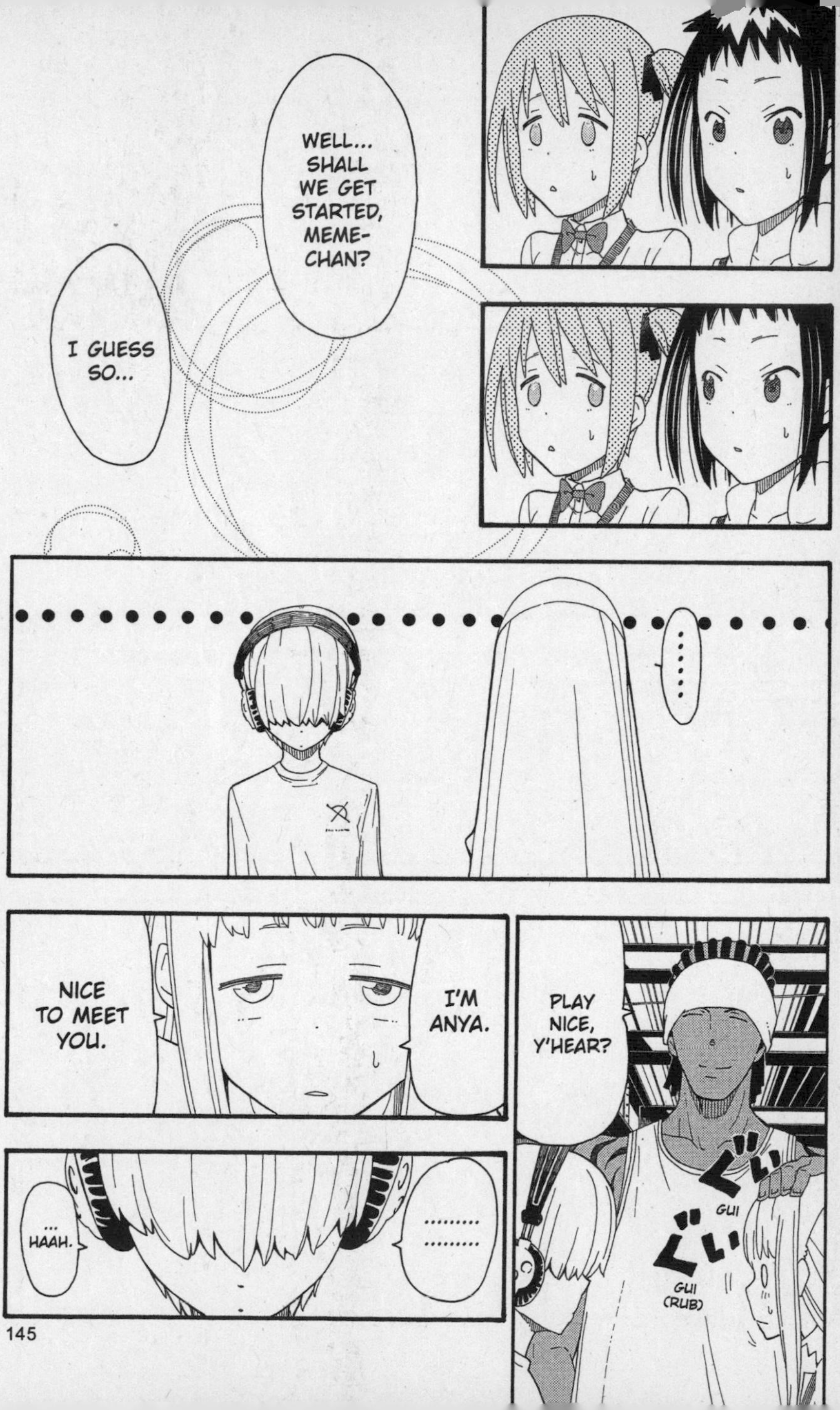
WELL... SHALL WE GET STARTED, MEME-CHAN?
I GUESS SO...
......
PLAY NICE, Y'HEAR?
GUI
GUI (RUB)
I'M ANYA.
NICE TO MEET YOU.
....
... HAAH.

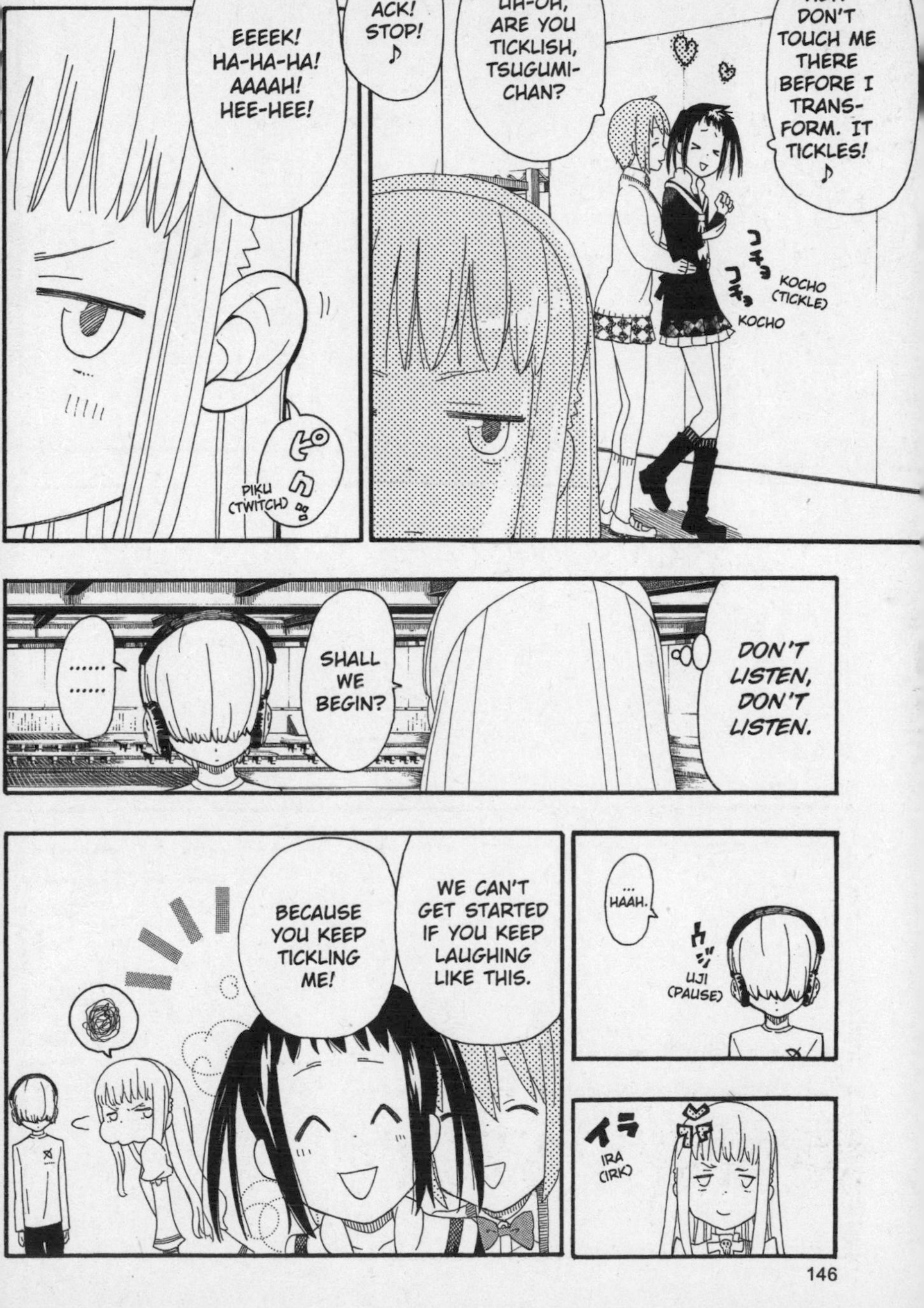
HEY! DON'T TOUCH ME THERE BEFORE I TRANS-FORM. IT TICKLES! ♪
UH-OH, ARE YOU TICKLISH, TSUGUMI-CHAN?
ACK! STOP! ♪
KOCHO (TICKLE)
KOCHO
EEEEK! HA-HA-HA! AAAAH! HEE-HEE!
PIKU (TWITCH)
DON'T LISTEN, DON'T LISTEN.
SHALL WE BEGIN?
....
... HAAH.
UJI (PAUSE)
IRA (IRK)
WE CAN'T GET STARTED IF YOU KEEP LAUGHING LIKE THIS.
BECAUSE YOU KEEP TICKLING ME!

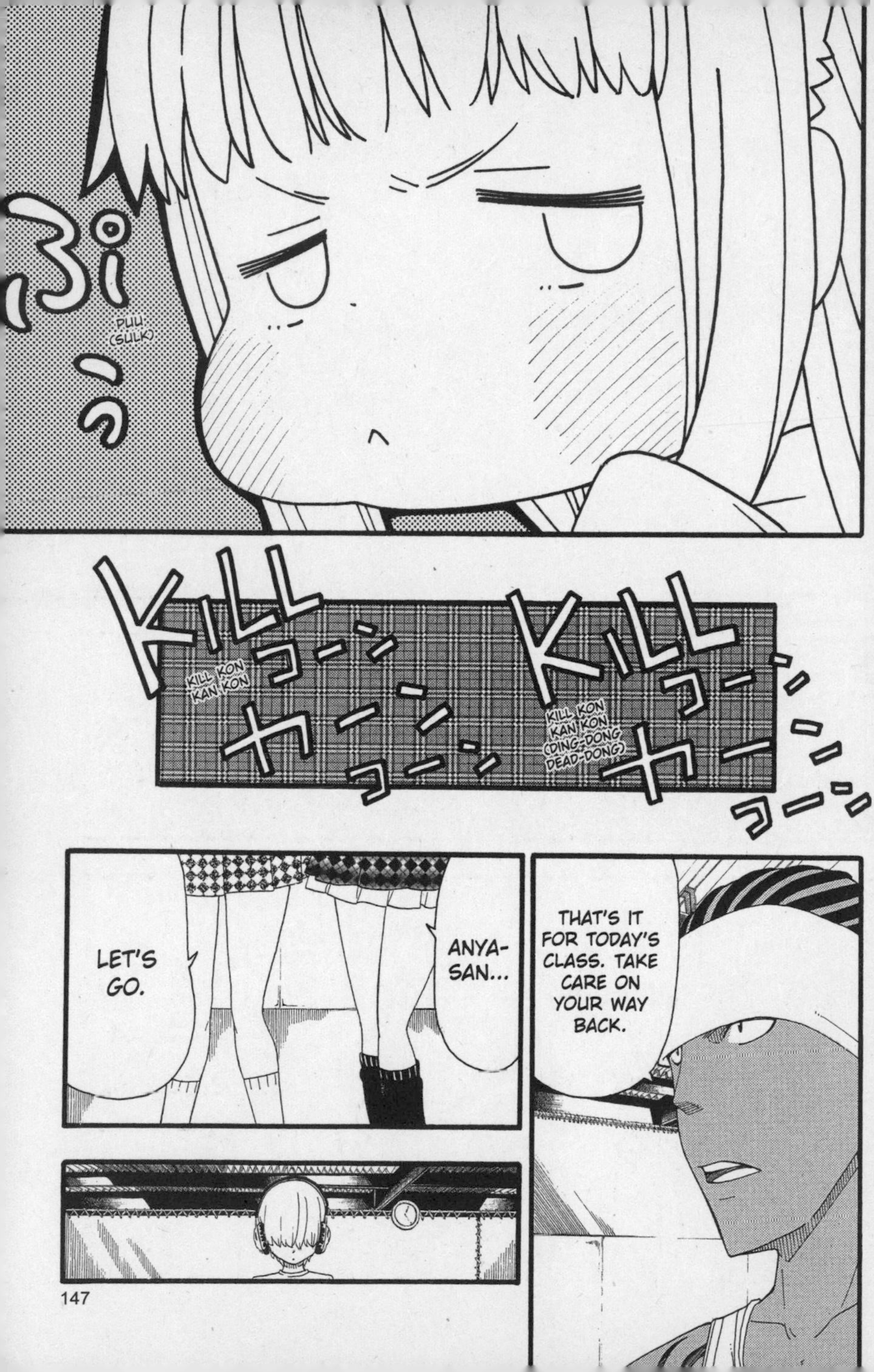
PUU (SULK)
KILL KON KAN KON (DING-DONG DEAD-DONG)
KILL KON KAN KON
THAT'S IT FOR TODAY'S CLASS. TAKE CARE ON YOUR WAY BACK.
ANYA-SAN...
LET'S GO.

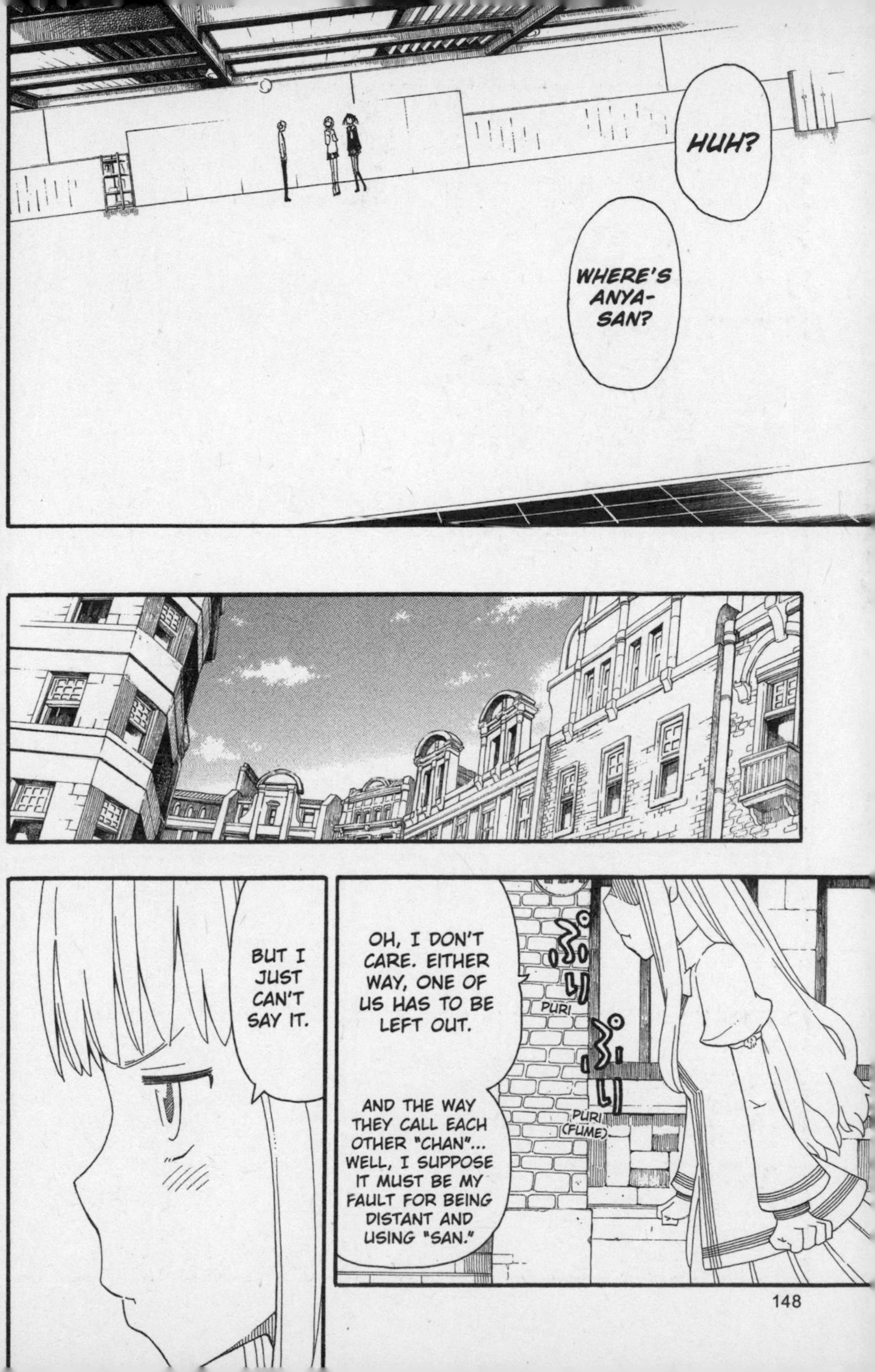
HUH?
WHERE'S ANYA-SAN?
OH, I DON'T CARE. EITHER WAY, ONE OF US HAS TO BE LEFT OUT.
PURI
PURI (FUME)
AND THE WAY THEY CALL EACH OTHER "CHAN"... WELL, I SUPPOSE IT MUST BE MY FAULT FOR BEING DISTANT AND USING "SAN."
BUT I JUST CAN'T SAY IT.

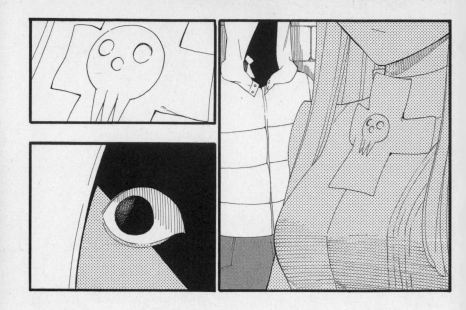

YOU'RE
FROM
DWMA.

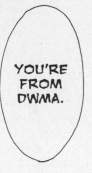

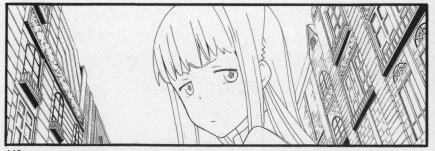

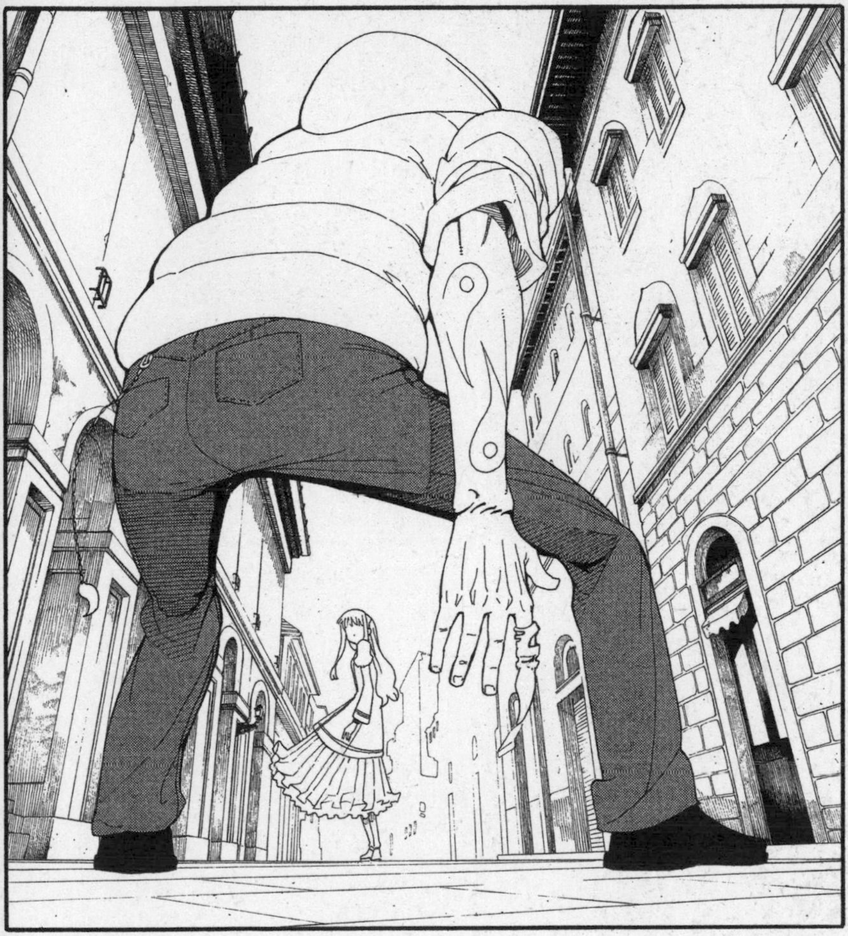

DID YOU
SLEEP WELL LAST
NIGHT?

SOUL EATER NOT!

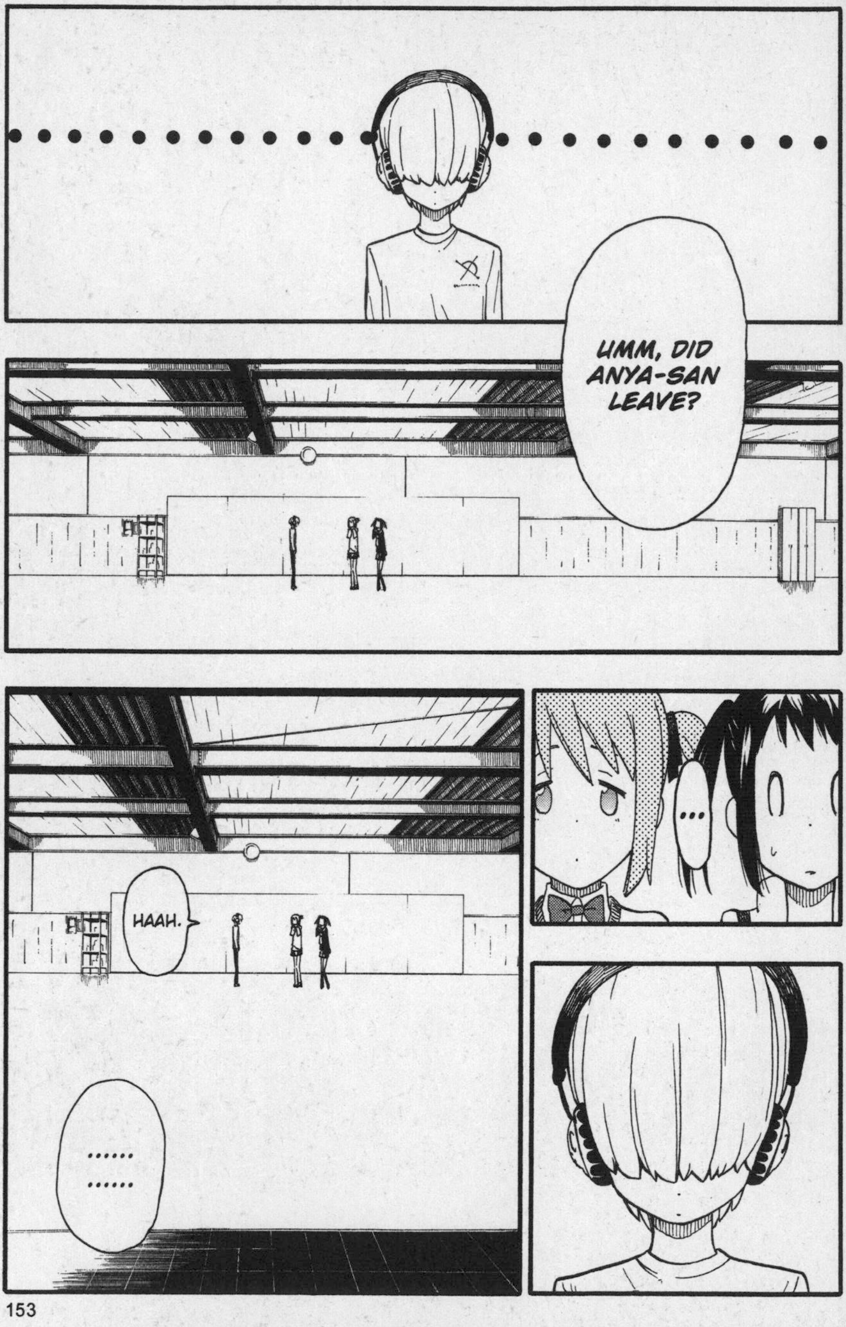
UMM, DID ANYA-SAN LEAVE?
...
HAAH.
......
......

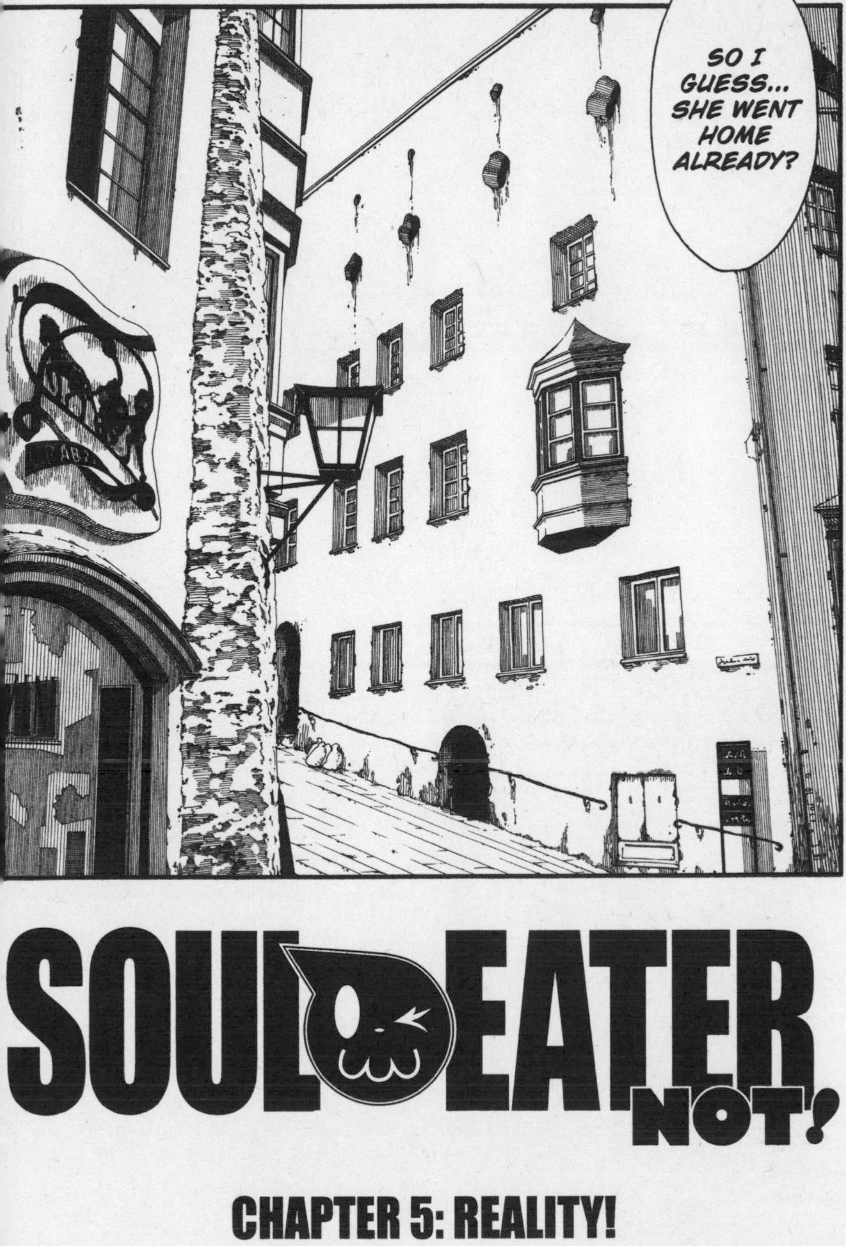
SO I GUESS... SHE WENT HOME ALREADY?

SOUL EATER NOT!

CHAPTER 5: REALITY!

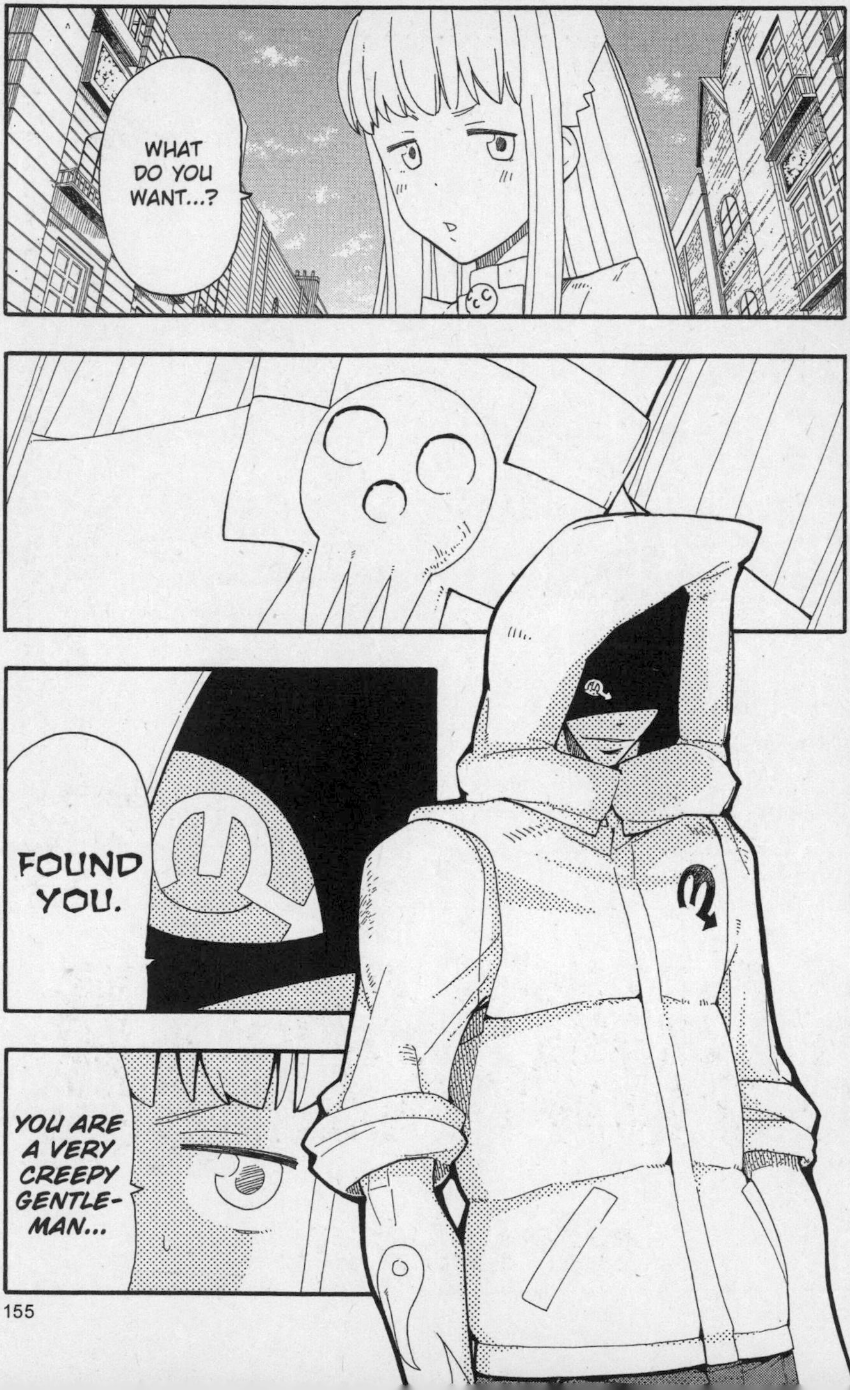
WHAT DO YOU WANT...?
FOUND YOU.
YOU ARE A VERY CREEPY GENTLE-MAN...

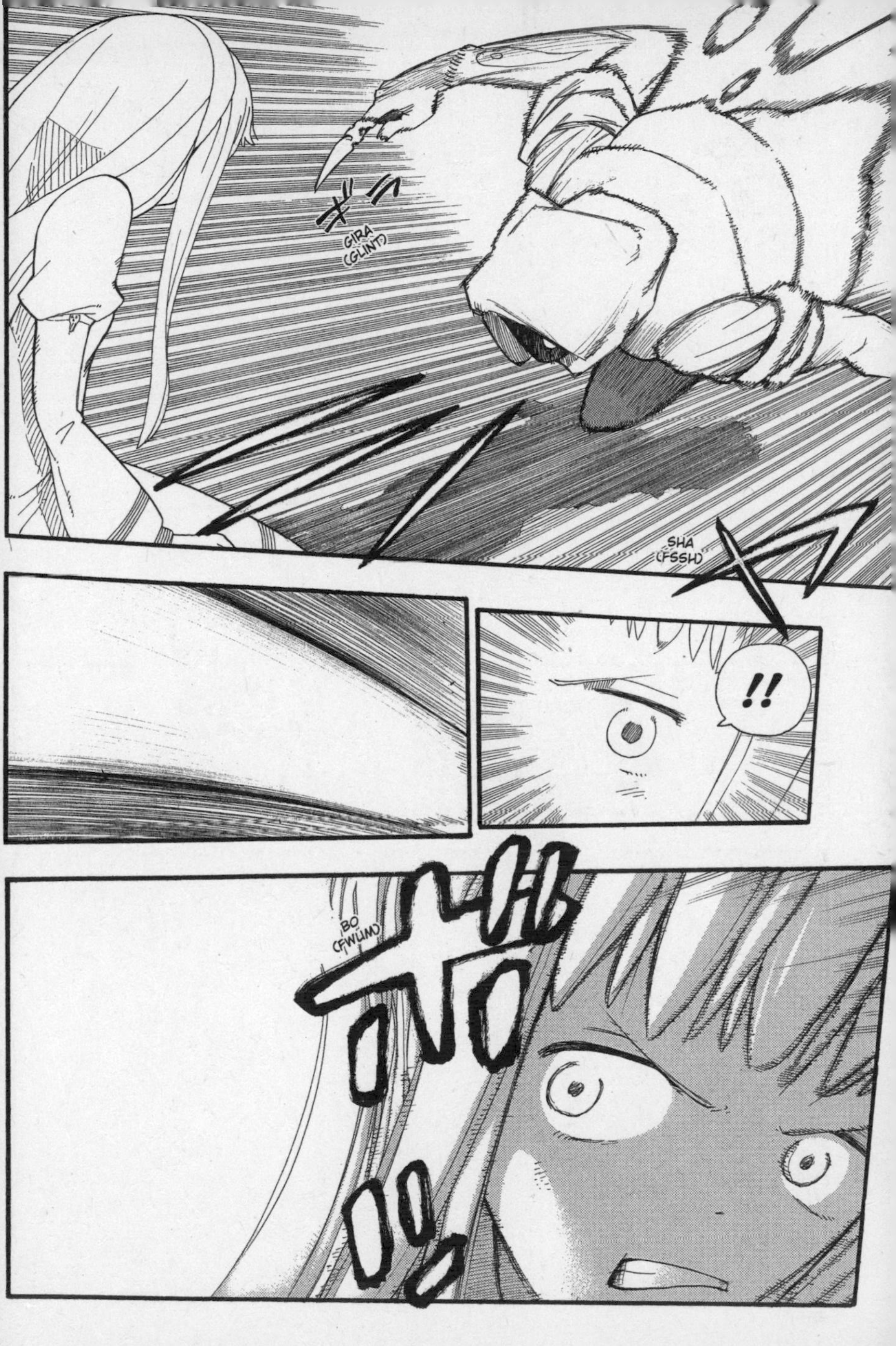
GIRA (GLINT)
SHA (FSSH)
!!
BO (FWUM)

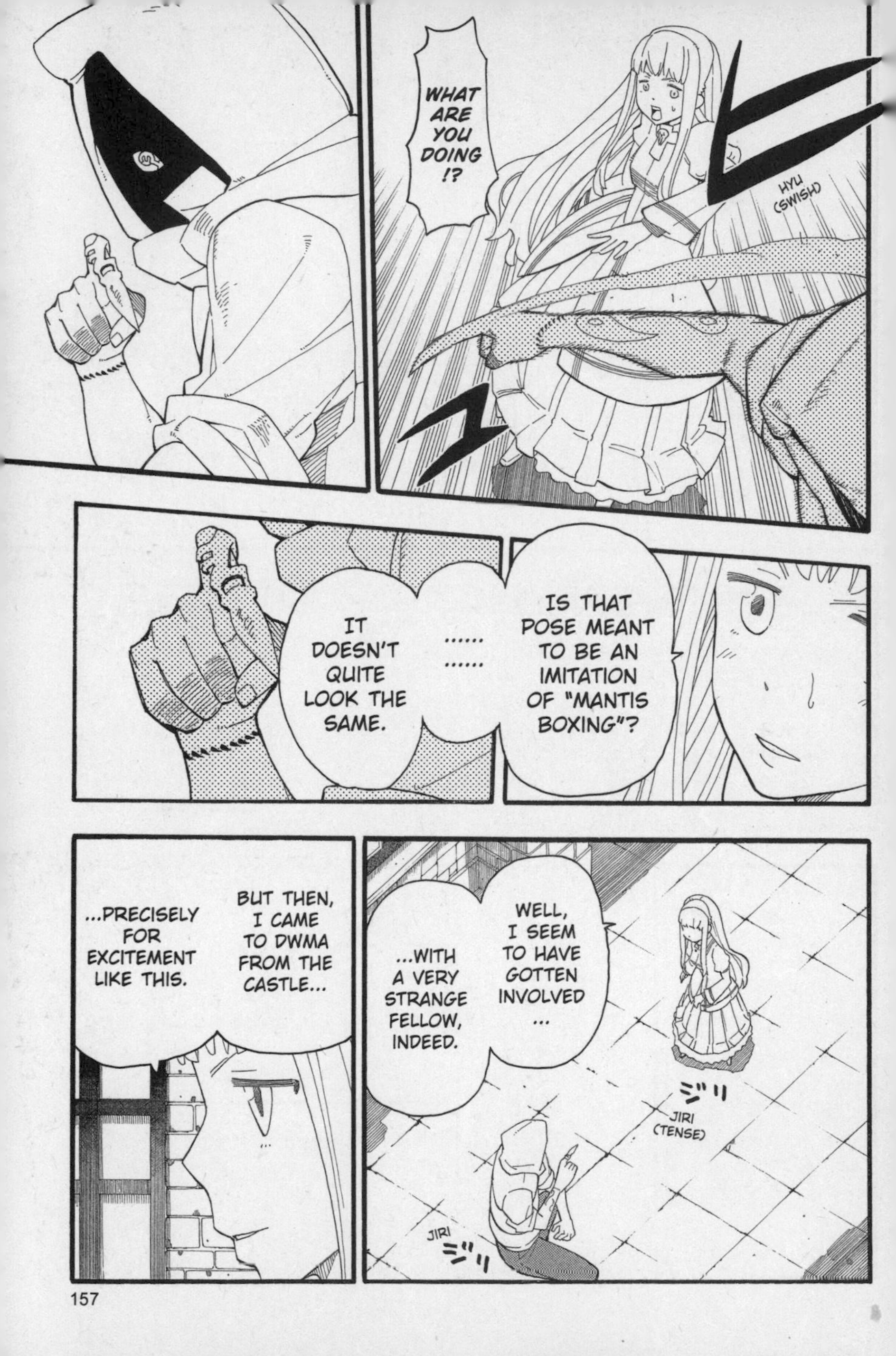

WHAT ARE YOU DOING !?
HYU (SWISH)
IS THAT POSE MEANT TO BE AN IMITATION OF "MANTIS BOXING"?
....
IT DOESN'T QUITE LOOK THE SAME.
WELL, I SEEM TO HAVE GOTTEN INVOLVED ...
...WITH A VERY STRANGE FELLOW, INDEED.
ジリ
JIRI (TENSE)
JIRI
ジリ
BUT THEN, I CAME TO DWMA FROM THE CASTLE...
...PRECISELY FOR EXCITEMENT LIKE THIS.

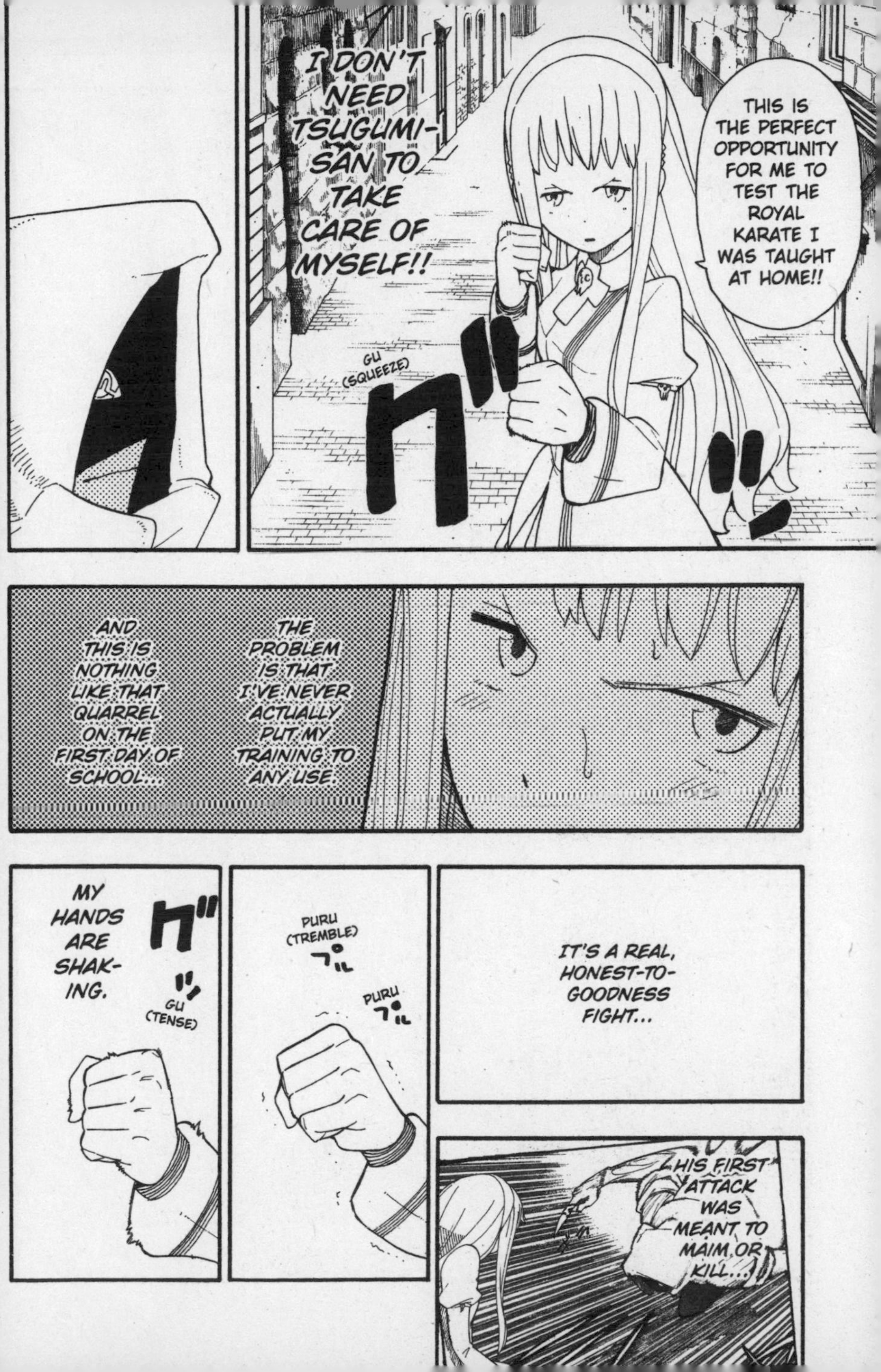
THIS IS THE PERFECT OPPORTUNITY FOR ME TO TEST THE ROYAL KARATE I WAS TAUGHT AT HOME!!
I DON'T NEED TSUGUMI-SAN TO TAKE CARE OF MYSELF!!
GU (SQUEEZE)
THE PROBLEM IS THAT I'VE NEVER ACTUALLY PUT MY TRAINING TO ANY USE.
AND THIS IS NOTHING LIKE THAT QUARREL ON THE FIRST DAY OF SCHOOL...
IT'S A REAL, HONEST-TO-GOODNESS FIGHT...
HIS FIRST ATTACK WAS MEANT TO MAIM OR KILL...
PURU (TREMBLE)
PURU
MY HANDS ARE SHAKING.
GU (TENSE)

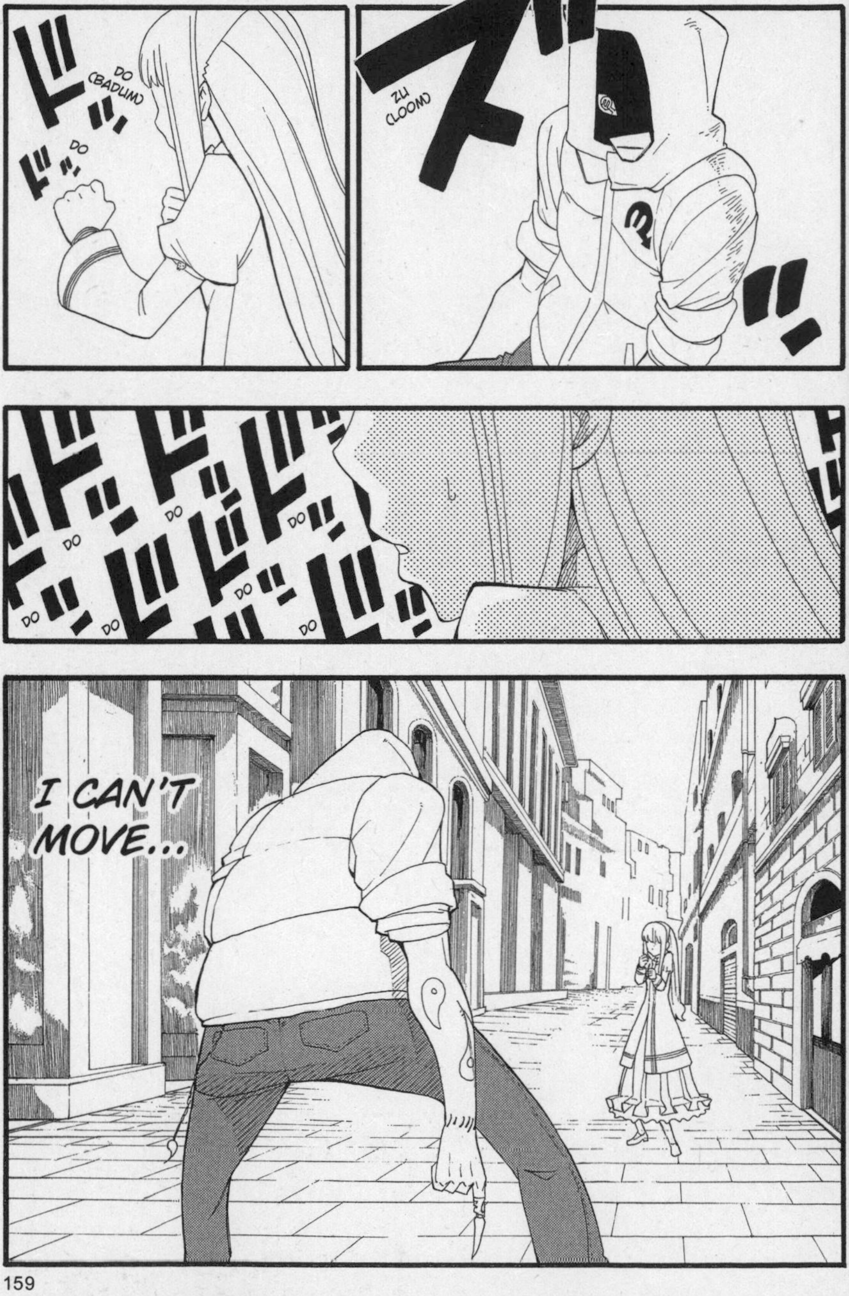
ZU
(LOOM)
DO
(BADUM)
DO
DO
DO
DO
DO
DO
DO
I CAN'T MOVE...

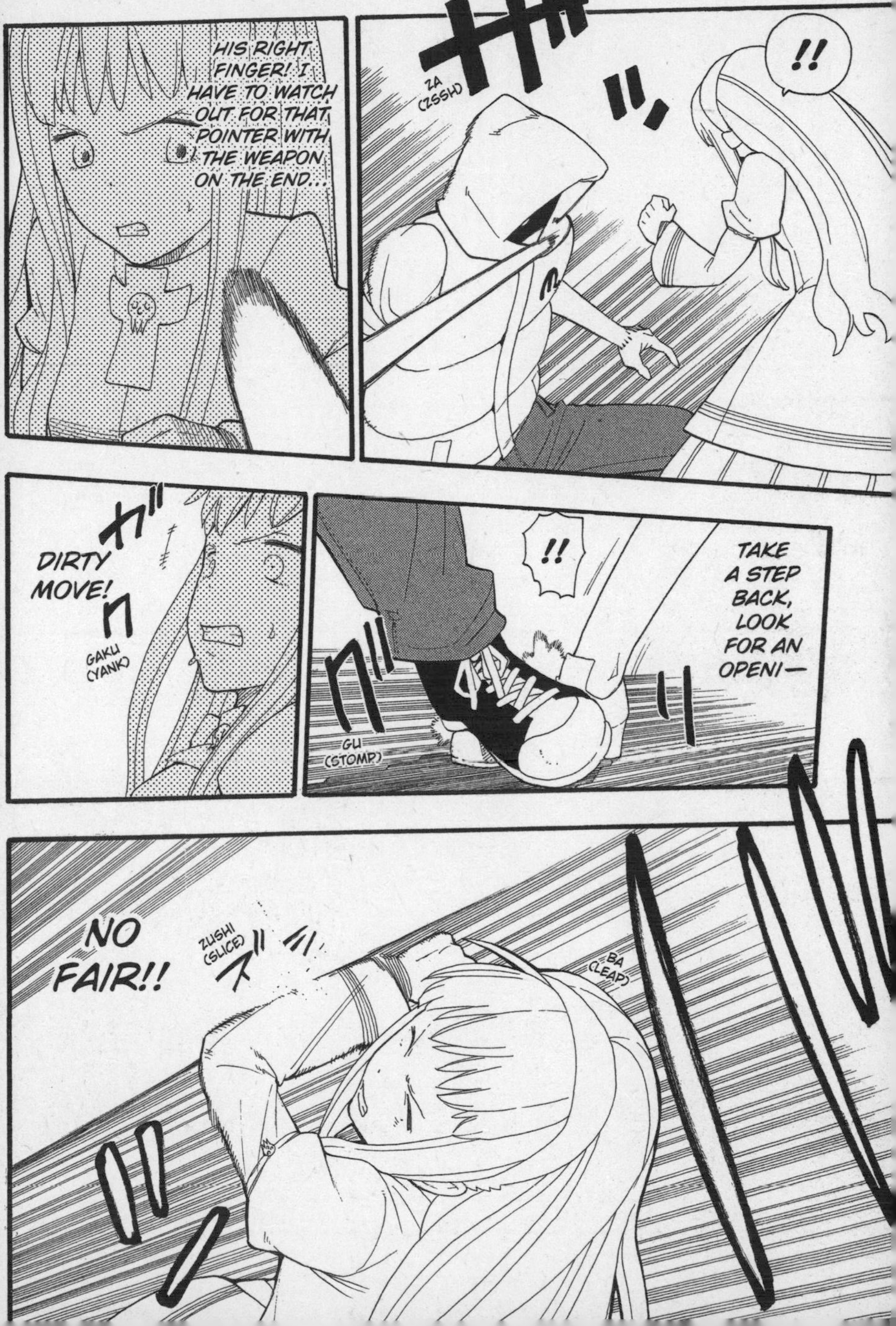
!!
ZA (ZSSH)
HIS RIGHT FINGER! I HAVE TO WATCH OUT FOR THAT POINTER WITH THE WEAPON ON THE END...
TAKE A STEP BACK, LOOK FOR AN OPENI—
!!
GU (STOMP)
DIRTY MOVE!
GAKU (YANK)
BA (LEAP)
ZUSHI (SLICE)
NO FAIR!!

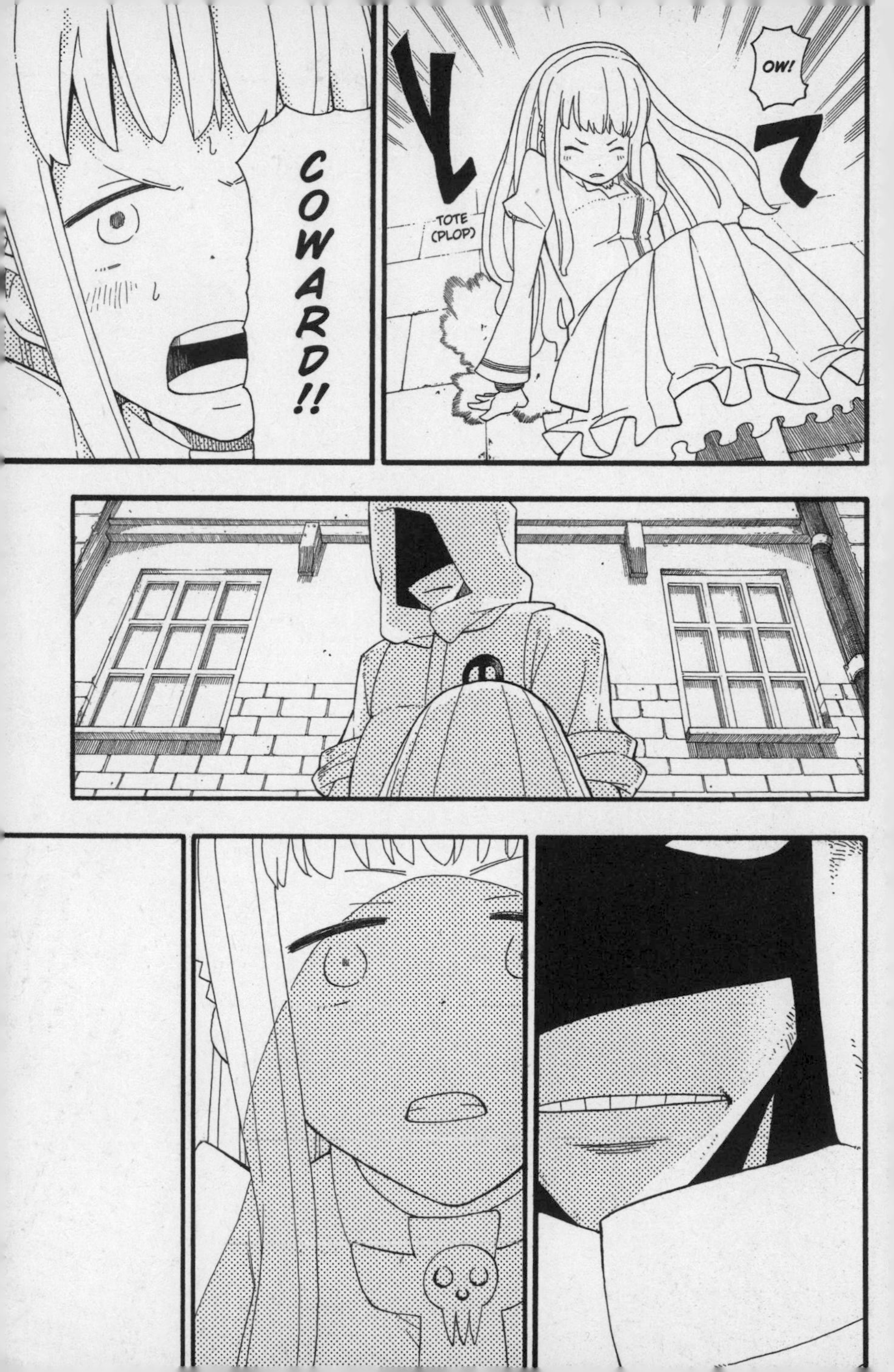
OW!
TOTE
(PLOP)
COWARD!!

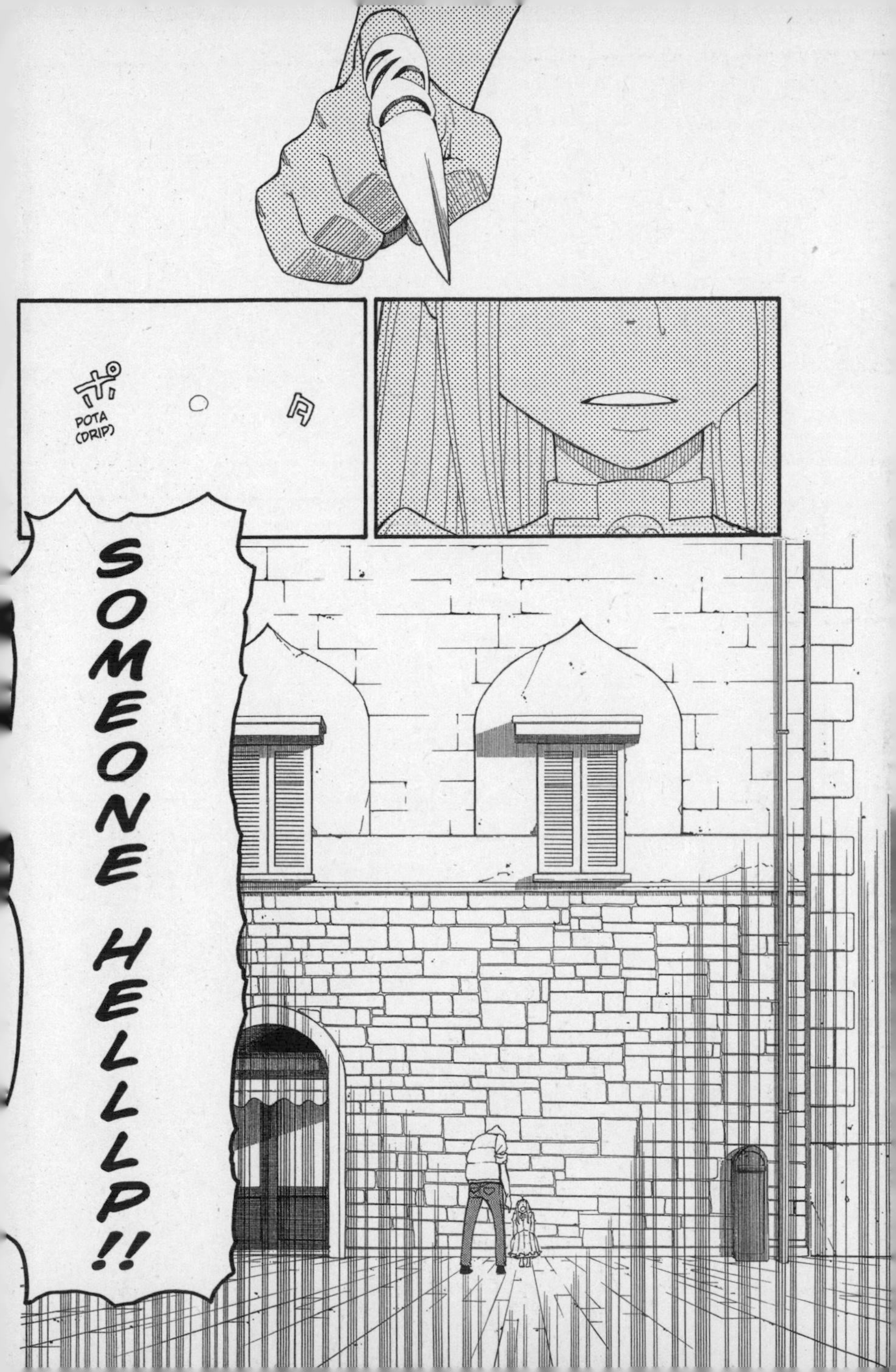
ポ
POTA
(DRIP)
SOMEONE HELLLP!!

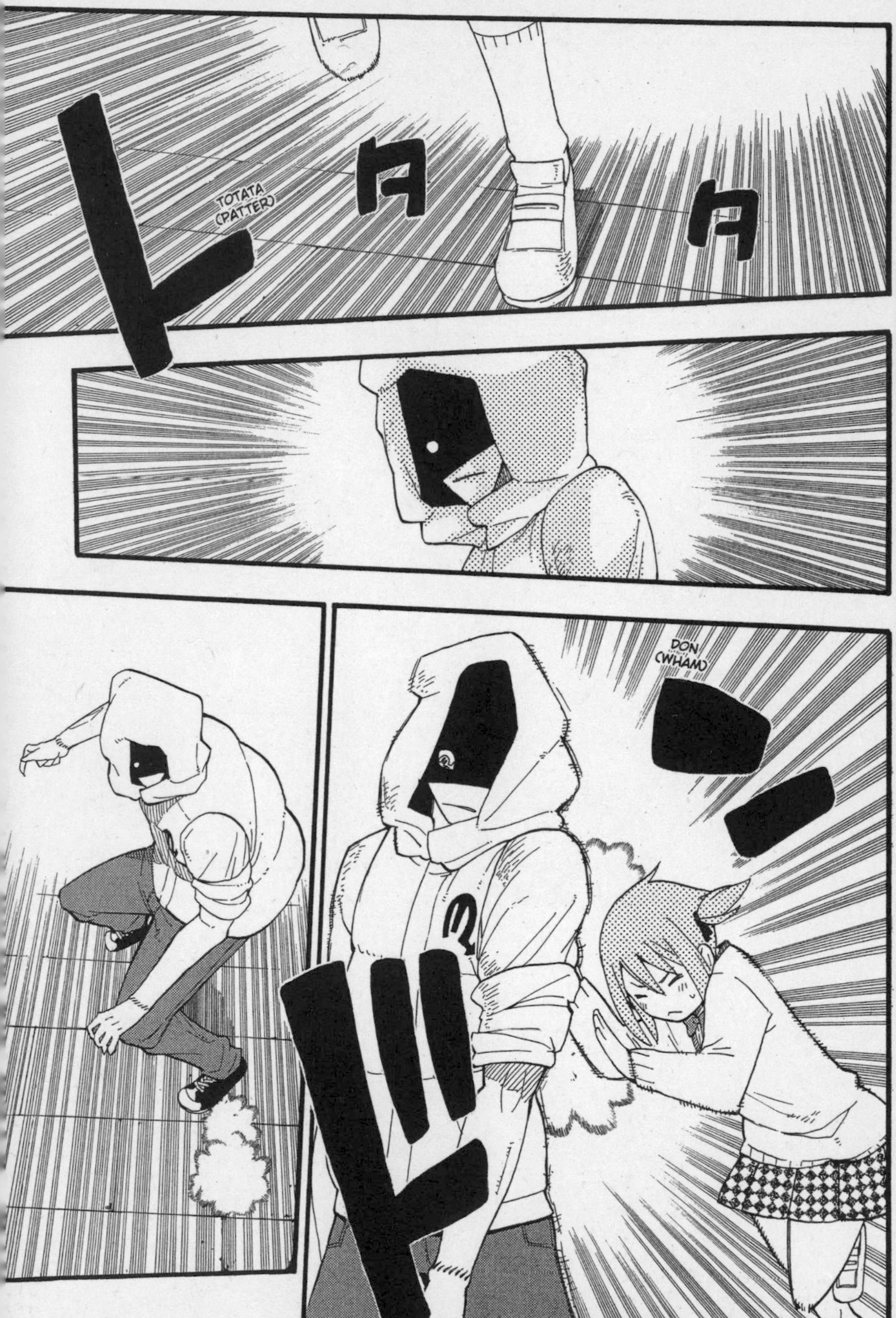
TOTATA
(PATTER)
DON
(WHAM)

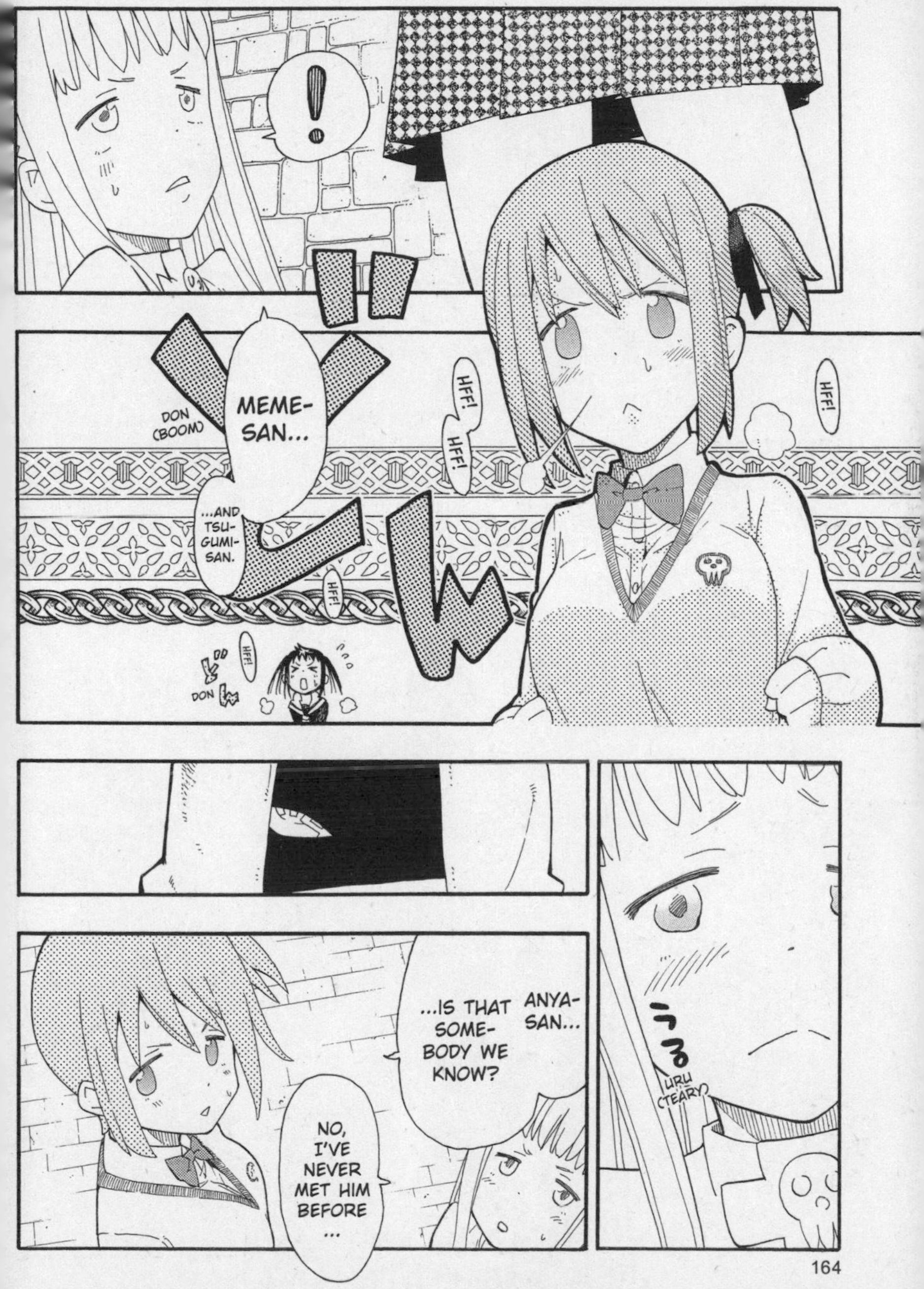
!
HFF!
HFF! HFF!
MEME-SAN...
DON (BOOM)
...AND TSUGUMI-SAN.
HFF!
HFF!
DON DON
URU (TEARY)
ANYA-SAN...
...IS THAT SOMEBODY WE KNOW?
NO, I'VE NEVER MET HIM BEFORE...

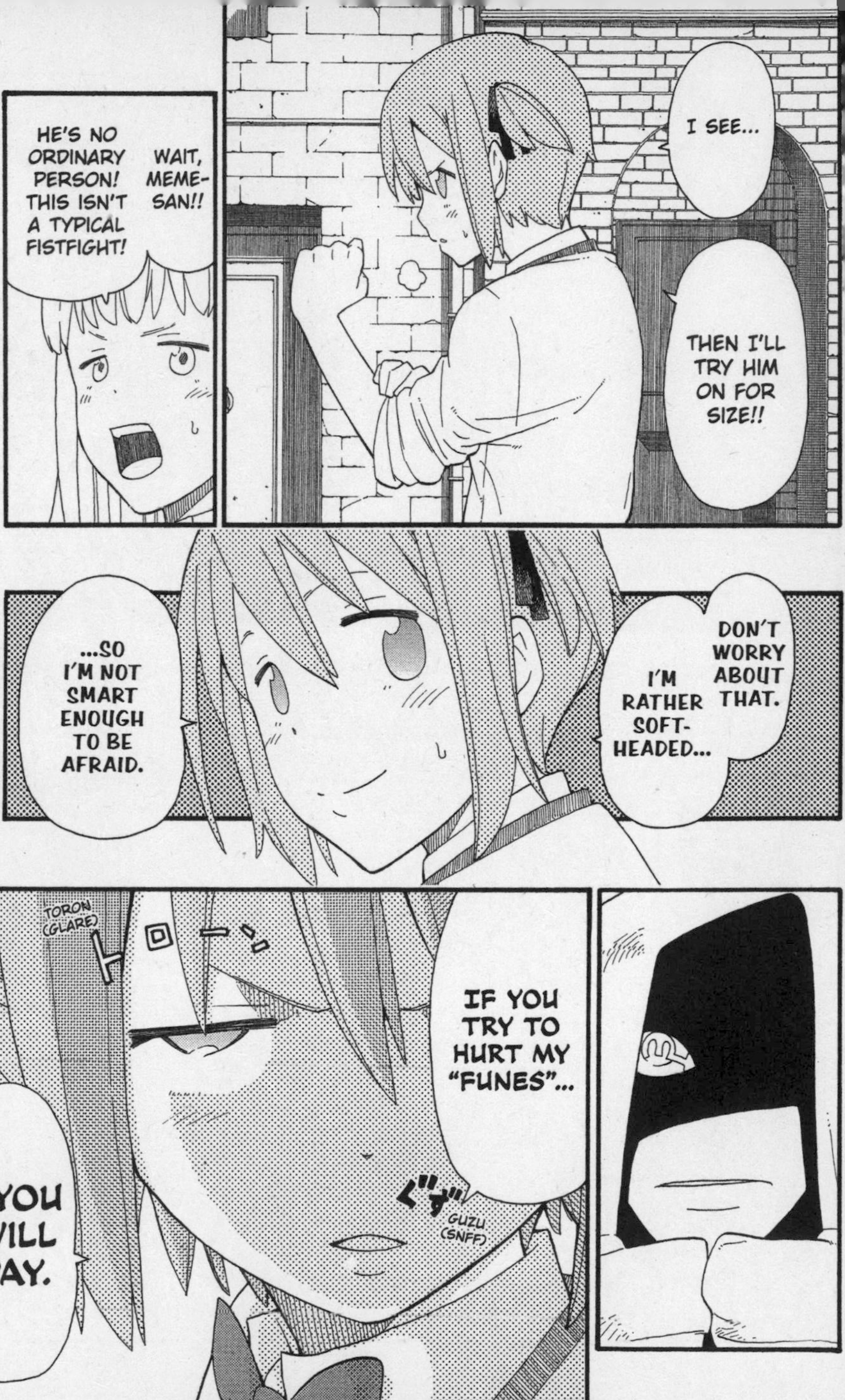

I SEE...
THEN I'LL TRY HIM ON FOR SIZE!!
WAIT, MEME-SAN!!
HE'S NO ORDINARY PERSON! THIS ISN'T A TYPICAL FISTFIGHT!
DON'T WORRY ABOUT THAT.
I'M RATHER SOFT-HEADED...
...SO I'M NOT SMART ENOUGH TO BE AFRAID.
トローン
TORON (GLARE)
IF YOU TRY TO HURT MY "FUNES"...
ぐず
GUZU (SNFF)
...YOU WILL PAY.

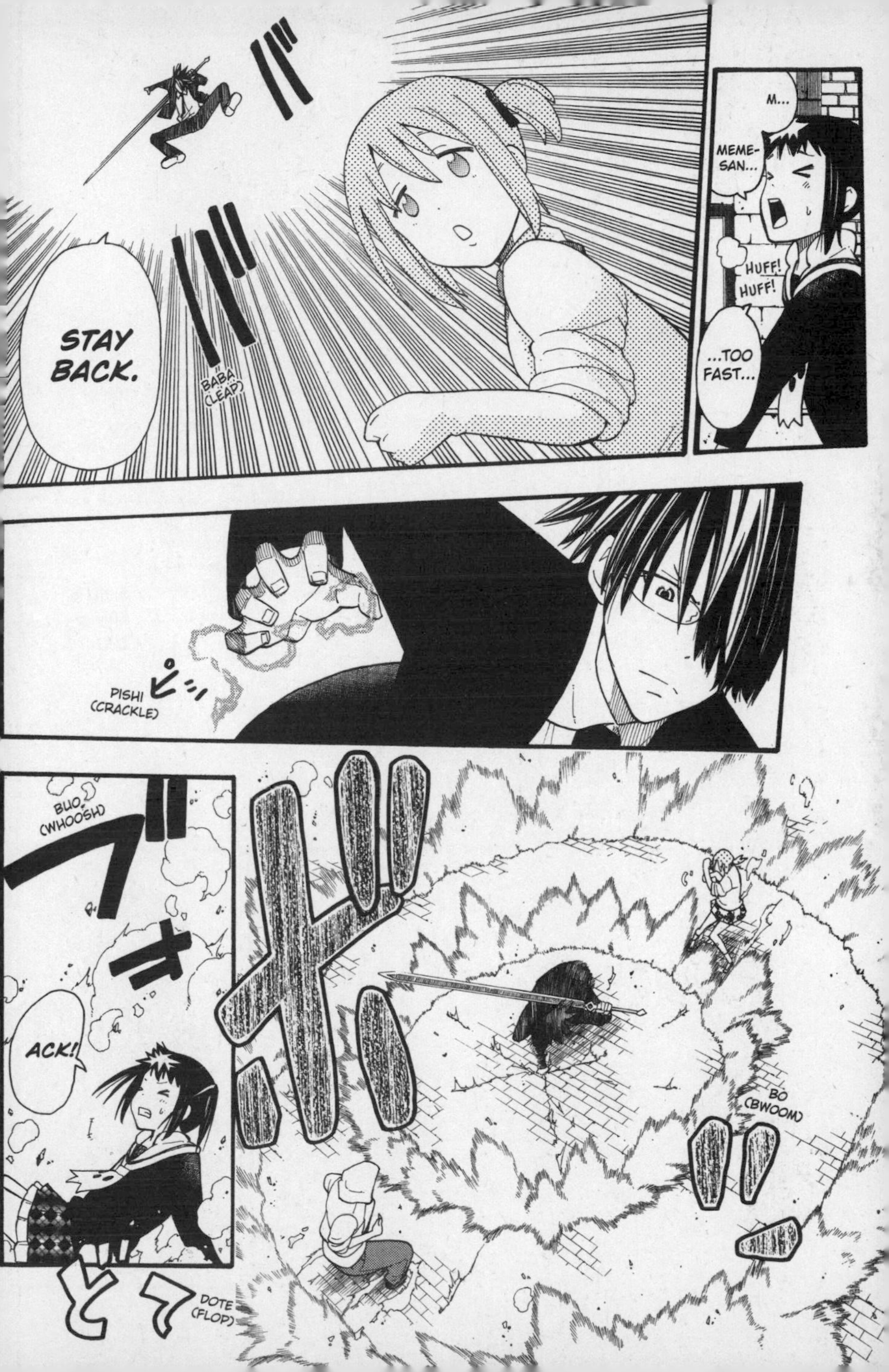
M...
MEME-SAN...
HUFF! HUFF!
...TOO FAST...
STAY BACK.
BABA (LEAP)
PISHI (CRACKLE)
BO (BWOOM)
BUO (WHOOSH)
ACK!
DOTE (FLOP)

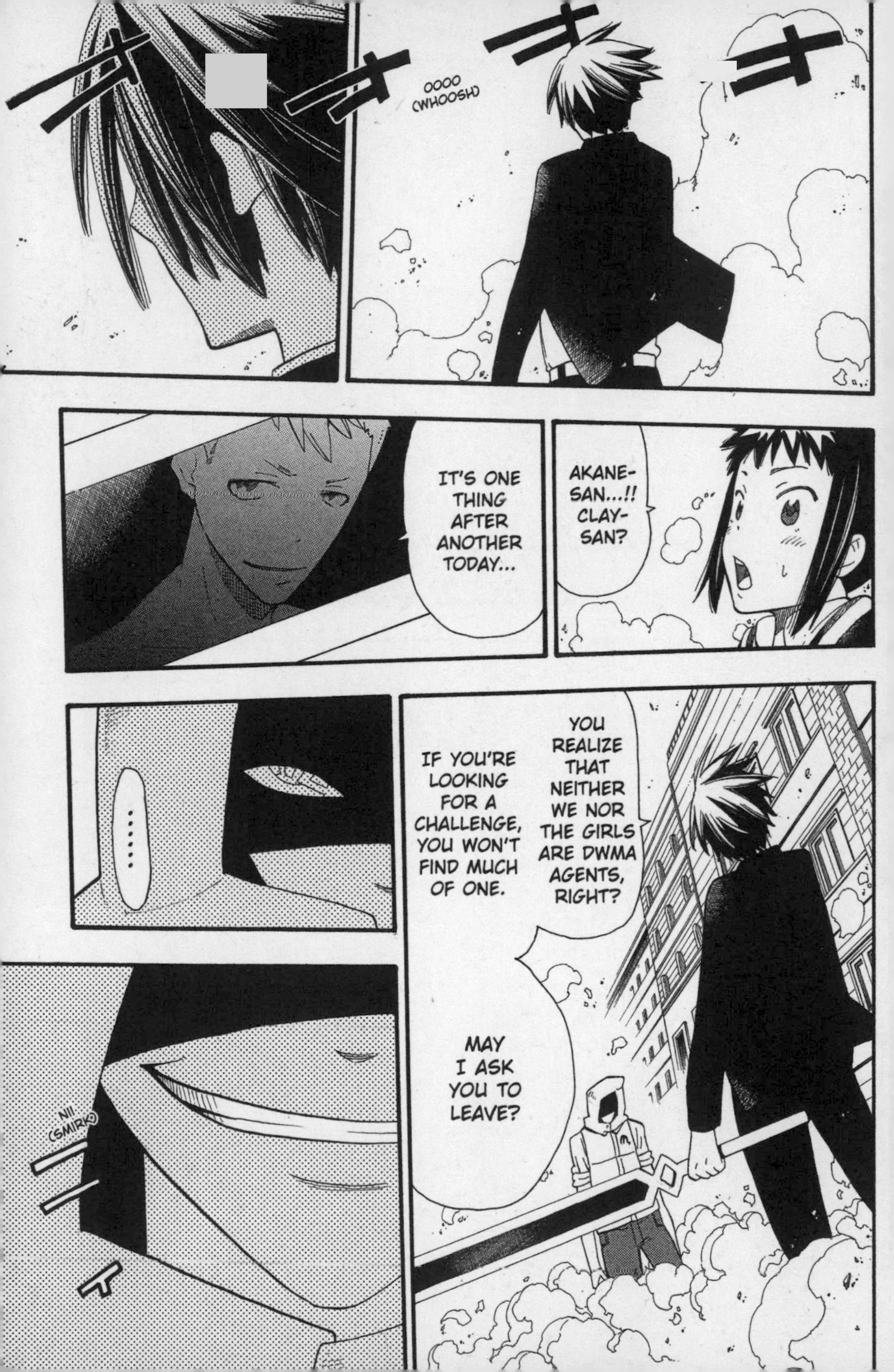
OOOO (WHOOSH)
AKANE-SAN...!! CLAY-SAN?
IT'S ONE THING AFTER ANOTHER TODAY...
YOU REALIZE THAT NEITHER WE NOR THE GIRLS ARE DWMA AGENTS, RIGHT?
IF YOU'RE LOOKING FOR A CHALLENGE, YOU WON'T FIND MUCH OF ONE.
MAY I ASK YOU TO LEAVE?
......
NII (SMIRK)

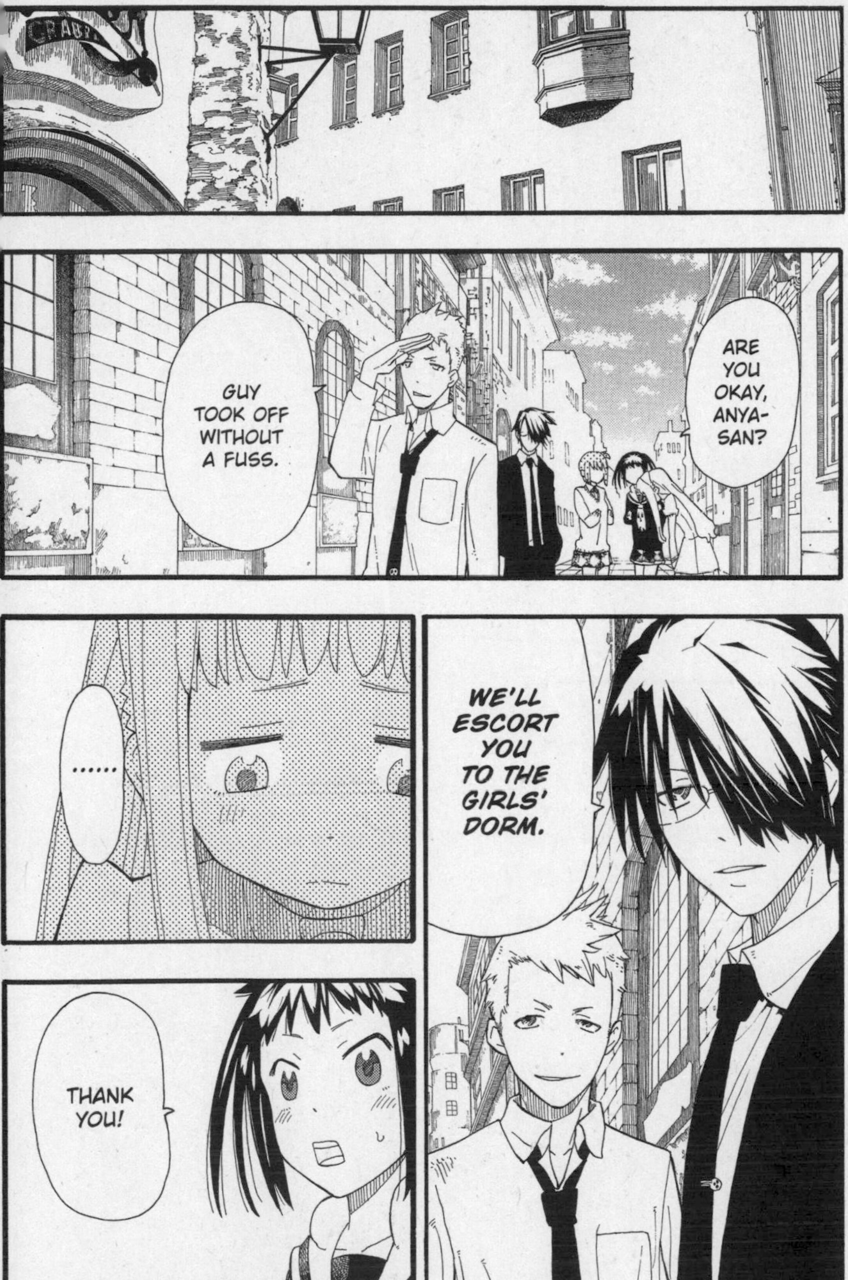
ARE YOU OKAY, ANYA-SAN?
GUY TOOK OFF WITHOUT A FUSS.
WE'LL ESCORT YOU TO THE GIRLS' DORM.
......
THANK YOU!

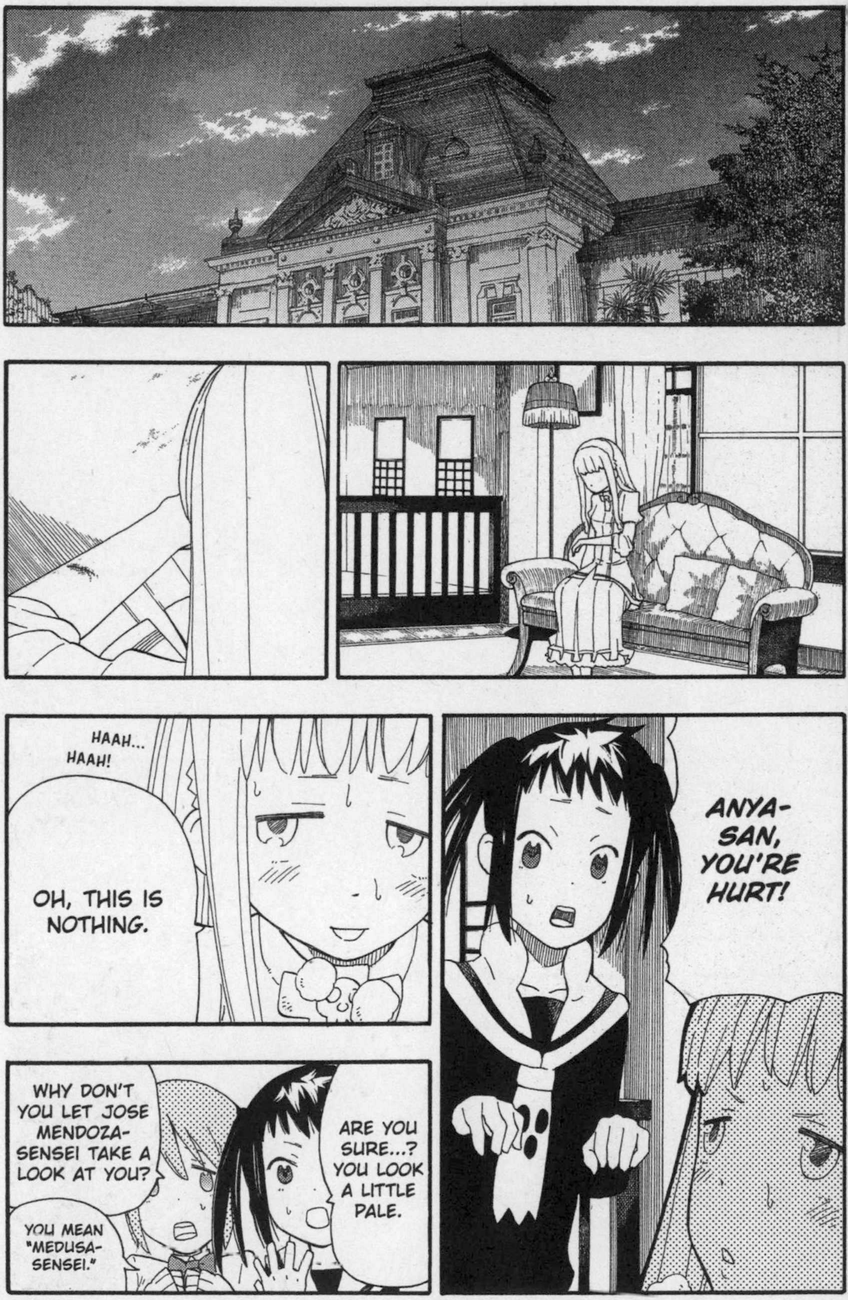
ANYA-SAN, YOU'RE HURT!
HAAH... HAAH!
OH, THIS IS NOTHING.
ARE YOU SURE...? YOU LOOK A LITTLE PALE.
WHY DON'T YOU LET JOSE MENDOZA-SENSEI TAKE A LOOK AT YOU?
YOU MEAN "MEDUSA-SENSEI."

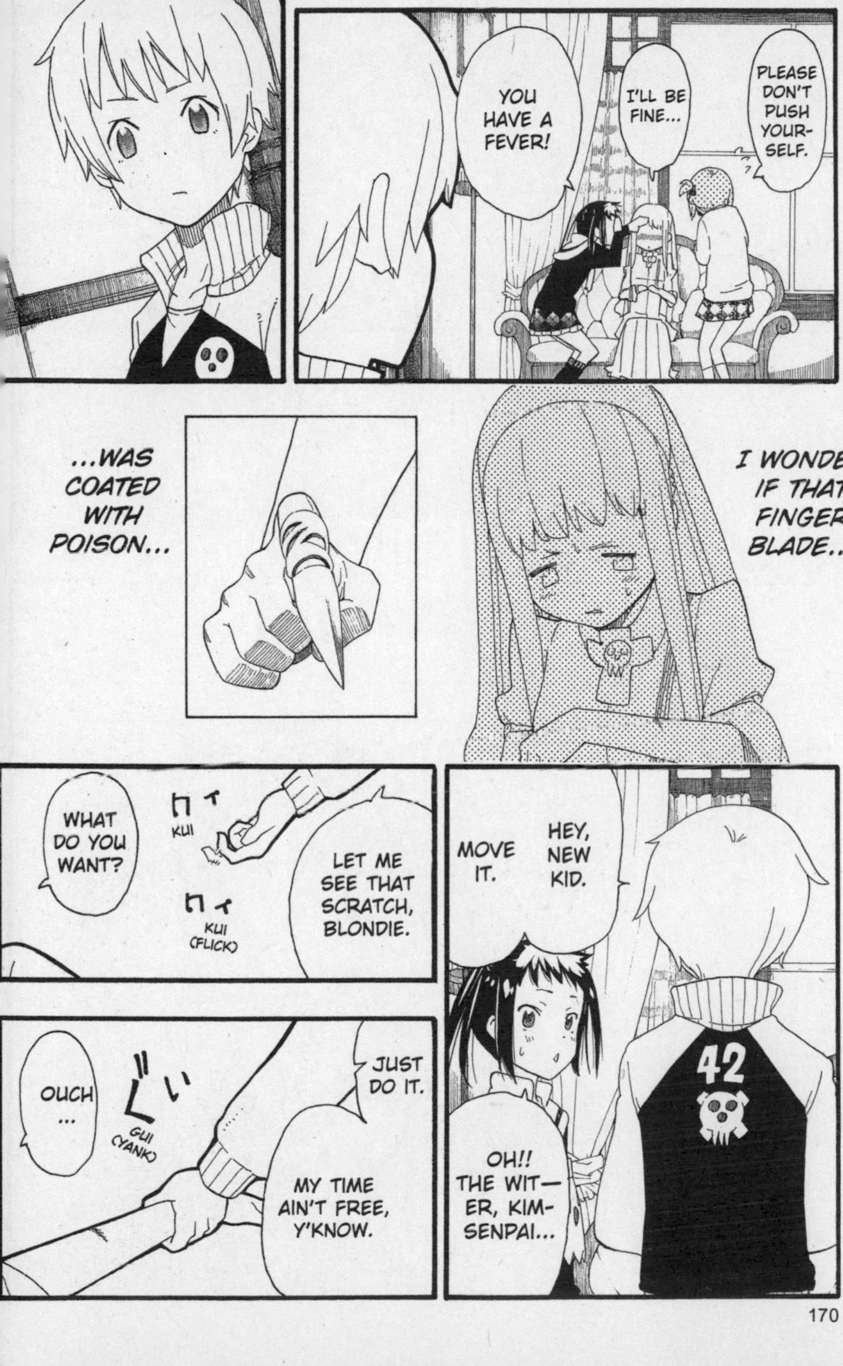
PLEASE DON'T PUSH YOURSELF.
I'LL BE FINE...
YOU HAVE A FEVER!
I WONDER IF THAT FINGER BLADE...
...WAS COATED WITH POISON...
HEY, NEW KID.
MOVE IT.
OH!! THE WIT— ER, KIM-SENPAI...
LET ME SEE THAT SCRATCH, BLONDIE.
クイ
KUI
クイ
KUI (FLICK)
WHAT DO YOU WANT?
JUST DO IT.
MY TIME AIN'T FREE, Y'KNOW.
グい
GUI (YANK)
OUCH...

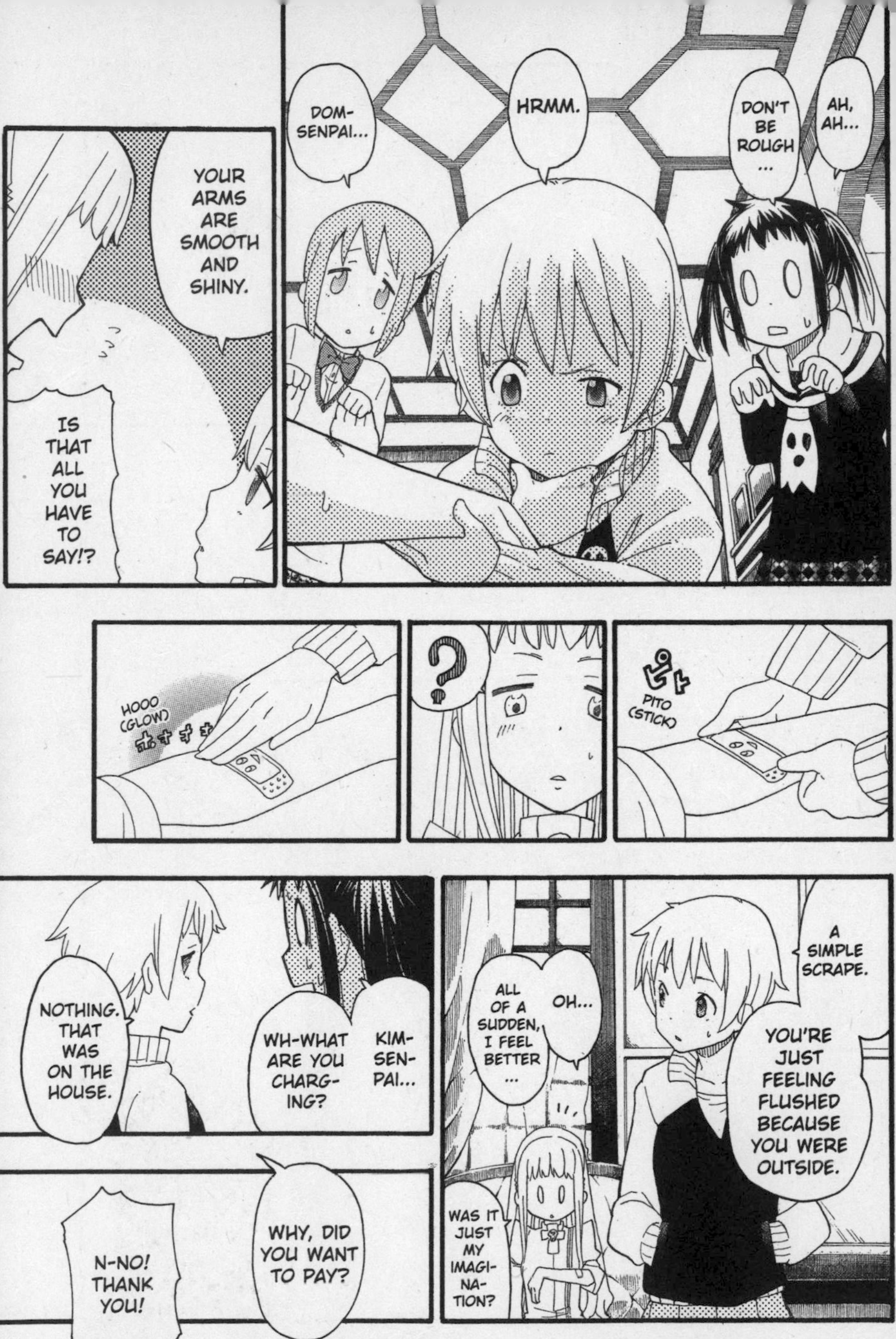
AH, AH...
DON'T BE ROUGH ...
HRMM.
DOM-SENPAI...
YOUR ARMS ARE SMOOTH AND SHINY.
IS THAT ALL YOU HAVE TO SAY!?
PITO (STICK)
?
HOOO (GLOW)
A SIMPLE SCRAPE.
YOU'RE JUST FEELING FLUSHED BECAUSE YOU WERE OUTSIDE.
OH...
ALL OF A SUDDEN, I FEEL BETTER ...
WAS IT JUST MY IMAGINATION?
KIM-SENPAI...
WH-WHAT ARE YOU CHARGING?
NOTHING. THAT WAS ON THE HOUSE.
WHY, DID YOU WANT TO PAY?
N-NO! THANK YOU!

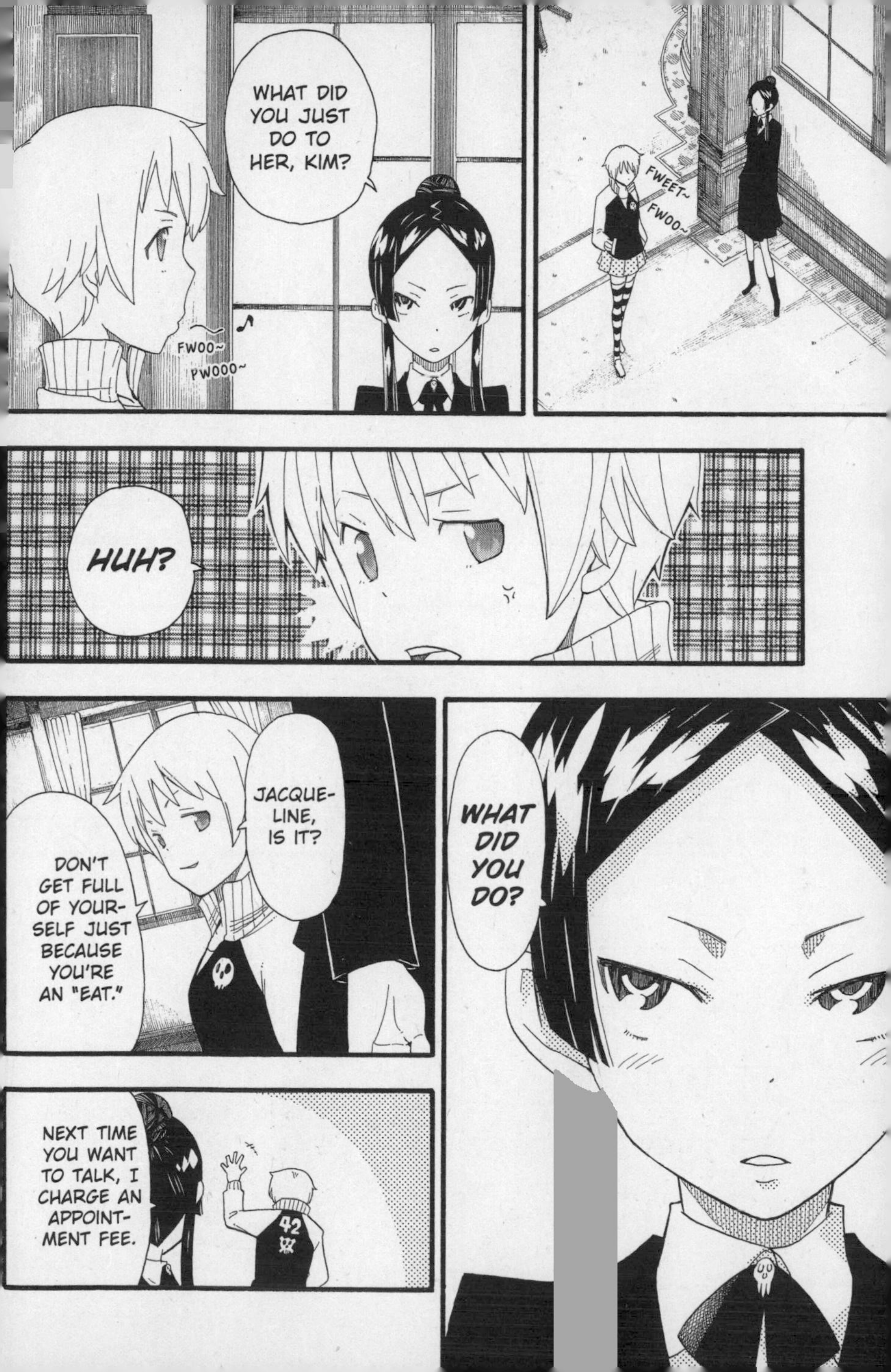
FWEET~
FWOO~
WHAT DID YOU JUST DO TO HER, KIM?
FWOO~
PWOOO~
HUH?
WHAT DID YOU DO?
JACQUELINE, IS IT?
DON'T GET FULL OF YOURSELF JUST BECAUSE YOU'RE AN "EAT."
NEXT TIME YOU WANT TO TALK, I CHARGE AN APPOINTMENT FEE.
42

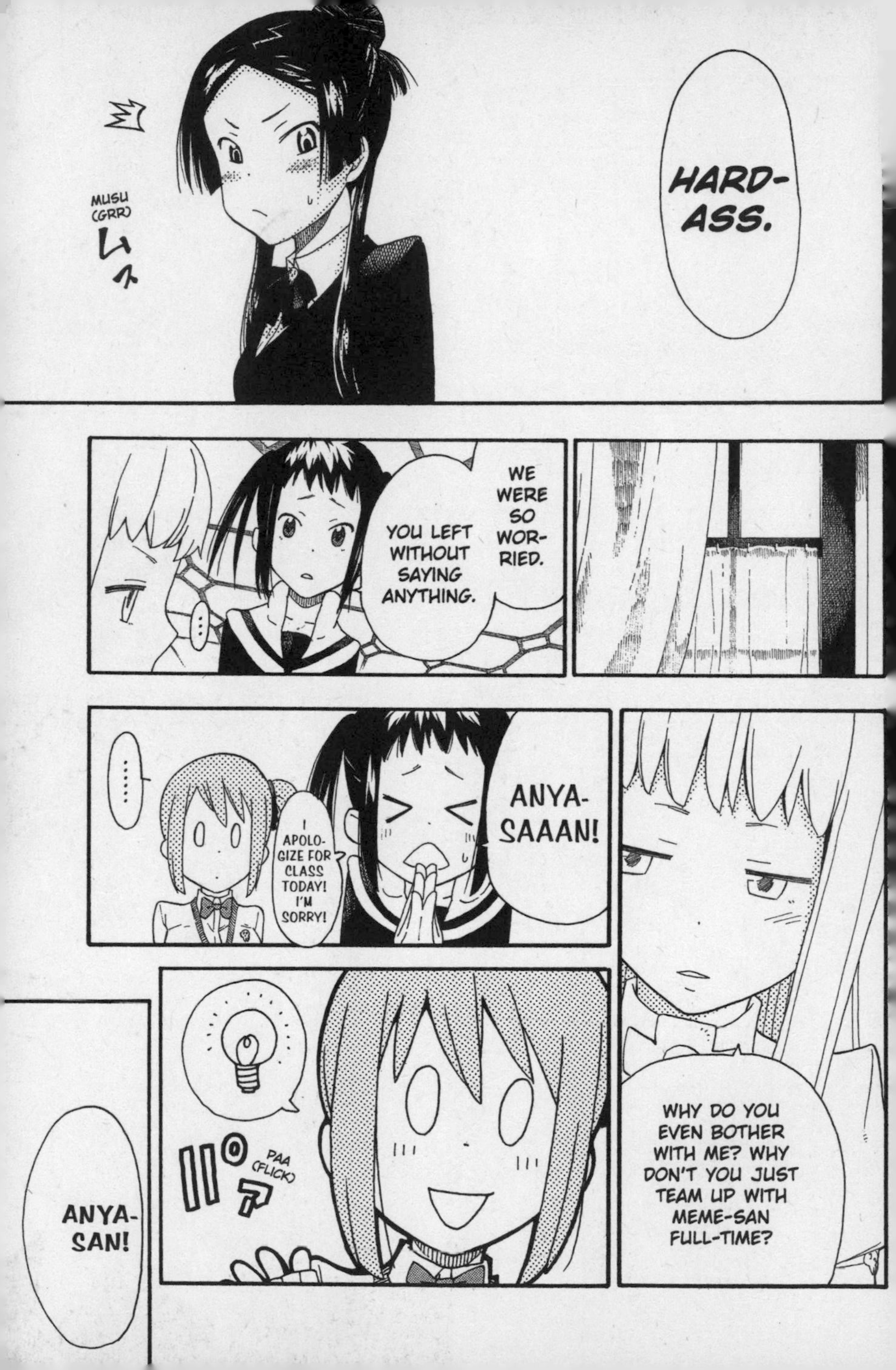
HARD-ASS.
MUSU (GRR)
ムッ
WE WERE SO WORRIED.
YOU LEFT WITHOUT SAYING ANYTHING.
…
WHY DO YOU EVEN BOTHER WITH ME? WHY DON'T YOU JUST TEAM UP WITH MEME-SAN FULL-TIME?
ANYA-SAAAN!
I APOLOGIZE FOR CLASS TODAY! I'M SORRY!
……
PAA (FLICK)
パッ
ANYA-SAN!

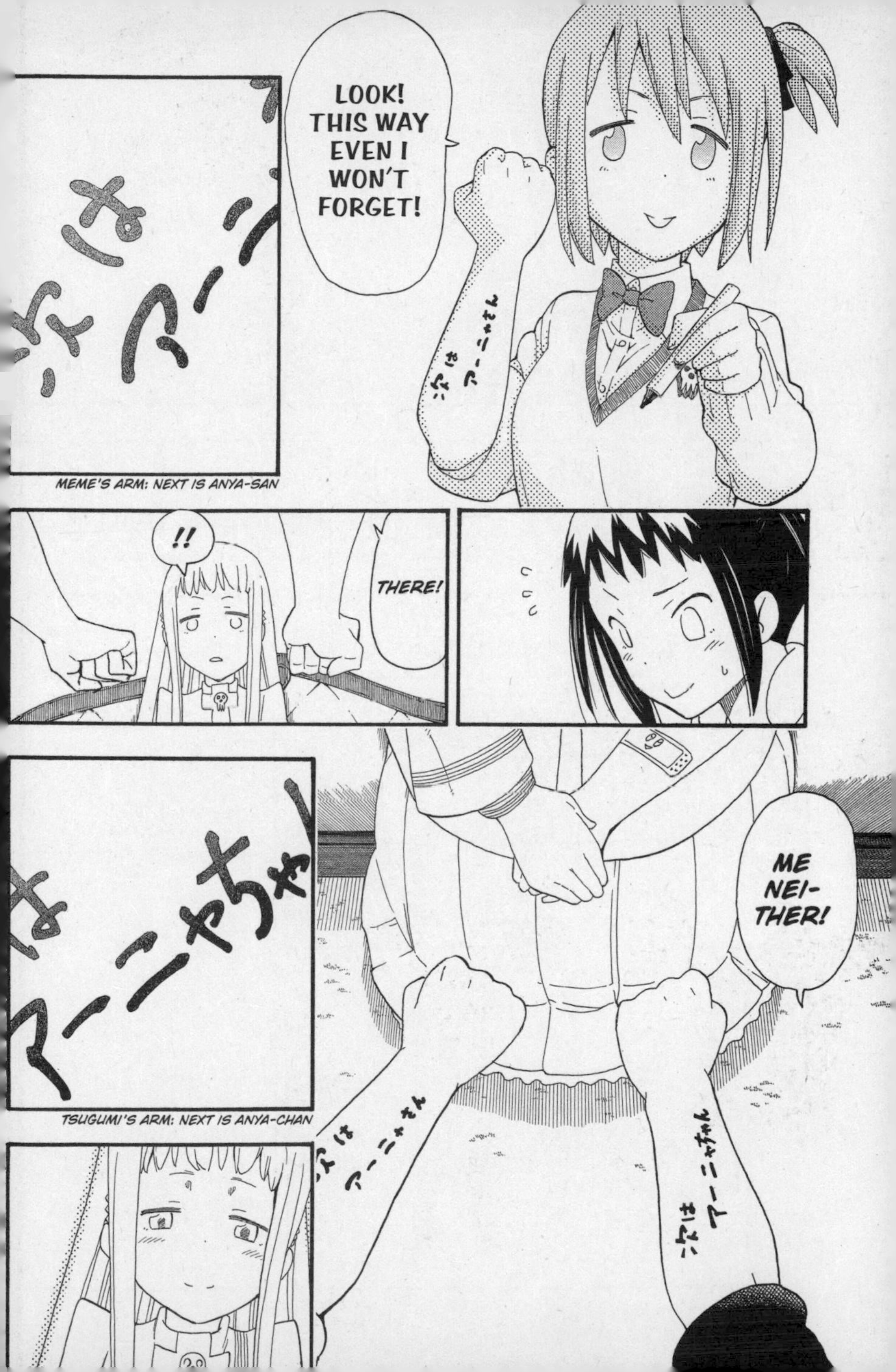
LOOK! THIS WAY EVEN I WON'T FORGET!
次はアーニャさん
MEME'S ARM: NEXT IS ANYA-SAN
!!
THERE!
ME NEI-THER!
次はアーニャちゃん
次はアーニャさん
TSUGUMI'S ARM: NEXT IS ANYA-CHAN

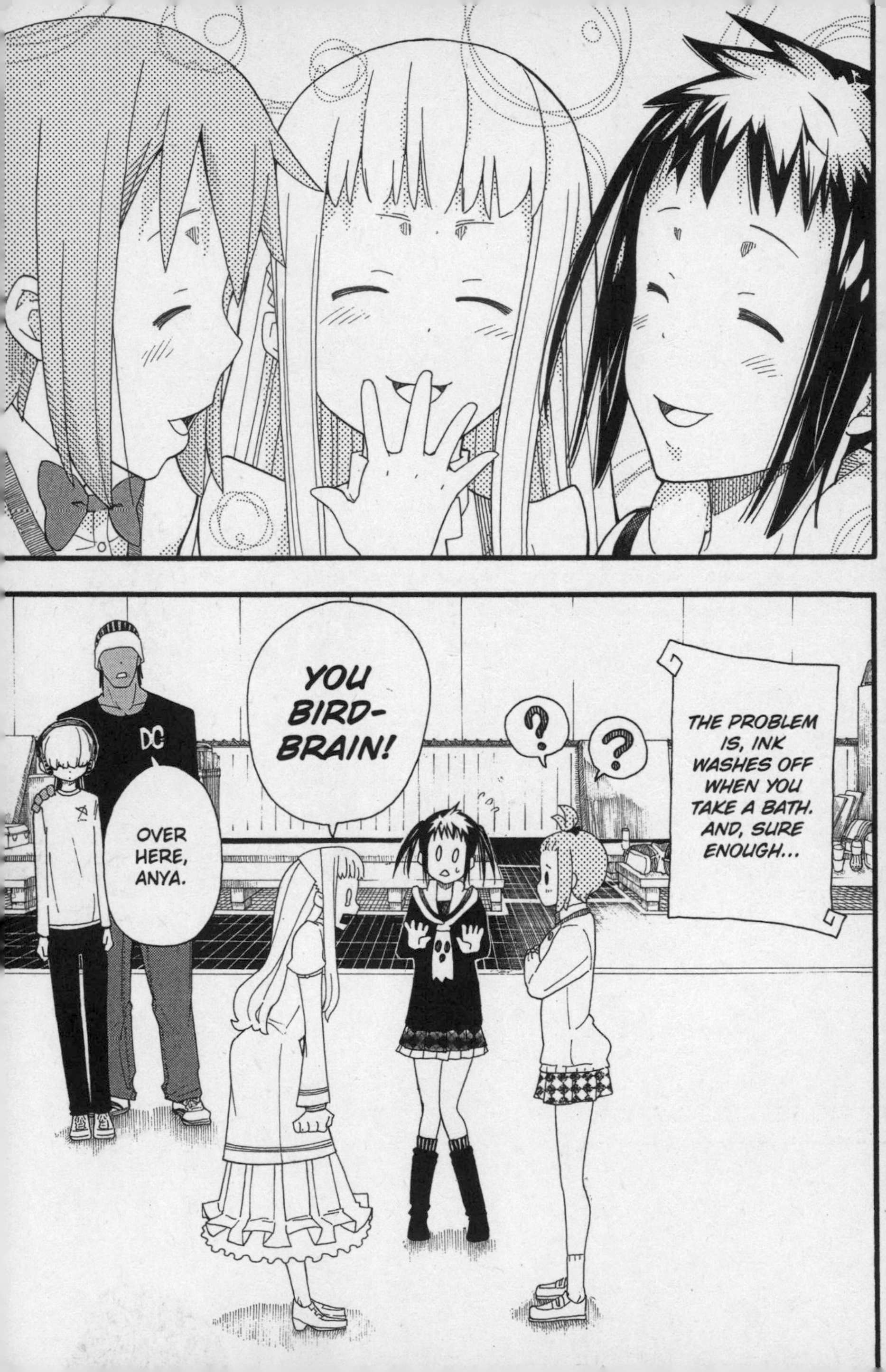
THE PROBLEM IS, INK WASHES OFF WHEN YOU TAKE A BATH. AND, SURE ENOUGH...
?
?
YOU BIRD-BRAIN!
OVER HERE, ANYA.

SOUL EATER
NOT!

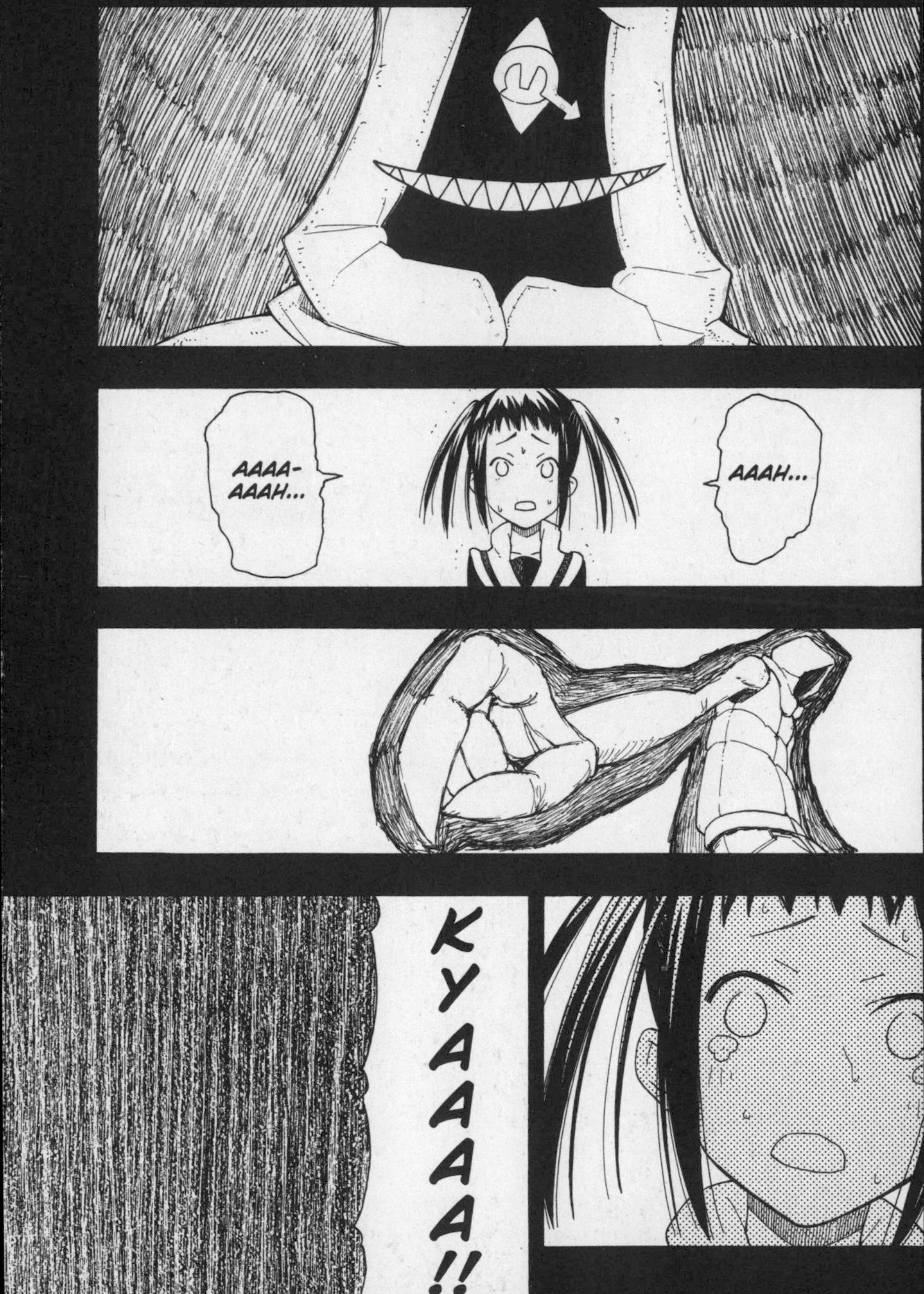
AAAH...
AAAA-AAAH...
KYAAAAA!!

SOUL EATER NOT!

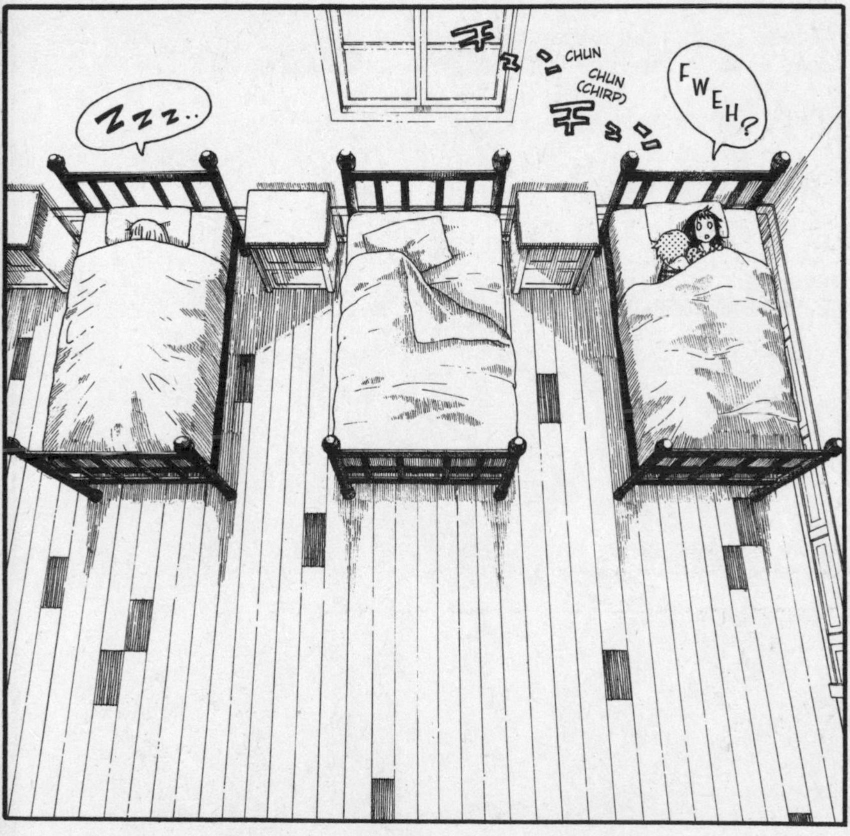
FWEH?
CHUN
CHUN
(CHIRP)
Zzz..

CHAPTER 6: HOW TO!

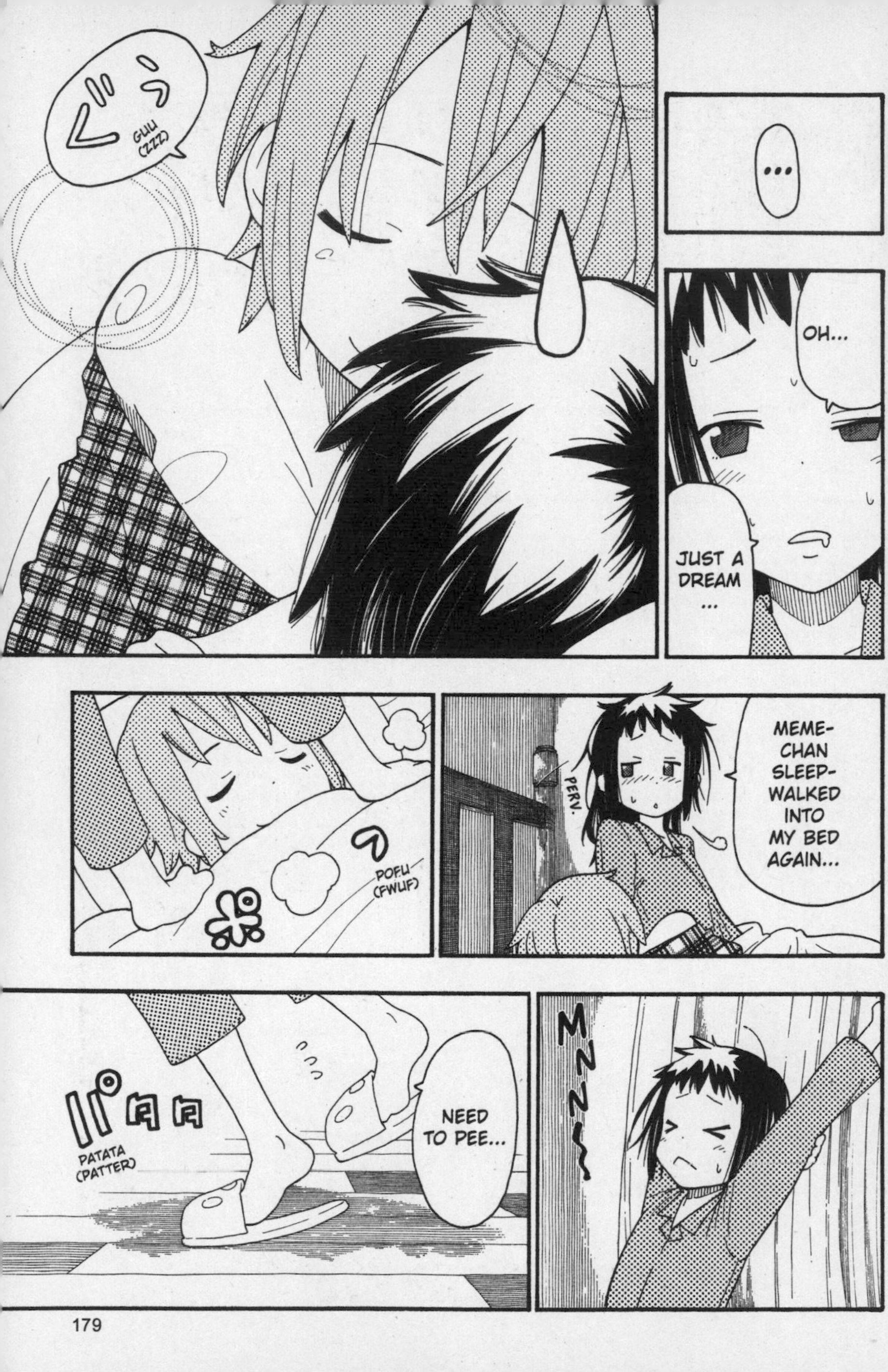

...
OH...
JUST A DREAM...
ぐう
GUU (ZZZ)
MEME-CHAN SLEEP-WALKED INTO MY BED AGAIN...
PERV.
POFU (FWUF)
MNN~
NEED TO PEE...
パタタ
PATATA (PATTER)

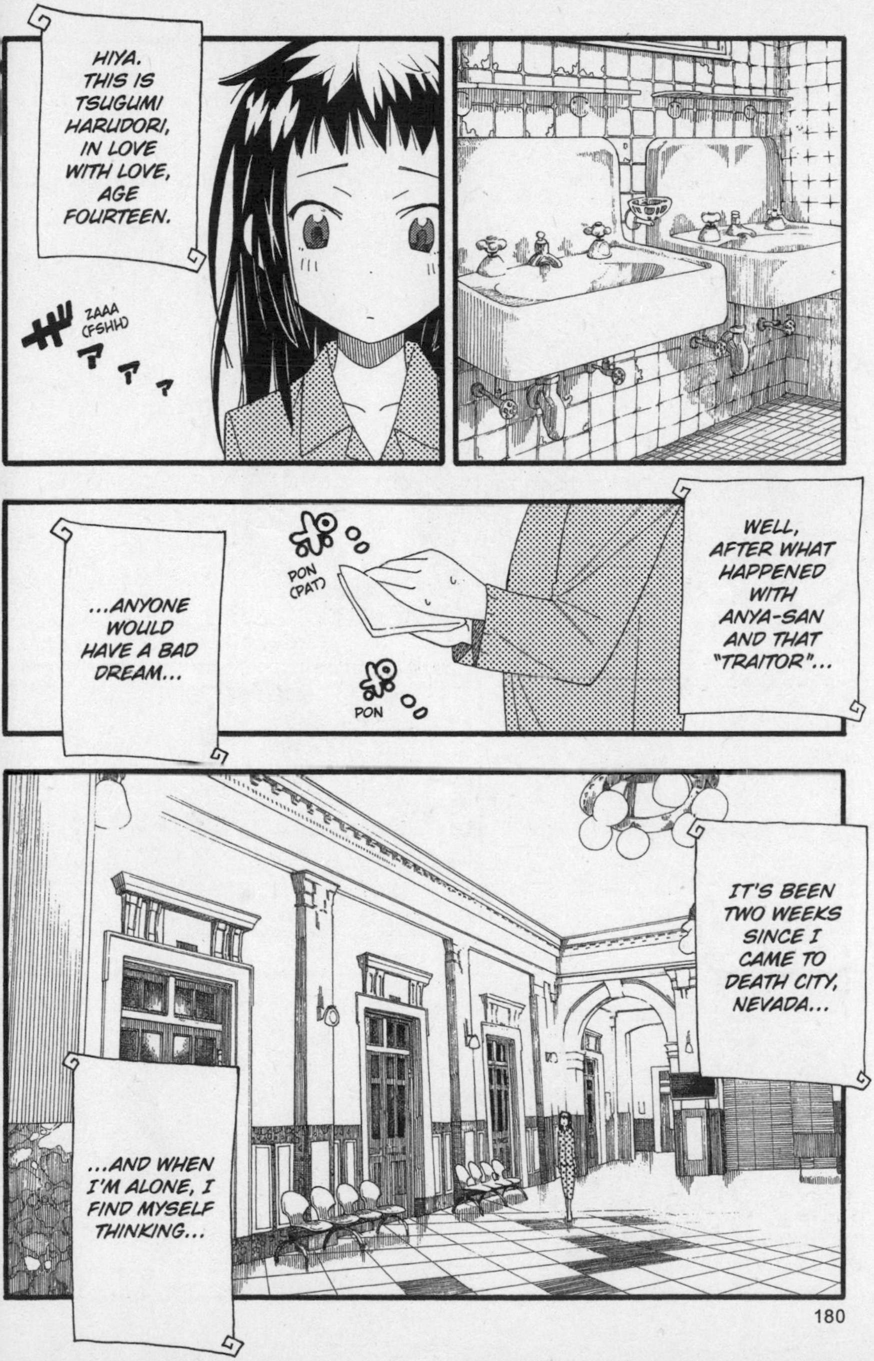
HIYA. THIS IS TSUGUMI HARUDORI, IN LOVE WITH LOVE, AGE FOURTEEN.
ZAAA (FSHH)
WELL, AFTER WHAT HAPPENED WITH ANYA-SAN AND THAT "TRAITOR"...
PON (PAT)
PON
...ANYONE WOULD HAVE A BAD DREAM...
IT'S BEEN TWO WEEKS SINCE I CAME TO DEATH CITY, NEVADA...
...AND WHEN I'M ALONE, I FIND MYSELF THINKING...

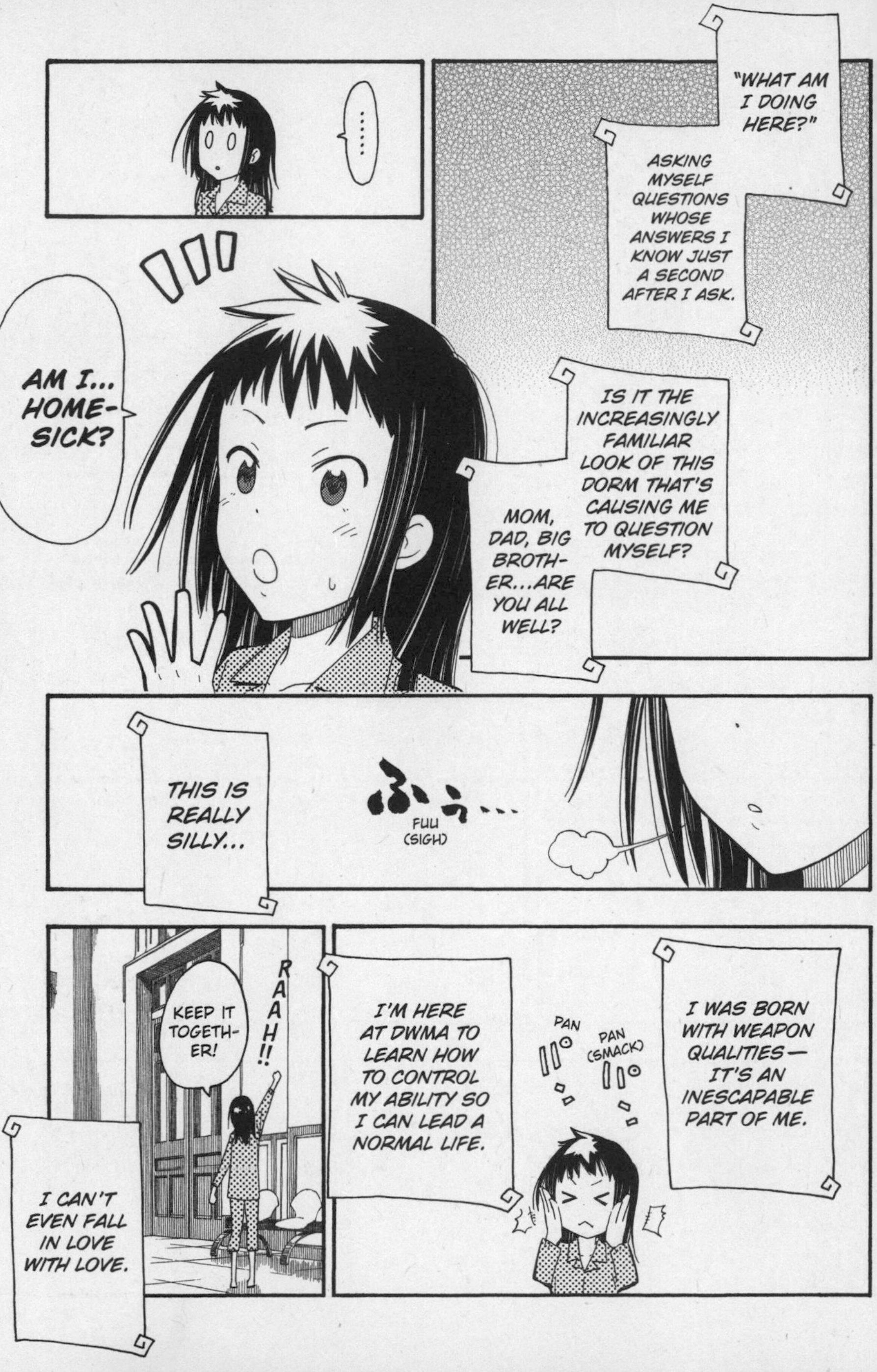
"WHAT AM I DOING HERE?"
ASKING MYSELF QUESTIONS WHOSE ANSWERS I KNOW JUST A SECOND AFTER I ASK.
......
IS IT THE INCREASINGLY FAMILIAR LOOK OF THIS DORM THAT'S CAUSING ME TO QUESTION MYSELF?
MOM, DAD, BIG BROTHER...ARE YOU ALL WELL?
AM I... HOME-SICK?
ふぅ...
FUU (SIGH)
THIS IS REALLY SILLY...
I WAS BORN WITH WEAPON QUALITIES— IT'S AN INESCAPABLE PART OF ME.
PAN
PAN (SMACK)
I'M HERE AT DWMA TO LEARN HOW TO CONTROL MY ABILITY SO I CAN LEAD A NORMAL LIFE.
RAAH!!
KEEP IT TOGETH-ER!
I CAN'T EVEN FALL IN LOVE WITH LOVE.

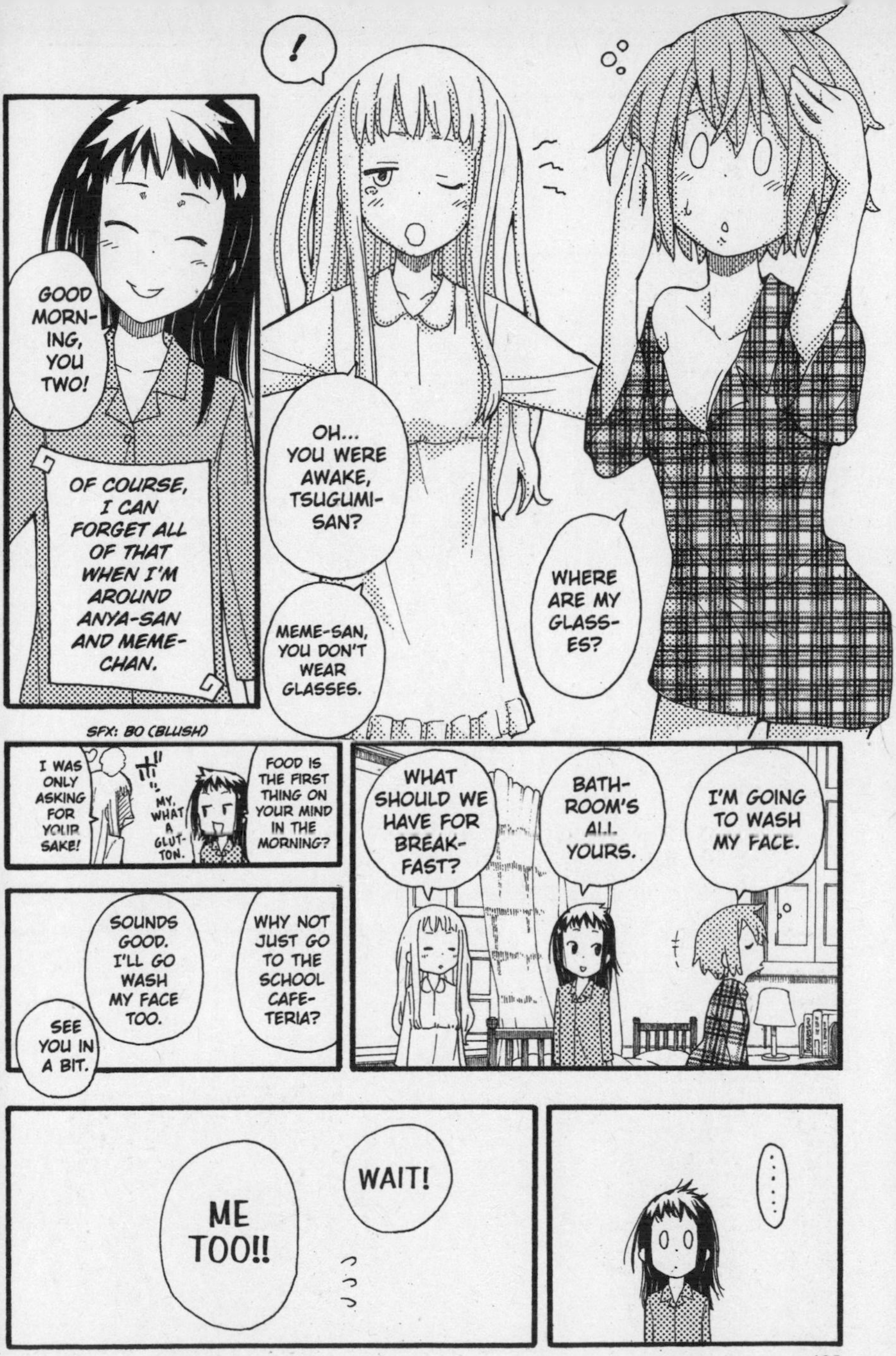
!
WHERE ARE MY GLASSES?
OH... YOU WERE AWAKE, TSUGUMI-SAN?
MEME-SAN, YOU DON'T WEAR GLASSES.
GOOD MORNING, YOU TWO!
OF COURSE, I CAN FORGET ALL OF THAT WHEN I'M AROUND ANYA-SAN AND MEME-CHAN.
SFX: BO (BLUSH)
I'M GOING TO WASH MY FACE.
BATHROOM'S ALL YOURS.
WHAT SHOULD WE HAVE FOR BREAKFAST?
FOOD IS THE FIRST THING ON YOUR MIND IN THE MORNING?
MY, WHAT A GLUTTON.
I WAS ONLY ASKING FOR YOUR SAKE!
WHY NOT JUST GO TO THE SCHOOL CAFETERIA?
SOUNDS GOOD. I'LL GO WASH MY FACE TOO.
SEE YOU IN A BIT.
......
WAIT!
ME TOO!!

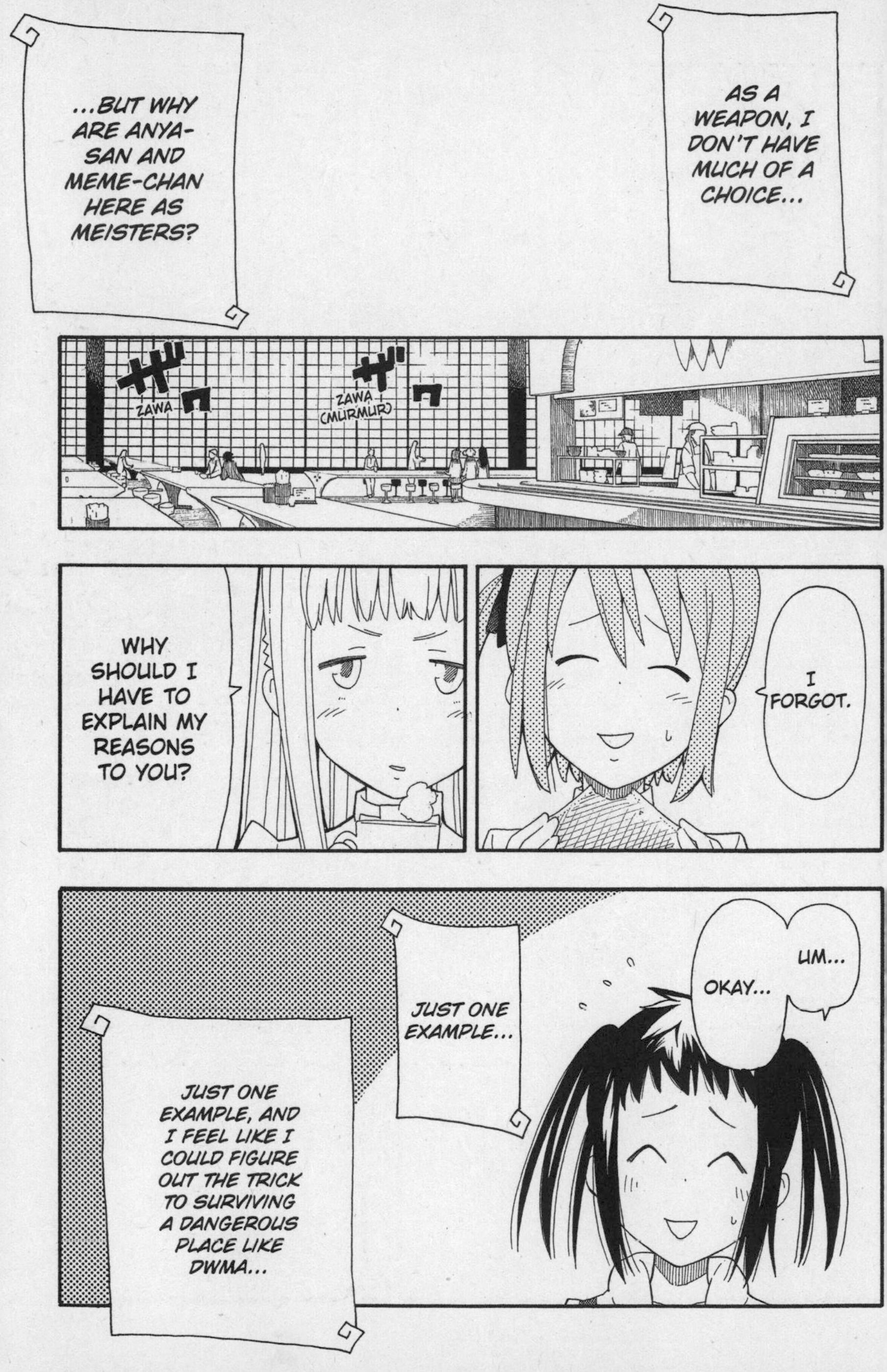
AS A WEAPON, I DON'T HAVE MUCH OF A CHOICE...
...BUT WHY ARE ANYA-SAN AND MEME-CHAN HERE AS MEISTERS?
ザワ
ZAWA (MURMUR)
ザワ
ZAWA
I FORGOT.
WHY SHOULD I HAVE TO EXPLAIN MY REASONS TO YOU?
UM... OKAY...
JUST ONE EXAMPLE...
JUST ONE EXAMPLE, AND I FEEL LIKE I COULD FIGURE OUT THE TRICK TO SURVIVING A DANGEROUS PLACE LIKE DWMA...

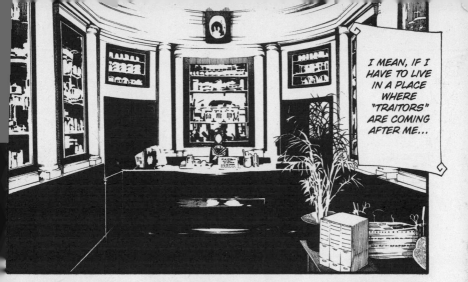

I MEAN, IF I HAVE TO LIVE IN A PLACE WHERE "TRAITORS" ARE COMING AFTER ME...

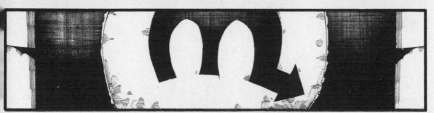

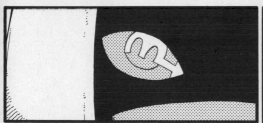

SU
(SHHP)

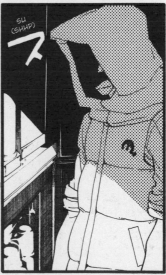

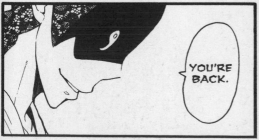

YOU'RE BACK.

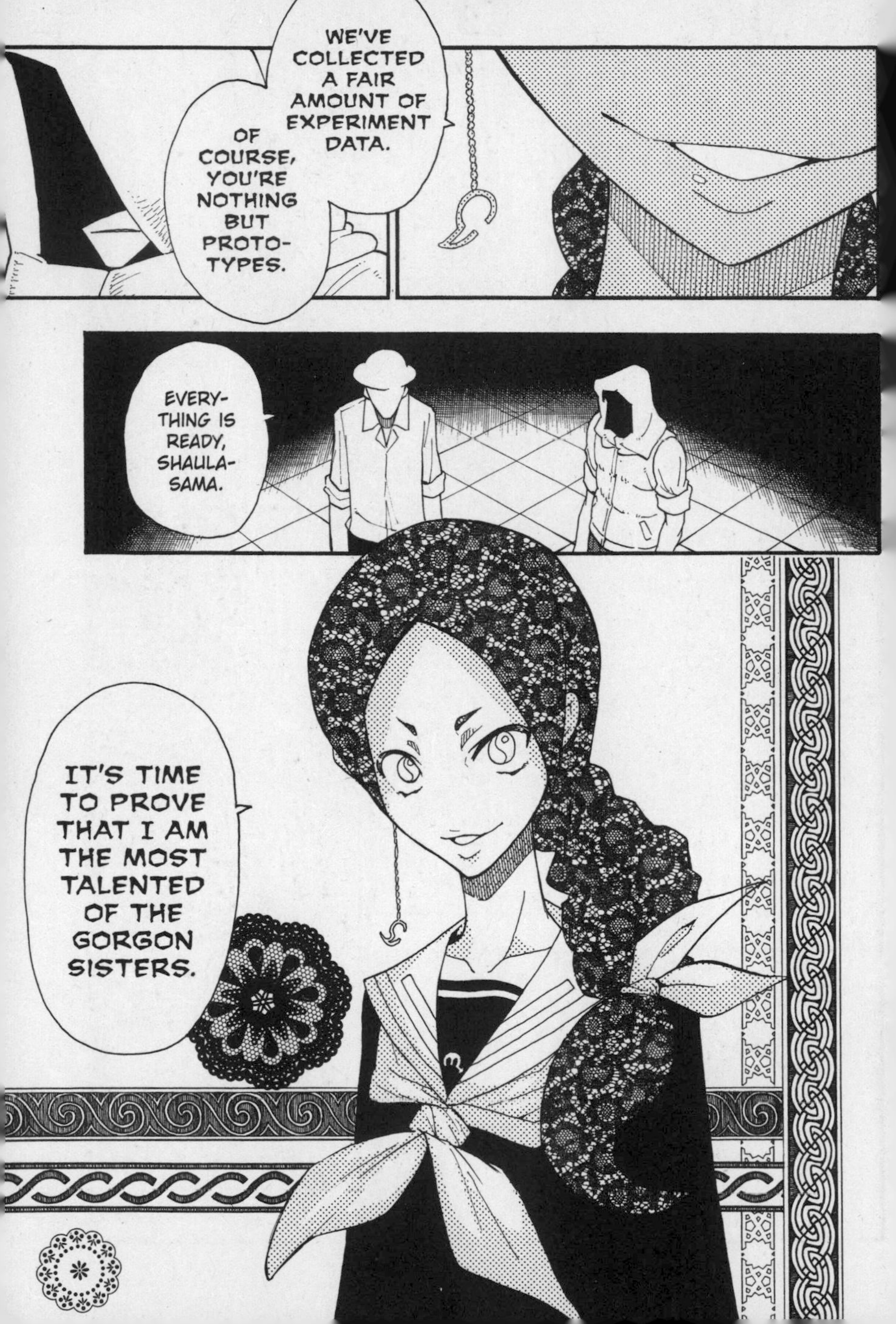
WE'VE COLLECTED A FAIR AMOUNT OF EXPERIMENT DATA.
OF COURSE, YOU'RE NOTHING BUT PROTO-TYPES.
EVERY-THING IS READY, SHAULA-SAMA.
IT'S TIME TO PROVE THAT I AM THE MOST TALENTED OF THE GORGON SISTERS.

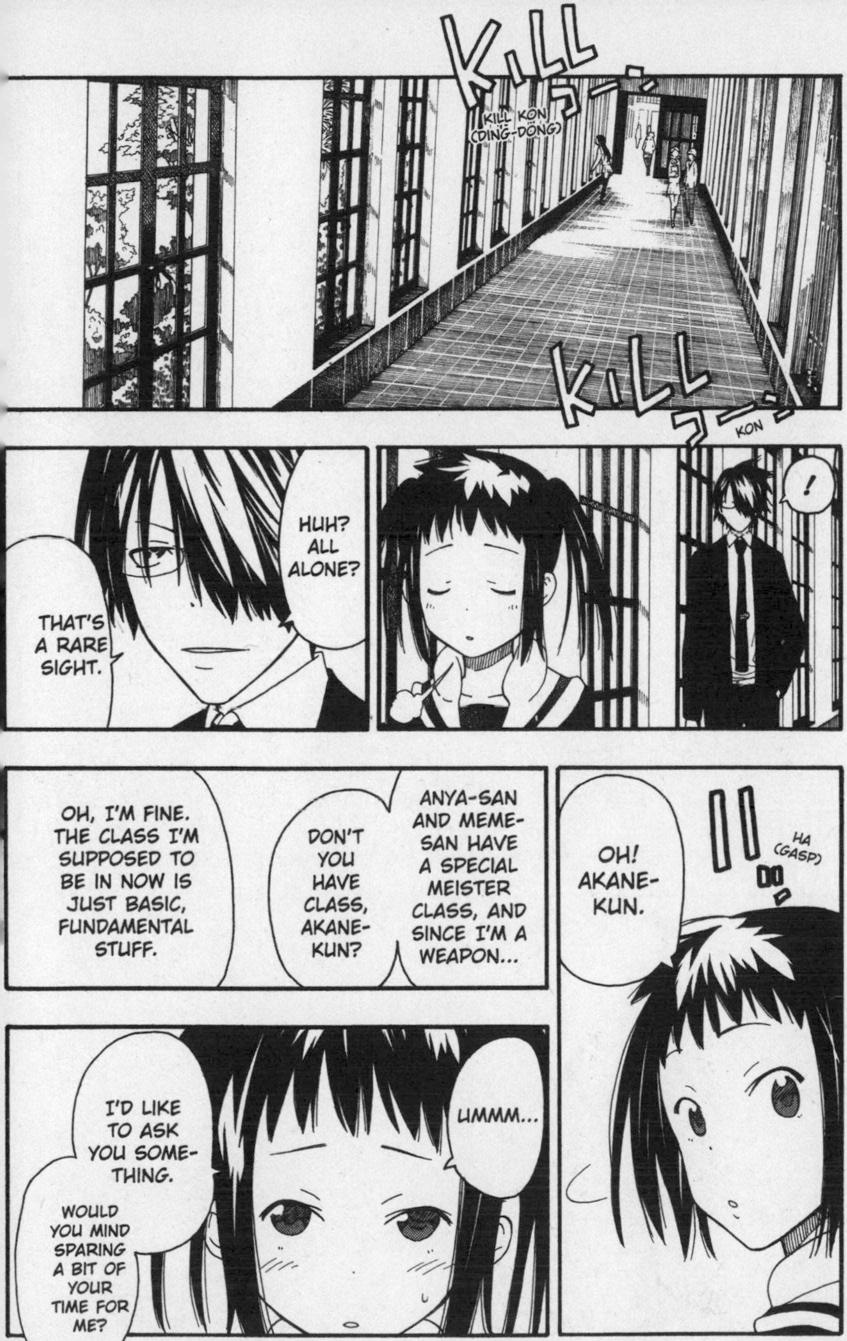
KILL
KILL KON (DING-DONG)
KILL
KON
!
HUH? ALL ALONE?
THAT'S A RARE SIGHT.
HA (GASP)
OH! AKANE-KUN.
ANYA-SAN AND MEME-SAN HAVE A SPECIAL MEISTER CLASS, AND SINCE I'M A WEAPON...
DON'T YOU HAVE CLASS, AKANE-KUN?
OH, I'M FINE. THE CLASS I'M SUPPOSED TO BE IN NOW IS JUST BASIC, FUNDAMENTAL STUFF.
UMMM...
I'D LIKE TO ASK YOU SOMETHING.
WOULD YOU MIND SPARING A BIT OF YOUR TIME FOR ME?

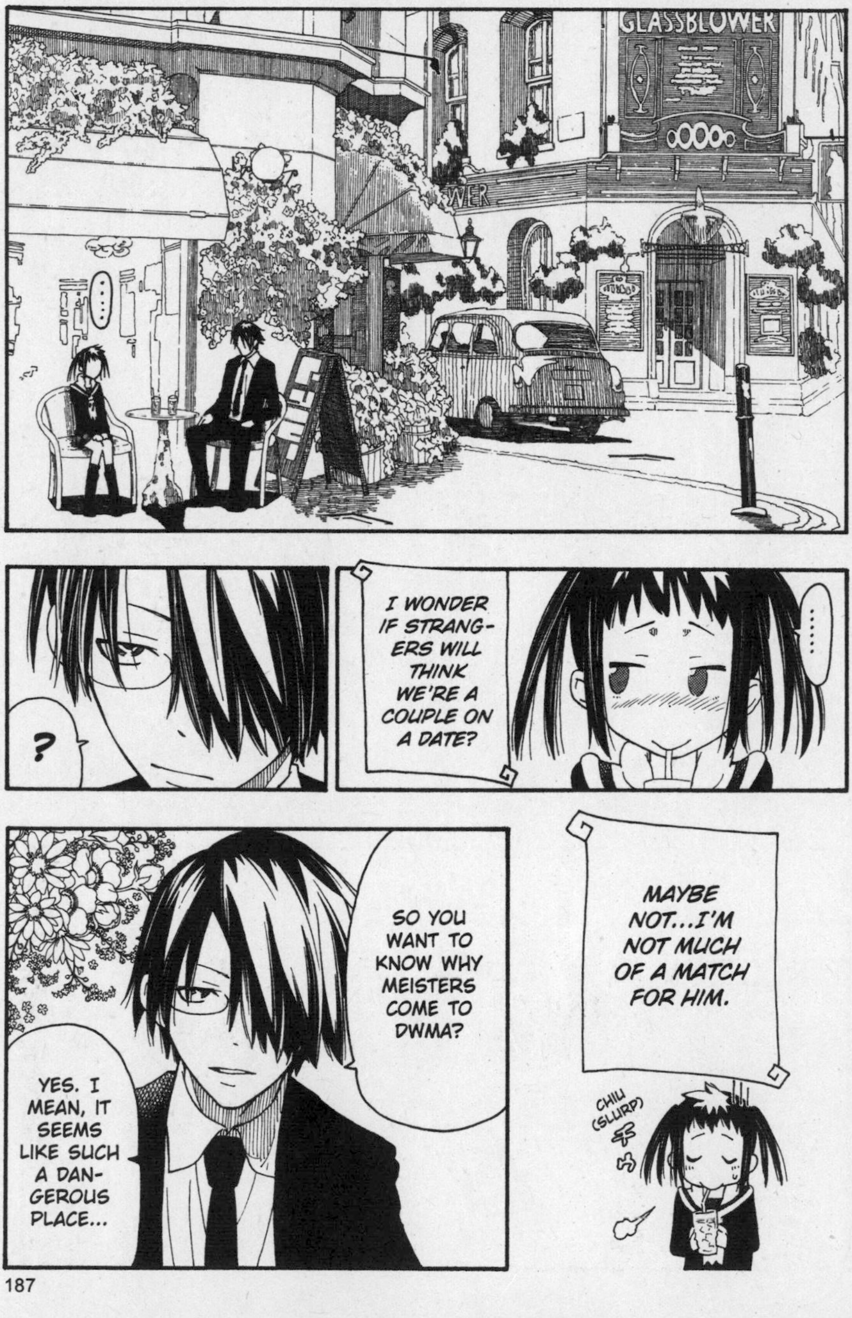
GLASSBLOWER
……
I WONDER IF STRANGERS WILL THINK WE'RE A COUPLE ON A DATE?
……
?
MAYBE NOT...I'M NOT MUCH OF A MATCH FOR HIM.
CHIU (SLURP)
SO YOU WANT TO KNOW WHY MEISTERS COME TO DWMA?
YES. I MEAN, IT SEEMS LIKE SUCH A DANGEROUS PLACE...

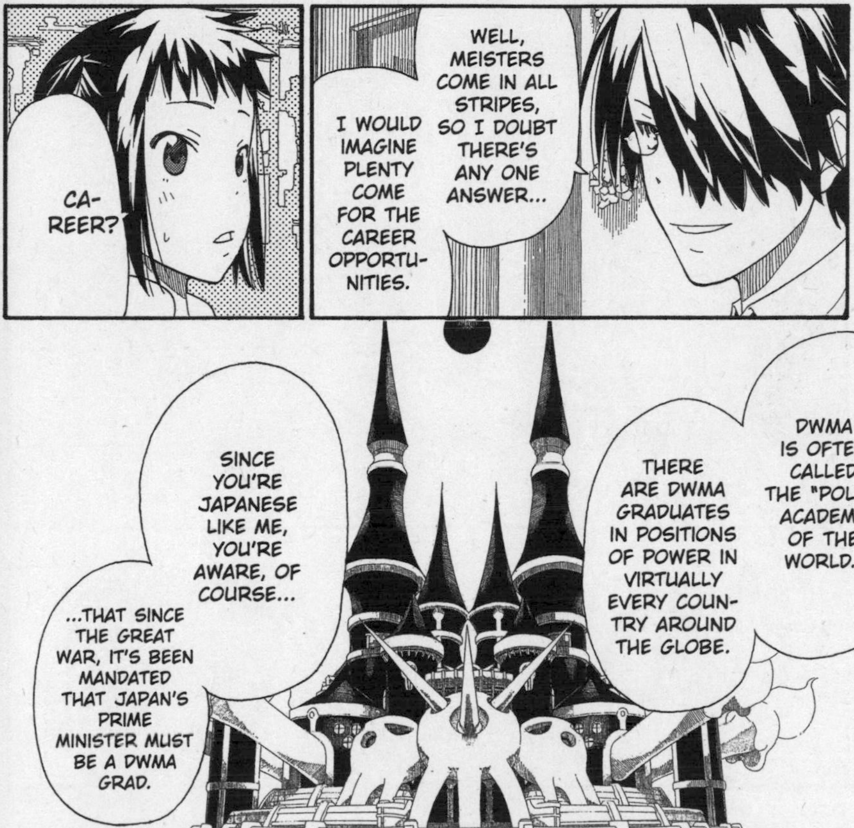
WELL, MEISTERS COME IN ALL STRIPES, SO I DOUBT THERE'S ANY ONE ANSWER...
I WOULD IMAGINE PLENTY COME FOR THE CAREER OPPORTUNITIES.
CA-REER?
DWMA IS OFTEN CALLED THE "POLICE ACADEMY OF THE WORLD."
THERE ARE DWMA GRADUATES IN POSITIONS OF POWER IN VIRTUALLY EVERY COUNTRY AROUND THE GLOBE.
SINCE YOU'RE JAPANESE LIKE ME, YOU'RE AWARE, OF COURSE...
...THAT SINCE THE GREAT WAR, IT'S BEEN MANDATED THAT JAPAN'S PRIME MINISTER MUST BE A DWMA GRAD.
NOW THAT YOU MENTION IT, I THINK I HEARD THAT IN SOCIAL STUDIES CLASS...
THE LEVEL OF TRUST PLACED IN DWMA IS ABSOLUTE, AND THE SCHOOL RECEIVES FUNDING FROM MOST OF THE COUNTRIES IN THE WORLD.
THAT'S WHY WE HAVE PLENTY OF MONEY FOR THE FACILITIES.
WORLD PEACE IS PRETTY CHEAPLY OBTAINED IF YOU CAN BUY IT WITH MONEY.

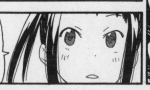

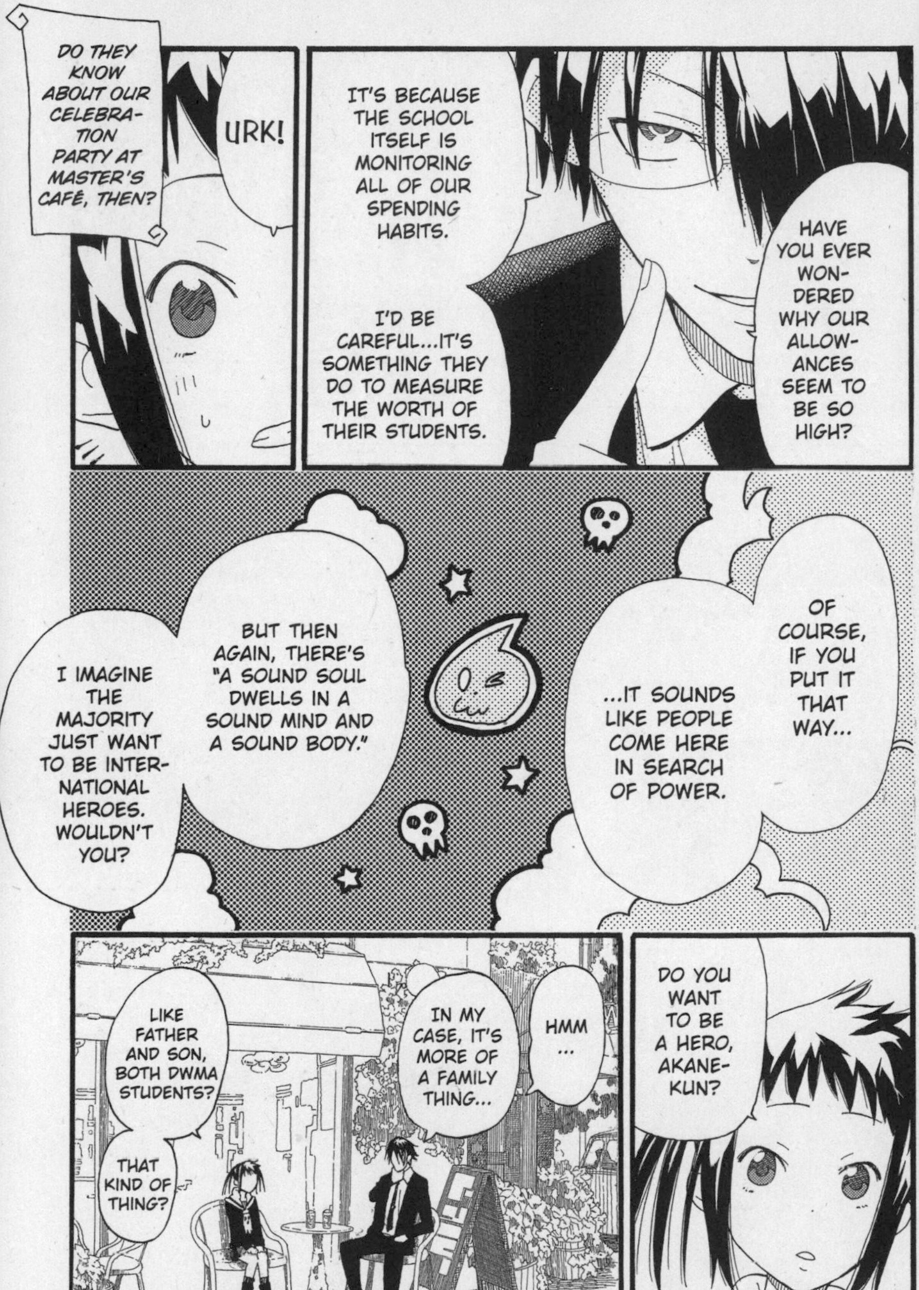
HAVE YOU EVER WONDERED WHY OUR ALLOWANCES SEEM TO BE SO HIGH?
IT'S BECAUSE THE SCHOOL ITSELF IS MONITORING ALL OF OUR SPENDING HABITS.
I'D BE CAREFUL...IT'S SOMETHING THEY DO TO MEASURE THE WORTH OF THEIR STUDENTS.
URK!
DO THEY KNOW ABOUT OUR CELEBRATION PARTY AT MASTER'S CAFÉ, THEN?
OF COURSE, IF YOU PUT IT THAT WAY...
...IT SOUNDS LIKE PEOPLE COME HERE IN SEARCH OF POWER.
BUT THEN AGAIN, THERE'S "A SOUND SOUL DWELLS IN A SOUND MIND AND A SOUND BODY."
I IMAGINE THE MAJORITY JUST WANT TO BE INTERNATIONAL HEROES. WOULDN'T YOU?
DO YOU WANT TO BE A HERO, AKANE-KUN?
HMM ...
IN MY CASE, IT'S MORE OF A FAMILY THING...
LIKE FATHER AND SON, BOTH DWMA STUDENTS?
THAT KIND OF THING?

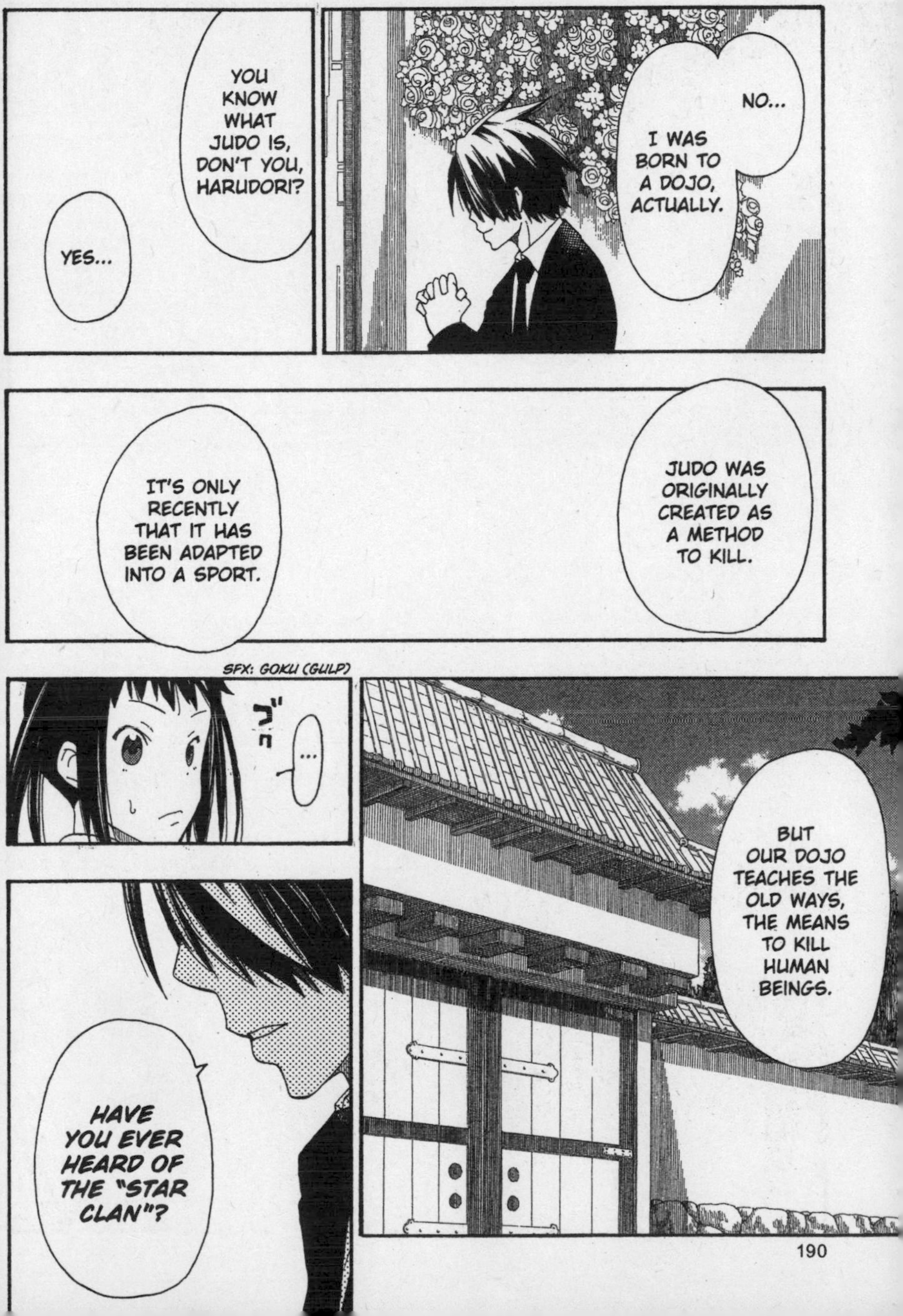
NO...
I WAS BORN TO A DOJO, ACTUALLY.
YOU KNOW WHAT JUDO IS, DON'T YOU, HARUDORI?
YES...
JUDO WAS ORIGINALLY CREATED AS A METHOD TO KILL.
IT'S ONLY RECENTLY THAT IT HAS BEEN ADAPTED INTO A SPORT.
BUT OUR DOJO TEACHES THE OLD WAYS, THE MEANS TO KILL HUMAN BEINGS.
SFX: GOKU (GULP)
ゴク
...
HAVE YOU EVER HEARD OF THE "STAR CLAN"?

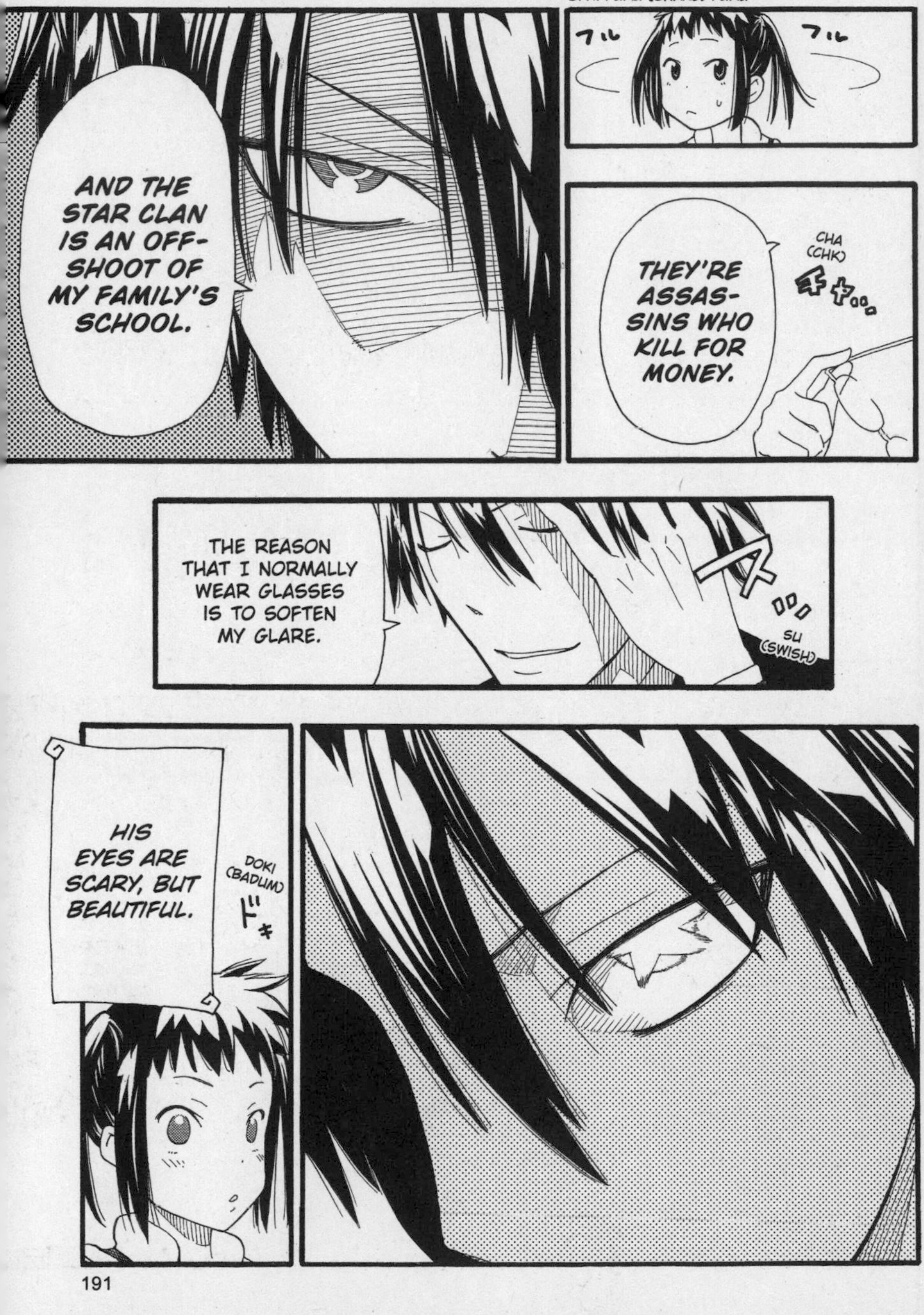
SFX: FURU (SHAKE) FURU
フル フル
THEY'RE ASSAS-SINS WHO KILL FOR MONEY.
CHA (CHK)
AND THE STAR CLAN IS AN OFF-SHOOT OF MY FAMILY'S SCHOOL.
SU (SWISH)
THE REASON THAT I NORMALLY WEAR GLASSES IS TO SOFTEN MY GLARE.
DOKI (BADUM)
HIS EYES ARE SCARY, BUT BEAUTIFUL.

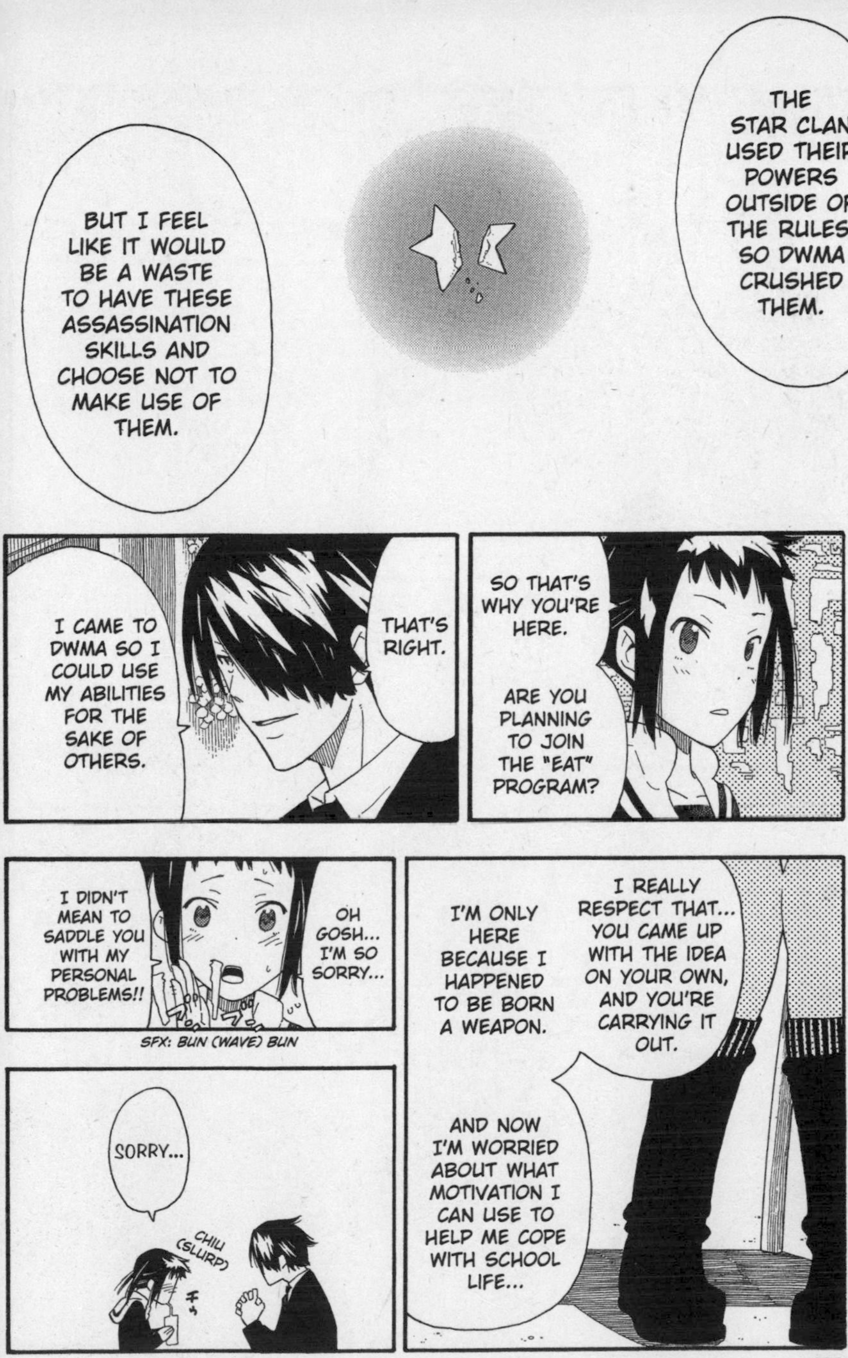
THE STAR CLAN USED THEIR POWERS OUTSIDE OF THE RULES, SO DWMA CRUSHED THEM.
BUT I FEEL LIKE IT WOULD BE A WASTE TO HAVE THESE ASSASSINATION SKILLS AND CHOOSE NOT TO MAKE USE OF THEM.
SO THAT'S WHY YOU'RE HERE.
ARE YOU PLANNING TO JOIN THE "EAT" PROGRAM?
THAT'S RIGHT.
I CAME TO DWMA SO I COULD USE MY ABILITIES FOR THE SAKE OF OTHERS.
I REALLY RESPECT THAT... YOU CAME UP WITH THE IDEA ON YOUR OWN, AND YOU'RE CARRYING IT OUT.
I'M ONLY HERE BECAUSE I HAPPENED TO BE BORN A WEAPON.
AND NOW I'M WORRIED ABOUT WHAT MOTIVATION I CAN USE TO HELP ME COPE WITH SCHOOL LIFE...
OH GOSH... I'M SO SORRY...
I DIDN'T MEAN TO SADDLE YOU WITH MY PERSONAL PROBLEMS!!
SFX: BUN (WAVE) BUN
SORRY...
CHIU (SLURP)

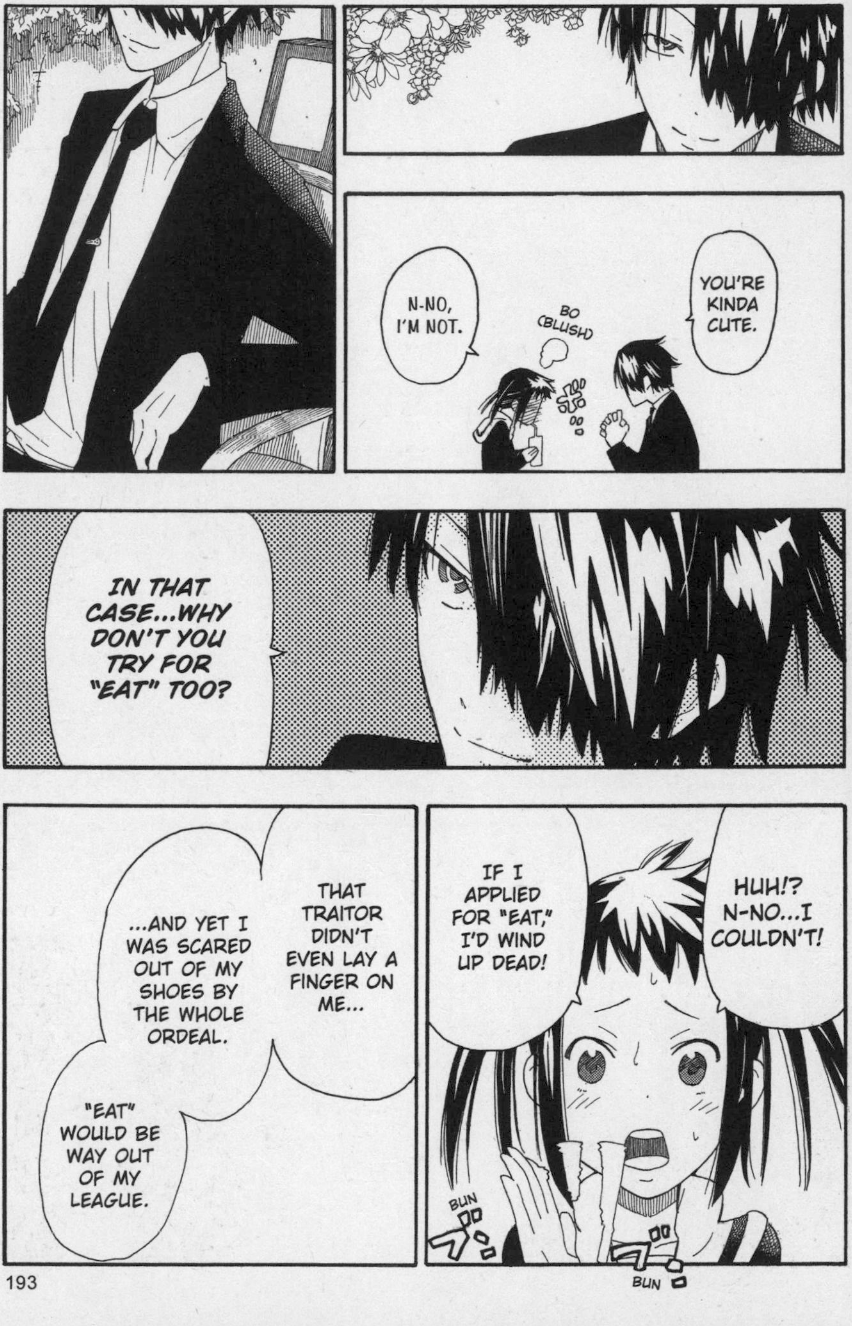
YOU'RE KINDA CUTE.
BO (BLUSH)
N-NO, I'M NOT.
IN THAT CASE...WHY DON'T YOU TRY FOR "EAT" TOO?
HUH!? N-NO...I COULDN'T!
IF I APPLIED FOR "EAT," I'D WIND UP DEAD!
BUN
BUN
THAT TRAITOR DIDN'T EVEN LAY A FINGER ON ME...
...AND YET I WAS SCARED OUT OF MY SHOES BY THE WHOLE ORDEAL.
"EAT" WOULD BE WAY OUT OF MY LEAGUE.

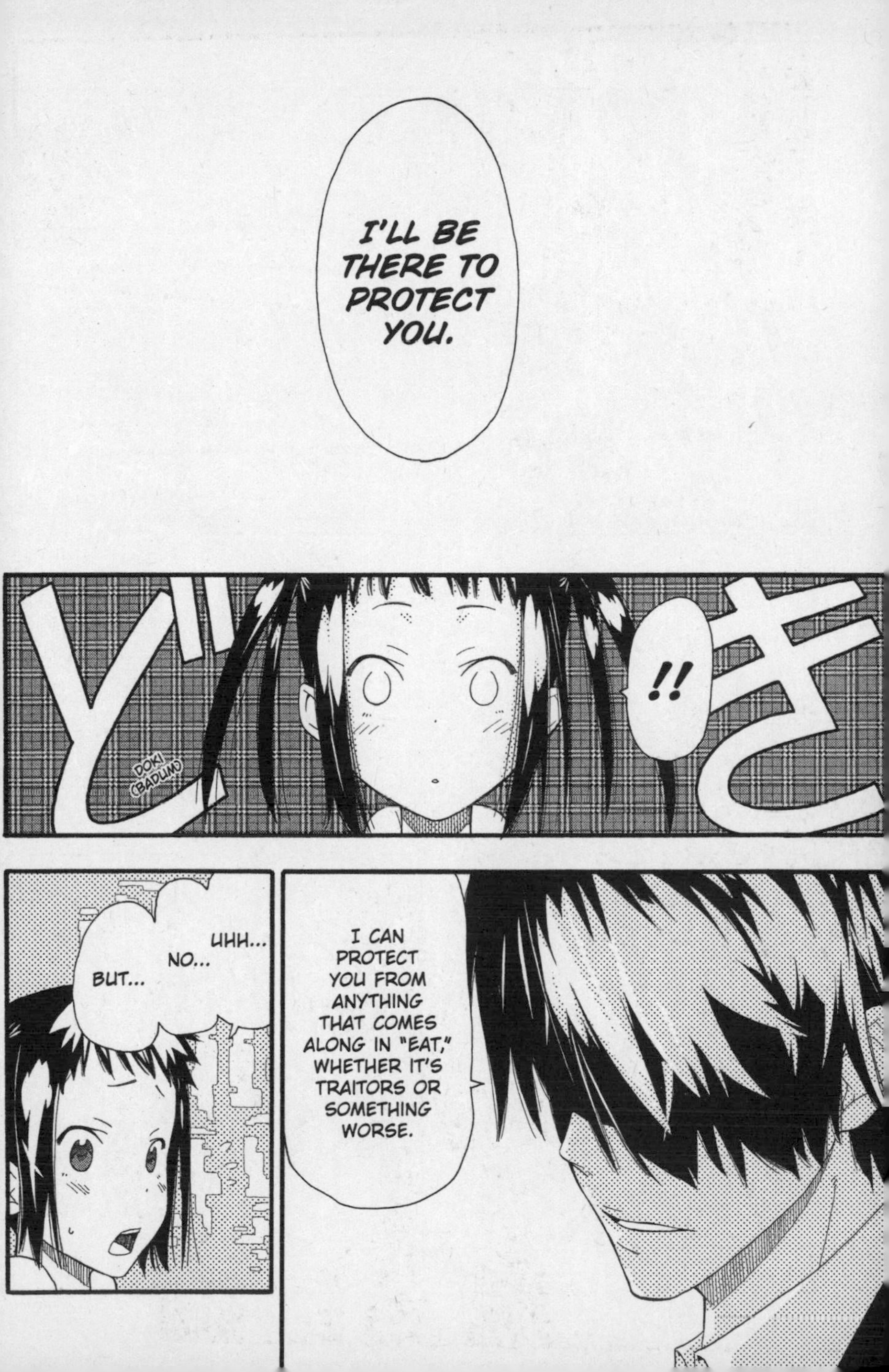
I'LL BE THERE TO PROTECT YOU.
!!
どき
DOKI (BADUM)
I CAN PROTECT YOU FROM ANYTHING THAT COMES ALONG IN "EAT," WHETHER IT'S TRAITORS OR SOMETHING WORSE.
UHH... NO... BUT...

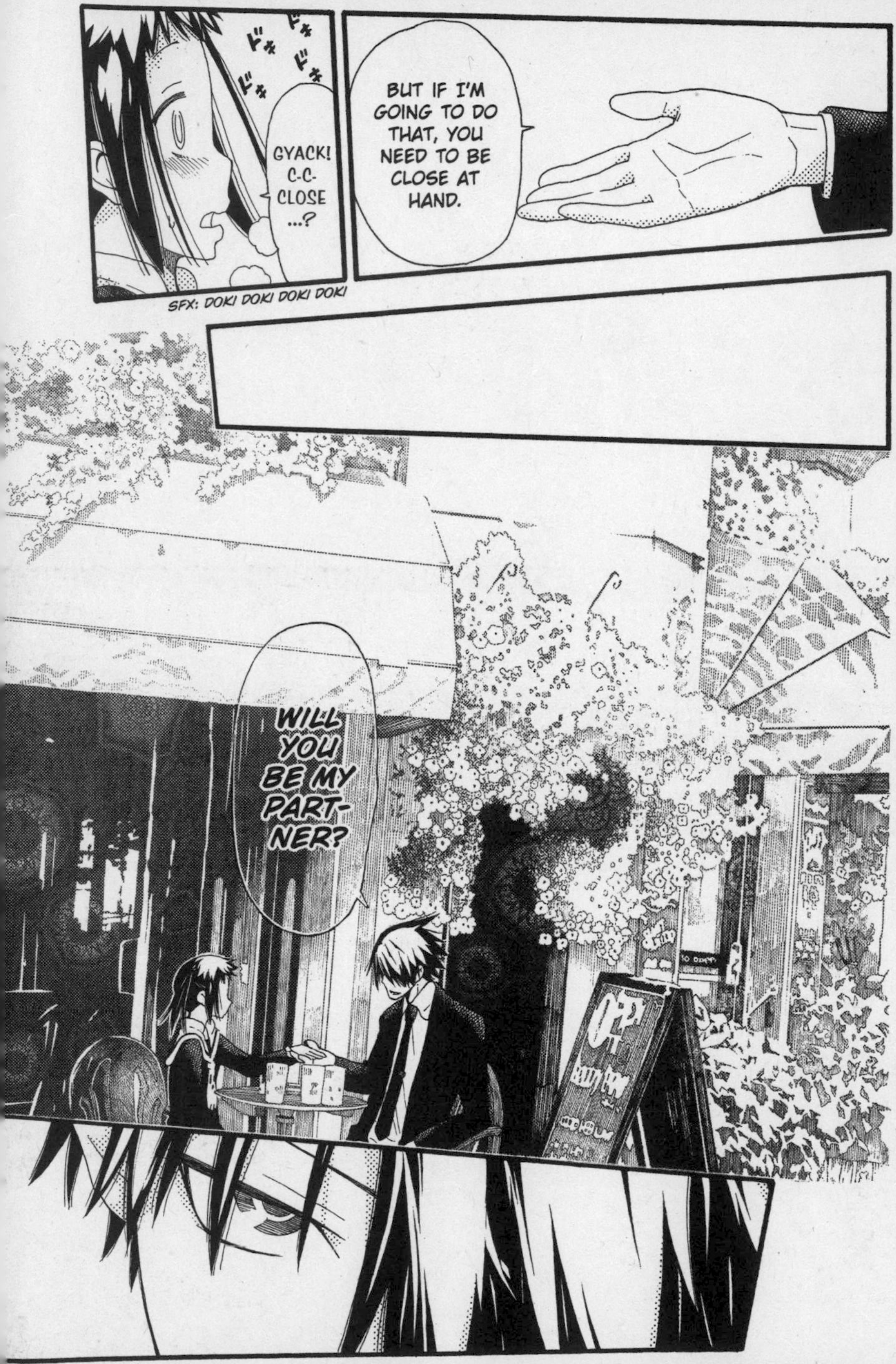
BUT IF I'M GOING TO DO THAT, YOU NEED TO BE CLOSE AT HAND.
ドキ ドキ ドキ ドキ
GYACK! C-C-CLOSE ...?
SFX: DOKI DOKI DOKI DOKI
WILL YOU BE MY PART-NER?

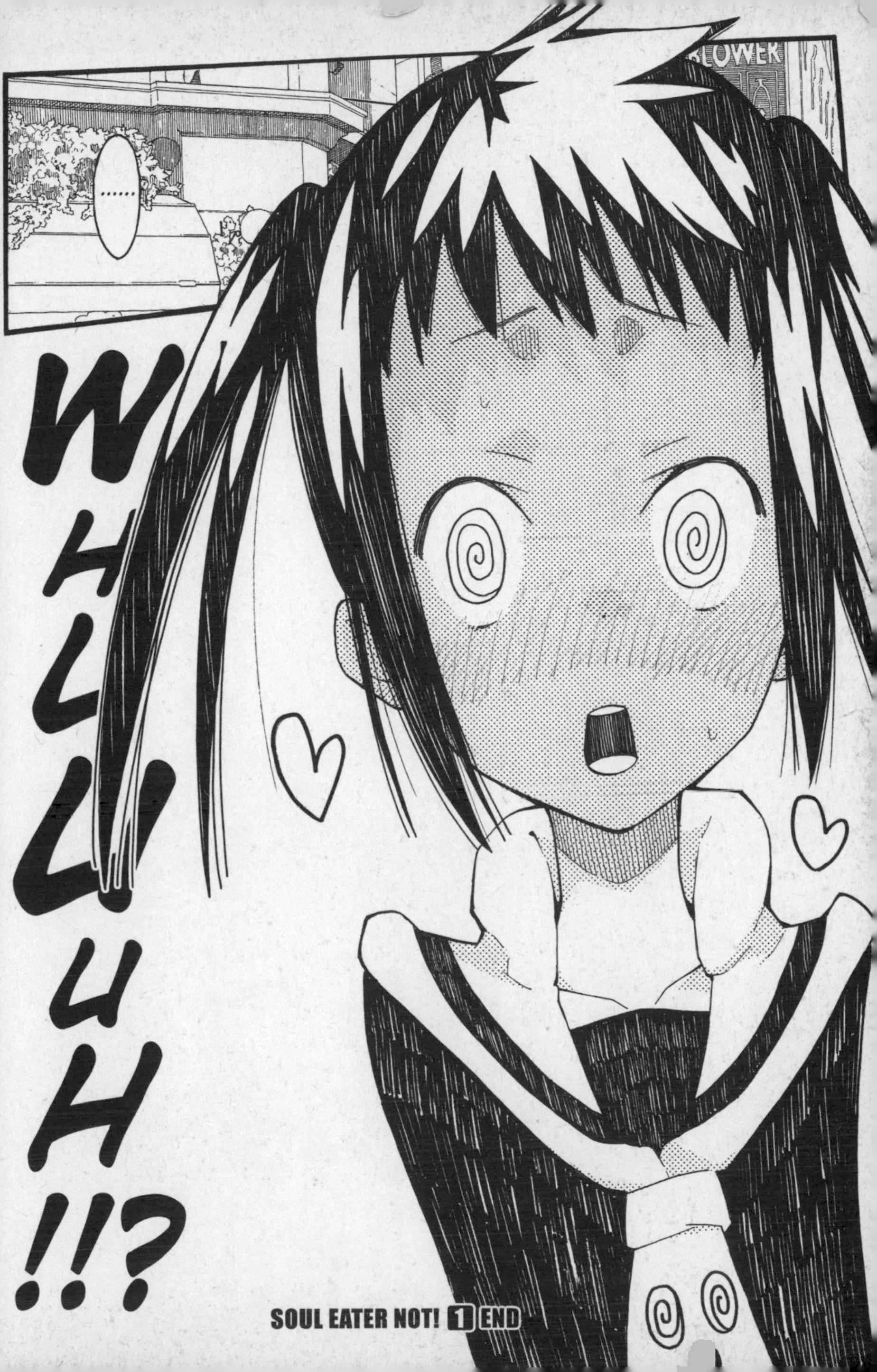

BLOWER
......
WHUUUH!!?

SOUL EATER NOT! 1 END

SOUL EATER NOT!

PREVIEW

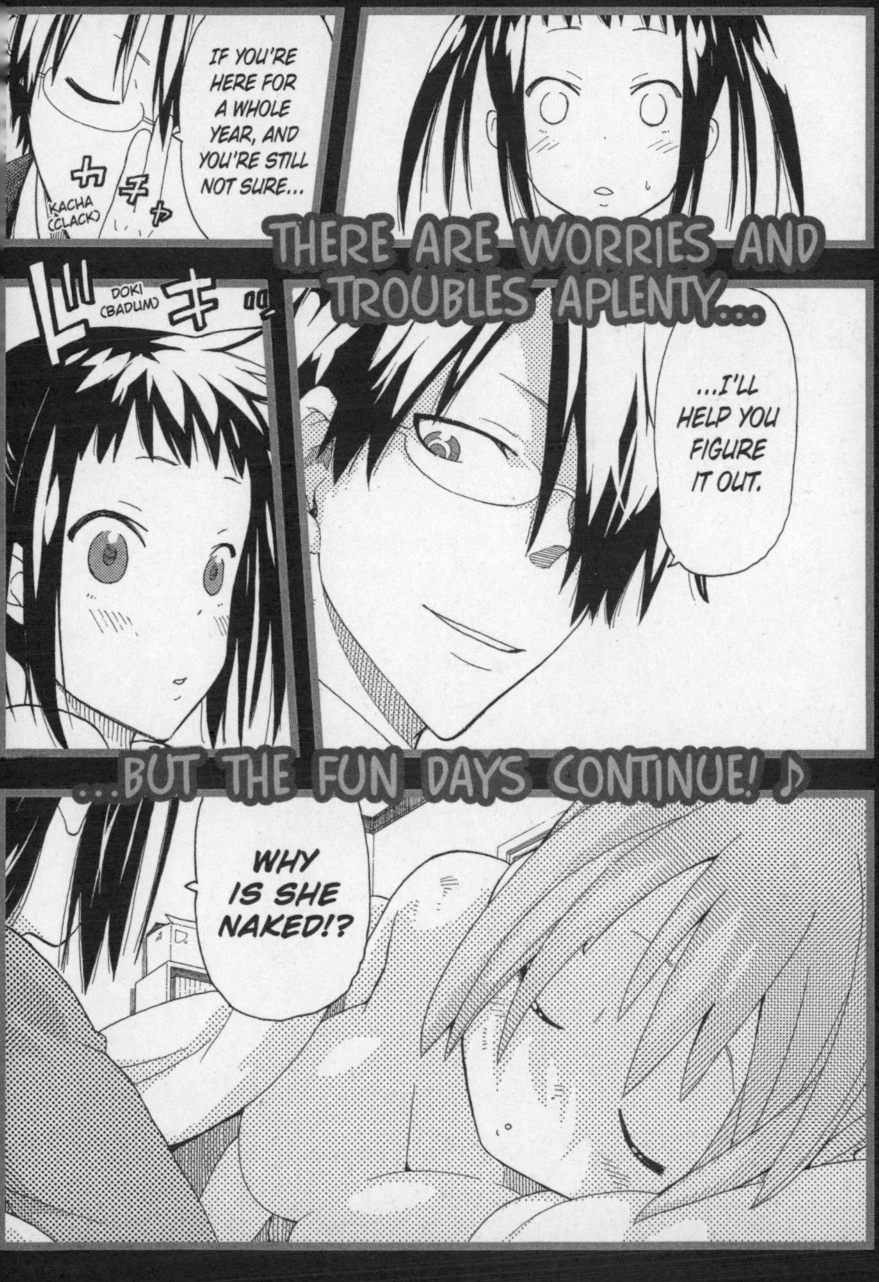
IF YOU'RE HERE FOR A WHOLE YEAR, AND YOU'RE STILL NOT SURE...
KACHA (CLACK)
THERE ARE WORRIES AND TROUBLES APLENTY...
...I'LL HELP YOU FIGURE IT OUT.
DOKI (BADUM)
...BUT THE FUN DAYS CONTINUE! ♪
WHY IS SHE NAKED!?

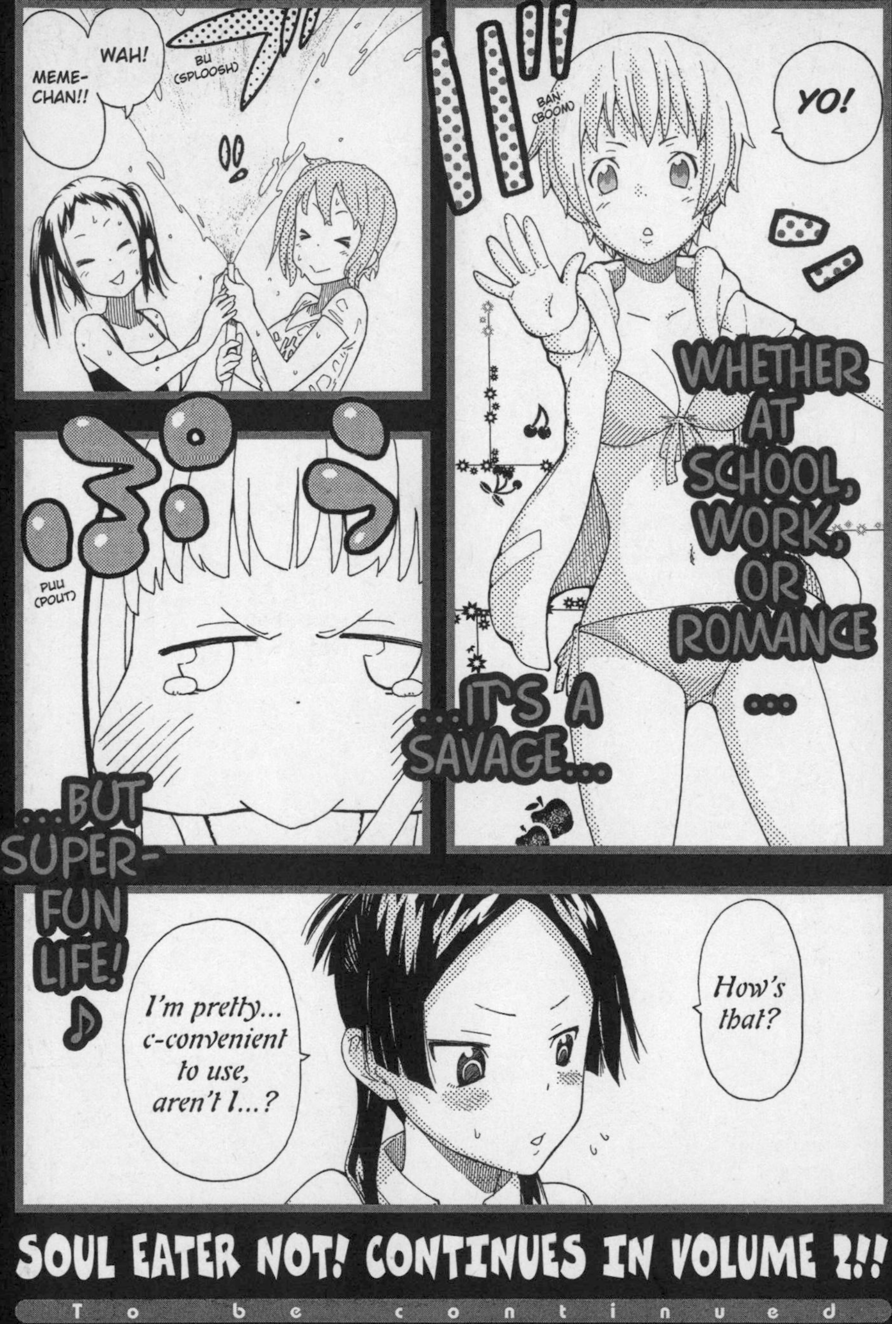
BAN (BOOM)
YO!
WHETHER AT SCHOOL, WORK, OR ROMANCE...
...IT'S A SAVAGE...
WAH!
MEME-CHAN!!
BU (SPLOOSH)
PUU (POUT)
...BUT SUPER-FUN LIFE! ♪
How's that?
I'm pretty... c-convenient to use, aren't I...?
SOUL EATER NOT! CONTINUES IN VOLUME 2!!
To be continued

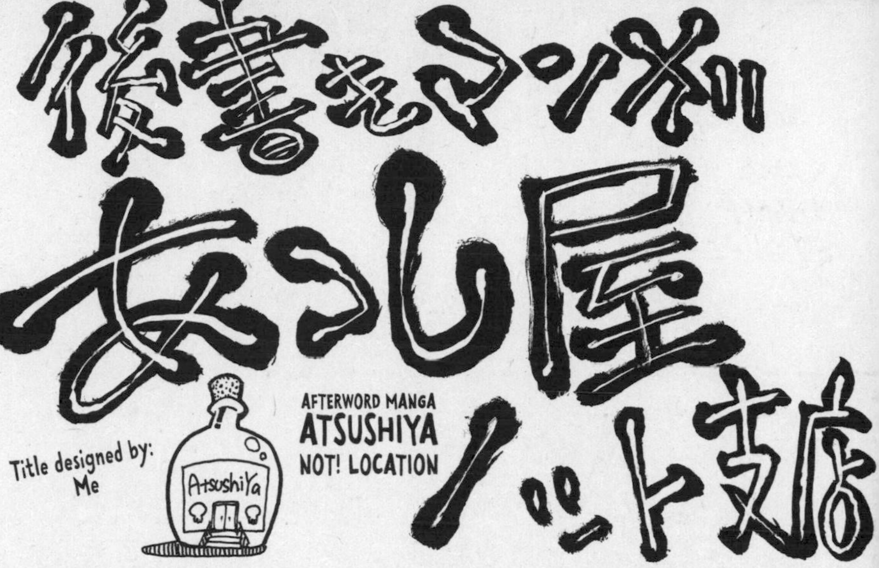
後書きマンガ
あつし屋
ノット支店
AFTERWORD MANGA
ATSUSHIYA
NOT! LOCATION
Title designed by: Me
AtsushiYa

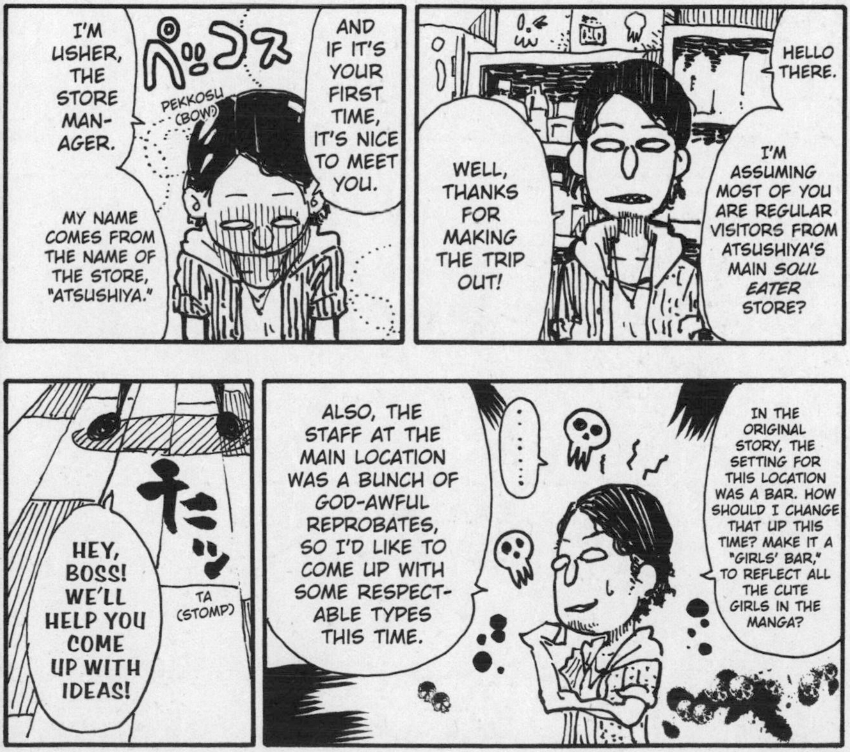
HELLO THERE.
I'M ASSUMING MOST OF YOU ARE REGULAR VISITORS FROM ATSUSHIYA'S MAIN *SOUL EATER* STORE?
WELL, THANKS FOR MAKING THE TRIP OUT!
AND IF IT'S YOUR FIRST TIME, IT'S NICE TO MEET YOU.
ペッコス
PEKKOSU (BOW)
I'M USHER, THE STORE MANAGER.
MY NAME COMES FROM THE NAME OF THE STORE, "ATSUSHIYA."
IN THE ORIGINAL STORY, THE SETTING FOR THIS LOCATION WAS A BAR. HOW SHOULD I CHANGE THAT UP THIS TIME? MAKE IT A "GIRLS' BAR," TO REFLECT ALL THE CUTE GIRLS IN THE MANGA?
....
ALSO, THE STAFF AT THE MAIN LOCATION WAS A BUNCH OF GOD-AWFUL REPROBATES, SO I'D LIKE TO COME UP WITH SOME RESPECTABLE TYPES THIS TIME.
たッ
TA (STOMP)
HEY, BOSS! WE'LL HELP YOU COME UP WITH IDEAS!

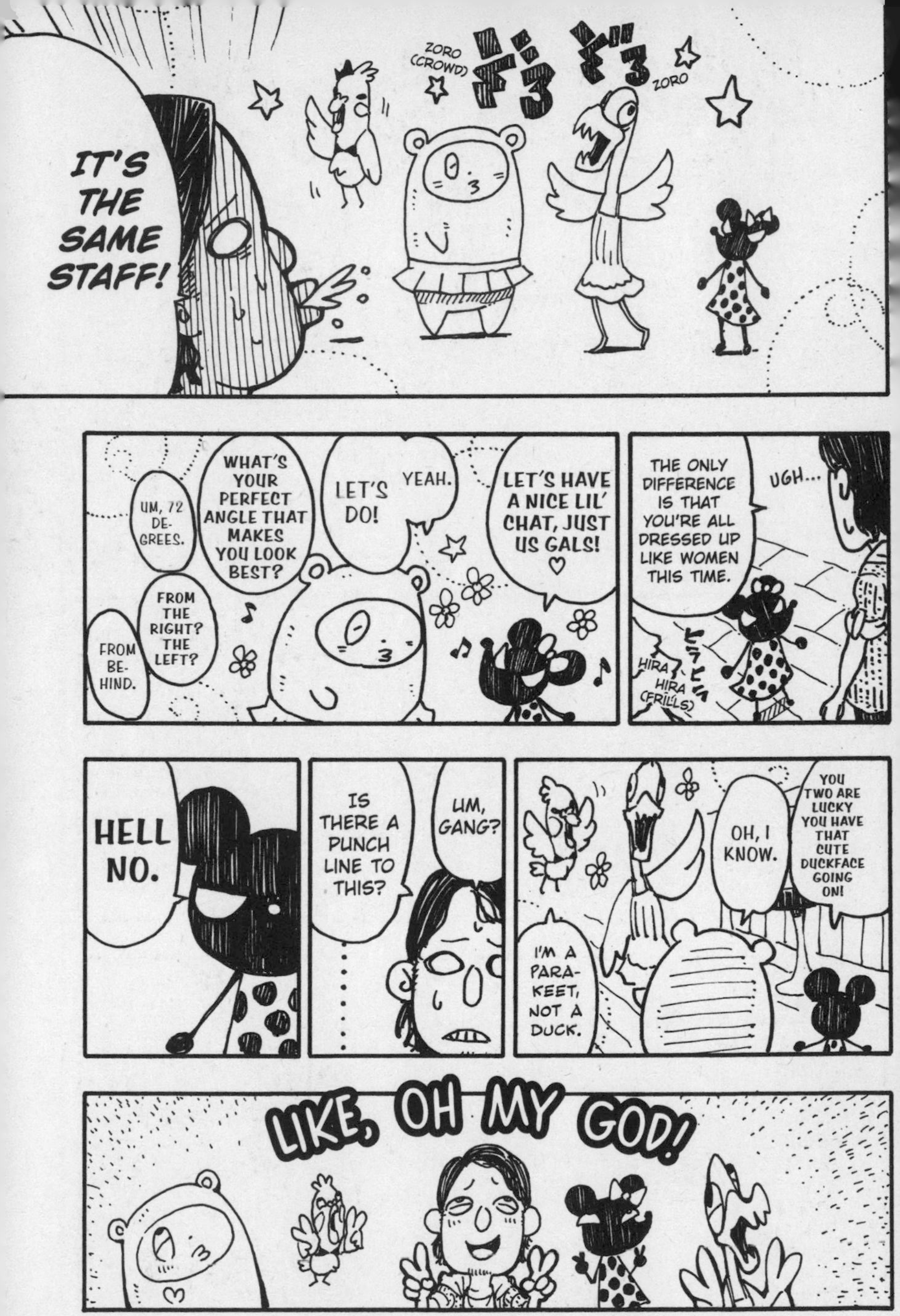
ZORO
ZORO (CROWD)
IT'S THE SAME STAFF!
UGH...
THE ONLY DIFFERENCE IS THAT YOU'RE ALL DRESSED UP LIKE WOMEN THIS TIME.
HIRA HIRA (FRILLS)
LET'S HAVE A NICE LIL' CHAT, JUST US GALS! ♡
YEAH.
LET'S DO!
WHAT'S YOUR PERFECT ANGLE THAT MAKES YOU LOOK BEST?
UM, 72 DEGREES.
FROM THE RIGHT? THE LEFT?
FROM BEHIND.
YOU TWO ARE LUCKY YOU HAVE THAT CUTE DUCKFACE GOING ON!
OH, I KNOW.
I'M A PARAKEET, NOT A DUCK.
UM, GANG?
IS THERE A PUNCH LINE TO THIS?
HELL NO.
LIKE, OH MY GOD!

Translation Notes

Common Honorifics

no honorific: Indicates familiarity or closeness; if used without permission or reason, addressing someone in this manner would constitute an insult.

-san: The Japanese equivalent of Mr./Mrs./Miss. If a situation calls for politeness, this is the fail-safe honorific.

-sama: Conveys great respect; may also indicate that the social status of the speaker is lower than that of the addressee.

-kun: Used most often when referring to boys, this indicates affection or familiarity. Occasionally used by older men among their peers, but it may also be used by anyone referring to a person of lower standing.

-chan: An affectionate honorific indicating familiarity used mostly in reference to girls; also used in reference to cute persons or animals of either gender.

-senpai: A suffix used to address upperclassmen or more experienced coworkers.

-sensei: A respectful term for teachers, artists, or high-level professionals.

Page 43
Halberd: Tsugumi's weapon transformation is a pun of sorts. Her family name, Harudori, literally means "spring bird." But the pronunciation for halberd (*harubaado*) also contains the Japanese transliteration for the English word "bird" (*baado*).

Page 62
Commoners of Flanders: This fictional book is a parody of the English novel *A Dog of Flanders* by Marie Louise de la Ramée. The story, set in Belgium and detailing the adventures of a boy named Nello and his dog Patrasche, is wildly popular in Japan and has been adapted into multiple anime TV series.

Hade Kilabiya: The Japanese equivalent of a joke name like "Gaudy McFlashy," the very opposite of the image of the plain-Jane "Mary Smith."

Page 68
Misery: A reference to the psychotic character Annie Wilkes from the Stephen King novel, *Misery*. Annie Wilkes is obsessed with the Misery series by novelist Paul Sheldon, whom she nurses to health after a car accident. She demands that he write more while confined to his bed and tortures him.

Page 70
Sleeping Fist: A parody of the "Drunken Fist" kung fu style popularized by the Jackie Chan film, *Drunken Master*.

Page 85
Kakesoba: A bowl of buckwheat soba noodles with a special soba broth poured on top (*kake* means "poured on" or "placed on"). Sliced scallions and peppers are often added for flavor.

Page 97
Master: In Japanese, the manager/proprietor/barman of a café or bar is usually referred to by the title "Master."

Page 121
Tsu-goober: In the original Japanese, Anya follows up "tsu" with "gumin," which means "ignorant masses" or "vulgar fools."

Page 123
Traitor: In *Soul Eater Not!* the term "traitor" is written with the kanji for "dojo destroyer," which refers to one who visits dojos that teach various martial arts or weapon disciplines and challenges the head sensei to a duel to prove their worth.

Page 165
Funes: A reference to the short story, "Funes El Memorioso" (Funes the Memorious), by Argentinean magical realist writer Jorge Luis Borges. Funes is a boy who hits his head falling off a horse and from that point on has perfect memory.

Page 200
Usher: When written in Japanese, "Usher" is *Assha* (あっしゃ), which contains the same letters as Atsushiya (あつしや).

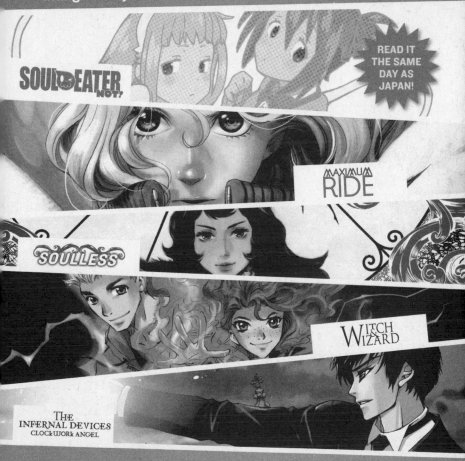
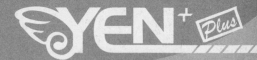

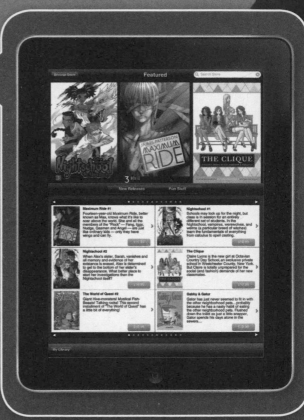
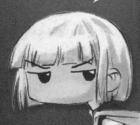

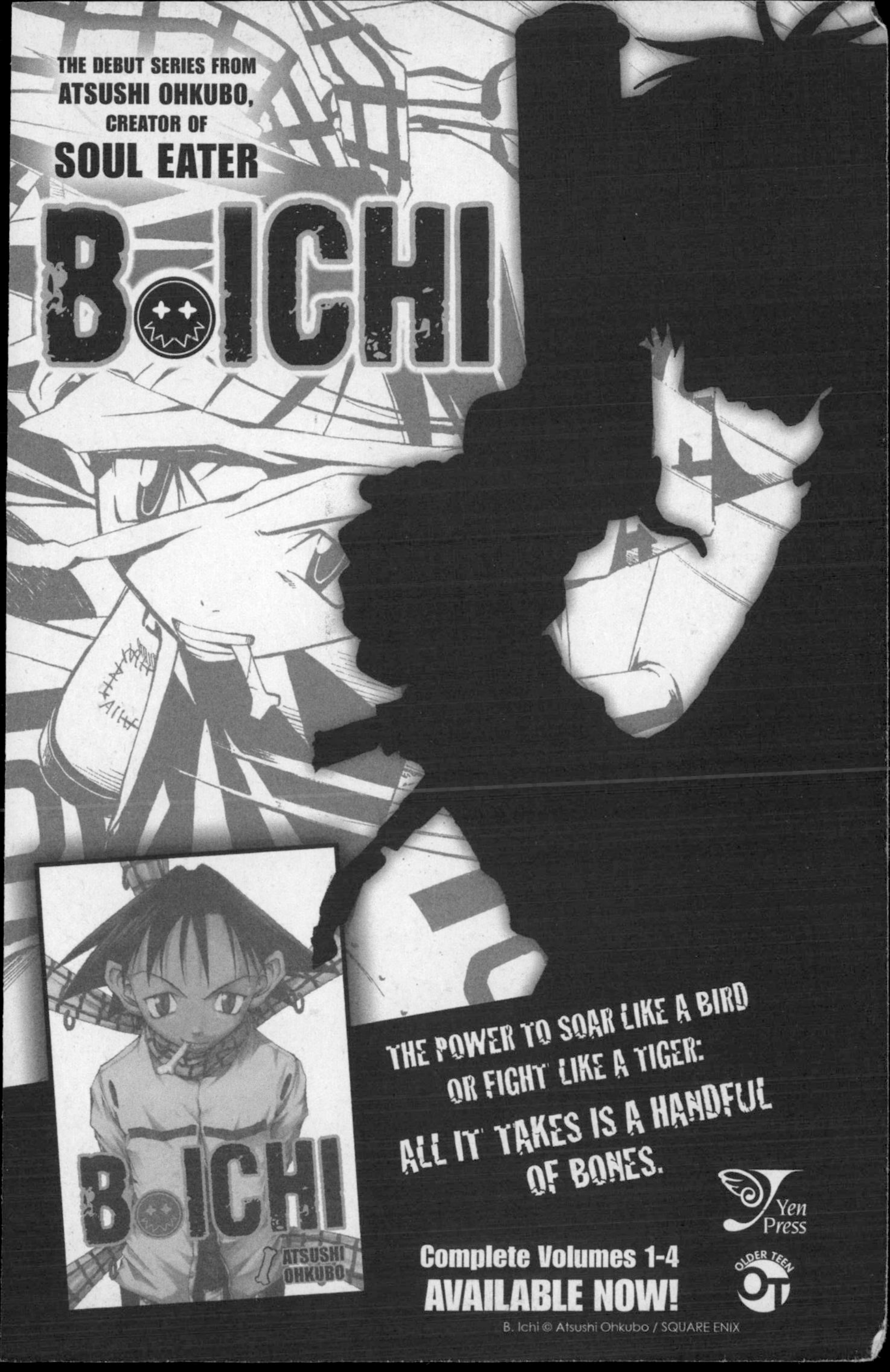
THE DEBUT SERIES FROM
ATSUSHI OHKUBO,
CREATOR OF
SOUL EATER
B.ICHI
B.ICHI
ATSUSHI OHKUBO
THE POWER TO SOAR LIKE A BIRD
OR FIGHT LIKE A TIGER:
ALL IT TAKES IS A HANDFUL
OF BONES.
Yen Press
Complete Volumes 1-4
AVAILABLE NOW!
OLDER TEEN
OT
B. Ichi © Atsushi Ohkubo / SQUARE ENIX

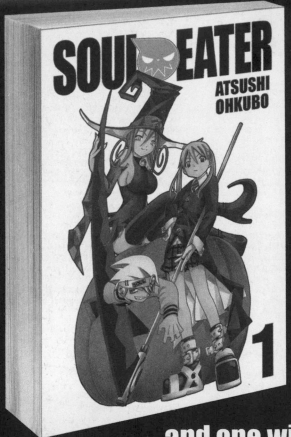

SOUL EATER NOT! ❶

ATSUSHI OHKUBO

Translation: Stephen Paul

Lettering: Abigail Blackman

SOUL EATER NOT! Vol. 1 © 2011 Atsushi Ohkubo / SQUARE ENIX. All rights reserved. First published in Japan in 2011 by SQUARE ENIX CO., LTD. English translation rights arranged with SQUARE ENIX CO., LTD. and Hachette Book Group through Tuttle-Mori Agency, Inc.

Translation © 2012 by SQUARE ENIX CO., LTD.

Yen Press
Hachette Book Group
1290 Avenue of the Americas, New Yo

www.HachetteBookGroup.com
www.YenPress.com

Yen Press is an imprint of Hachette Book Group, Inc. The Yen Press name and logo are trademarks of Hachette Book Group, Inc.

First Yen Press Edition: July 2012

ISBN: 978-0-316-21362-2

10 9 8

BVG

Printed in the United States of America

D0008628